OXFORD COMPARATIVE CONSTITUTIONALISM

Series Editors

RICHARD ALBERT

William Stamps Farish Professor of Law,
The University of Texas at Austin School of Law

ROBERT SCHÜTZE

Professor of European and Global Law,
Durham University and College of Europe

The Global South and Comparative Constitutional Law

OXFORD COMPARATIVE CONSTITUTIONALISM

Series Editors

Comparative constitutional law has a long and distinguished history in intellectual thought and in the construction of public law. As political actors and the people who create or modify their constitutional orders, they often wish to learn from the experience and learning of others. This cross-fertilization and mutual interaction has only accelerated with the onset of globalization, which has transformed the world into an interconnected web that facilitates dialogue and linkages across international and regional structures. Oxford Comparative Constitutionalism seeks to publish scholarship of the highest quality in constitutional law that deepens our knowledge of local, national, regional, and global phenomena through the lens of comparative public law.

ADVISORY BOARD

The Global South and Comparative Constitutional Law

Edited by

PHILIPP DANN, MICHAEL RIEGNER,
and MAXIM BÖNNEMANN

OXFORD
UNIVERSITY PRESS

OXFORD
UNIVERSITY PRESS

Great Clarendon Street, Oxford, OX2 6DP,
United Kingdom

Oxford University Press is a department of the University of Oxford.
It furthers the University's objective of excellence in research, scholarship,
and education by publishing worldwide. Oxford is a registered trade mark of
Oxford University Press in the UK and in certain other countries

First Edition published in 2020
Impression: 1

Published in the United States of America by Oxford University Press
198 Madison Avenue, New York, NY 10016, United States of America

British Library Cataloguing in Publication Data
Data available

Library of Congress Control Number: 2020937991

ISBN 978–0–19–885040–3

Printed and bound by
CPI Group (UK) Ltd, Croydon, CR0 4YY

Acknowledgements

This book has a really long history, even for standards of publishing edited volumes in legal academia. It is based on the proceedings of a conference that took place in 2017 at Humboldt University in Berlin. But this is not its entire pedigree. Rather, the conference and with it this book grew out of the fifty-year history of the journal *Verfassung und Recht in Übersee/World Comparative Law* (*VRÜ/WCL*) that we commemorated and celebrated with the 2017 conference. Founded in the late 1960s in Hamburg, Germany (of all places) out of sheer curiosity about the constitutional developments in the then 'newly independent countries', the *VRÜ/WCL* became a platform for a global exchange about public law in the Global South for decades to come. It was founded by Professor Herbert Krüger, who also created an academic association to feed into the journal (the 'Arbeitskreis für überseeische Verfassungsvergleichung'), and edited many years in particular by Professor Brun-Otto Bryde and Professor Philip Kunig, who also continued to organize the association.

We are immensely grateful to the daughter of the founder, Gabriele Krüger, who has continued to generously support the journal and the academic association ever since and the 2017 conference in particular. We also thank in particular Brun-Otto Bryde for his continued support in all these *VRÜ*-related endeavours, and the larger editorial board.

Philipp Dann—Michael Riegner—Maxim Bönnemann
Berlin, March 2020

Summary Contents

Detailed Contents

List of Contributors

Diego Werneck Arguelhes (LLM, JSD, Yale Law School; LLB., MA, State University of Rio de Janeiro) is Associate Professor at Insper–Institute for Education and Research, in São Paulo, Brazil. Mr Arguelhes was previously a Professor of Law at the Getulio Vargas Foundation Law School in Rio de Janeiro (FGV Direito Rio), and has been a fellow at NYU Law School (Hauser), the Information Society Project at Yale Law School, and the Max Planck Institute in Heidelberg, Germany.

David Bilchitz is Professor of Fundamental Rights and Constitutional Law at the University of Johannesburg and Director of the South African Institute for Advanced Constitutional, Public, Human Rights and International Law (SAIFAC). He is also Professor of Law at the University of Reading and Vice-President of the International Association of Constitutional Law. He was elected to the South African Young Academy of Science in 2015. In 2016, he was awarded a Von Humboldt Foundation Fellowship and wrote his contribution to this volume during his time as a Visiting Research Professor at the Humboldt University in Berlin. He has a BA (Hons) LLB cum laude from the University of the Witwatersrand and an MPhil and PhD from the University of Cambridge. He clerked for Deputy Judge-President (then) Langa of the South African Constitutional Court in 2000.

Maxim Bönnemann is Research Fellow at Humboldt University Berlin. He has been visiting researcher at National Law University (Delhi) in 2015 and at the Centre for Policy Research (Delhi) in 2017 and has completed a monograph on constitutionalism and economic transformation in India. Recent publications include articles and book chapters on comparative law and legal theory. He is managing editor of *Verfassung und Recht in Übersee/World Comparative Law*.

Weitseng Chen is Associate Professor at National University of Singapore (NUS) Faculty of Law. He specializes in comparative Chinese law in Greater China, with an emphasis on law and development. He recently published books entitled *The Beijing Consensus? How China has Changed the Western Ideas of Law and Economic Development* (CUP 2017) and *Authoritarian Legality in Asia* (CUP 2020). Weitseng Chen received his JSD from Yale Law School and worked as a Hewlett Fellow at Stanford University before joining NUS.

Sujit Choudhry (WZB Berlin Social Science Research Centre) has written widely on comparative constitutional law. He is currently working on the public law theory of political parties. His edited volumes include *The Migration of Constitutional Ideas* (CUP), *Constitutional Design for Divided Societies* (OUP), the *Oxford Handbook of the Indian Constitution* (OUP), *Territory and Power in Constitutional Transitions* (OUP), and *Security Sector Reform in Constitutional Transitions* (OUP). He has advised constitutional processes in Cyprus, Egypt, Jordan, Libya, Myanmar, Nepal, South Africa, Tunisia, Ukraine, and Yemen.

Philipp Dann is Full Professor at the Law Faculty of Humboldt University Berlin. He received his law degrees from the state of Berlin (1. and 2. state examination), Frankfurt University (PhD and post-doctoral habilitation), and Harvard Law School (LLM). He has published three monographs and several edited volumes in the area of public international law, European Union law, and constitutional law theory. He is the co-editor-in-chief of the quarterly journal *Verfassung und Recht in Übersee/World Comparative Law* (published by Nomos), a journal on comparative constitutional law and the Global South. In recent years, he has published intensively in the area of law and development, comparative constitutional law, and institutional law.

Roberto Gargarella is Senior Researcher at CONICET (Argentina); Doctor in Law (University of Buenos Aires, 1991); Master in Law (University of Chicago, 1992); Doctor in Law (University of Chicago, 1993). Post-doctoral studies at Balliol College, Oxford (1995). He received a John Simon Guggenheim grant (1999) and also a Harry Frank Guggenheim grant (2002). He has published numerous books and articles, including, *The Legal Foundations of Inequality* (CUP 2010) and *Latin American Constitutionalism* (OUP 2013).

Florian Hoffmann is Professor of Law at the Pontifícia Universidade Católica do Rio de Janeiro (PUC-Rio), Brazil, and an associate researcher in the Núcleo de Direitos Humanos (Human Rights Center) of the Law Department. Prior to this he was the Franz Haniel Chair of Public Policy (2010–2016) and the Director of the Willy Brandt School of Public Policy (2012–2015) at the University of Erfurt (Germany). Before this he taught at the London School of Economics and Political Science (LSE) (2008–2010) and the PUC-Rio (2003–2008). He works, inter alia, on human rights, the theory of international law, and law and development. He is, with Anne Orford, the co-editor of the *Oxford Handbook on the Theory of International Law* (2016).

Heinz Klug is Evjue-Bascom Professor of Law, University of Wisconsin Law School and Visiting Professor in the School of Law at the University of the Witwatersrand, Johannesburg, South Africa. He holds an SJD from Wisconsin Law School, a JD from the University of California–Hastings College of Law, and a BA(Hons) from the University of Natal. He participated in the anti-apartheid struggle and the constitutional transition in South Africa and taught law at the University of the Witwatersrand in Johannesburg from 1991 to 1996. His book on South Africa's democratic transition, *Constituting Democracy*, was published by Cambridge University Press in 2000.

Jedidiah J Kroncke is Associate Professor of Law at the University of Hong Kong, with a undergraduate degrees and a doctorate in anthropology from Berkeley and a law degree from Yale. His work focuses on transnational legal history and alternative property and labour institutions, drawing on comparative analysis emphasizing US, Chinese, and Brazilian law. His articles have addressed these topics, as well law and development, authoritarian law, comparative constitutionalism, legal education, and economic republicanism. His book *The Futility of Law and Development: China and the Dangers of Exporting American Law* was published by Oxford University Press in 2018.

Zoran Oklopcic is Associate Professor at the Department of Law and Legal Studies, Carleton University, Ottawa. He holds an SJD from Toronto University, and LLM from Central European University, an Executive MA from Amsterdam University, and an LLB from Zagreb University. His research focuses on the vocabulary of peoplehood in the context of state-formation at the intersection of constitutional theory, normative political theory, and international law, on which he published *Beyond the People: Social Imaginary and Constituent Imagination* (OUP 2018).

Roberto Niembro Ortega is Professor of Constitutional Law at the Instituto Tecnológico Autónomo de México. He holds a PhD in Law from the Universidad Complutense de Madrid, a Master's in Legal Theory from New York University (Hauser Global Scholar), and a law degree from the Escuela Libre de Derecho in Mexico City. He is author of the book *La justicia constitucional de la democracia deliberativa* (Marical Ponso 2019) and co-editor of *Constitucionalismo popular en Latinoamérica* (Porrúa 2013) together with Micaela Alterio and of *Constitucionalismo progresista: Retos y Perspectivas. Un homenaje a Mark Tushnet* (IIJ-UNAM 2016) together with Roberto Gargarella.

Michael Riegner is Postdoctoral Researcher at the Law Faculty of Humboldt University Berlin. He holds a PhD in law from Humboldt University, an LLM from New York University School of Law, and studied law in Germany and Switzerland. He has published a monograph on international institutional law, a co-edited volume on comparative constitutional justice in Southeast Europe, and articles on international and comparative law in the Yale Journal of International Law, Transnational Legal Theory, International Organizations Law Review, and other journals. He is the co-editor-in-chief of the quarterly journal *Verfassung und Recht in Übersee/World Comparative Law* and is currently a principal investigator in the multinational research project *Varieties of constitutionalism: Contestations of liberal constitutionalism in comparative constitutional law*.

Christine Schwöbel-Patel is Associate Professor at Warwick Law School where she is also co-Director of the Centre for Critical Legal Studies. Her research focuses on issues of conflict and humanitarianism, mass atrocities and institutions of law, and decoloniality and pedagogy. These themes are brought together through a political economy and aesthetics critique. She is the author of *Global Constitutionalism in International Legal Perspective* (Brill 2011) and the editor of *Critical Approaches to International Criminal Law: An Introduction* (Routledge 2014).

1

The Southern Turn in Comparative Constitutional Law

An Introduction

Philipp Dann, Michael Riegner, and Maxim Bönnemann[*]

A. Introduction and Argument

Comparative constitutional law is not what it used to be. As a field of study, it has globalized geographically, diversified methodologically, and pluralized epistemologically. Constitutional orders in Asia, Africa, and Latin America have expanded the Euro-American horizon of the discipline. Critical comparatists and social scientists have provided new methodological tools to study constitutional orders across the North–South divide. 'Southern voices' are more present in constitutional conversations, and the 'Global South' is increasingly invoked in comparative debates.[1]

And yet, the Global South still seems to punch under its weight in constitutional conversations. While it represents 'most of the world'[2] in terms of population and constitutions, it remains vastly under-represented in global constitutional debates, teaching materials, publications, and conferences. Unlike in neighbouring disciplines, the Global South remains under-theorized

* We would like to thank Daniel Bonilla Maldonado, Deval Desai, James Fowkes, Florian Hoffmann, and Michaela Hailbronner for valuable comments on an earlier version of this chapter. The text has also greatly benefited from discussions and conversations with presenters and participants during and after the fiftieth anniversary conference of the *Verfassung und Recht in Übersee/World Comparative Law* journal in 2017.

[1] See only William Twining (ed), *Human Rights, Southern Voices: Francis Deng, Abdullahi An-Na'im, Yash Ghai and Upendra Baxi* (CUP 2009); Daniel Bonilla Maldonado (ed), *Constitutionalism of The Global South: The Activist Tribunals of India, South Africa, and Colombia* (CUP 2013); Michaela Hailbronner, 'Transformative Constitutionalism: Not Only in the Global South' (2017) 65 (3) American Journal of Comparative Law 527.

[2] Partha Chatterjee, *The Politics of the Governed: Reflections on Popular Politics in Most of the World* (Columbia UP 2006).

Philipp Dann, Michael Riegner, and Maxim Bönnemann, *The Southern Turn in Comparative Constitutional Law* In: *The Global South and Comparative Constitutional Law.* Edited by: Philipp Dann, Michael Riegner, and Maxim Bönnemann, Oxford University Press (2020). © Oxford University Press. DOI: 10.1093/oso/9780198850403.003.0001

as a concept, and no equivalent to 'Third World Approaches to International Law' has emerged in comparative constitutional law.[3]

Against this background, this volume posits that it is high time for a 'Southern turn' in comparative constitutional scholarship. It aims to take stock of existing scholarship on the Global South and comparative constitutional law and to move the debate forward. It brings together authors who all hail from, or are based in, the Global South and who represent a range of regions, perspectives, and methodological approaches. The volume emerged from a conference on the occasion of the fiftieth anniversary of the journal *Verfassung und Recht in Übersee/World Comparative Law* (VRÜ/WCL), which has been dedicated since 1968 to legal developments outside Euro-America and has become an important platform for and archive of South–North dialogue.[4] Our own scholarly approach is informed by our work as editors of this journal, and by a number of other long-term scholarly projects connecting Southern and Northern constitutionalism.[5]

In this introductory chapter, we contextualize, describe, and frame this Southern turn in comparative constitutional scholarship. Our argument has three elements: first, we observe that 'Global South' has already become a term used productively in neighbouring disciplines and legal scholarship, even though in very different and sometimes under-theorized ways. From this follows the question of how we could make sense of the notion in comparative constitutional law.

We argue, secondly, that the 'Global South' is a useful concept to capture and understand a distinctive constitutional experience. This experience is shaped

[3] Zoran Oklopcic, 'The South of Western Constitutionalism: A Map Ahead of a Journey' (2016) 37 (11) Third World Quarterly 2080. On TWAIL see Obiora Okafor, 'Critical Third World Approaches to International Law (TWAIL): Theory, Methodology, or Both?' (2008) 10 (4) International Community Law Review 371; James Gathii, 'TWAIL: A Brief History of Its Origins, Its Decentralized Network, and a Tentative Bibliography' (2011) 3 Trade, Law, and Development 26; Luis Eslava and Sundhya Pahuja, 'Beyond the (Post)colonial: TWAIL and the Everyday Life of International Law' (2012) 45 (2) VRÜ/WCL 195.

[4] For a history of WCL (formerly *Law and Politics in Asia, Africa, and Latin America*), see Brun-Otto Bryde, '50 Years of "VRÜ/Law and Politics in Asia, Africa and Latin America": History and Challenges' (2018) 51 (1) VRÜ/WCL 3. We discuss our role and position as Northern scholars in this context below in the conclusion, see section E.

[5] Philipp Dann, 'Federal Democracy in India and the European Union: Towards Transcontinental Comparison of Constitutional Law' (2011) 44 (2) VRÜ/WCL 160; Philipp Dann and Felix Hanschmann, 'Post-colonial Theories and Law' (2012) 45 (2) VRÜ/WCL 123; Michael Riegner, 'Access to Information as a Human Right and Constitutional Guarantee. A Comparative Perspective' (2017) 50 (4) VRÜ/WCL 332; Michael Riegner, 'Comparative Foreign Relations Law between Centre and Periphery: Liberal and Postcolonial Perspectives' in Helmut Aust and Thomas Kleinlein (eds), *Encounters between Foreign Relations Law and International Law* (CUP 2020), forthcoming; ; Maxim Bönnemann and Laura Jung, 'Critical Legal Studies and Comparative Constitutional Law' in Rainer Grote, Frauke Lachenmann, and Rüdiger Wolfrum (eds), *Max Planck Encyclopedia of Comparative Constitutional Law* (OUP 2017).

by the *distinctive context* that emerges from the history of colonialism and the peripheral position of the South in the geopolitical system, placing Southern constitutionalism in a dialectical relationship with its Northern counterpart. Three *distinctive themes*, so we continue to argue, characterize Southern constitutionalism: constitutionalism as an experience of socio-economic transformation; constitutionalism as a site of struggle about political organization; and constitutionalism as denial of, and access to, justice. Southern constitutionalism is hence a shared experience, shaped by similar macro-dynamics but also profoundly heterogeneous micro-dynamics. It is distinct from, and at the same time deeply entangled with, constitutionalism in the Global North.

From this observation of the South–North entanglement follows the third element of our argument—namely that taking the Global South seriously has implications for comparative constitutional scholarship as a whole. The Southern turn implies an approach to *doing* comparative law that improves our understanding of constitutional law in both North and South. Thinking about and with the 'Global South' denotes a specific epistemic, methodological, and institutional sensibility that reinforces the ongoing move towards more epistemic reflexivity, methodological pluralism, and institutional diversification in comparative constitutional scholarship generally. In that sense, the Southern turn is a double turn: after the pivot to the South, it turns back to the North and to the world as a whole.

The remainder of this chapter mirrors this argument and proceeds in three steps: first, we describe the use of the notion of 'Global South' in neighbouring disciplines, as well as in comparative constitutional scholarship historically and today (B). We then sketch what we consider to be distinct about the constitutional experience in the South (C). From this we move on to describe the implications for comparative constitutional scholarship generally, mapping the contours of how to do 'world comparative law' (D). We conclude with a short self-reflection of our own positionality and role in the Southern turn (E).

B. Towards a Southern Turn in Comparative Constitutional Law

If comparative constitutional law wants to remain relevant in a multipolar world, it urgently requires a broader foundation. A discipline whose very *raison d'être* is to transcend individual legal orders but which continues to exclude most of the world is bound to lose relevance.[6] Less than ever, the comparatist can afford overgeneralizations based on an unrepresentative sample of Western legal orders.[7] But not only the discipline's quest for relevance urges us to turn to the Global South. Recognizing the constitutional experiences of the Global South is also a genuine question of epistemic justice. From colonial times to contemporary rule of law projects, Euro-American law has been exported, imposed, and mimicked elsewhere, while other legal traditions have been either ignored or relegated to the sphere of the 'local', 'indigenous', or 'premodern'.[8] Taking these legal traditions seriously also highlights the deep entanglements, past and present, that continue to shape constitutional orders in both North and South and that require a transregional dialogue beyond the universalism–particularism dichotomy. A final reason for engaging with the Global South in comparative constitutional law is rather simple: it is intellectually productive. It not only adds innovative legal material for comparison, but also offers fresh theoretical perspectives, alternative ways of thinking, and necessary irritations of disciplinary orthodoxies. Many of the themes in current global debates have been under discussion in Southern constitutional law for quite some time: the globalization of constitutional law; democratic constitutionalism beyond homogenous nation states; contestations of liberal constitutionalism and non-liberal varieties of constitutional government; the constitutionalization of social rights and welfare guarantees; the relationship between globalized capitalism, inequality, and democratic constitutionalism; judicial review and state power; methodological debates between comparative constitutional law and comparative constitutional studies. The Global South speaks to all these debates, and offers a wealth of insights.[9]

Considering these reasons for a Southern turn, we first want to understand better its context—in three steps: we first analyse the history of the term and its productive use in other disciplines (1). We then turn to legal scholarship

[6] On this understanding of comparative law as general jurisprudence see William Twining, *General Jurisprudence: Understanding Law from a Global Perspective* (CUP 2009).

[7] An exemplary error arising from an unrepresentative comparative sample is pointed out by Upendra Baxi's review of David Dyzenhaus, 'The Unity of Public Law' (2004) 14 *Law and Politics Book Review* 799, 804: It is 'plainly and surprisingly wrong' to state that the Canadian Supreme Court established in 1999 'for the first time in the common law world a general duty for administrative decision-makers to give reasons for their decisions . . . The Indian Supreme Court has already, and reiteratively, further with multiplier impacts in South public law jurisprudence, performed this feat ever since 1950!'

[8] Teemu Ruskola, *Legal Orientalism: China, the United States, and Modern Law* (Harvard UP 2013); Turan Kayaoğlu, *Legal Imperialism: Sovereignty and Extraterritoriality in Japan, the Ottoman Empire, and China* (CUP 2013).

[9] See only Boaventura de Sousa Santos, 'A New Vision of Europe: Learning from the South' in Gurminder K Bhambra and John Narayan (eds), *European Cosmopolitanism: Colonial Histories and Postcolonial Societies* (Routledge 2017) 173.

and trace the treatment of Southern constitutionalism in comparative (constitutional) law over time (2). We end with a brief overview of contemporary approaches to constitutional law in the South (3).

1. The notion of the Global South and its use in neighbouring disciplines

Using the notion of 'Global South' is an endeavour that requires explanation. Sceptics criticize that the term is too fuzzy to be analytically useful, that it lumps together very different legal orders with little normative common ground, or that there is nothing distinctive about the constitutional experience of the Global South.[10] Indeed, comparatists may rightfully ask whether this vastly heterogeneous array of constitutional orders has something in common that justifies the label Global South, and at the same time sets it apart from its logical other, the Global North. Are highly aggregated concepts like 'Global South' heuristically valuable at all?

A bit of context is useful here. Commonly, the Global South is considered as the heir to the notion of the 'Third World', which emerged in the early 1950s as the confident self-description of the newly independent and non-aligned states in the South. 'Third World' was a reference to Abbé Sieyès' notion of the 'third estate' during the French revolution, which had formulated the demand of the democratic majority of citizens to end aristocratic rule in the eighteenth century.[11] In the era of 'decolonization', the notion easily conveyed the idea that now the democratic majority of peoples in the world demanded their voice to be heard on the world stage.[12] It quickly caught on in political and academic language, as it expressed a common agenda based on a shared historical experience. This common agenda, however, fell apart under the dichotomous pressures of the Cold War and the increasingly different paths of the countries in this group. In the North, the notion was also routinely misinterpreted as meaning a hierarchy of the first (capitalist), second (communist), and third

[10] Ran Hirschl, *Comparative Matters: The Renaissance of Comparative Constitutional Law* (OUP 2014) 218. Sceptic as to the distinctiveness is Hailbronner, 'Transformative Constitutionalism' (n 1).

[11] Alfred Sauvy, 'Trois mondes, une planète' *L'Observateur* (Paris, 14 August 1952); on the history of the notion: Vijay Prashad, *The Darker Nations: A People's History of the Third World* (The New Press 2007) 6–11.

[12] Luis Eslava, Michael Fakhri, and Vasuki Nesiah, 'The Spirit of Bandung' in Luis Eslava, Michael Fakhri, and Vasuki Nesiah (eds), *Bandung, Global History, and International Law: Critical Pasts and Pending Futures* (CUP 2017) 3; Jochen von Bernstorff and Philipp Dann, 'The Battle for International Law in the Decolonization Era: An Introduction' in Jochen von Bernstorff and Philipp Dann (eds), *The Battle for International Law in the Decolonization Era* (OUP 2019) 1–31.

or last world of 'developing countries' and hence took on a rather derogative meaning. In the early 1990s, with the end of the Cold War, the notion lost its appeal and resonance.

And yet, there seemed to have been a demand to capture the non-OECD group of states and peoples in one notion. In the 1990s, the notion of the 'Global South' emerged and started a productive intellectual career less in the formalized political arena but rather in the grassroots political sphere and especially in social sciences and humanities. In these disciplines, 'Global South' is a widely established term, while its specific meaning and contours remain subject to debate.

In international political economy and international relations, the 'Global South' is not only associated with the rise of emerging economies, especially by the BRICS, but also with the unequal distribution of wealth and benefits in a unified globalized economy.[13] This distribution, however, does not necessarily follow the methodological nationalism of GDP figures but also entails massive internal inequalities. In this vein, in area studies, re-energized and to some extent displaced by 'Global Studies', the concept does not primarily emphasize a North/South divide but rather highlights entanglements and uneven developments.[14] Areas of the Global South can be found in racialized urban ghettos of North America, as much as the Global North can exist in gated communities of the rich in Rio, Lagos, or Mumbai.

Postcolonial theorists, by contrast, use the term to emphasize that much of our knowledge, categories, and methods, which claim to be universal, turn out to be deeply provincial when we take a closer look.[15] In a similar vein, certain strands of anthropology and sociology have developed a rich body of 'Southern theory' which tries to escape the trap of methodological nationalism (and parochialism) and puts subaltern knowledge and experiences centre stage.[16]

[13] BS Chimni and Siddharth Mallavarapu (eds), *International Relations: Perspectives for the Global South* (Pearson 2012); Amitav Acharya and Barry Buzan, *The Making of Global International Relations: Origins and Evolution of IR at its Centenary* (CUP 2019); Siba Grovogui, 'A Revolution Nevertheless: Global South in International Relations' (2011) 5 (1) The Global South 175; Thomas Eriksen, 'What's Wrong with the Global North and the Global South?' in Andrea Hollington and others (eds), *Concepts of the Global South: Voices From Around the World* (Global South Studies Center Cologne 2015) <https://kups.ub.uni-koeln.de/6399/1/voices012015_concepts_of_the_global_south.pdf> accessed 8 March 2020.

[14] See eg Katja Mielke and Anna-Katharina Hornridge (eds), *Area Studies at the Crossroads* (Palgrave 2017).

[15] Dipesh Chakrabarty, *Provincializing Europe: Postcolonial Thought and Historical Difference* (2nd edn, Princeton UP 2009); Walter D Mignolo and Catherine E Walsh, *On Decoloniality: Concepts, Analytics, Praxis* (Duke UP 2018).

[16] Jean Comaroff and John L Comaroff, *Theory from the South, or, How Euro-America is Evolving toward Africa* (Paradigm 2012); Julian Go, 'Globalizing Sociology, Turning South: Perspectival Realism and the Southern Standpoint' [2016] (2) Sociologica 1; Shalini Randeria and Sebastian Conrad (eds), *Jenseits des Eurozentrismus* (Campus Verlag 2014).

Thus, the Global South can also be understood as a political concept that gains its critical potential from its geographical imprecision: it allows negotiating an array of geographic scales from planet to neighbourhood 'to understand how forces that seek to impose exploitative and hegemonic economic and political forms have been and can be resisted'.[17]

In this light, the Global South is not only, or even primarily, a place, but rather a sensibility and perspective, a way of looking at the world as a whole. This relative flexibility and imaginative resonance may explain its relative popularity over possible contenders, such as the more technical developed/developing distinction, the politically explicit 'most of the world' or centre-periphery opposition, or the geographically more precise 'Asia, Africa and Latin America'.

2. The Global South in comparative constitutional law: a brief intellectual history

Law has not been entirely absent from these debates. Anthropologists, sociologists, and postcolonial theorists alike have discussed the distinctive features of law and its role in the Global South.[18] Lawyers in the South, of course, have reflected on their respective legal systems. Yet, as a distinctively theoretical perspective, the South has been developed mostly in public international law. Since the 1990s, 'Third World Approaches to International Law' (TWAIL) have brought together scholars from the South and fellow travellers in a shared intellectual project that has gained some internal coherence, theoretical sophistication, and critical traction in global legal discourse.[19]

By contrast, in comparative law, up to date no equivalent to TWAIL has emerged, be it in private, criminal, or constitutional law.[20] The reasons for this gap are surely manifold.[21] But of course, this does not mean that there has been no comparative study of constitutional law of the South. In fact, there

[17] Leigh Anne Duck, 'The Global South via the US South' in Andrea Hollington and others (eds), *Concepts of the Global South* (Global South Studies Center Cologne 2015) <https://kups.ub.uni-koeln.de/6399/1/voices012015_concepts_of_the_global_south.pdf> accessed 8 March 2020.

[18] Jean Comaroff (ed), *Law and Disorder in the Postcolony* (University of Chicago Press 2006); Chatterjee, *The Politics of the Governed* (n 2).

[19] Luis Eslava and Sundhya Pahuja, 'Beyond the (Post)Colonial: TWAIL and the Everyday Life of International Law' (2012) 45 (2) VRÜ/WCL 195.

[20] But see Pablo Ciocchini and George Radics (eds), *Criminal Legalities in the Global South* (Routledge 2019).

[21] On possible reasons, see Oklopcic (n 3) (arguing that competing critical projects (such as transnational law or political economy approaches) as well as the much more complex political agenda of critical comparison in domestic law (in contrast to critical international law) have hindered the emergence).

is a particular history of comparative law engagement with Southern constitutional orders that comparatists should be aware of. Occasions for comparative engagement often arose at founding moments.[22] When Latin American constitution-makers first drafted independence constitutions in the nineteenth century, they looked to other constitutional orders for inspiration—mostly the US and Europe, not necessarily because of their perceived superiority but for a perceived lack of alternative examples of constitutional government.[23] Similarly, constitution-making during the twentieth century decolonization era in Asia and Africa was accompanied by comparative studies.[24] Ultimately, however, these processes generated much less scholarly engagement as one would have thought and wished for—and much is still to be discovered.

One reason is that in the second half of the twentieth century, comparative legal studies very much remained in the shadow of the Cold War.[25] The 'law and development' movement of the 1960s and 1970s, which was a primary place of scholarly legal engagement between South and North, was gripped by modernization theory and the concept of development, thus being more preoccupied with legally remaking developing economies in the image of industrialized nations than with comparing constitutional foundations of political government.[26] At the same time, there was hardly any engagement with the emerging new constitutions of the South. Even though the new objects of study

[22] Daniel Bonilla Maldonado and Michael Riegner, 'Decolonization' in Rainer Grote, Frauke Lachenmann, and Rüdiger Wolfrum (eds), *Max Planck Encyclopedia of Comparative Constitutional Law* (2020, online); Mara Malagodi, Luke McDonagh, and Thomas Poole, 'New Dominion Constitutionalism at the Twilight of the British Empire: An Introduction' (2019) 17 (4) ICON 1166.

[23] Roberto Gargarella, *Latin American Constitutionalism, 1810–2010: The Engine Room of the Constitution* (OUP 2013) 2.

[24] James S Read, 'Bills of Rights in "The Third World": Some Commonwealth Experiences' (1973) 6 (1) VRÜ/WCL 21; Gordon Woodman, 'British Legislation as a Source of Ghanaian Law: From Colonialism to Technical Aid' (1974) 7 (1) VRÜ/WCL 19; AS Fadlalla, 'Fundamental Rights and the Nigerian Draft Constitution' (1977) 10 (4) VRÜ/WCL 543; Ebitimi E Chikwendu, 'Considerations of the Freedom Value in a Military Regime. A Decade of Military Rule in Nigeria' (1977) 10 (4) VRÜ/WCL 531; Zdenek Červenka, 'Rhodesia Five Years after the Unilateral Declaration of Independence' (1971) 4 (4) VRÜ/WCL 9. In retrospect see Harshan Kumarasingham (ed), *Constitution Making in Asia: Decolonisation and State-building in the Aftermath of the British Empire* (Routledge 2016); Charles Parkinson, *Bills of Rights and Decolonization: The Emergence of Domestic Human Rights Instruments in Britain's Overseas Territories* (OUP 2007); Kwasi Prempeh, 'Africa's "Constitutionalism Revival": False Start or New Dawn?' (2007) 5 (3) ICON 469; see also Kevin Tan, *Constitutional Foundings in Southeast Asia* (Hart Publishing 2020).

[25] Ugo Mattei, 'The Cold War and Comparative Law: A Reflection on the Politics of Intellectual Discipline' (2017) 65 (3) American Journal of Comparative Law 567;

[26] David Trubek and Marc Galanter, 'Scholars in Self-estrangement: Some Reflections on the Crisis in Law and Development Studies in the United States' [1974] Wisconsin Law Review 1062; David Trubek, 'Toward a Social Theory of Law: An Essay on the Study of Law and Development' (1972) 82 (1) Yale Law Journal 1; for a recent day reflection, David Trubek, 'Law and Development: Forty Years after "Scholars in Self-Estrangement"' (2016) 66 (3) University of Toronto Law Journal 301. For exceptions, see eg Kenneth Karst and Keith Rosenn, *Law and Development in Latin America: A Case Book*, vol 28 (University of California Press 1975).

were plentiful, studies are rare in legal scholarship—and if existent were often shaped by Cold War logics.[27] This dearth of comparative constitutional studies looking at the South was no outlier, however, when looking at the state of comparative constitutional law more generally. While comparative studies in the area of private law blossomed and professionalized, the comparative studies of constitutions even with regard to Northern constitutions was rather dormant during the cold war era.

Notable counterexamples only highlight this point. Most prominent is maybe India, whose Constitution has not only been studied intensely from early on[28] but also attracted wider comparative attention.[29] But then again, India's constitution is also the unusual example of a postcolonial constitution that had been debated intensely even before independence, was soon defended by a confident Supreme Court, and not hollowed out by constant constitutional change or poisonous constitutional politics.[30] Another fascinating exception to the overall rule of Northern ignorance towards Southern constitutionalism is the history of our journal, *Verfassung und Recht in Übersee/World Comparative Law* (VRÜ/WCL), formerly with the English subtitle 'Law and Politics in Asia, Africa and Latin America'. The journal was founded in 1968 in the spirit of decolonization and a cooperative new beginning, and its trajectory is a good indicator of the developments in scholarship. Initially it covered constitutional developments in Asia, Africa, and Latin America with a range of authors from all world regions.[31] Up to the late 1970s, it was a global and plural platform for public law reflections. However, with authoritarian regimes increasingly displacing constitutional governments, the journal more and more turned to

[27] For a fascinating exchange on new Southern constitutions and the role of German scholars from East and West, see (the East German communist) Gerhard Brehme and Klaus Hutschenreuter, 'Zur Rolle der westdeutschen Staats- und Rechtswissenschaft im System des Neokolonialismus' (1970) 19 (8) Staat und Recht 1254; and the replique by (the West German liberal) B-O Bryde, 'Überseerecht und Neokolonialismus' (1971) 4 (1) VRÜ/WCL 51.

[28] HM Seerwai, *Constitutional Law of India* (1st edn, Tripathi 1967).

[29] Granville Austin, *The Indian Constitution: Cornerstone of a Nation* (Clarendon Press 1966); Marc Galanter, '"Protective Discrimination" for Backward Classes in India' (1961) 3 (1) Journal of the Indian Law Institute 39; Dieter Conrad, 'Limitation of Amendment Procedures and the Constituent Power' (1970) 15–16 Indian Year Book of International Affairs 1966–1967 375.

[30] On the Indian constitutional history only Arun K Thiruvengadam, *The Constitution of India: A Contextual Analysis* (Hart Publishing 2017).

[31] See for the opening statement of the journal Herbert Krüger, 'Verfassung und Recht in Übersee' (1968) 1 (1) VRÜ/WCL 3; for an example of the early contributions on constitutional developments around the world see only SC Sen, 'Constitutional Storm in India' (1974) 7 (1) VRÜ/WCL 33; KM de Silva, 'Sri Lanka (Ceylon): The New Republican Constitution' (1972) 5 (3) VRÜ/WCL 239; Hector Fix-Zamudio, 'México: El Organismo Judicial (1950–1975)' (1977) 10 (3) VRÜ/WCL 391; Kwame Opoku, 'African Law: Existence and Unity' (1976) 9 (1) VRÜ/WCL 65.

international law as a less ominous site of legal engagement by and with the Third World.[32]

The overall situation changed in the 1990s. Interest in comparative constitutional law resurged after the end of the Cold War, when waves of democratization brought about new constitutions in the former Third World and post-Soviet states. Northern scholars took an interest in the 'rise of world constitutionalism' and the 'inevitable globalization of constitutional law'.[33] At the same time, Southern scholars like Upendra Baxi began to challenge the eurocentrism of purportedly universal categories of comparative constitutional law and argued for a reconceptualization of constitutionalism from a subaltern perspective.[34] In a similar vein, critical legal comparatists turned to the Global South and especially began to use insights from postcolonial theory for the theory and practice of comparative law.[35] The situation and reception of VRÜ/WCL changed, too; a new generation of authors and editors began to realize the opportunities of an already well-established journal for reflection of South–North comparative constitutionalism.

Yet, while in public international law TWAILers were busy forging a scholarly movement, constitutionalists did not follow suit for some time. Neither questions of poverty, colonial past, and global asymmetries, nor the challenge of inequality, marginalization, and distributive justice acquired prominence in a discipline whose epistemic horizon was limited by the idea and experience of liberal democracy. It took until 2013 for a volume to see the light of day in which the Global South explicitly became title and scholarly programme in *The Constitutionalism of the Global South*.[36]

[32] See for a reflection on the role and use of international law in the history of the journal Philip Kunig, 'Völkerrecht und Übersee' (1997) 30 (4) VRÜ/WCL 465.

[33] Bruce Ackerman, 'The Rise of World Constitutionalism' (1997) 83 (4) Virgina Law Review 771; Mark Tushnet, 'The Inevitable Globalization of Constitutional Law' (2009) 50 (1) Virginia Journal of International Law 985.

[34] Upendra Baxi, 'Constitutionalism as a Site of State Formative Practices' (1999–2000) 21 Cardozo Law Review 1183; Twining, *Human Rights, Southern Voices* (n 1).

[35] Nathaniel Berman, 'Aftershocks: Exoticization, Normalization, and the Hermeneutic Compulsion' [1997] (2) Utah Law Review 281; Lama Abu-Odeh, 'Comparatively Speaking: The "Honor" of the "East" and the "Passion" of the "West"' [1997] (2) Utah Law Review 287; Teemu Ruskola, 'Legal Orientalism' (2002) 101 (1) Michigan Law Review 179; Bönnemann and Jung, 'Critical Legal Studies' (n 5); Sherally Munshi, 'Comparative Law and Decolonizing Critique' (2017) 65 (suppl 1) American Journal of Comparative Law 207; Judith Schacherreiter, 'Postcolonial Theory and Comparative Law: On the Methodological and Epistemological Benefits to Comparative Law through Postcolonial Theory' (2016) 49 (3) VRÜ/WCL 291.

[36] Bonilla Maldonado, *Constitutionalism of the Global South* (n 1).

3. Approaches in contemporary constitutional scholarship

Today, Southern constitutions are part of the global comparative conversation, some more (like the Indian, Brazilian, Colombian, or South African constitution), some less; academic journals have evolved and provide platforms for global exchange; new voices have emerged.[37] But the approaches to these constitutions vary considerably—with significant implications. At the risk of oversimplifying, we propose to distinguish three ideal-typical approaches: comparative constitutional law *for*, *with*, and *from* the Global South. Each approach is characterized by a combination of scholarly concerns and has distinct epistemic and political implications. They ultimately differ by the importance they give to the constitutional experience in the South.

(a) Comparative constitutional law for the Global South

A first approach might be called 'comparative constitutional law for the Global South'. It is concerned with the production of knowledge about constitutional law in the North for consumption in the South, be it in the form of colonial export, law and development initiatives, rule of law projects, constitutional octroi, or contemporary projects of constitutional advice and reform that draw on templates of Western liberal constitutionalism.[38] Here, the constitutional law and experience of the South does not feature as particularly relevant but more as an object to be reformed and shaped. Such scholarship has initially been driven mostly by European and American actors, international organizations, or bilateral aid agencies with little input from the Global South. Its main concern is the transplantation, or diffusion, of Western liberal constitutionalism to new contexts in the Global South.[39] Epistemically and politically, these approaches are highly ambivalent: while studying these processes descriptively may be heuristically valuable, advocating them normatively has been increasingly complex, politically dubious, and practically impossible where transplantation is accompanied by violent imposition or economic coercion.

[37] Today, three international English-language journals aim to reflect comparative constitutional law in general (with no regional or particular thematic focus): *VRÜ/WCL*, *International Journal of Constitutional Law* (ICON), and *Global Constitutionalism*.

[38] For analysis and critique of these dynamics, see Philipp Dann and Zaid Al Ali, 'Internationalized Pouvoir constituant' (2006) 10 (1) Max Planck Yearbook of United Nations Law 423; Constance Grewe and Michael Riegner, 'Internationalized Constitutionalism in Ethnically Divided Societies: Bosnia-Herzegovina and Kosovo Compared' (2011) 15 (1) Max Planck Yearbook of United Nations Law 1; Jedidiah Kroncke, *The Futility of Law and Development: China and the Dangers of Exporting American Law* (OUP 2016).

[39] This thematic orientation is evident, for instance, in many contributions to journals such as *Global Constitutionalism* and *The Hague Journal of the Rule of Law*.

(b) Comparative constitutional law with the Global South

The second approach—*with* the Global South—is to include Southern constitutional law in the comparison and practice and treat it as an equally important object of study. Two varieties of this approach can be distinguished, depending on the further intentions and epistemic awareness connected to them.

In a rather neutral version, authors of this approach simply want to broaden the sample for comparison, or to globalize the 'gene pool' of comparative constitutional law.[40] Reasons for this can be intellectual curiosity but also a methodological concern with representativeness of their case selection.[41] The notion of the Global South (if used at all) describes this geographical and thematic expansion but is not used as an identity marker or theoretical concept.[42] Proponents of social-scientific and quantitative comparative studies have argued that quantitative methods have an egalitarian impetus because they treat all observations alike, whether they concern the constitution of the US or Gambia.[43] Overall, however, the epistemic and political implication is that this approach extends the existing framework to new materials: it allows for addition, but not for more.

In a more deliberate variety, Southern constitutionalism is more than an equal object of study and appears as an original producer of legal knowledge, ideas, and innovation. Scholars in this camp emphasize the production of comparative constitutional law scholarship by and in the Global South.[44] Methodologically, this variety tends to use qualitative approaches that emphasize the specific contexts of constitutional law in the Global South (as much as in the Global North).[45] Most authors seem comfortable with a global pluralism that allows for a peaceful coexistence of North and South as equals, each with

[40] Cheryl Saunders, 'Towards a Global Constitutional Gene Pool' (2009) 4 (1) National Taiwan University Law Review 1.

[41] Hirschl (n 10); Tom Ginsburg, *Judicial Review in New Democracies: Constitutional Courts in Asian Cases* (CUP 2003); David Law and Tom Ginsburg, 'Constitutional Drafting in Latin America: A Quantitative Perspective' in Colin Crawford and Daniel Bonilla Maldonado (eds), *Constitutionalism in the Americas* (Edward Elgar 2018) 217.

[42] See Hirschl (n 10) 207–23.

[43] ibid 223.

[44] Heinz Klug, *Constituting Democracy: Law, Globalism, and South Africa's Political Reconstruction* (CUP 2000); Theunis Roux, *The Politico-Legal Dynamics of Judicial Review* (CUP 2018); Gary Jeffrey Jacobsohn, *The Wheel of Law: India's Secularism in Comparative Constitutional Context* (Princeton UP 2003); James Fowkes, 'Texts in a Time of Imposition: Lessons from Two Imposed Constitutions in Africa' in Richard Albert and others (eds), *The Law and Legitimacy of Imposed Constitutions* (Routledge 2018) 243; Michaela Hailbronner, 'Constitutional Legitimacy and the Separation of Powers in Africa: Looking forward' in Charles Fombad (ed), *Stellenbosch Handbooks in African Constitutional Law, Volume 1: The Separation of Powers* (OUP 2016) 385.

[45] Klug, *Constituting Democracy* (n 44).

their own distinctive constitutional outlook. The epistemic framework is thus pluralized but remains intact for the North itself.

(c) Comparative constitutional law from the Global South

Finally, in a third and more fundamental approach, some scholars demand to rethink comparative constitutional law *from* the perspective of the Global South and use the South as a tool for critique of constitutional orthodoxy. Here, the notion of the Global South functions as a lens to rethink comparative constitutional law in its entirety. This approach brings together authors from both North and South who are critical of orthodoxies in comparative constitutional discourse. The primary concern of this approach is to revise the epistemic framework of the discipline and to dismantle the hierarchy of legal ideas and scholarship dominated by Northern scholars and institutions.[46] Many scholars here insist on the originality of Southern constitutionalism and its distinctive constitutional themes and experiences.[47] Often, this includes recovering experiences in the South that would not count as 'constitutional' within an orthodox framework. Approaches belonging to this modus are often intertwined with critical legal theory and question the Western script of liberal constitutionalism with a distinctively emancipatory agenda in mind.[48] To this end, the notion of the Global South is used as a central theoretical concept, characterized by its ex-centric perspective outside Euro-America. At their most radical, its proponents perceive the Global South as an alternative lens to understand the world.[49] Methodologically, scholars belonging to this approach reject positivism and formalism as tools of legal scholarship and turn to other sources of knowledge such as anthropology, sociology of knowledge,

[46] Daniel Bonilla Maldonado, 'The Political Economy of Legal Knowledge' in Colin Crawford and Daniel Bonilla Maldonado (eds), *Constitutionalism in the Americas* (Edward Elgar 2018) 29; Jorge L Esquirol, *Ruling the Law: Legitimacy and Failure in Latin American Legal Systems* (CUP 2020); Baxi, 'Constitutionalism as a Site of State Formative Practices' (n 34) 1210. Boaventura de Sousa Santos, *The End of the Cognitive Empire: The Coming of Age of Epistemologies of the South* (Duke UP 2018).

[47] Philipp Dann and Arun Thiruvengadam (eds), *Democratic Constitutionalism in Continental Polities: EU and India Compared* (Edward Elgar 2021); Siri Gloppen and others (eds), *Courts and Power in Latin America and Africa* (Palgrave 2010); Armin von Bogdandy and others (eds), *Transformative Constitutionalism in Latin America: The Emergence of a New Ius Commune* (OUP 2017).

[48] Boaventura de Sousa Santos, 'Plurinationaler Konstitutionalismus und experimenteller Staat in Bolivien und Ecuador: Perspektiven aus einer Epistemologie des Südens' (2012) 45 (2) Kritische Justiz 163; Heiner Fechner, *Emanzipatorischer Rechtsstaat: Praxistheoretische Untersuchung soziokultureller Inklusion durch Recht am Beispiel Venezuelas* (Nomos 2016); Baxi, 'Constitutionalism as a Site of State Formative Practices' (n 34); Upendra Baxi, 'Postcolonial Legality: A Postscript from India' (2012) 45 (2) VRÜ/WCL 178; Roger Merino, 'Reimagining the Nation-State: Indigenous Peoples and the Making of Plurinationalism in Latin America' (2018) 31 (4) Leiden JIL 773.

[49] Oklopcic (n 3); Jedidiah J Kroncke, 'Legal Innovation as a Global Public Good: Remaking Comparative Law as Indigenization' (in this volume) 110; Florian Hoffmann, 'Facing *South*: On the Significance of An/Other Modernity in Comparative Constitutional Law' (in this volume) 41.

political economy, or post-structuralism.[50] The main epistemic and political implication is a challenge to existing structures of global knowledge production in comparative constitutional law.

C. Southern Constitutionalism as Distinctive Constitutional Experience

The authors of this volume contribute to the Southern turn in comparative constitutional law in a variety of ways and do not follow a unified theory or approach. They can be located in the latter two approaches outlined above (*with* and *from* the Global South) and thus reflect the internal plurality of Southern constitutionalism. From this plurality, however, emerge some recurring patterns and shared experiences that we want to highlight and develop further in this introductory chapter. We do not attempt to summarize each author's contribution here but rather highlight key thoughts at relevant points throughout the text.

Our own argument in this section is that the Global South is a useful concept to capture and understand a distinctive constitutional *experience*. Southern constitutionalism is, first and foremost, a shared experience, shaped by homogenous macro-dynamics and profoundly heterogeneous micro-dynamics. This constitutional experience is distinct from, and at the same time deeply entangled with, constitutionalism in the Global North. This distinctiveness of the Southern constitutional experience results from a combination of contextual and normative, historical and contemporary, global and local factors. It resides as much in the object of analysis as in the perspective of those who collectively identify with this experience.

We describe and analyse this distinctiveness on two levels: first, we argue that the history of colonialism and the position of the South in the geopolitical system are a *distinctive context* that shapes the experience of Southern constitutionalism in a dialectical relationship with its Northern counterpart (1). Secondly, we identify three *distinctive themes* that characterize Southern constitutionalism: constitutionalism as an experience of socio-economic

[50] See, for instance, the early observation by Baxi, 'Constitutionalism as a Site of State Formative Practices' (n 34) 1209: 'As a non-hegemonic epistemic enterprise, comparative constitutionalism needs to transform itself into constitutional ethnography, or the anthropology of power-fields'; Ruskola, *Legal Orientalism* (n 8); Kroncke (n 38).

transformation; constitutionalism as a site of struggle about political organization; and constitutionalism as denial of, and access to, justice (2).[51]

We hope that using the concept of the Global South helps not only to capture distinctive features and entanglements, but also to guard against some pitfalls of a global comparison, namely against essentializing, othering, and subordinating constitutional experiences from outside Euro-America. The Global South is a polythetic category, ie not all its members necessarily share all its distinctive features. Besides, the North–South divide is not a strict dichotomy. The adjective 'Global' highlights that the South is not a strictly geographical notion, and 'distinctiveness' (rather than 'difference') accentuates features that are particularly salient for the (self)description of the South but may be present in the North, too.

1. Context: the colonial experience and geopolitical asymmetries

As several authors in this volume emphasize, one starting point to grasp the distinct nature of constitutionalism in the South lies in the history of colonialism and the geopolitical asymmetries it entrenched.[52] Most societies in the South share the experience of having been colonized—at least in a wider sense of having been in the periphery of a global order that was centred around the North Atlantic. Conversely, the Northern/Western constitutional experience is shaped by its position at the centre of this global order. Or to put it more bluntly: historically, the North has been the colonizer, the South the colonized—and both have been bound together in an imperially structured global order.

Surely, the colonial experience is a heterogeneous one, and its impact on constitutionalism is modulated by a range of factors: the identity of the colonizer (Spanish, Portuguese, British, French, German empires, etc), the nature of colonialism (eg settler vs exploitation colonialism), the type of imperial rule

[51] These three themes are not meant as an exhaustive and comprehensive list capturing all aspects of Southern constitutionalism, and other themes remain possible. Cultural diversity, for example, could be another important trait of Southern constitutionalism, which we however treat as a cross-cutting dimension that is relevant across all of our three themes. Another area for further exploration would be the relationship of constitutional law in the South to international law, see Riegner, 'Comparative Foreign Relations Law between Centre and Periphery' (n 5).

[52] Christine Schwöbel-Patel, '(Global) Constitutionalism and the Geopolitics of Knowledge' (in this volume) 67; Heinz Klug, 'Transformative Constitutionalism as a Model for Africa?' (in this volume) 141; Sujit Choudhry, 'Postcolonial Proportionality: *Johar*, Transformative Constitutionalism and Same Sex Rights in India' (in this volume) 190.

(direct vs indirect), the duration and intensity of the colonial encounter and the time of decolonization (Latin America vs Asia and Africa), and the type of transition to independence (negotiated vs liberation war). The constitutional legacy of colonialism in Latin America thus differs in important respects from that in Africa and Asia, and former settler colonies like the USA and Australia are another category unto themselves.[53]

Yet, the colonial experience typically had some recurring features: a substantial period of foreign domination that interrupted autonomous evolution and replaced indigenous ideas, institutions, and elites with foreign ones; a colonial state structured by an imperial modality of resource extraction and social administration predicated on European superiority; a legal system imported from or heavily influenced by the metropolis which entrenched structures of political oppression, economic exploitation, racism, and physical violence; and the forced integration of colonized societies into a hierarchically structured global order, in which power and wealth was increasingly centred in Europe and North America.[54]

With respect to these experiences, formal 'decolonization' was both a moment of rupture and continuity. Colonial institutions both perished and persisted after independence. On the one hand, independence constitutions symbolized a break with the past and provided a foundation for a new political community with emancipatory possibilities unavailable under imperial rule. On the other hand, colonial institutions and laws persisted in practice, local elites replaced foreign ones, and new states appropriated colonial instruments of domination and exploitation. As importantly, the constitutional imagination and possibilities of postcolonial societies were heavily conditioned by the grammar of modern constitutionalism and the unequal global order in which they remained embedded. Postcolonial constitution-making thus has been an uneven process of constitutional mimicry (or 'transplantation' and 'migration'), poesis, and hybridization.[55]

One might object that constitutionalism in the North is equally marked by ruptures and continuities, especially in the French tradition of revolutionary

[53] Baxi, 'Postcolonial Legality' (n 48); Bonilla Maldonado and Riegner, 'Decolonization' (n 22); Kevin Bruyneel, 'Review Essay: On Settler Colonialism' (2020) 82 (1) The Review of Politics 145.

[54] Arudra Barra, 'What is "Colonial" About Colonial Laws?' (2016) 31 (1) American University International Law Review 137; Brenna Bhandar, *Colonial Lives of Property: Law, Land, and Racial Regimes of Ownership* (Duke UP 2018); Upendra Baxi, 'The Colonialist Heritage' in Pierre Legrand and Roderick JC Munday (eds), *Comparative Legal Studies: Traditions and Transitions* (CUP 2003) 46; Mahmood Mamdani, *Citizen and Subject: Contemporary Africa and the Legacy of Late Colonialism* (Princeton UP 2018).

[55] Bonilla Maldonado and Riegner, 'Decolonization' (n 22); Baxi, 'Postcolonial Legality' (n 48).

constitutionalism.[56] Nevertheless, there are differences: revolutionary constitutionalism in the North and its experience of rupture and continuity were predominantly an internal, domestic struggle. In the South, in contrast, external imperial forces (ideas, elites, powers, etc.) played a significant, if not dominant role, degrading and supressing endogenous developments. This co-governance from the outside is distinct and persists often long after formal decolonization.[57]

A second difference relates to the historical evolution of European modernity and its alternatives. Statehood, constitutionalism, secularism, capitalism, industrialization, and other features of European modernity developed over centuries and in a particular historical sequence. In contrast, imperialism suppressed similar or alternative processes in the colonies, and decolonization often compressed these processes into much shorter timespans. Many former colonies acquired formal attributes of statehood—territory, people, government, sovereignty, constitutions, a national economy, etc—practically overnight and had to achieve a lot at the same time: functioning state institutions, developing economies, mass democracy, constitutional systems, etc. To the extent that decolonization was a rupture, it was thus also a moment of overload. The experience of rupture and continuity in Southern constitutional development was hence profoundly different in many cases.[58]

For the geopolitical system, decolonization was also a moment of rupture and continuity. While formal empires dissolved and colonies acquired independence, most Southern nations continue to occupy a peripheral position in the global order. Economically, many of them remain dependent on commodity exports, capital imports, and asymmetric trade and debt relations.

[56] Constitutional theory has juxtaposed two types of constitutionalism, namely revolutionary and evolutionary constitutionalism, based on their understanding of the connection between law and politics, see in particular Christoph Möllers, 'Pouvoir Constituant—Constitution—Constitutionalism' in Armin von Bogdandy and Jürgen Bast (eds), *Principles of European Constitutional Law* (Hart & CH Beck 2009) 170; Hannah Arendt, *On Revolution* (Penguin Books 1963). For a global view of revolutionary constitutionalism see Bruce A Ackerman, *Revolutionary Constitutions: Charismatic Leadership and the Rule of Law* (Harvard UP 2019). The distinction between Northern and Southern revolutionary constitutionalism remains an important subject of further comparative research, especially with regard to the interplay of decolonial and revolutionary dynamics in the South.

[57] Surely, foreign European powers also sought to intervene in European revolutions (Prussian monarchists in France, for example) and constitutional ideas and practices were deeply entangled within Europe. But these external influences were of a different quality than imperial rule, although some of the struggles with foreign overbearance especially in areas of former European land empires might display some structural parallels with decolonization, see below section D.1 and James Fowkes and Michaela Hailbronner, 'Decolonizing Eastern Europe: A Global Perspective on 1989 and the World It Made' (2019) 17 (2) ICON 497.

[58] On the relevance of historical sequence in political, economic, and constitutional development see Sudipta Kaviraj, 'An Outline of a Revisionist Theory of Modernity' (2005) 46 (3) European Journal of Sociology 497.

Decolonization-era attempts to reform the international legal system, which pre-existed most postcolonial states, did not fundamentally change its structure.[59] Cold war tensions and US-American or Soviet hegemony limited the space for autonomous Southern politics. Global knowledge regimes continued to reflect epistemic hierarchies, which subordinate the South as space and subject of knowledge production. This geopolitics of knowledge, as Christine Schwöbel-Patel calls it in this volume, affects not least the production of legal knowledge and the discipline of comparative constitutional law.[60]

In sum, taking into account colonial legacies and geopolitical asymmetries is an analytical imperative of the Southern turn in comparative constitutional law. One cannot understand Southern constitutionalism without this context. At the same time, neither colonialism nor geopolitics furnishes monocausal and linear explanations of constitutional development, and more often than not ruptures and continuities create distinctly hybrid constitutional assemblages. Moreover, the global context itself is changing in response to the geopolitical rise of some emerging economies, and there is considerable variation in how Southern constitutional orders respond to, reject or vernacularize global influences. The respective local contexts thus remain a crucial factor in understanding the distinct constitutional experience of the Global South.

2. Themes: socio-economic transformation, political struggle, and justice

The constitutional experience of the Global South is characterized by three distinctive themes that recur both in the chapters of this volume and in the wider literature. The first theme relates to how constitutions are experienced as vehicles of socio-economic transformation (a). The second theme encompasses experiences of constitutionalism as site of state formative practices and of struggle about political organization between democratic and authoritarian forces (b). The third theme relates to the profoundly ambivalent nature of the state and its law, which leads to contradictory experiences of constitutionalism as both a denial of justice and as means of access to justice (c).

[59] Jochen von Bernstorff and Philipp Dann (eds), *The Battle for International Law: South–North Perspectives on the Decolonization Era* (OUP 2019).

[60] Schwöbel-Patel (n 52). See also Bonilla Maldonado, 'The Political Economy of Legal Knowledge' (n 46); Esquirol, *Ruling the Law* (n 46); Sousa Santos, *The End of the Cognitive Empire* (n 46).

(a) Constitutionalism as socio-economic transformation

Southern constitutionalism often encapsulates a distinctive response to experiences of poverty, exclusion, inequality, and historical injustice inherited from colonialism and perpetuated by the postcolonial state system. Poverty has been a deeply formative experience for the Global South, frequently associated with practices of exclusion based on gender, ethnicity, race, caste, geography, or socio-economic status. Southern states have been marked by high levels of internal economic inequality, much higher than within the North. And despite the rise of 'emerging economies', the North–South divide still reflects significant economic disparities between states.

This socio-economic context has deeply shaped the nature of statehood and constitutionalism across the Global South. For one, Southern states have largely been developmental states.[61] Beginning with early decolonization in Latin America, postcolonial states emerged with a modernizing impetus and sought to 'catch up' economically, politically and socially with European metropolises. During the high point of decolonization in the twentieth century, statehood became the universal vehicle for 'modernization', industrialization, and development across the Global South. State-led development policies (such as import substitution industrialization) sought to accelerate processes of socio-economic transformation that had taken over a century in Europe and North America. Inspired by dependency theorists and ideas for a New International Economic Order, some developmental states sought to achieve this aim and to overcome economic dependency by nationalizing key industries and natural resources.[62] Yet unlike nineteenth-century Europe and North America, developmental states of the twentieth century were defined and constrained by Eurocentric notions of development, external influence, and internal legacies of colonial administration and social stratification.[63]

In this context, constitutions and constitutional law in the Global South are conceived as symbols and instruments of fundamental social transformation,

[61] Meredith Woo-Cummings (ed), *The Developmental State* (Cornell UP 1999). The notion of 'developmental state' is sometimes limited to a few economically successful Asian states, but is used much more broadly here. See also Pinar Bilgin and Adam David Morton, 'Historicising Representation of "Failed States"' (2002) 23 (1) Third World Quarterly 55.

[62] Marion Mushkat, 'The Needs of the Developing Countries and the Shifting Views of International Law' (1971) 4 (1) VRÜ/WCL 1; Zdenek Červenka, 'Africa and the New International Economic Order' (1976) 9 (2) VRÜ/WCL 187; Emmanuel G Bello, 'The Pursuit of Rights and Justice in International Law by the Developing Nations' (1981) 14 (2) VRÜ/WCL 171.

[63] Luis Eslava, 'The Developmental State: Independence, Dependency, and History of the South' in Dann and Bernstorff (n 59) 71–100; Merino (n 48); Shalini Randeria, 'Cunning States and Unaccountable International Institutions' (2003) 44 (1) European Journal of Sociology 27; Marie von Engelhardt, *International Development Organizations and Fragile States* (Palgrave 2018).

aimed at dismantling socio-economic hierarchies and inequalities.[64] In contemporary comparative debates, this dynamic dimension is captured in particular by the concept of transformative constitutionalism, but it has a much older and broader lineage. Many independence constitutions of postcolonial states aimed at a decisive break with the past and at the foundation of a new political community. The revolutionary constitutions of Haiti were an early attempt to replace colonial slavery with an emancipatory black citizenship.[65] The Mexican Constitution of 1917 envisaged socio-economic rights and land reform as proto-transformative elements.[66] Some postcolonial constitutions, especially in Asia and Africa, envisioned a socialist transformation, and many allowed for the nationalization of natural resources, constitutionalizing the idea of permanent sovereignty over natural resources.[67] Beyond socialism, the idea of a 'directive constitution' (*constituição dirigente*), which drives a political, social, and economic transformation, was influential especially in Latin America and embraced by Brazil's constitution of 1988.[68] In an exemplary fashion, the Indian constitution of 1950 was envisioned from the outset as an anti-colonial, transformative document. As Sujit Choudhry reminds us in this volume, it conferred on the state and its courts an express mandate to attack social hierarchies and to redistribute economic and political power away from elites towards the hitherto politically powerless and economically deprived majority.[69]

Today, 'transformative constitutionalism' is sometimes conceived as a distinctive feature of constitutional states in the Global South and as a counter-concept to the 'liberal constitutionalism' of the Global North.[70] One reason

[64] 'Symbolic' in this context refers to the cultural importance of constitutions in processes of collective identity formation and should not be misunderstood as necessarily implying their ineffectiveness.

[65] Adom Getachew, 'Universalism After the Post-colonial Turn: Interpreting the Haitian Revolution' (2016) 44 (6) Political Theory 821.

[66] Gargarella (n 23) 101; Judith Schacherreiter, *Das Landeigentum als Legal Transplant in Mexiko: Rechtsvergleichende Analysen unter Einbezug postkolonialer Perspektiven* (Mohr Siebeck 2014); Schacherreiter, 'Tierra y libertad. Trasplantes jurídicos y rupturas en el derecho agrario mexicano' (2009) 3 Cuadernos de Literatura Jurídica 188; Javier Garciadiego, 'The Revolution' in Pablo Escalante (ed), *A New Compact History of Mexico* (El Colegio de México 2013) 229, 255.

[67] Julian Go, 'A Globalizing Constitutionalism?' (2003) 18 (1) International Sociology 71.

[68] Gilberto Bercovici, 'A problemática da constituição dirigente: algumas considerações sobre o caso brasileiro' (1999) 36 (142) Revista de Informação Legislativa 35; Luis Virgílio Afonso da Silva, *The Constitution of Brazil: A Contextual Analysis* (Hart Publishing 2019).

[69] Choudhry (n 52); Baxi, 'Constitutionalism as a Site of State Formative Practices' (n 34) 1205; Rohit De, *A People's Constitution: The Everyday Life of Law in the Indian Republic* (Princeton UP 2018); Gautam Bhatia, *The Transformative Constitution: A Radical Biography in Nine Acts* (Harper Collins India 2019).

[70] Upendra Baxi, 'Preliminary Notes on Transformative Constitutionalism' in Oscar Vilhena Vieira, Upendra Baxi, and Frans Viljoen (eds), *Transformative Constitutionalism: Comparing the Apex Courts of Brazil, India, and South Africa* (Pretoria University Law Press 2013) 19; David Bilchitz, 'Constitutionalism, the Global South, and Economic Justice' in Daniel Bonilla Maldonado (ed),

for this view is genealogical: the concept was initially used to characterize the South African post-apartheid constitution of 1996 (even though initially coined by US-American scholar Karl Klare). In this sense, transformative constitutionalism designates 'an enterprise of inducing large-scale social change through nonviolent political processes grounded in law'.[71] This idea travelled to other Southern constitutional orders with comparable contexts like India, Colombia, Brazil, and Bolivia.[72] Since then, comparatists have also identified substantive commonalities that characterize transformative constitutionalism in the Global South: an interventionist state that actively promotes social change; a fundamental rights doctrine that emphasizes social and collective rights, positive state obligations and horizontal effect among private parties; an activist role of constitutional courts, including broad access and innovative remedies; and an anti-formalist interpretive and legal culture geared towards dynamic change.[73]

Taken together, these elements characterize a constitutional type that is distinct from preservative constitutions that emphasize stability, negative rights, and a less interventionist state. The US federal constitution is maybe the clearest example of such a preservative, structural-liberal type—but also probably rather exceptional.[74] In fact, transformative elements can be found in various liberal-democratic constitutions in the Global North, especially in continental Europe. Constitutionalism emerging from the French revolution aimed at the transformation of feudal society, replacing old status hierarchies with an egalitarian promise. Across Europe, certain elements of the welfare state, whether social-liberal or social-democratic in origin, have been constitutionalized over

Constitutionalism of the Global South: The Activist Tribunals of India, South Africa, and Colombia (CUP 2013) 41–94.

[71] Karl Klare, 'Legal Culture and Transformative Constitutionalism' (1998) 14 (1) South African Journal on Human Rights 146, 150. See also Pius Langa, 'Transformative Constitutionalism' (2006) 17 (3) Stellenbosch Law Review 351; James Fowkes, 'Transformative Constitutionalism and the Global South: The View from South Africa' in Bogdandy and others (n 47) 97–121.

[72] Oscar Vilhena Vieira, Upendra Baxi, and Frans Viljoen (eds), *Transformative Constitutionalism: Comparing the Apex Courts of Brazil, India, and South Africa* (Pretoria University Law Press 2013); Bonilla Maldonado, *Constitutionalism of the Global South* (n 1); Boaventura de Sousa Santos, *Refundacíon del Estado en América Latina* (Siglo XXI 2010); Bogdandy and others, *Transformative Constitutionalism in Latin America* (n 47).

[73] Hailbronner, 'Transformative Constitutionalism' (n 1) 540f; Alun Gibbs, 'Theorizing Transformative Constitutional Change and the Experience of Latin American Constitutionalism' [2017] Law, Culture & the Humanities 1, 9f; Oscar Vilhena Vieira, Upendra Baxi, and Frans Viljoen, 'Some Concluding Thoughts on an Ideal, Machinery and Method' in Vieira, Baxi, and Viljoen (n 72) 617, 620.

[74] Michael Dowdle and John Wilkinson, 'On the Limits of Constitutional Liberalism: In Search of Constitutional Reflexivity' in Michael W Dowdle and Michael Wilkinson (eds), *Constitutionalism beyond Liberalism* (CUP 2017) 17–37.

time. The German Basic Law not only guided a post-authoritarian transformation, but also envisaged a social state actively shaping economy and society in an egalitarian direction.[75] Yet, these individual features remain less dominant in most Northern constitutional experiences and do not envisage the same kind of deep, constitutionally driven transformation. While constitutional courts play their role, the European welfare state remains, after all, primarily a legislative project. This difference becomes particularly evident in the area of socio-economic rights: their judicialization is rightfully considered an innovative hallmark of Southern constitutionalism that remains unmatched by the case law of Northern constitutional courts.[76]

But then again, if the activist role of courts is a distinctive feature of transformative constitutionalism in the Global South, it is also a contested one. Recent literature has differentiated the court-centrism of early accounts and highlighted the interplay of all branches of government as feature of transformative constitutionalism. In his contribution to this volume, Diego Werneck Arguelhes echoes this point when he argues that the transformation in Brazil was driven as much by the political branches as by courts. He also cautions against generalizing the framework of transformative constitutionalism too easily: relatively successful cases like the Colombian Constitutional Court are not necessarily representative, and constitutional texts, courts, lawyers, and the political branches may diverge in the extent to which they embrace a transformative vision. What ultimately matters is whether transformative norms and judgements are actually implemented, which is much harder to assess. Heinz Klug develops this thought when he suggests that transformative constitutionalism may be a useful yardstick for sociological analysis of different constitutional orders: is a constitution actually being implemented or floating meaninglessly above society? Is it used to support, challenge, or change the status quo? Like Arguelhes, Klug emphasizes that transformative constitutionalism is not limited to rights enforcement but also depends on a progressive interpretation of the structural elements of the constitution that advance democratic participation and transformative politics.

Our authors' reflections point to two open questions that are relevant for both the distinctiveness and the success of 'transformative constitutionalism': for one, one has to ask whether transformative constitutionalism has a distinctive substance beyond court-enforced rights, especially with respect

[75] This argument is forcefully made by Hailbronner, 'Transformative Constitutionalism' (n 1) 541ff. See generally Michaela Hailbronner, *Traditions and Transformations: The Rise of German Constitutionalism* (OUP 2015).

[76] Klug (n 52).

to the economic order it envisages? The constitutional history of the developmental state reminds us that economic constitutionalism can go well beyond the redistribution of (some) *public* resources through social rights litigation. Does transformative constitutionalism, with its frequent invocations of 'economic justice' and the 'democratization of the economy', have something distinctive to say about the structure of economic institutions that affect the initial distribution in the first place, such as private property, market economy, and corporate capitalism?[77] A second and similar question can be asked with respect to the relationship between transformative constitutionalism and the political system it envisages. As Roberto Gargarella argues, rights alone will not counter deeply entrenched inequality as long as the 'engine room' of the constitution, the organization of political power, remains unreformed.[78] This raises constitutional questions about political representation and electoral systems, political parties and campaign finance, legislative process and public scrutiny, and the political economy of transformative constitutionalism—in short: does transformative constitutionalism have its own, distinctive 'law of democracy' that favours a *transformative politics*?[79]

(b) Constitutionalism as site of struggle about political organization

Constitutionalism in the Global South also reflects the immense challenges of state-building and political organization in postcolonial, heterogeneous, and hierarchical societies. Constitutionalism is experienced not as stable order tending towards linear progress, but as site of state formative practices and of struggle about political organization between democratic and authoritarian forces.[80]

[77] On the one hand, transformative constitutionalism is not socialism: all constitutions discussed under this label accept, in principle, private property, markets, and corporations. On the other hand, they incorporate a considerable variety of potentially transformative economic elements, ranging from the social and ecological function of property to indigenous land rights, public ownership over natural resources, mixed economies, and state capitalist structures. See eg Jedidiah J Kroncke and Michael Riegner, 'Corporation' in Rainer Grote, Frauke Lachenmann, and Rüdiger Wolfrum (eds),*Max Planck Encyclopedia of Comparative Constitutional Law* (2020) ; Helena Alviar García, 'Looking beyond the Constitution: The Social and Ecological Function of Property' in Rosalind Dixon and Tom Ginsburg (eds), *Comparative constitutional law in Latin America* (Edward Elgar 2017) 176.

[78] Roberto Gargarella, 'Inequality and the Constitution: From Equality to Social Rights' (in this volume) 235, and Gargarella (n 23) 172ff.

[79] See Samuel Issacharoff, 'Comparative Constitutional Law as a Window on Democratic Institutions' in Erin F Delaney and Rosalind Dixon (eds), *Comparative Judicial Review* (Edward Elgar 2018) 60–82; Dann and Thiruvengadam (eds), *Democratic Constitutionalism in Continental Polities* (n 47); also Philipp Dann and Michael Riegner, 'Parliaments' in De Feyter and others (eds), *Law and Development Encyclopedia* (Edward Elgar 2020).

[80] Baxi, 'Constitutionalism as a Site of State Formative Practices' (n 34).

In most places, these challenges hark back to the moment of decolonization and the political form it took, the nation state. Under the dominant European vision of international law and modern constitutionalism, nation statehood was the only viable form of political organization to achieve self-determination.[81] Mimicking the European (nation) state offered colonized peoples a path to decolonization with a well-defined end point, but also implied limitations and difficulties for internal political organization and self-determination. For one, statehood implied the acceptance of colonial borders that imperial powers had imposed without regard to the diversity of groups and identities populating the territory, and it rejected alternative forms of political organization that would have undone colonial spatial ordering, such as pan-national federations based on religious, linguistic or cultural variables.[82] In this context, the idea of a homogenous nation as the subject of self-determination—one state, one nation, etc—clashed violently with the cultural, racial, and religious diversity of postcolonial societies, contributing to internal divisions, violent conflict, civil war, secession, and partition.

In addition, independent nation states inherited the authoritarian legacy of colonialism: repressive institutions and laws, legalized practices of violence, executive discretion unconstrained by law, permanent states of exception, unaccountable government, as well as practices of racist subordination and economic exploitation. These authoritarian instruments and practices often remained in place after independence, and new elites deployed them to quell dissent and divisions within the heterogeneous populace. As Weitseng Chen points out (in this volume), the sedition laws used today in Hong Kong against democratic protestors are of colonial origin.[83] Colonialism had also inhibited the emergence of the democratic culture and institutions commonly thought to enable democracy in Euro-America, such as a public sphere, political parties, and civil society.[84] Where they did evolve in the South, they took hybrid forms, eg political parties sometimes formed not along ideological but ethnic or religious lines. The autonomous development of political institutions and

[81] Eslava, 'The Developmental State' (n 62); Bonilla Maldonado and Riegner, 'Decolonization' (n 22).

[82] Adom Getachew, *Worldmaking after Empire: The Rise and Fall of Self-determination* (Princeton UP 2019); Margaret Kohn and Keally D McBride, *Political Theories of Decolonization: Postcolonialism and the Problem of Foundations* (OUP 2011) 18ff.

[83] Weitseng Chen, 'Same Bed, Different Dreams: Constitutionalism and Legality in Asian Hybrid Regimes' (in this volume) 250. See also Klug (n 52); Mara Malagodi, 'Dominion Status and the Origins of Authoritarian Constitutionalism in Pakistan' (2019) 17 (4) ICON 1235. For the impact of pre-colonial and post-colonial state structures, see Pierre Englebert, *State Legitimacy and Development in Africa* (Lynne Rienner 2000).

[84] See only Boaventura de Sousa Santos, 'Public Sphere and Epistemologies of the South' (2012) 37 (1) African Development 43.

culture was further inhibited by the Cold War tensions, foreign intervention, and the economic pressures and interdependencies of a globalized economy.[85]

Under these difficult circumstances, constitutions in the Global South had the task of creating the very conditions considered to be prerequisites of their own existence. Southern constitutionalism has been a site of state formative practices and—often violent—nation-building projects.[86] These practices and projects have evolved over time in democratic or authoritarian directions, with fits and starts, and recurring phases of constitutional crisis and stability. From this unsteady process emerges, on the one hand, a rich practice of innovation and adaptation of democratic institutions. In processes of hybridization, alternatives to the single-nation state emerged, namely the idea of state-nations and pluri-national states.[87] Institutionally, federalism, territorial autonomies, legal pluralism, and the recognition of collective linguistic and cultural rights became common strategies to accommodate diversity. At the same time, also in successful constitutional democracies like India, electoral processes, political representation, and political parties reflect the diversity of postcolonial societies as much as they continue to struggle with the legacies of colonial subordination and exclusion.[88]

On the other hand, many Southern constitutions pursued the process of state- and nation-building not by limiting public power and protecting individual rights, but by concentrating power in imperial presidencies or unconstrained executives.[89] As Heinz Klug reminds us, 'constitutions without constitutionalism'[90] or 'thin constitutionalism' have been a long-standing feature of postcolonial statehood in Africa, along with weak administrations, patrimonial forms of governance, coups, and authoritarianism. One explanation, according to Klug, lies in the distinctive nature of the postcolonial state

[85] Odd Arne Westad, *The Global Cold War: Third World Interventions and the Making of our Times* (CUP 2005); Prashad, *The Darker Nations* (n 11); Michael Dowdle, 'On the Regulatory Geography of Modern Capitalism: Putting "rule of law" in its Place' <https://www.law.ox.ac.uk/sites/files/oxlaw/dowdle_putting_rule_of_law_in_its_place.pdf> accessed 8 March 2020.

[86] Baxi, 'Constitutionalism as a Site of State Formative Practices' (n 34).

[87] Mostafa Rejai and Cynthia H Enloe, 'Nation-States and State-Nations' (1969) 13 (2) International Studies Quarterly 140; Boaventura de Sousa Santos, *Refundación del Estado en América Latina: Perspectivas desde una epistemología del Sur* (3rd edn, Siglo XXI 2010) 81ff; Alfred Stepan, Juan Linz, and Yogendra Yadav, *Crafting State-Nations* (Johns Hopkins UP 2011).

[88] Dann and Thiruvengadam, *Democratic Constitutionalism in Continental Polities* (n 47), in particular Hailbronner and Thayyil therein.

[89] Gargarella (n 23); Jose Cheibub, Zachary Elkins, and Tom Ginsburg, 'Still the Land of Presidentialism? Executives and the Latin American Constitution' in Detlef Nolte and Almut Schilling-Vacaflor (eds), *New Constitutionalism in Latin America: Promises and Practices* (Ashgate 2012) 73–98; Prempeh (n 24).

[90] Okoth-Ogendo, 'Constitutions Without Constitutionalism: Reflections on an African Political Paradox' in Douglas Greenberg and others (eds), *Constitutionalism and Democracy: Transitions in the Contemporary World* (OUP 1993) 65–82. See also Klug (n 52).

and the institutional legacies of colonialism that remain dominant within societies and were not fundamentally transformed by negotiated independence constitutions that primarily facilitated the transfer of power to local elites.

Besides, constitutions have thus also been instruments of authoritarian legality. This aspect has regained prominence in recent comparative debates about constitutions in authoritarian regimes and the resurgence of illiberal governments across North and South.[91] In this literature, 'authoritarian constitutionalism' designates a system of political rule in which constitutions do not effectively constrain the political leadership but nevertheless perform certain governance functions, such as coordinating ruling elites, controlling lower-level agents, incentivizing economic activity, and providing political legitimacy.[92] Primary examples are the economically successful developmental states in Asia, analysed by Weitseng Chen in his chapter on constitutionalism and legality in Asian hybrid regimes.[93] These constitutional systems have proved relatively stable and functional. Moreover, they have become less authoritarian over time as they incorporate elements of liberal democratic constitutionalism, at least on paper. In practice, however, they remain characterized by a distinct form of authoritarian legality, marked by a pragmatic, instrumental commitment to constitutionalism that promotes governmental performance and economic development. This stabilizes the system and makes a linear transition to liberal democratic constitutionalism anything but assured. For Chen, studying these constitutional orders uncovers alternative, sometimes functionally equivalent constitutional concepts and mechanisms that pluralize our understanding of constitutionalism in all its variants.

The dichotomy between liberal and authoritarian constitutionalism is further complicated by Roberto Niembro Ortega's chapter in this volume on the constitutional development of Mexico.[94] According to Niembro, what makes a constitution authoritarian is not necessarily its content but the mentality of those who wield power under it. Even a constitution with power-limiting features on paper, like the Mexican one, can thus become authoritarian in practice. This observation is all the more salient as authoritarian tendencies resurface

[91] Tom Ginsburg and Alberto Simpser (eds), *Constitutions in Authoritarian Regimes* (CUP 2014); Mark A Graber, Sanford Levinson, and Mark V Tushnet (eds), *Constitutional Democracy In Crisis?* (OUP 2018); Helena Alviar García and Günter Frankenberg (eds), *Authoritarian Constitutionalism: Comparative Analysis and Critique* (Edward Elgar 2019).

[92] Tom Ginsburg and Alberto Simpser, 'Introduction: Constitutions in Authoritarian Regimes' in Ginsburg and Simpser (n 91) 1–18; Mark Tushnet, 'Authoritarian Constitutionalism' (2015) 100 (2) Cornell Law Review 392.

[93] See Chen (n 83).

[94] Roberto Niembro Ortega, 'The Challenge of Transforming Mexican Authoritarian Constitutionalism' (in this volume) 270.

within liberal constitutional states in Europe and even in the US. This further unsettles the dichotomy between liberal and authoritarian constitutions and opens conceptual space for comparison of other forms of hybrid arrangements and overlaps, for instance the transitional justice approaches to authoritarian legacies in democratic constitutional states, or the 'liberal authoritarianism' seen by some as undemocratic imposition of economic liberalization, austerity, and structural adjustment, be it within the EU or the Global South.[95] These debates across the globe question the narrative of linear progress inherent in some accounts of liberal constitutionalism. While Euro-America may not necessarily be evolving towards the South, Southern constitutionalism appears to offer a more complicated, and possibly more realistic, narrative of constitutional development.

(c) Constitutionalism as denial of and access to justice

The two earlier elements converge in a third, distinctive theme—namely, the profoundly ambivalent, sometimes even contradictory, nature of the state and its law in the Global South. Like the metaphorical Janus, state and law often have two faces: one looks forward, one backward; one is strong, one weak; one emancipatory, one oppressive. Constitutionalism is thus experienced as both a denial of justice, and as means of access to justice.

States in the Global South are often two-faced in that they are, on the one hand, strong states: as 'developmental states' they organize economic activity, they keep together extremely heterogeneous societies without a strong unitary identity, and they use the repressive and authoritarian instruments inherited from the colonial state. On the other hand, many Southern states were often 'instant states', created overnight, without functional institutions and local elites, sufficient public resources, and social legitimacy. Many remain dependent on external support and are vulnerable to global economic shocks, while waves of liberalization, privatization, and structural adjustment have weakened state capacity to provide public services and governance.

As much as there is an ambivalence in the state, there is an ambivalence in the perception of its law. On the one hand, law is an instrument of emancipation and liberation—for the society at large (the right to self-determination) and for the individual and disadvantaged groups (rights, affirmative action,

[95] Michael A Wilkinson, 'Authoritarian Liberalism in the European Constitutional Imagination: Second Time as Farce?' (2015) 21 (3) ELJ 313; Hermann Heller, 'Authoritarian Liberalism?' (2015) 21 (3) ELJ 295.

etc).[96] Transformative constitutionalism embodies this emancipatory face of law. On the other hand, law is often also perceived as an instrument of oppression, subordination, and exploitation—for societies, social groups, and individuals alike. Constitutionalism is perceived as entrenching these structures of subordination and exploitation and insulating them from democratic change.

This ambivalence is not exclusive to the South. It is in fact a core of Marxist critique of the state and its law in general.[97] However, it is interesting to realize that in response to these ambivalences and contradictions, the legal and constitutional orders of the South display more pronounced, flexible, and multifaceted reactions to the law of the state. For one, the social legitimacy and normativity of law is more precarious. The Latin American adage—'*obedece mas no cumple*' (one obeys but doesn't comply)—illustrates the fraught relationship of citizens and public officials with state law across many parts of the Global South. Law is enforced and complied with selectively. Informal rules, institutions, and practices gain a distinct importance in understanding how law really works in action. Citizens often turn to non-state collectives and their norms, such as religious or ethnic groups, indigenous peoples, social movements, trade unions, or business associations.[98] The result is diverse forms of legal pluralism and non-state justice systems, which are increasingly recognized by constitutions across the South. One example is personal laws in India, another self-governed indigenous territories in Bolivia.[99] Even without formal recognition, such intermediary collectives play an important role in struggles about the interpretation and application of constitutions, as debates about societal constitutionalism or 'constitutionalism from below' attest.[100]

[96] On this ambivalence see Baxi, 'Postcolonial Legality' (n 48); on the historical roots of attitudes towards the law see Yves Dezalay and Bryan Garth, *Asian Legal Revivals* (University of Chicago Press 2010).

[97] At the same time, one has to point out the Northern stereotype about the presumed inefficacy of law in the South, from which many Northern scholars conclude that it is worthless to study them. The question of laws' efficacy strikes us as a gradual question (and many examples of ineffective Northern laws could be gathered). This point is forcefully made by Daniel Bonilla Maldonado, 'Introduction: Toward a Constitutionalism of the Global South' in Daniel Bonilla Maldonado (ed), *Constitutionalism of the Global South: The Activist Tribunals of India, South Africa, and Colombia* (CUP 2013) 1–38; Jorge Esquirol, 'The Failed Law of Latin America' (2008) 56 (1) American Journal of Comparative Law 75. It is also implicit in Trubek and Galanter, 'Scholars in Self-estrangement' (n 26).

[98] Siddharth de Souza, 'Non-State Justice Systems' in Rainer Grote, Frauke Lachenmann, and Rüdiger Wolfrum (eds), *Max Planck Encyclopedia of Comparative Constitutional Law* (2019, online).

[99] Tanja Herklotz, 'Dead Letters? The Uniform Civil Code through the Eyes of the Indian Women's Movement and the Indian Supreme Court' (2016) 49 (2) VRÜ/WCL 148; Merino (n 48).

[100] Schwöbel-Patel (n 52); Gavin Anderson, 'Societal Constitutionalism, Social Movements, and Constitutionalism from Below' (2013) 20 (2) Indiana Journal of Global Legal Studies 881; Boaventura de Sousa Santos and Cesar Rodriguez-Garavito (eds), *Law and Globalization from Below: Towards a Cosmopolitan Legality* (CUP 2005); Bonilla Maldonado, 'Introduction' (n 97).

Another distinctive element of Southern constitutionalism is the emergence of alternative and partly collectivized avenues and instruments to use the law but also to resist the law and the state.[101] These avenues can often be found under the notion of 'access to justice'.[102] As David Bilchitz argues in his chapter, access to justice is a core capability citizens need to realize substantive claims to socio-economic rights. In the context of poverty and inequality, access is facilitated by innovative procedural devices that 'bring justice within the reach of the poor masses', as the Supreme Court of India put it.[103] Examples for such procedures are the '*tutela*'/'*amparo*' in Latin America or 'public interest litigation' in India.[104] Often, these instruments are used in strategic litigation by civil society organizations or social movements that seek to defend and enforce collective rights of the groups they represent. A similar function is performed by state institutions constitutionally empowered to represent citizens' and collective interests, such as the Ministério Publico in Brazil or the Public Protector in South Africa.[105] But access to justice can also refer to dispute settlement within non-state justice systems, such as religious institutions, indigenous tribunals, or the Nyaya Panchayats in India. In these situations, access to justice leads away from the state and may be a way of resisting its law.[106]

Again, it is useful and necessary to juxtapose presumed Southern experiences against those in the North. And yes, Northern legal systems also know instruments like legal aid and clinics. But then again, such devices are hardly at the core of their constitutional identity.[107] It seems that 'access to justice' responds to distinctly Southern experiences with law and constitutionalism. At the same time, it is increasingly recognized in international and comparative discourse, most prominently in Sustainable Development Goal 16 of the UN's Agenda 2030.[108] From a Southern perspective, this globalization is ambivalent.

[101] Julia Eckert (ed), *Law Against the State: Ethnographic Forays into Law's Transformations* (CUP 2014); Partha Chatterjee, *Lineages of the Political Society* (Columbia UP 2011).

[102] See only David Mason, 'Access to Justice in South Africa' (1999) 17 Windsor Yearbook of Access to Justice 230; Mauro Cappelletti and Bryant Garth, *Access to Justice: The Worldwide Movement to Make Rights Effective* (AW Sijthoff 1978).

[103] *People's Union for Democratic Rights v Union of India*, 1982 AIR 1473.

[104] Anuj Bhuwania, *Courting the People: Public Interest Litigation in Post-Emergency India* (CUP 2017); Allan Brewer-Carías, 'The Amparo as an Instrument of a Ius Constitutionale Commune' in Bogdandy and others (n 47) 171–90. As early as 1970, an article in VRÜ/WCL discussed the '*amparo*'-remedies in Latin America: see Juan Jose Reyven, 'Der Grundrechtsschutz (Habeas Corpus, Recurso de Amparo) im argentinischen Recht' (1970) 3 (2) VRÜ/WCL 179.

[105] Klug (n 52).

[106] Souza (n 98). As early as 1968, an article in *VRÜ/WCL* discussed the 'Nyaya Panchayats' in India: see Detlef Kantowsky, 'Indische Laiengerichte. Die Nyaya Panchayats in Uttar Pradesh' (1968) 1 (2) VRÜ/WCL 140.

[107] But see on the underlying problems Deborah L Rhode, *Access to Justice* (OUP 2004).

[108] SDG 16 reads: "Promote peaceful and inclusive societies for sustainable development, provide access to justice for all and build effective, accountable and inclusive institutions at all levels . . ." See also

On the one hand, access to justice risks becoming a narrow technical term or a broad superficial label for rule of law promotion projects.[109] On the other hand, it can also provide an opportunity for what Florian Hoffmann in this volume calls 'meridionalization',[110] in this case of the global rule of law discourse. Access to justice can, and should, be understood as a conceptual space for rethinking key constitutional concepts *from* the South, by rooting them in concrete experiences of injustice *in* the South. These injustices only begin with the lack of access to the legal system; they also relate to the entire enterprise of pursuing justice by legal means. 'Justice' thus acquires multiple meanings—social justice, distributive justice, racial justice, gender justice, environmental justice, climate justice, etc. Those who are denied 'access to justice' are excluded from this entire enterprise of pursuing justice through law. Understood in this broader sense, access to justice evokes diverse social struggles for justice and subaltern perspectives on constitutionalism, a 'constitutionalism of the wretched'.[111] At the same time, 'access' to justice emphasizes that constitutionalism is not identical with justice, but can only, and ideally, provide a path towards it. Making access to justice a central constitutional concept thus opens up a critical and emancipatory horizon within comparative constitutional law, all while acknowledging its inherent limitations.

D. Implications for Comparative Constitutional Scholarship: South as Sensibility

So far, we have argued that the concept of the Global South is useful to understand a distinctive constitutional experience that can pluralize and enrich comparative constitutional law. In the following section, we take this argument further and contend that taking the Global South seriously has implications for comparative constitutional scholarship as a whole: the Southern turn also implies an approach to *doing* comparative law that improves our understanding of constitutional law in both North and South. In other words, the 'Global South'

Michael Trebilcock and Ronald Daniels, *Rule of Law Reform and Development: Charting the Fragile Path of Progress* (Edward Elgar 2008) 236ff.

[109] Critically Günter Frankenberg, *Comparative Law as Critique* (Edward Elgar 2016) 205ff.

[110] Hoffmann (n 49) 42.

[111] Vidya Kumar, 'Towards a Constitutionalism of the Wretched: Global Constitutionalism, International Law and the Global South' (*Völkerrechtsblog*, 27 July 2017) DOI 10.17176/20170727-141227, <https://voelkerrechtsblog.org/towards-a-constitutionalism-of-the-wretched/> accessed 8 March 2020.

also denotes a specific epistemic, methodological, and institutional sensibility of the comparatist. This sensibility reinforces three movements that are already underway in the discipline: towards epistemic reflexivity (1), methodological pluralism (2), and institutional diversification (3).

The Global South thus acquires a double meaning: it is not only a concept that captures a distinct constitutional *experience*, but also an epistemic, methodological, and institutional *approach* to doing comparative law. This double understanding also promises new insights for constitutional law in the Global North. For one, our notion of distinctiveness highlights features that are particularly salient for the (self-)description of the South, but may equally be present in the North and deserve closer attention there. Besides, the entangled nature of North and South means that one cannot be understood without the other. Finally, the complementary notion of the Global North may, *mutatis mutandis*, be useful in rethinking the distinctive constitutional experience of Euro-America in a global framework. To achieve a deeper understanding of the distinctiveness and entanglements of both North and South, we thus need an epistemically, methodologically, and institutionally sensitive approach to doing comparative constitutional law generally. In that sense, the Southern turn is also a double turn: after the pivot to the South, it turns back to the North and to the world as a whole. We sought to capture this double turn when we gave our journal, formerly the *Law and Politics in Asia, Africa and Latin America*, the new English name in 2018, namely *World Comparative Law*.[112]

1. Epistemic reflexivity

The first implication of a Southern turn for comparative constitutional law is the need for epistemic reflexivity. Epistemic reflexivity concerns the way in which the comparatist approaches the foundations of knowledge production—the very grammar of our discipline, the basic concepts and theoretical assumptions, the voices that speak, and the silences this entails. It describes a particular research ethos that does not rush to find 'solutions' to pre-defined 'problems' but rethinks the questions we ask, the categories we use, the perspectives we take. Reflexivity requires us to complete several epistemic moves already under way in the discipline.

[112] For a parallel formulation and partial demonstration of this approach, see Philipp Dann and Arun Thiruvengadam, 'Framing a Comparative Law of Democracy: An Introduction' in Dann and Thiruvengadam, *Democratic Constitutionalism in Continental Polities* (n 47) 1.

The first is the move from epistemic hierarchy to recognizing epistemic injustice and aiming for epistemic equality. It is important to step back first and reflect how constitutional scholarship has so far neglected and subordinated Southern forms of knowledge at great cost for individuals, collectives, and scholarship itself.[113] The recognition of this injustice and its proactive correction strikes us as an important first step to then reach some kind of epistemic equality. As a global discipline, comparative constitutional law must accord 'equal dignity' to all constitutional discourses in North and South.[114] This implies that Southern and Northern authors, texts, concepts, histories are equally legitimate reference points in constitutional discourse. Noting *distinctive* features or differences does not imply a hierarchization, and the comparatist needs to take into account the 'power effects of history' on both theories and socio-political constellations.[115] Epistemic equality also demands fundamental conceptual openness, requiring us to accept phenomena as 'constitutional' that may not qualify as such from the perspective of Western liberal constitutionalism.[116] This may include, for instance, various forms of societal constitutionalism from below, indigenous approaches to constitutionalism including rights of nature, or a rethinking of the nation state as a vehicle for collective self-determination in pluri-national contexts.[117] Such openness includes the willingness of Northern scholars to effectively learn from and import Southern institutions, concepts, and theoretical approaches, and transform their own.[118] This point is also forcefully made by Jedidiah Kroncke in his contribution to this volume when he argues that the role of the comparatist ought to be that of an 'indigenizer' of foreign legal knowledge, scanning globally for legal innovations and adapting them to one's own legal context.[119]

[113] Daniel Bonilla Maldonado, 'The Political Economy of Legal Knowledge' in Colin Crawford and Daniel Bonilla Maldonado (eds), *Constitutionalism in the Americas* (Edward Elgar 2018) 29–78; Sousa Santos, *The End of the Cognitive Empire* (n 46).

[114] Baxi, 'Constitutionalism as a Site of State Formative Practices' (n 34) 1210. See also Bonilla Maldonado, 'Introduction' (n 97).

[115] Ina Kerner, 'Beyond Eurocentrism: Trajectories towards a Renewed Political and Social Theory' (2018) 44 (5) Philosophy & Social Criticism 550.

[116] Zoran Oklopcic, 'Comparing as (Re-)Imagining: Southern Perspective and the World of Constitutions' (in this volume) 86; Schwöbel-Patel (n 52) 84: 'A constitutionalism from below may stretch the term so far that it becomes unrecognizable.'

[117] See eg Merino (n 48); conceptualizing India and the EU as continental polities, see contributions in Dann and Thiruvengadam, *Democratic Constitutionalism in Continental Polities* (n 47).

[118] For example, it might be productive to ask what can be learned from post- and decolonial approaches and experiences in the South for understanding contemporary constellations of post-authoritarian constitutionalism and its struggle with foreign overbearance, especially in areas of former European land empires in East and Southeast Europe. See eg Fowkes and Hailbronner, 'Decolonizing Eastern Europe' (n 57); Bonilla Maldonado and Riegner, 'Decolonization' (n 22); Jan Komarek, 'Waiting for the Existential Revolution in Europe' (2014) 12 (1) ICON 190; Ivan Krastev and Stephen Holmes, *The Light that Failed: A Reckoning* (Allen Lane 2019).

[119] Kroncke (n 49) 128ff.

The second move is towards multi-perspectivity: there is no one privileged standpoint for comparison, and the comparatist must adopt multiple perspectives. This implies, as Florian Hoffmann argues in this volume, a decentring of Euro-American perspectives—not only by addition of new materials, but by provincializing its theoretical approach with respect to the scope of their claims to validity and applicability; by engaging in inter-contextual dialogue; by decentring the thematic focus or agenda setting in order to go beyond constellations of the Euro-Atlantic world.[120] This requires 'distancing' and 'differencing' on the part of the Northern comparatist.[121] It may require, for instance, taking a subaltern perspective that 'define[s] the experience of constitutional development from the standpoint of constitutional losers, not winners'.[122] To do so, one might try to develop the idea of access to justice, as we have suggested above.

A third move is towards relationality. Even though we study other jurisdictions as 'foreign', it would be wrong to think of each other as separate entities with fixed identities. As postcolonial legal theory teaches us, (legal) culture is an inherently hybrid phenomenon, marked by conflicts, contradictions, and global entanglements.[123] This puts the comparatist in a somewhat precarious position: on the one hand, the hybrid character of culture requires us to avoid essentialist and fixed depictions of legal systems. At the same time, however, it would be equally dangerous to deny differences for the sake of universalizing problems and experiences. Comparative constitutional law thus might be described as a navigating exercise between those two poles, as an endeavour which uses this tension to understand similarity and difference. [124]

2. Methodological pluralism

The second implication is the need for methodological pluralism. This means several things: first, doctrinal and formalist approaches alone are not sufficient to understand the constitutional experiences in either North or South in their

[120] Hoffmann (n 49); Kerner (n 115). For an application across the North-South divide, see Smarika Lulz and Michael Riegner, 'Freedom of Expression and Hate Speech Law', in Dann and Thiruvengadam, *Democratic Constitutionalism in Continental Polities* (n 47), forthcoming.

[121] Günter Frankenberg, 'Critical Comparisons: Rethinking Comparative Law' (1985) 26 (2) Harvard International Law Journal 411.

[122] Baxi, 'Constitutionalism as a Site of State Formative Practices' (n 34) 1185.

[123] Daniel Bonilla Maldonado, 'The Concept of Culture and the Cultural Study of Law: An Essay' (2019) 52 (3) VRÜ/WCL 297.

[124] Judith Schacherreiter, 'Postcolonial Theory and Comparative Law: On the Methodological and Epistemological Benefits to Comparative Law through Postcolonial Theory' (2016) 49 (3) VRÜ/WCL 291.

multiple contexts. Despite its limitations, an enlightened functionalist approach can still be a useful starting point.[125] As Weitseng Chen demonstrates in his chapter, functional analysis of non-liberal legal orders may uncover functional equivalents to liberal constitutional institutions that help us understanding both the functioning of authoritarian systems and its democratic counterparts.[126] But ultimately this functionalism must be contextualized.

Second, while hardly anyone disputes anymore that a meaningful comparative endeavour requires us to embed the law in its societal contexts, it is far less obvious to which neighbouring disciplines we should talk to when doing comparative legal research.[127] At first glance, the answer to this question seems obvious: the discipline we engage with depends on the questions we ask and the research design we pick. Yet, looking at the distinct constitutional experiences we have mapped in part three of this introduction, some neighbouring disciplines impose themselves more than others for context-sensitive comparison from and with the South. Understanding the impact of colonialism and formal decolonization on the state, for instance, is not possible without reference to various fields of history, be it political history, economic history, or history from below. Likewise, once we have acknowledged the central role of global and domestic inequality for the constitutional systems in the Global South, there is no way around deepening our conversation with political economy. Though political economy has reflected for a long time on many of the questions that are at the heart of the socio-economic dimension of constitutional law (put simply: who gets what), the interaction between law and political economy has only recently began to intensify.[128] And finally, the need to capture the emic perspective on Southern constitutional *experiences* makes anthropology another important partner for contextual comparison. No matter if we try to understand how injustice is perceived on the ground and battled with legal instruments, whose knowledge and social reality counts in constitution-making, or how 'radically different conceptions of law' evolve—all those elements of

[125] See for a convincing reconstruction of functionalist thought Ralf Michaels, 'The Functional Method of Comparative Law' in Reinhard Zimmermann and Mathias Reimann (eds), *The Oxford Handbook of Comparative Law* (OUP 2006) 340–380.

[126] Chen (n 83).

[127] On the need for interdisciplinarity in comparative constitutional scholarship see Hirschl (n 10).

[128] David Kennedy, 'Law and the Political Economy of the World' (2013) 26 (1) Leiden Journal of International Law 7; Katharina Pistor, The *Code of Capital: How the Law Creates Wealth and Inequality* (Princeton UP 2019); David Singh Grewal and Jedediah Purdy, 'Introduction: Law and Neoliberalism' (2014) 77 (4) Law and Contemporary Problems 1; David Singh Grewal, Amy Kapczynski, and Jedediah Purdy, 'Law and Political Economy: Toward a Manifesto' (*Law and Political Economy*, 6 November 2017) <https://lpeblog.org/2017/11/06/law-and-political-economy-toward-a-manifesto/> accessed 8 March 2020.

world constitutionalism cannot be studied with doctrinal legal methods but rather by engaging in 'thick descriptions' of local legal contexts. [129]

It is important to emphasize that these methodological tools are to be deployed with respect to constitutional experiences in South and North alike: to understand entanglements and interdependencies between Southern and Northern constitutional experiences, we need to understand the *global* history of colonialism and decolonization; the *global* political economy; and the processes of *glocalization* of norms that are ongoing across the North–South divide. Given what we have said about epistemic reflexivity, interdisciplinarity should not become a tool of othering the South yet again by means of methodology.

This epistemic concern also leads to a third methodological consideration, namely the equal relevance of formalist and doctrinal comparison with and from the South. While interdisciplinarity is important, we should not dismiss the value of constitutional experiences in the South *as law* by limiting comparison to legal realist or social scientific approaches.[130] Law has a relative autonomy and internal rationality that should be taken seriously across the North–South divide. Comparative *law* ultimately is *also* a hermeneutic exercise of understanding legal meaning. What is required is a layered narrative that takes into account constitutional text, interpretation, underlying theoretical and ideological assumptions, as well as the multifaceted contexts beyond the law.[131]

3. Institutional diversification, collaboration, slow comparison

The third and final implication concerns the institutional and organizational dimension of doing comparative constitutional law research. The epistemic and methodological requirements we describe above make comparison a complex and demanding enterprise that an individual comparatist will struggle to pursue well in a short amount of time. There are thus certain institutional and organizational prerequisites that are rarely discussed but highly important in

[129] In a similar vein, cultural studies and law and literature may be a promising way to understand processes of othering and collective identity formation that are crucial for legal consciousness, see eg Munshi (n 35).

[130] Jorge Esquirol, 'The Geopolitics of Constitutionalism in Latin America' in Colin Crawford and Daniel Bonilla Maldonado (eds), *Constitutionalism in the Americas* (Edward Elgar 2018) 79–108.

[131] Günter Frankenberg, 'Comparing Constitutions: Ideas, Ideals, and Ideology—Toward a Layered Narrative' (2006) 4 (3) ICON 439; Baxi, 'Constitutionalism as a Site of State Formative Practices' (n 34) 1188–89.

practice. What is required are a diversification of the scholarly infrastructure of comparative law, new modes of collaboration, and slow comparison.

Up to date, the majority of prestigious law schools, widely cited journals, and powerful think tanks remains in the Western hemisphere. Southern voices, by contrast, are still facing numerous hurdles both in terms of access and recognition. Targeting those asymmetries thus requires us to think about modes of collaboration and questions of organization.[132] This begins with seemingly technical questions such as setting a conference location or a reimbursement policy, continues with issues of copyright and open access to research publications, and extends to the very question of how we organize comparative research. If the age of the solitary comparatist is over, we must turn to new modes of organization such as dialogical and collaborative forms of research in which there is time to reflect and understand each other without the pressure to produce easy comparative 'take-aways'. Making such collaborative settings work is not only a question of time and resources, but also of diversity. This includes geographical diversity, but also—and equally important—diversity in terms of gender, race, language, and socio-economic background.[133] All this can be a challenging exercise—as is perhaps best demonstrated by this book. While we succeeded to convene authors from diverse geographies across the Global South, the volume does not reflect the diversity of experiences in other dimensions in the same way that our journal has done over the years.[134]

Taken together, the epistemic, methodological, and institutional demands and challenges of sophisticated comparative constitutional scholarship require one particularly valuable thing that is in particularly short supply in today's academia: time. This is especially true once we move into a much larger pool of experiences and formations, where complexity and strangeness risks leading to superficiality. What is thus needed is an approach that has been termed 'slow comparison'.[135] Like slow food, the notion of 'slow comparison' emphasizes the

[132] Dann and Thiruvengadam, *Democratic Constitutionalism in Continental Polities* (n 47) 1; Annelise Riles, 'From Comparison to Collaboration: Experiments with a New Scholarly and Political Form' (2015) 78 (1) Law and Contemporary Problems 147.

[133] We recognize that the dominance of English in global academic conversations is a major barrier to other voices and traditions. At the same time, we aim to contribute to a common and global discussion, not one separated by region and language. In this dilemma, we opted for English—but we try to complement this with funds for the translation of works from other languages for publication in our journal. On the problem of language, see Gabriel Lentner, 'Law, Language and Power: English and the Production of Ignorance in International Law' (2020) 8 International Journal of Language and Law 50.

[134] In particular, female scholars and scholars of colour remain under-represented among the authors in this book, and we readily acknowledge this as a problem. We had invited a higher number of them as contributors to this book and to the conference on which it is based than are now represented in the final volume. There are many reasons for this, which require further efforts to overcome obstacles to diversification.

[135] Dann and Thiruvengadam, 'Framing a Comparative Law of Democracy' (n 112) 4–7.

process in which comparative knowledge emerges in a necessarily longer, often difficult and cumbersome process, in which the ingredients need careful selection, flavours emerge slowly, and taste is only acquired over time. This might be an anomaly in today's academic system. It requires a profound contextual understanding of one's own constitutional order, a certain level of 'bi-legalism', an ability to deal with 'comparative confusion', and, well, patience. But it (hopefully) generates better and longer lasting results.

E. Conclusion

This volume in general and our introductory chapter in particular call for a plural, 'worldlier' approach to comparative constitutional scholarship. This call starts with a reconsideration of the notion 'Global South' that we consider a useful lens to understand constitutional experiences around the world; it continues with an attempt to capture what is distinct about the constitutional experience in the South, including its entanglement with the North; and it leads finally beyond the South to a refocused understanding of constitutional scholarship in general, ie in the South as much as in the North.

The Southern turn also raises an important question that we have avoided so far: what is the position and role of us as authors of this text and editors of this volume, who happen to be three white male scholars writing from a privileged position in the North? Such a self-reflection triggers questions about the place of sincere and respectful scholars in the North in debates about Southern constitutionalism. A tentative answer to this question should begin by acknowledging the necessity of the question and a reflection about positionality here. Our own views and assumptions are necessarily shaped by the socialization we have received, the circumstances under which we work and live. Recognizing the particularity of our perspective is a necessary step to engage with other voices in mutual respect.

But in our view, the consequence of our positionality cannot be that we remain on the sidelines as bystanders of the Southern turn. We believe that scholars like us can perform four useful roles in global constitutional conversations: listeners, enablers, contributors, and translators. As listeners, we should be receptive to Southern experiences and voices and engage in a conversation with, not about, the South.[136] In this vein, we chose not to speak at the fiftieth anniversary conference of our journal which formed the basis for this volume,

[136] Michael Dowdle, 'Constitutional Listening' (2012) 88 (1) Chicago-Kent Law Review 115.

but rather listened first. As enablers, we offer fora for exchange and procure necessary resources, be it as organizers of conferences or editors of our journal or this book. As contributors, we offer the results of our own intellectual engagement with Southern constitutionalism, by authoring this chapter all while reflecting our own positionality as much as we can. Finally, as translators we seek to promote mutual understanding of various scholarly communities hampered by linguistic, national, methodological, or ideological barriers. This may include literal translation from and to English, for which our journal will make available some extra resources. But it also includes translation between different scholarly traditions and 'camps' often pitted against each other, be it formalists against crits, liberals against conservatives, or otherwise. While many value-based differences of opinion may be irreducible, remaining in a conversation across dividing lines remains a value in itself in times of increasing polarization and 'filter-bubbles'.

We attempt to fulfil these four roles in various individual projects but also and importantly in our common endeavour, which is the editing of the journal *VRÜ/WCL*. The journal has a long tradition in organizing such a plural and respectful exchange about law and politics in the Global South. And it can serve as a major (and perhaps unique) archive of the difficulties and complexities of such conversation. At the same time, we are working to make it a more inclusive, plural organ—on various fronts: while it has always had a plurality of voices, this plurality has increasingly become reflected in the board of editors. In sum, we hope that our journal makes a modest contribution to the research field and agenda we have laid out in this chapter. The renaming of our journal expresses this hope and approach, and we cordially invite you all to contribute to this adventure of *World Comparative Law* in the future.

PART I

THEORIZING THE GLOBAL SOUTH IN COMPARATIVE CONSTITUTIONAL LAW

2

Facing *South*

On the Significance of An/Other Modernity in Comparative Constitutional Law

Florian Hoffmann

A. Prolegomenon

A, by necessity, concise reflection on the epistemological significance of the *Global South* for comparative constitutional law is bound to ride roughshod over the term's conceptual history, the complex empirical reality it purports to represent, as well as the sizable literature that has been and is being produced on the subject.[1] Almost everything surrounding it is contested, beginning with its (trans-)disciplinary framing as comparative constitutional law, comparative constitutional studies, or, indeed, comparative constitutional inquiry,[2] and ending with the fundamental questioning of the very possibility of either

[1] See, amongst (many) others, contributions Tom Ginsburg and Rosalind Dixon (eds), *Comparative Constitutional Law* (Edward Elgar 2011); Mauro Bussani and Ugo Mattei (eds), *The Cambridge Companion to Comparative Law* (CUP 2012); Roger Masterman and Robert Schütze (eds), *The Cambridge Companion to Comparative Constitutional Law* (CUP 2019); Ran Hirschl, *Comparative Matters: The Renaissance of Comparative Constitutional Law* (OUP 2014); Michel Rosenfeld and András Sajó (eds), *The Oxford Handbook of Comparative Constitutional Law* (OUP 2012); Mark V Tushnet, *Advanced Introduction to Comparative Constitutional Law* (Edward Elgar 2014); Mathias Reimann and Reinhard Zimmermann (eds), *The Oxford Handbook of Comparative Law* (OUP 2006); Nico Krisch, *Beyond Constitutionalism: The Pluralist Structure of Postnational Law* (OUP 2010); Petra Dobner and Martin Loughlin (eds), *The Twilight of Constitutionalism?* (OUP 2010); Jeffrey Dunoff and Joel Trachtman (eds), *Ruling the World: Constitutionalism, International Law and Global Governance* (CUP 2009); Antje Wiener and Tony Lang (eds), *Handbook of Global Constitutionalism* (Edward Elgar 2016); Daniel Bonilla Maldonado (ed), *Constitutionalism of the Global South: The Activist Tribunals of India, South Africa, and Colombia* (CUP 2013); BS Chimni, 'A Just World Under Law: A View from the South' (2006) 100 Proceedings of the ASIL Annual Meeting 17; Michaela Hailbronner, 'Transformative Constitutionalism: Not Only in the Global South' (2017) 65 American Journal of Comparative Law 527; Upendra Baxi, 'Constitutionalism as a Site of State Formative Practices' (2000) 21 Cardozo Law Review 1183; as well as Conrado Hübner Mendes and Roberto Gargarella, *Oxford Handbook of Constitutional Law in Latin America* (OUP 2020).

[2] See Ginsburg and Dixon, *Comparative Constitutional Law* (n 1); Günter Frankenberg, *Comparative Constitutional Studies: Between Magic and Deceit* (Edward Elgar 2018); Michel Rosenfeld, 'The Politics of Comparative Constitutional Inquiry: At the Crossroads of Law, Political Science, and Ideology' (2016) 66 University of Toronto Law Journal 273; and generally, Pierre Legrand and Roderick Munday (eds), *Comparative Legal Studies: Traditions and Transitions* (CUP 2003).

Florian Hoffmann, *Facing* South In: *The Global South and Comparative Constitutional Law.* Edited by: Philipp Dann, Michael Riegner, and Maxim Bönnemann, Oxford University Press (2020). © Oxford University Press.
DOI: 10.1093/oso/9780198850403.003.0002

comparativism, or a *Southern* perspective, or both.[3] Of the many possible strategies to deal with this predicament, the one chosen here, both for reasons of space and argument, is likely to contribute to this contestability, as it seeks to advance a number of hypotheses that are premised on particular perspectives and positions.[4] Unlike some of the other contributions in this volume, it will, hence, not query positionality and perspectivity as such—though it will frame them differently from certain established bodies of literature—but it will attempt to outline a number of particular contentions about comparative (constitutional) law and the *Global South*, as yet in rather rough brushstrokes.

It will, in particular, argue that taking the *Global South* seriously in and for comparative constitutional law must mean transcending its use either as a mere marker of supressed difference or as a critical wedge against the hegemony of *Western/modern* constitutional concepts. The *Global South* must, instead, be unlocked as the real locus—not in a geographical but in a cognitive sense—of constitutional modernity the world over. This, it is suggested, should happen by means of a number of methodological moves, the most important of which will here be termed the *de-Weberianization* of the fundamental terms and normative ideals of comparative constitutional law. For it is the stylized ideal types of the *Weberian* world—which, as will be shown, is itself an ideal type of the much more differentiated and ambivalent thought of the real Weber—that frames and, therefore, blurs the cognitive horizon of the legal comparativist. They provide the cornerstones of the mainstream/Eurocentric constitutional *mappa mundi* that locks the complex and often fuzzy constitutional reality of both the *Global South* and the *Global North* into a preordained and cognitively closed framework which tends to engender an under-complex and often contradictory account of how (constitutional) law works 'on the ground'.

De-Weberianization through a *Southern* lens is, therefore, not meant to be limited to an ideology critique of *Western modernity* but is a project to provide a more realist vision of that modernity and, thereby, a deeper understanding of 'how the world works'. This modernity, which is not seen as complementary or parallel, as it is in part of the *Southern* theory in the context of which this contribution is situated, but as alternative and global, is, thus, *meridional* (aka *Southern*) and the methodological agenda associated with it is, accordingly, the *meridionalization* of comparative (constitutional) law. One crucial

[3] See, in particular, Zoran Oklopcic, 'Comparing as (Re-)imagining: Southern Perspective and the World of Constitutions' in this volume; Zoran Oklopcic, 'The South of Western Constitutionalism: A Map Ahead of a Journey' (2016) 37 Third World Quarterly 2080.

[4] See Florian Hoffmann, 'International Legalism and International Politics' in Anne Orford and Florian Hoffmann (eds), *Oxford Handbook of the Theory of International Law* (OUP 2016) 954.

instrument of this endeavour is an ethnographic perspective that seeks to discern and decipher the myriad ways in which the law operates in the everyday life of states, societies, and people across the globe—without being constrained by the (*Weberian*) categories that form the *Western* legal canon. It requires, amongst others, a new sensitivity to and openness for existing and new ethnographic and methodologically related research that seeks to re-frame *Weberian* configurations, such as people, self-government, citizen, rights, equality, autonomy, nation, or popular sovereignty, in light of concrete experiences in the *Global South*. In this way, the big themes of mainstream comparative constitutional law, notably how the state, the rule of law and democratic legitimacy are conceived and conceivable, can gradually be reworked in a *Southern* key, with some, thereby, dissolving entirely, and others being re-signified in fundamentally different terms. Needless to say, this project can only be outlined here, as one—certainly contestable but hopefully productive—way, amongst the several others presented in this volume, to approach the contemporary predicament of comparative constitutional law in relation to the *Global South*.

B. On Nomenclature

At the beginning, hence, stands Weber—Max Weber, that is—and, in particular, his ideal types. By way of warning it should be pointed out that this will not be what Richard Rorty would have termed an historical reconstruction of Weber's thought, but rather what he saw as a rational reconstruction thereof that uses the concept of *Weberianism*—which is, of course, itself an ideal type—as a representation of Western constitutional modernity within a specific (and contemporary) argument about legal comparativism.[5] This may be seen as an idiosyncratic as well as problematic choice, as Weber evidently represents but one aspect of *Western* modernity's narrative about itself, and one that, in addition, has been much contested in terms of its historical accuracy and explanatory value.[6] Moreover, Weber himself was, of course, highly circumspect of undue generalization and extrapolation and was also distinctly ambivalent about *Western* modernity's connotation in the wider, global historical scheme

[5] Richard Rorty, 'The Historiography of Philosophy: Four Genres' in Richard Rorty, Jerome Schneewind, and Quentin Skinner (eds), *Philosophy in History* (CUP 1984) 49.

[6] Hans Joas and Wolfgang Knöbl, *Social Theory: Twenty Introductory Lectures* (CUP 2009) 20; Sven Eliaeson, *Max Weber's Methodologies: Interpretation and Critique* (Polity 2002); Walter G Runciman, *A Critique of Max Weber's Philosophy of Social Science* (CUP 2002).

of things.[7] Indeed, the 'real' Weber is, arguably, much less an example of epistemic Eurocentrism than both his reputation in certain quarters and his stylization into the denominator of *Weberianism* (in this contribution) would have it.[8] However, many of Weber's central categories, such as the state, rational administration, the rule of law, or instrumental rationality, have entered the canon of *Western* constitutionalism and form the essential elements of its representation of the world, its dominant cognitive map as it is articulated in the comparativist mainstream, quite apart and beyond Weber's own aspirations.[9] Indeed, as will be seen, part of the present argument seeks to argue with Weber against *Weber(ianism)*, or, put differently, it seeks to mobilize some of Weber's own methodological insights against the hypostatization of his conceptual apparatus into constitutionalism's reality.[10] However, this, too, is here merely explorative and points to the need of a much deeper engagement with Weber's thought as part of the wider research agenda set out in this contribution.

Back to ideal types. These were, to Weber

> formed by the one-sided accentuation of one or more points of view and by the synthesis of a great many diffuse, discrete, more or less present and occasionally absent, concrete individual phenomena, which are arranged according to those one-sidedly emphasized viewpoints into a unified analytical construct . . . . in its conceptual purity, this mental construct . . . . cannot be found empirically anywhere in reality.[11]

As such, ideal types do not purport to be representations of reality but merely heuristic devices meant to organize and orient—as well as simplify—the observer's thought on reality, notably as condensed aggregate terms that express certain sets of phenomena or objects in an abstract, though, therefore, also necessarily partial and imprecise way. In the present case, not only are ideal types probably the only way to pursue the intended argument, but the

[7] See, *inter alia*, Jane Bennett, 'Modernity and its Critics' in John Dryzek, Bonnie Honig, and Anne Phillips, *The Oxford Handbook of Political Theory* (OUP 2006) 211; Herbert Krüger, 'Die Modernität des Modernen Staates' (1973) 6 VRÜ/WCL 5.

[8] John A Hall, 'Confessions of a Eurocentric' (2001) 16 International Sociology 488.

[9] Ivan Szelényi, 'Entzauberung: Notes on Weber's Theory of Modernity' (2015) 8 International Political Anthropology 5; Wolfgang Schluchter, *The Rise of Western Rationalism* (University of California Press 1981); Harold J Berman, 'Some False Premises of Max Weber's Sociology of Law' (1987) 65 Washington University Law Quarterly 758.

[10] Max Weber, *Gesammelte Aufsätze zur Wissenschaftslehre* (3rd edn, Mohr Siebeck 1968) 191; see also Max Weber, 'Objectivity in Social Science and Social Policy' in Max Weber, *The Methodology of the Social Sciences* (Free Press 1949); Frigga Haug, Fritz Haug, and Wolfgang Küttler, 'Idealtypus' (2004) 47 Forum Kritische Psychologie 112.

[11] Weber, 'Objectivity' (n 10) 90.

multiplicity of overlapping terms for (roughly) similar phenomena would seem to leave no alternative but to select certain general ciphers, as reductive and stylized as these then necessarily are.[12]

This is certainly the case for the key concept underlying this volume, the *Global South*: as a term, its age spans no more than two decades, though its pedigree reaches back to the 1950s and the idea of a Third World which brought together Cold War developmental taxonomy with the earlier concept of a formerly excluded third estate (*tiers etat*) staking a claim for recognition and representation.[13] Today, the *Global South* alludes less to a geographical than to a socio-economic and an epistemic divide, not least as the common 'one third/two thirds' demarcation between states is cross cut by transnational categories such as social class, (post-)coloniality, or subalternity.[14] The continuing salience of the idea of the *Global South* derives, thus, from its quality as a heuristic concept that subsumes different locations, conditions, and concerns.

The same, in the inverse, goes, of course, for the *Global South*'s antipode, the *Global North*, which traditionally stands for two further ciphers, notably *Europe* and (*North*) *America* (sometimes referred to as *Euroamerica*), or for any number of defining attributes given to the former, such as industrialized world, developed countries, or advanced economies.[15] More importantly, it also stands for a particular epistemic horizon within which the modern world is seen as being in and of the *Global North* which, in turn, is constructed as the opposite to the *Global South*.[16]

Yet, here begins the terminological muddle, as, traditionally, this *Global North* has mostly been known as the *West* which, in turn, was originally constructed in opposition to the *East*.[17] This betrays, of course, that the terminology involving the four cardinal directions was never limited to a mere geographical signification linked to specific socio-economic indicators but to

[12] Haug, Haug, and Küttler (n 10).

[13] Classically Carl Oglesby, 'Vietnamism has Failed . . . The Revolution can only be Mauled, Not Defeated' (1969) Commonweal 90; Willy Brandt, *North–South: A Programme for Survival: Report of the Independent Commission on International Development Issues* (MIT Press 1980); The South Commission, *The Challenge to the South: The Report of the South Commission* (OUP 1990); see further Justin Dargin (ed), *The Rise of the Global South: Philosophical, Geopolitical, and Economic Trends of the 21st Century* (World Scientific 2013); Annette Trefzer and others (eds), 'The Global South and/in the Global North: Interdisciplinary Investigations' (2014) 8 The Global South 1.

[14] Arif Dirlik, 'Global South: Predicament and Promise' (2007) 1 The Global South 12; Jonathan Rigg, *An Everyday Geography of the Global South* (Routledge 2007); Juan Obarrio, 'Pensar al Sur' (2013) 3 Intersticios de la Política y la Cultura 5.

[15] John Comaroff and Jean Comaroff, *Theory from the South: Or, How Euro-America is Evolving Toward Africa* (Paradigm 2012).

[16] Luis Eslava, Michael Fakhri, and Vasuki Nesiah (eds), *Bandung, Global History, and International Law: Critical Pasts and Pending Futures* (CUP 2017).

[17] Eric Sheppard and Richa Nagar, 'From East–West to North–South' (2004) Antipode 557.

a particular position within a dynamic matrix made up of space, specific historical trajectory, and relations of (socio-economic) inter-dependence. Indeed, the socio-economic indicators that are now taken to assign particular places or peoples on either side of either cardinal dichotomy (*West/East* or *North/South*) are merely the effects of their respective position within the matrix at any one moment of time. The recently prefixed *global* to the *South/North* dichotomy is meant to express this geographical diffusion, though it will, in the following argument, fall victim to reductive ideal-typization—and, thus, be omitted henceforth.[18] Moreover, the association of the elements that make up the cardinal dichotomies with states and societies is evidently also an ideal-typical stylization, for it really starts with the internal stratification within each state and society, so that each of these has, in turn, its own hierarchically ordered *South* and *North* or *West* and *East* beyond any actual geographical significance. These socio-economic *Souths* and *Norths* are, in turn, transnationally interconnected and form a patchwork of stratified constituencies that cross cut—and irritate—both national politics and international governance.[19]

There has, however, always also been a more abstract meaning to the cardinal dichotomies, notably one in which they indicate a person's or a state's position in relation to the notion of *civilization*, which, in turn, has come to be merged with the concept of *modernity*, which, in turn, has come to be merged with the notion of the *West*, which, in turn, has been constructed in opposition to a *non-West* located, on the 'civilizational' compass card, at the opposite end of the *Northern* pole, namely in the *South*. It is an associational chain summed up early on by Norbert Elias, who contended that the concept of *civilization*

> ... expresses the self-consciousness of the West ... [it] sums up everything in which Western society of the last two or three centuries believes itself superior to earlier societies or 'more primitive' contemporary ones. By this term Western society seeks to describe what constitutes its special character and what it is proud of: the level of its technology, the nature of its manners, the development of its scientific knowledge or view of the world, and much more ...[20]

[18] Alfred J López, 'Introduction: The (Post) Global South' (2007) 1 The Global South 1.

[19] Caroline Thomas and Peter Wilkin (eds), *Globalization and the South* (St Martin's Press 1997); Neil Brenner, 'The Space of the World: Beyond State-Centrism?' in David Palumbo-Liu, Nirvana Tanoukhi, and Bruce Robbins (eds), *Immanuel Wallerstein and the Problem of the World: System, Scale, Culture* (Duke UP 2011) 101–37; Tanja Aalberts and Thomas Gammeltoft-Hansen, 'Sovereignty Games: Law and Politics in World Society' in Tanja Aalberts and Thomas Gammeltoft-Hansen, *The Changing Practices of International Law* (CUP 2018).

[20] Norbert Elias, *The Civilizing Process: Sociogenetic and Psychogenetic Investigations* (Blackwell 2000) 5.

Hence, on this level, the cardinal divide between *North* and *South* is deeply entangled with the narrative construction of colonialism (and neo-colonialism) and its main corollary, namely the vertical differentiation between the *West* ('civilized') and the *Rest* (not (yet) 'civilized'), on which the well-known linear progress narrative leading up to the *West* (aka the *North* aka *modernity* aka *civilization*) is based. And so on.[21] In terms of a simplified—and contestable—working nomenclature, the two contrasting concepts shall henceforth for the most part be the *South* and the *West*.[22]

It might at this point be objected that, given this terminological muddle, only a careful hermeneutic reconstruction of the historical trajectories of each of these terms, a proper *Begriffsgeschichte* (conceptual history), could do any justice to the *South* (in comparative constitutional law), and not its stylization into an abstract ideal type.[23] In fact, this hypothetical objection lies at the core of the overall question explored here, namely how to 'understand' the *South* for the purposes of comparative methodology. For one of the key contentions of the present exploration is that epistemology matters and that the methodology by which the *South* is 'understood' implies an ultimately political choice about the nature and purpose of knowledge and science, of law and constitution, and of the complex reality within which they are set.[24] The argument here pursued is, thus, twofold: it seeks to outline different ways to 'understand' the *South* and its epistemic value for comparative methodology, and it aims to show the wider implications of these different 'understandings' on how comparative lawyers (can) see themselves and their discipline.[25]

[21] See Niall Ferguson, *Civilization: The West and the Rest* (Penguin 2012); Thomas Skouteris, *The Notion of Progress in International Law Discourse* (Springer 2008); Pierre Alexandre Cardinal and Frédéric Mégret, 'The Other "Other": Moors, International Law and the Origin of the Colonial Matrix' in Ignacio de la Rasilla del Moral and Ayesha Sahid (eds), *International Law and Islam* (Brill 2018).

[22] This is, of course, also problematic, less so, perhaps, in relation to the *South*, but certainly so in relation to the *West*, which is here meant to encompass both the conceptual *West* and *North*; at least in relation to Latin America, this conflation may be particularly complicated, as, in traditional socio-historical terms, the region is often considered to be both part of the *South* and of the *West*, thereby cross-cutting the *South/West* dichotomy: see eg José G Merquior, 'The Other West: On the Historical Position of Latin America (1991) 6 International Sociology 149.

[23] Reinhart Koselleck and Todd Samuel Presner, *The Practice of Conceptual History: Timing History, Spacing Concepts* (Stanford UP 2002); Martin Clark, 'Ambivalence, Anxieties/Adaptations, Advances: Conceptual History and International Law' (2018) 31 Leiden Journal of International Law 747.

[24] See Philipp Dann 'Of Apples and Mangoes: Comparing the European Union and India' (2016) Indian Yearbook of Comparative Law 1; and again, Okplocic, 'Comparing as (Re)Imagining' (n 3); 'The South of Western Constitutionalism' (n 3).

[25] See Max Weber, *Economy and Society: An Outline of Interpretive Sociology* (University of California Press 1978); Charles Camic, Philip S Gorski, and David M Trubek, *Max Weber's Economy and Society: A Critical Companion* (Stanford UP 2005); as well as Wolfgang Schluchter, 'Handlungs- und Strukturtheorie nach Max Weber' (2000) 10 Berliner Journal für Soziologie 125; and John R Hall, *Cultures of Inquiry: From Epistemology to Discourse in Sociohistorical Research* (CUP 1999) 129.

For this venture, Weber is, of course, both a necessary and a problematic starting point, as his thought has itself been stylized into an ideal type for the 'understanding' of modernity as *Western/Northern*. It lies at the heart of the *West/non-West* (or *West/East* or *North/South*) dualism that, arguably, still dominates the (self-)representation of modernity and that forms the mental map of a world in which the compass' needle is oriented to the *North*. It is from his particular 'understanding' of the social, political, economic, and legal history of the *West/North* that the (ideal typical) conceptions of the building blocks of the modern world are derived. Hence, the Weberian semantic of such key terms as capitalism, statehood, political power, constitutional government, professional administration, or, indeed, (modern) law still informs at least the subconscious of comparativism (in law and elsewhere).[26]

However, in Weber's own conception, ideal types are not representational but heuristic devices and, hence, as an ideal type, the prevailing *Weberianism* in comparative law is neither a representation of the entire tradition of *Western* social, political, and economic thought nor of Weber's own complex and often ambivalent diagnostic of modernity.[27] Instead, *Weberianism* draws on two specific aspects of Weber's work: on a substantive level on his contention that the Euro-American variety of (instrumental) rationality has been the primary driving force of modernization, an interpretation that a priori localizes modernity in the *West/North*;[28] and on an epistemological level his adoption of methodological individualism as the framework of reference according to which social reality can and ought to be observed.[29] The significance of these Weberian moves is, of course, that they stylize a set of localized historical processes into a universal intellectual development and thereby create an a priori equivalence between modernity and the *West/North*.[30]

This constellation, arguably, goes back to Weber's original predicament, which was to avoid what he saw as the flaws of the two alternative epistemologies

[26] Chantal Thomas, 'Re-Reading Weber in Law and Development: A Critical Intellectual History of "Good Governance" Reform' (2008) 118 Cornell Law Faculty Publications 10.

[27] See Thomas (n 26); Berman (n 9); as well as Sigfried Weichlein, 'Max Weber, der modern Staat und die Nation' in Andreas Anter and Stefan Breuer (eds), *Max Webers Staatssoziologie* (Nomos 2007); Hall (n 25).

[28] Max Weber, 'Die Protestantische Ethik und der Geist des Kapitalismus' (2001) 1 Archiv für Sozialwissenschaften und Sozialpolitik 1; Weber, *Economy and Society* (n 25); and generally, Jürgen Habermas, *Theorie des kommunikativen Handelns* (Suhrkamp 1981).

[29] Weber, *Economy and Society* (n 25); see also Christian List and Kai Spiekermann, 'Methodological Individualism and Holism in Political Science: A Reconciliation' (2013) 107 American Political Science Review 629.

[30] Jaime Pastor Verdú, 'Los movimientos sociales: De la crítica de modernidad a la denuncia de la globalización' (2006) 15 Psychosocial Intervention 133; Paul Gilroy, *The Black Atlantic: Modernity and Double Consciousness* (Harvard UP 1993).

with which he engaged, notably (scientific) positivism and Marxism, both of which he considered as falling to fundamental category mistakes. On one hand, positivism's exclusive focus on the causal explanation of phenomena deemed to be external from the observer was, to Weber, notoriously inadequate for an incipient social science the object of which was to 'understand' social action on the basis of the (subjective) meaning attributed by actors to their conduct.[31] In line with his neo-Kantian premises, such meaning-making was, to Weber, necessarily rational and, thus, irreducible to mere psychological impulses—a contention he associated with the positivist economics of the Austrian School.[32] On the other hand, however, Weber also took pains to differentiate himself from Marx's (Hegelian) epistemology which insisted that thought and understanding were necessarily entangled with the actual (material) structure of society. Against this he insisted, again in neo-Kantian fashion, on a strict separation between what he saw as an ultimately chaotic and intractable reality and the rational forms of thought by which it is 'understood'.[33] While these rational forms of thought derive from the (subjective) experience of life in 'real' societies, they can never be more than heuristic devices to 'understand' specific phenomena, in contrast to the total epistemic transparency promised by Marx's historical materialism.[34] Indeed, Weber's ideal types, which are not representational of either the totality of social relations nor of reality itself, are just such heuristic devices.[35]

This particular architecture is, arguably, the reason why *Weberianism* has become the ideal type for the description of legal modernity as *Western*—and, therefore, as definitive of the non-*West* (aka the *South*).[36] For by historicizing modernity—against positivism—yet by simultaneously denying that its historicity follows deeper structural patterns—against Marx—he universalizes the historically evolved 'forms of thought' of the *West* as modernity. It is through these 'forms of thought' that the *West* describes itself as modern and reduces the *Rest* to mere approximations thereof.[37] It is, hence, a stylized and partial

[31] Weber, *Economy and Society* (n 25); Schluchter, 'Handlungs-und Strukturtheorie' (n 25) 125.

[32] Haug, Haug and Küttler (n 10) 116.

[33] ibid 118.

[34] See, again, Haug, Haug, and Küttler (n 10); see also China Miéville, *Between Equal Rights: A Marxist Theory of International Law* (Brill 2005); Robert Knox, 'Marxist Approaches to International Law' in Anne Orford and Florian Hoffmann (eds), *The Oxford Handbook of the Theory of International Law* (OUP 2016) 306.

[35] Haug, Haug, and Küttler (n 10); JWN Watkins, 'Ideal Types and Historical Explanation' (1952) 3 British Journal for the Philosophy of Science 22.

[36] Bryan S Turner, *Max Weber: From History to Modernity* (Routledge 2002).

[37] Silvia Federici, *Enduring Western Civilization* (Praeger 1995); Stuart Hall, 'The West and the Rest: Discourse and Power' in Tania Das Gupta and others (eds), *Race and Racialization: Essential Readings* (Canadian Scholars' Press 2007).

version of *Western* history that is normalized into the constitutional imaginary as articulated in classical comparativism.[38]

This is, again, neither new nor any longer particularly surprising to anyone informed by critical thought—from classical critical theory, via post-structural deconstruction and to the post- and decolonial critique of *Western* epistemic hegemony[39]—yet the consequences of this critique, not least for comparative methodology and comparative law have, arguably, still not been mapped out in sufficient detail to have instigated any paradigm shift in the wider discipline.[40] One reason for this is, arguably, the high stakes involved in moving out of the established *Weberian* paradigm as well as the rather different political projects associated with such moves. Some of this will briefly be set out below.

C. Facing (the) *South* in Legal Modernity

In the epilogue to his recent *Comparative Constitutional Studies: Between Magic and Deceit*, Günter Frankenberg, the *praeceptor* of critical legal comparativism in Germany (and elsewhere) observes that

> the state of exception seems to have mutated from a distinctive event with specific connotations arising at a limited location to a collective singular of numerous crises happening all at once . . . their dynamics devour the rules and benchmarks of normality . . . . what had been designed in theory—out of naivety or in bad faith—is now turned into practice: the triumph of the exception's cannibalism.[41]

[38] See Thomas, 'Re-Reading Weber' (n 26); Berman (n 9).

[39] See Maxim Bönnemann and Maximilan Pichl, 'Postkoloniale Rechtstheorie' in Sonja Buckel, Ralph Christensen, and Andreas Fischer Lescano, *Neue Theorien des Rechts* (3rd edn, UTB/Mohr Siebeck 2020); Judith Schacherreiter, 'Postcolonial Theory and Comparative Law' (2016) 49 VRÜ/WCL 291; Partha Chatterjee, 'Introduction: Postcolonial Legalism' (2014) 34 Comparative Studies of South Asia, Africa and the Middle East 224.

[40] See eg Costas Douzinas, *Critical Jurisprudence: The Political Philosophy of Justice* (Hart 2005); Edward W Said, *Orientalism* (Penguin Books 1973); Christopher C Lee (ed), *Making a World after Empire: The Bandung Moment and its Political Afterlives* (Ohio UP 2010); Robert JC Young, 'Postcolonialism: From Bandung to the Tricontinental' (2005) 5 Historein 11; Rosalind O'Hanlon and David Washbrook, 'After Orientalism: Culture, Criticism, and Politics in the Third World (1992) 34 Comparative Studies in Society and History 141; Dipesh Chakrabarty, *Provincializing Europe: Postcolonial Thought and Historical Difference* (Princeton UP 2000); Arif Dirlik, *The Postcolonial Aura: Third World Criticism in the Age of Global Capitalism* (Westview Press 1998); Partha Chatterjee, *Nation and its Fragments: Colonial and Postcolonial Histories* (Princeton UP 1993); Achille Mbembé, *On the Postcolony* (University of California Press 2001); Aimé Césaire, *Discourse on Colonialism* (Monthly Review Press 2000); Walter D Mignolo, *Local Histories/Global Designs: Coloniality, Subaltern Knowledges, and Border Thinking* (Princeton UP 2012); Jochen V Bernstorff and Philipp Dann, *The Battle for International Law: South–North Perspectives on the Decolonization Era* (OUP 2019).

[41] Frankenberg, *Comparative Constitutional Studies* (n 2) 290.

The implication here is not only that, as he frames it, 'the world is experienced as having come apart at its seams' because the reality purportedly enshrined and eternalized in constitutional law is being challenged from the outside. For what is being challenged is actually the very reality of the reality at the base of constitutionalism, notably the modern world that the *West* has constructed in broadly *Weberian* terms. The shock and horror that this latter challenge produces among those socialized into *Weberian* normality is much deeper than that occasioned by a mere external attack, as it situates the source of the exception within the *West* itself, notably in form of the suspicion that everything might, in fact, be different, that the exception is, actually, the norm and that the 'world as it is known', the world represented in the constitution of the modern mind, the modern state, and modern society is but an illusion, an ephemeral fairy tale bereft of reality.[42]

If true, this would leave 'the moderns' not only blind and unprepared for the *real* world, but it would also mean that its very *raison d'être*, namely the idea that modernity is humanity's self-redemption, the product of evolutionary progress towards the end of history, was always only premised on the violent suppression of others, framed as exceptions, and on the always only tenuous dominance such violence implies.[43] Modern constitutions would then be, as hinted in Frankenberg's title, merely instruments of self-deceit, ideological frameworks meant to veil the real world by performing the strict division between the inside normal and the outside exception. And comparison would be but an authoritarian exercise in the adequation of divergence/exception with a preordained normality, a normative science meant to shield the *West* against the *South*'s intrusion.

None of this is new, and none of this should be unsettling to scholars of comparative constitutional law.[44] Yet, the consequences of this critical insight have,

[42] See eg Bruno Latour, *We Have Never Been Modern* (Harvard UP 2012).

[43] Enrique Dussel, 'Eurocentrism and Modernity' (1993) 2 Boundary 65; Susan Marks, 'The End of History? Reflections on Some International Legal Theses' (1997) 3 European Journal of International Law 449; Mike Featherstone, Scott Lash, and Roland Robertson (eds), *Global Modernities* (Sage 1995).

[44] See eg early and seminally Günter Frankenberg, 'Critical Comparisons: Re-Thinking Comparative Law' (1985) 26 Harvard International Law Journal 411; as well as Pierre Legrand, 'Comparative Legal Studies and Commitment to Theory' (1995) 58 Modern Law Review 262; William Twining, 'Globalization and Comparative Law' (1999) 6 Maastricht Journal of European and Comparative Law 225; Mark V Tushnet, 'The Possibilities of Comparative Constitutional Law' (1999) 108 Yale Law Journal 1225; Mark Van Hoecke and Mark Warrington, 'Legal Cultures, Legal Paradigms, and Legal Doctrine: Towards a New Model for Comparative Law' (1998) 47 International and Comparative Quarterly 495; George P Fletcher, 'Comparative Law as a Subversive Discipline' (1998) 46 American Journal of Comparative Law 683; David Kennedy, 'New Approaches to Comparative Law: Comparativism and International Governance' (1997) 1997 Utah Law Review 545; John C Reitz, 'How To Do Comparative Law' (1998) 46 American Journal of Comparative Law 617; Peer Zumbansen, 'Comparative Law's Coming of Age? Twenty Years after Critical Comparisons' (2005) 6 German Law Journal 1074; Simon Glanert and Pierre Legrand, 'Law, Comparatism, and Epistemic

arguably, not yet been worked out in all their complexity; to be sure, critical reactions to this (late) modern predicament abound, but rarely have they been framed as an explicit response to the ontological, epistemological, and ethical challenge posed by what Frankenberg calls the 'exception's cannibalism'.[45] There are certainly more questions than answers: who represents the exception?[46] Is the exception itself generated by modernity or is it its primordial nemesis?[47] Is there one (modern) world, the complexity of which has simply not yet been mapped, or is modernity the representation of but one world among many and, if so, how do we approach these other worlds?[48] Is (constitutional) law but the ideological framework of modernity or does its indeterminate performativity give it an autonomous standpoint capable of irritating its own (modern) premises?[49] Is (legal) comparativism a form of ideology critique?[50] And would it, then, chiefly serve to integrate the exception into the map of its world, or could it, potentially, also reach out towards other worlds?[51]

These are, of course, questions well beyond the remit of a short contribution on comparative constitutional law, but they nonetheless delineate the nature of the quest on which anyone wishing to engage with Frankenberg's scenario has to embark. For the purposes of this argument, two aspects of this endeavour shall (briefly) be examined: one is the idea that the exception is the *South*, that is, that the *South* is here taken to represent the outside of the modern (*Weberian*) world, its constitutive other which, in Frankenberg's vision, is now crawling through the cracks and fissures of the *West's* normality.[52]

Governance: There Is Critique and Critique' (2017) 18 German Law Journal 701; Michael Riegner, 'Transformativer Konstitutionalismus und offene Staatlichkeit im regionalen Verfassungsvergleich mit Lateinamerika' (2019) 67 Jahrbuch des öffentlichen Rechts der Gegenwart 265; Oscar Vilhena, Upendra Baxi, and Frans Viljoen (eds), *Transformative Constitutionalism: Comparing the Apex Courts of Brazil, India and South Africa* (Pretoria University Law Press 2013).

[45] Frankenberg, *Comparative Constitutional Studies* (n 2) 290.

[46] See Frankenberg's own reflection in ibid 261.

[47] Max Horkheimer and Theodor W Adorno, *Dialectic of Enlightenment* (Stanford UP 2002).

[48] Eduardo Viveiros De Castro, *Cannibal Metaphysics* (University of Minnesota Press 2015); Bethania Assy and Florian Hoffmann, 'Towards a (Radically) Decolonial Anthropology: Revisiting the Iberian School of Peace's Encounter with (the Rights of) Amerindians' (2017) 51 Direito, Estado e Sociedade 10.

[49] Frankenberg, *Comparative Constitutional Studies* (n 2); Gunther Teubner, 'Legal Irritants: How Unifying Law Ends Up in New Divergences' in Peter A Soskice and David W Hall (eds), *Varieties of Capitalism: The Institutional Foundations of Comparative Advantage* (OUP 2001), 417.

[50] Günter Frankenberg, 'Comparing Constitutions: Ideas, Ideals, and Ideology: Toward a Layered Narrative' (2006) 4 International Journal of Constitutional Law 439; Duncan Kennedy, 'Political Ideology and Comparative Law' in Bussani and Mattei, *Cambridge Companion* (n 1) 35.

[51] H Patrick Glenn, 'Are Legal Traditions Incommensurable' (2001) 49 American Journal of Comparative Law 133; Pierre Legrand and Roderick Munday (eds), *Comparative Legal Studies: Traditions and Transitions* (CUP 2003); Richard Rorty, *Objectivity, Relativism, and Truth* (CUP 1991); Clifford Geertz, 'Local Knowledge and Its Limits' (1992) 5 Yale Journal of Criticism 129.

[52] See, classically, Antonio Gramsci, *The Southern Question* (tr P Verdicchio, Bordighera Press 2015); as well as Roberto M Dainotto, 'Does Europe Have a South? An Essay on Borders' (2011) 5

What is new here is not the contention that the *South* is constitutive of the *West*, but that this dependence is suddenly much less amenable to being supressed and (thus) rendered invisible and inconsequential (to the *West*). What reasons are attributed to this phenomenon depends on one's framework of reference; it may be the long-awaited crisis of late capitalism,[53] the social and economic fallout from neoliberal globalization,[54] the emergence of a virtual global public sphere,[55] the dawn of a new age of mass migration,[56] or, as a result of all of these, a new historical consciousness of the multiple exclusions of the *South* in the *West*'s self-image.[57]

What is more important than the precise reasons are the consequences, namely that the *South* is increasingly emerging into the *West* and that this profoundly challenges the *West*'s image of itself by revealing at once its inherent *Southernness* and the violence, epistemic and otherwise, that was always required to supress it.[58] Hence, turning towards the *South* in this context does not mean to merely look to the *Southern* half of the globe, or to the Third World, or the world's *poor*, or the *pre-modern* part of the world; instead, looking towards the *South* means to accept, firstly, that the dichotomy between the *West* and *South* is dissolving, and, secondly, that the *real* world beyond this dichotomy is not self-evidently given by the (*Weberian*) categories of the *West*. The second aspect to be looked into here derives from the first and concerns the question of what this epistemic provocation of the *South* does to our ways of thinking, notably to the way in which we conceive of comparative knowledge, of the idea

The Global South 37; Walter Mignolo, 'The Global South and World Dis/Order' (2011) 67 Journal of Anthropological Research 165.

[53] See, classically, Jürgen Habermas, 'What Does a Crisis Mean Today? Legitimation Problems in Late Capitalism' (1973) Social Research 643; David Harvey, *The Enigma of Capital and the Crises of Capitalism* (OUP 2011); see also Grietje Baars, *The Corporation, Law and Capitalism* (Brill 2019).

[54] Richard P Appelbaum and William I Robinson (eds), *Critical Globalization Studies* (Psychology Press 2005); Arjun Appadurai, *Globalization* (Duke UP 1998); Mike Featherstone and Scott Lash, 'Globalization, Modernity and the Spatialization of Social Theory: an introduction' in Featherstone, Lash, and Robertson, *Global Modernities* (n 43); Francois Venter, 'Globalization of Constitutional Law through Comparative Constitution-Making' (2008) 1 VRÜ/WCL 16.

[55] Manuel Castells, 'The New Public Sphere: Global Civil Society, Communication Networks, and Global Governance' (2008) 616 The Annals of the American Academy of Political and Social Science 78; Nancy Fraser, 'Transnational Public Sphere: Transnationalizing the Public Sphere: On the Legitimacy and Efficacy of Public Opinion in a Post-Westphalian World' (2007) 24 Theory, Culture & Society 7.

[56] Marc R Rosenblum and Daniel J Tichenor (eds), *The Oxford Handbook of the Politics of International Migration* (OUP 2012).

[57] See Oklopcic, 'The South of Western Consitutionalism' (n 3); Florian Hoffmann, 'Discourse' in Jean D'Aspremont and Sahib Singh, *Concepts for International Law* (Edward Elgar 2019) 201.

[58] See, classically, Gayatri Chakravorty Spivak, 'Can the Subaltern Speak?' in Cary Nelson and Lawrence Grosberg (eds), *Marxism and the Interpretation of Culture* (Macmillan 1988) 271; as well as Amy Allen, *The End of Progress: Decolonizing the Normative Foundations of Critical Theory* (Columbia UP 2016) 204.

of (a) constitution, and of (constitutional) law as a (*modern*) performative social practice.

Setting up the issue this way means, of course, to understand the concept of the *South* essentially as an instrument of ideology critique in the sense of 'classical' (and *Western*) critical theory.[59] Hence, the *South* is read into the *West* so as to reveal the discourse of modernity as an ideological construct meant to disguise its constitution by structural factors such as exploitation, colonialism, or imperialism.[60] Only once the ideological veil is pierced the many injustices that inhere in the actual constitution of (*Western*) modernity can be addressed—though there remains stark disagreement over whether the remedies for modernity's foundational ills can only come from itself or whether, on the contrary, modernity—and its *Weberian* self-description—must either be transcended or discarded to this end; indeed, these two meta-theoretical positions have provided the spectral range through which the role of the *South* in comparative methodology has been thematized.

At the beginning of such thematization stand a number of questions: is the *South* merely seen as the heretofore hidden underbelly of the *West* which, when put into the light, reveals an overall more complex but also more ambivalent world, or is it taken to represent another world entirely? What is the precise role of the *South* in the exposure of the *Western* self-image (aka *modernity*) as mere ideology? And what is the ultimate purpose of this exposure, is it about the recognition of difference or the affirmation of sameness? The latter distinction is important for two reasons: firstly, because it engages several key debates in the (*Western*) conception of knowledge, secondly because it is reflected in the specific types of responses so far given to the 'provocation of the *South*' in the context of comparative constitutional law.[61]

Put very broadly, these responses have been elaborated within either of two epistemic horizons: on one side of the spectrum lies the world of difference—or, perhaps, the difference of worlds—in which *West* and *South* are seen as each other's others and form a plurality of particulars, people, and communities at different moments of time that are not bound together by a common 'higher' denominator and that can, therefore, only be accessed from inside, immanently and ideographically. In law, as in other social sciences, these

[59] Hoffmann, 'International Legalism' (n 4) 954; Susan Marks, 'Big Brother Is Bleeping Us-with the Message That Ideology Doesn't Matter' (2001) 12 European Journal of International Law 109.

[60] Anthony Anghie, *Imperialism, Sovereignty and the Making of International Law* (CUP 2007); Ruth Buchanan and Sundya Pahuja, 'Legal Imperialism: Empire's Invisible Hand?' in Jodi Dean and Paul Passavant (eds), *Empire's New Clothes: Reading Hardt and Negri* (Routledge 2004) 73.

[61] See, classically, Peter Winch, *The Idea of a Social Science and Its Relation to Philosophy* (Routledge 2007).

worlds can, therefore, only be explored either hermeneutically, by historicizing modern law's 'real abstractions' and by uncovering their roots in colonialism, imperialism, capitalism, as well as in gender- and racialized hierarchies;[62] or ethnographically, by making real life beyond *Western* modernity and *Weberian* categories visible.[63] This perspective is, arguably, primarily motivated by two ethical demands, namely to expose and impeach the injustice of the epistemic suppression and subjection of the *South*, and to claim recognition—in the *West*—for what the real *South* is and does.

On the other side of the spectrum lies the world of sameness, that is, the idea of one world that is shaped by certain (structural) properties which have to be deciphered out of a multifarious reality. Here *West* and *South* are seen as part of the same continuum, shaped, in principle, by the same forces and displaying the same types of effects. Only that *Western* modernity has tended to conceive these forces and effects entirely on the basis of its own self-observation which essentially projects a *Weberian* reading of its particular historical trajectory and social makeup as the universal, normal, and only accurate way to describe this (one) world.[64] By, thus, rendering the *West* as 'the measure of the world', the *South* always appears as divergent and deficient, secondary and subordinate. It remains, at best, an exotic other that is inexorably intermediated by Eurocentric normative horizons and abridged, as Jean and John Comaroff have pointed out, to being 'a place of parochial wisdom, of antiquarian traditions, of exotic ways and means . . . above all, of unprocessed data [. . . not] sources of refined knowledge [. . . but] reservoirs of raw fact'.[65] Daniel Bonilla Maldonado has echoed this concern in his writings on comparative constitutional law in and of the *South* and the multiple biases it faces when received in and by the *West*.[66] Hence, he has identified several factors that underlie such devaluing

[62] For the 'turn to history', see Martti Koskenniemi, *Gentle Civilizer of Nations* (CUP 2004); Martti Koskenniemi, Walter Rech, and Manuel Jiménez Fonseca, *International Law and Empire: Historical Explorations* (OUP 2017); Thomas Skouteris, 'Engaging History in International Law' in José Maria Beneyto and David Kennedy, *New Approaches to International Law* (Springer 2012) 99; Rose Parfitt, *The Process of International Legal Reproduction: Inequality, Historiography, Resistance* (CUP 2018).

[63] See eg Fleur Johns, *Non-Legality in International Law: Unruly Law* (CUP 2013); Ben Boer and others, *The Mekong: A Socio-Legal Approach to River-Basin Management* (Routledge 2015); Luis Eslava, *Global Space, Local Life* (CUP 2015).

[64] Seminally Comaroff and Comaroff, *Theory from the South* (n 15) and forcefully BS Chimni, 'Third World Approaches to International Law: A Manifesto' (2006) 8 International Community Law Review 3; as well as Martti Koskenniemi, 'Histories of International Law: Dealing with Eurocentrism' (2011) 19 Rechtsgeschichte 152; Christine Schwöbel-Patel, 'Global Constitutionalism and the Geopolitics of Knowledge', in this volume.

[65] Comaroff and Comaroff, *Theory from the South* (n 15) 1.

[66] Bonilla Maldonado, *Constitutionalism* (n 1); see also Michael Riegner, 'How Universal are International Law and Development? Engaging with Postcolonial and Third World Scholarship from the Perspective of its Other' (2012) 45 VRÜ/WCL 232.

of the *Southern* experience by *Western* legal academia, amongst these the assumption that law in the *South* is comparatively weak(er), that it tends to be practised in simplistically formalist ways, that legal scholarship is dominated by *Western* academia, is allegedly more rigid and robust there, yet simultaneously encased in American parochialism and European selective openness. This, to him, produces three characteristics about Western (constitutional) comparativism, namely what he terms a *Western*-centric 'production well', a 'protected geographical indication' of *Western* constitutional scholarship, and the assumption that *Western* scholars are the more 'effective operators' of standard legal terms and processes. Bonilla's target is, thus, the *Western* 'epistemic arrogance' that ignores and disdains the distinct experiential horizon of the *South*.[67]

By contrast, the sameness perspective purports to invert this (a)symmetry by understanding the *South* as providing a view of the modern world that is unobstructed by the ideological screen maintained by the *Weberian* categories that are premised on the *Western* standpoint. The *South* is here not just the other of the *West*—as it is in the difference perspective—but it is the 'real' *West* insofar as the *West* signifies the modern world. The motivation behind this perspective is, hence, another type of epistemic justice, namely one that seeks to reveal the world in a *Southern* likeness and to, thereby, effect nothing less than a Copernican paradigm shift from a *Weberian* to a *meridional* account of that world. This spectrum, then, delineates how the category of the *South* has been used in (critical legal) comparativism, notably either as a tool for epistemic justice (in the *West*) or as an alternative paradigm (to the *West*). Both positions have brought forth a number of propositions about how to do (comparative) law that will briefly be outlined in the following.

D. The *South* in the *West*: Ideology Critique and Epistemic Justice

Both perspectives, arguably, have their common precursor in 'classical' (*Western*) critical legal studies (CLS) and its combination of legal realism, sociological jurisprudence, and critical theory in the wake of the Frankfurt School.[68] This agenda initially brought together interest-oriented socio-legal

[67] Bonilla Maldonado, *Constitutionalism* (n 1) 21.

[68] Classically Roberto Mangabeira Unger, 'The Critical Legal Studies Movement' (1982) 96 Harvard Law Review 561; and also Mark V Tushnet, 'Critical Legal Studies: A Political History' (1991) Yale Law Journal 1515; see also David Kennedy, 'Law and the Political Economy of the World' (2013) 26 Leiden Journal of International Law 1 and, importantly for the comparative context, Maxim Bönnemann

analysis with a general ideology critique of the structures of modern (capitalist) law, though by the time it percolated into comparative law's methodological self-reflection in the 1990s, a split along the difference/sameness dichotomy had produced two rather different research agendas. On the difference side, CLS and its Marxist undercurrents was itself being critiqued for a Eurocentric bias in its 'immanent' engagement with the history and language of modern (*Western*) law.[69] The basis for that critique was the incorporation into the critical horizon of a post-structural sensitivity for the contingency of language and historical narrative, resulting in the reframing of comparative (legal) methodology as, again in Frankenberg's words, an exercise in 'contextualizing, decentering, distancing and differencing'.[70] This programme, in turn, provided the backdrop for a 're-discovery' of the *South* through the lens of, first, the postcolonial and then the decolonial deconstruction of the *Weberian* (self-)image of the *West* and its law.[71]

A common starting point was the exposure of the deep structural entanglement of the history and language of modern law with what one of the doyens of the decolonial turn, Walter Mignolo, has termed the 'logic of coloniality'.[72] Epistemic decolonization is the central tenet of this critical programme, which seeks, according to Mignolo, to 'shift the geography of knowledge and recast critical theory within the frame of a geo- and bio-politics of knowledge, [with] the first step in the grammar of decolonization [... being] cast [... as] learning to unlearn'.[73] This alludes, of course, to earlier methodological interventions by a host of postcolonial and decolonial thinkers who dissected different aspects of (post)colonial subjectivity.[74] The 'learning to unlearn' agenda calls both for a historical deconstruction of the *modern* narratives deriving from the concrete colonial past—and, hence, for a methodological 'turn to history'—as well as

and Laura Jung, 'Critical Legal Studies and Comparative Constitutional Law' in Rainer Grote, Frauke Lachenmann, and Rüdiger Wolfrum (eds), *Max Planck Encyclopedia of Comparative Constitutional Law* (OUP 2017).

[69] James Gathii, 'International Law and Eurocentricity' (1998) 9 European Journal of International Law 184;

[70] Günter Frankenberg, 'Stranger Than Paradise: Identity and Politics in Comparative Law' (1997) 2 Utah Law Review 262.

[71] See Boike Rehbein, *Critical Theory after the Rise of the Global South* (Routledge 2015); Mukoma wa Ngugi (ed), 'Special Issue: Rethinking the Global South' [2012] Journal of Contemporary Thought; Paul Amar (ed), *The Middle East and Brazil: Perspectives on the New Global South* (Indiana UP 2014); Susanne Klengel and Alexandra Ortiz Wallner (eds), *Sur/South: Poetics and Politics of Thinking Latin America/India* (Iberoamericana 2016); Vijay Prashad, *The Poorer Nations: A Possible History of the Global South* (Verso 2012).

[72] Walter Mignolo, 'Delinking: The Rhetoric of Modernity, the Logic of Coloniality and the Grammar of De-Coloniality' (2007) 21 Cultural Studies 449.

[73] ibid 485.

[74] Frantz Fanon, *The Wretched of the Earth* (Penguin 1965); Dussel (n 43).

for the uncovering of the ever-present yet ever supressed alterity against which modern law is constructed—and which implies a parallel 'turn to language'.[75] The aim of this venture is, as Makau Mutua has put it in relation to comparative law's disciplinary sibling international law, to 'understand, deconstruct, and unpack the uses of . . . law as a medium for the creation and perpetuation of a racialised/genderized hierarchy of . . . norms and institutions that sub-ordinate non-Europeans and Europeans alike'.[76] The concept of the *South* is, here used as a tool to reverse the colonial epistemicide by which, as Ramon Grosfoguel has put it, the historical *South* has been reduced to 'first a place without culture, then a place without history, then a place without development, and, finally a place without democracy'.[77]

By revealing the *South* to be at once empirically different and epistemically supressed, this critique seeks to irritate the *West*'s *Weberian* (self-)image—as articulated, inter alia, in liberal constitutionalism and its attendant 'comparison-as-adequation' paradigm—and to, thereby, undermine its hegemony in an epistemic *Kampf um Anerkennung* ('fight for recognition').[78] The latter's methodological toolkit has come to a large extent from historical hermeneutics and has involved the reconstruction of the ways in which *Western* law is the product of the suppression of the *South* (and other 'others') by means of a deep reading of its historical text and texture, with a view to showing it—and the *modernity* it articulates—as an ideological curtain that covers up the harsh reality of *Western* domination but that is itself permeated by paradoxes and inconsistencies that render it fundamentally indeterminate. Concretely this has played out through a 'turn to history' in critical legal scholarship in which the liberal progress narrative of *Western* law is contested by the revisionist historization of its key concepts, protagonists, and formative moments.[79]

[75] Ngugi wa Thiong'o, *Globalectics: Theory and the Politics of Knowing* (Columbia UP 2012); and Andrea Gil and Thula Pires, 'From Binary to Intersectional to Imbricated Approaches: Gender in a Decolonial and Diasporic Perspective' (2019) 41 Contexto Internacional 275.

[76] Makau Mutua, 'What is TWAIL?' (2000) 94 American Society of International Law Proceedings 31; see also Ralph Wilde, 'Introduction to Queering International Law' (2007) American Society of International Law Proceedings of the Annual Meeting 119.

[77] Ramon Grosfoguel, 'Decolonizing Post-Colonial Studies and Paradigms of Political-Economy: Transmodernity, Decolonial Thinking, and Global Coloniality' (2011) 1 Transmodernity: Journal of Peripheral Cultural Production of the Luso-Hispanic World <http://dialogoglobal.com/texts/grosfoguel/Grosfoguel-Decolonizing-Pol-Econ-and-Postcolonial.pdf> accessed 10 August 2019; see also Malcolm Langford, 'Rights, Development and Critical Modernity' (2015) 46 Development and Change 777.

[78] See eg Bonilla Maldonado, *Constitutionalism* (n 1); see also Juan Pablo Scarfi, *The Hidden History of International Law in the Americas: Empire and Legal Networks* (OUP 2017).

[79] Matthew Craven, 'Theorizing the Turn to History in International Law' in Anne Orford and Florian Hoffmann (eds), *Oxford Handbook of the Theory of International Law* (OUP 2016) 21; Koskenniemi, 'Histories' (n 64) 152; and Outi Korhonen, 'Liberalism and International Law: A Center Projecting a Periphery' (1996) 65 Nordic Journal of International Law 481.

Here, the *South* provides the necessary contrast to make the deep structure of *Western* law visible, but it is the latter which remains the starting and the eventual end point of such critical hermeneutics. Indeed, in line with hermeneutic circularity, *Western* law is not re-described 'from outside', notably by reference to some overarching structural or functional logic that is deemed to determine its particular historical facticity, but it is rather dissected 'from within', by showing, through any number of historical or textual instances, how it has been constituting itself against its *Southern* other.[80] It is, hence, fundamentally left in place, *sous rature* (struck out), deeply problematic, yet inescapable. Given the depth of *Western* epistemicide over the past (roughly) five hundred years and the role legal concepts and forms have played in it, this remains a massive, if not uncontested endeavour.[81]

One such contestation derives from the hermeneutic-immanent character of these historical reconstructions and their, therefore, necessary fixation on the *West* and *Western* law. For even though the pre-/para-/post-colonial world that is represented by the *South* is meant to be made visible in the process of hermeneutic re-reading, the main purpose of this visibility is to highlight the injustice of its exclusion. The *South* here functions essentially as a de-encryption manual through which the historical text of *Western* law can be deciphered and revealed as what it is, namely Eurocentric, (neo-)colonial, white, male, and capitalist. However, to work as a recognizable marker thereof in *Western* law's text, the *South* ends up being itself reduced to an ideal type constructed from the elements of that text, that is, from the very generalizations and simplifications that lie at the basis of its exclusion. Ironically, then, the *South* is here always a part of the very *Western* legal text that is the object of critique, with the actual *South* remaining methodologically *hors-texte* and beyond the hermeneut's radar.[82]

This inherent limitation of historical hermeneutics has generated a response from within the difference perspective that has sought to avoid the inherent Eurocentrism of 'pure' hermeneutics. It has emerged from the critical formalism developed by Martti Koskenniemi and others in the context of

[80] See Alexandra Kemmerer, 'Sources in the Meta-Theory of International Law: Hermeneutical Conversations' in Samantha Besson and Jean D'Aspremont (eds), *The Oxford Handbook on the Sources of International Law* (OUP 2017); George Galindo, 'Martti Koskenniemi and the Historiographical Turn in International Law' (2005) 16 European Journal of International Law 539; Martti Koskenniemi, 'Histories of International Law: Significance and Problems for a Critical View' (2013) Temple International and Comparative Law Journal 215.

[81] See Jacques Derrida, *Of Grammatology* (Johns Hopkins UP 1997) and Gayatri Chakravorty Spivak, 'Tranlator's Preface' in Jacques Derrida, *Of Grammatology* (Johns Hopkins UP 1997) ix; Boaventura de Sousa Santos, *Epistemologies of the South: Justice against Epistemicide* (Paradigm 2014).

[82] Derrida, *Of Grammatology* (n 81) 158.

international law as an attempt to connect (critical) legal scholarship to (critical) legal practice.[83] Its starting point has been the same dual impulse that had motivated the original legal positivists, notably to, on one hand, provide an epistemic framework specific to law as an autonomous discourse irreducible to a mere epiphenomenon of deeper functional or structural determinants;[84] and, on the other hand, to make the normative claim that such an autonomous law is inherently capable of advancing progressive values such as peace, equity, human dignity, or, indeed, justice writ large.[85] However, unlike classical (legal) positivism, critical formalism could no longer take *Western* law at face value but, as was seen, has had to work with a discourse the manifold 'dark sides' of which had gradually been dragged into the light by successive iterations of critical re-reading.[86]

However, to retain the autonomous character of 'the law', its deeply problematic historical concretization as *Western* law could neither simply be discarded nor explained away, but had to be reframed from within, notably by making a virtue of its vice of indeterminacy and by, therefore, drawing on the inherently open-ended nature of legal discourse and its innermost nature as an argumentative *praxis* that 'brings out into the open the contradictions of the society in which it operates and the competition of opposite interests that are the flesh and blood of the legal every day'.[87] This theoretical move was meant to make it possible to turn the inherent structural bias of legal practice, that is, the a priori 'shared understanding of how the rules and institutions should be applied',[88] into the very wedge by which its concealed underside could be exposed and thereby undermined. This move hinges on the nature of legal practice which, through formalization, enables an open-ended process of argumentation among nominal equals that breaks down universalist claims into

[83] Martti Koskenniemi, 'Law, Teleology and International Relations: An Essay in Counterdisciplinarity' (2012) 26 International Relations 3; Jan Klabbers, 'Towards a Culture of Formalism? Martti Koskenniemi and the Virtues' (2013) 27 Temple International and Comparative Law Journal, 417; Jean d'Aspremont, *Formalism and the Sources of International Law: A Theory of the Ascertainment of Legal Rules* (OUP 2011).

[84] Martti Koskenniemi, *From Apology to Utopia* (2nd edn, CUP 2006); Florian Hoffmann, 'Teaching General Public International Law' in Jean D'Aspremont and Jörg Kammerhofer (eds), *International Legal Positivism in a Post-Modern World* (CUP 2014) 349; Jörg Kammerhofer, 'International Legal Positivism' in Anne Orford and Florian Hoffmann (eds), *Oxford Handbook of the Theory of International Law* (OUP 2016) 407.

[85] Martti Koskenniemi, 'The Politics of International Law: 20 Years Later' (2009) 20 European Journal of International Law 7; Wouter Werner, Marieke de Hoon, and Alexis Glán, *The Law of International Lawyers: Reading Martti Koskenniemi* (CUP 2017).

[86] Martti Koskenniemi, 'Vitoria and Us: Thoughts on Critical Histories of International Law' (2014) 22 Rechtsgeschichte/Legal History 119.

[87] Koskenniemi, 'Law, Teleology and International Relations' (n 83) 19.

[88] Koskenniemi, *From Apology to Utopia* (n 84) 608.

the particular positions and interests that drive them, while simultaneously enjoining its participants to make their particular claims (hypothetically) universalizable.[89] In other words, *Western* law's purpose is here interlinked with its promise and is thereby meant to open up a navigable passageway 'between the Scylla of empire and the Charybdis of fragmentation, [with] the culture of formalism resist[ing] reduction into substantive policy, whether imperial or particular'.[90]

Hence, in essence, critical formalism seeks to reframe legal practice as a form of hermeneutics, that is, as an exercise of continuous reinterpretation, according to formalized rules, of a given legal text and its history in relation to particular cases. These cases function, in best *Weberian* fashion, as ideal-types and, hence, as stylized yet ultimately arbitrary snapshots through which the injustices inscribed in legal *modernity* can be made visible and procedurally redeemed in a piecemeal fashion. Such a law-as-hermeneutic-practice is, therefore, no longer interested in taking an epistemological position on what the law is or how it can be known, but it marks a turn away from conventional epistemology all together, in the sense that it does not seek to generate theoretical knowledge (*episteme*), but, instead, practical knowledge (*phronesis*) through the practice of law before courts.[91] Law, thus, becomes synonymous with legal practice which, in turn, becomes synonymous with epistemic justice.

To be fair, critical formalism does not claim that this epistemic justice implies that legal process always results in substantively 'just' solutions to real-life disputes, nor that it always benefits subaltern (aka *Southern*) participants thereof. It is rather meant to signify the fundamental contestability of the modern (*Western*) production of knowledge (as *episteme*) and its inherent entanglement with power. *Western* science and its disciplines are here taken to enshrine this power-knowledge, whereas a law reconceived as an indeterminate process

[89] Tanja Aalberts and Ingo Venzke, 'Moving Beyond Interdisciplinary Turf Wars: Towards an Understanding of International Law as Practice' in Jean D'Aspremont and others (eds), *International Law as a Profession* (CUP 2017) 287; Geoff M Gordon, 'Universalism' in Jean D'Aspremont and Sahib Singh, *Concepts for International Law* (Edward Elgar 2019) 865.

[90] Jeffrey L Dunoff, 'From Interdisciplinarity to Counterdisciplinarity: Is There Madness in Martti's Method' (2013) 27 Temple International and Comparative Law Journal 309.

[91] Jan Klabbers, 'Towards a Culture of Formalism? Martti Koskenniemi and the Virtues' (2013) 27 Temple International and Comparative Law Journal 417; Roberto Vilchez Yamato and Florian Hoffmann, 'Counter-disciplining the Dual Agenda: Towards a (Re-) Assessment of the Interdisciplinary Study of International Law and International Relations' (2018) 61 Revista Brasileira de Política Internacional 1; David Roth-Isigkeit, 'The Blinkered Discipline? Martti Koskenniemi and Interdisciplinary Approaches to International Law' (2017) 9 International Theory 410; see, however, Anthea Roberts, *Is International Law International?* (OUP 2017); and Ralf Michaels' comment 'Beyond Universalism and Particularism in International Law: Insights from Comparative Law and Private International Law' (2019) 99 Boston University Law Review 18.

that produces practical judgement vis-à-vis concrete cases is a potential irritant to *Western* epistemic hegemony.[92]

The law, thus, functions as a wedge against epistemic domination, that is, as a discursive practice that is able to challenge the various disciplines of power-knowledge wedded to the overarching functional and structural precepts of the *West*. Law is, thus, effectively transformed into a 'counterdiscipline' that is not a scientifically 'disciplined' meta-language by which the workings of public or private (legal) relations might be understood (and/or explained), nor an object of study to be described in terms of the meta-language of another discipline (such as international relations, political science, sociology, anthropology, comparative literature, continental or analytical philosophy, psychoanalysis, or economic theory (or else)). Instead, it is a practice which can be 'known' properly only through its enactment and from the (internal) position of a participant. This law as a 'counterdiscipline' is, thus, conceived as a framework for the empowerment and emancipation of the *South* as much as of the *West*,[93] one that allegedly escapes disciplinary essentialization and functionalization and that is, instead, 'non-scientistic, non-traditional, oppositional, transformative',[94] or, as Balakrishnan Rajagopal has framed it, 'plainly counterhegemonic'.[95]

E. The *South* as the *West*: Towards (a) Meridional Modernity

Yet, how counterhegemonic can such 'counterdisciplinarity' be for the legal comparativist if the actual *South* remains epistemically unreachable and, therefore, ultimately irrelevant to understanding the *West*? For it would seem that the critique of the reductionism and bias of the *Weberian* account of modernity becomes, in its counterdisciplinarian variant, a critique of (*Western*) epistemology itself, notably as a form of power-knowledge that is always bound to resolve difference into a hierarchical relation dominated by the *West* and its

[92] Gunther Teubner, 'Legal Irritants: Good Faith in British Law or How Unifying Law Ends Up In New Divergences (1998) 61 Modern Law Review 11; and Gunther Teubner, *Constitutional Fragments: Societal Constitutionalism and Globalization* (OUP 2012).

[93] Koskenniemi, 'Law, Teleology and International Relations' (n 83); Yamato and Hoffmann, 'Counter-disciplining the Dual Agenda' (n 91); Anne Orford, 'Scientific Reason and the Discipline of International Law' (2014) 25 European Journal of International Law 369.

[94] For the initial argument see again Frankenberg, 'Stranger Than Paradise' (n 70).

[95] Balakrishnan Rajagopal, 'Counterhegemonic International Law: Rethinking Human Rights and Development as a Third World Strategy' (2006) 27 Third World Quarterly 767; Balakrishnan Rajagopal, *International Law From Below: Development, Social Movements, and Third World Resistance* (CUP 2003); yet Isabel Feichtner, 'Critical Scholarship and Responsible Practice of International Law: How Can the Two Be Reconciled?' (2016) 29 Leiden Journal of International Law 979.

Weberian categories. The legal scholar must, therefore, abstain from seeking to 'know' the *South*, yet for the price that the latter must remain inconsequential to the (self-)understanding of the *West*. The *South* becomes here visible (only) through its contestation of *Western* hegemony in the context of legal process or by way of an ethnographic narrative that refrains from comparison, extrapolation, or generalization. Ironically, this files an epistemic injunction not only against *Weberianism* but also against its historical antipode *Marxism*—as both are premised on the idea that either the material world or our knowledge thereof is structured by the same fundamental properties.[96]

Yet, if any form of common epistemic horizon is rejected outright, the question of whether the *West*'s (*Weberian*) description of modernity does justice both to the 'real-existing' *West* as much as to the *South* cannot even be broached. Nor could the *South* be understood as potentially providing a more accurate and plausible account of the modern world than the *Weberian* categories. It is, instead, bound to remain an abstract idea, a mere epistemic provocation, and a bloodless other—and as such but another incarnation of Eurocentrism.[97]

To look beyond the (Eurocentric) cliché of the *South*, a new comparative methodology must seek to reach the concrete *South* and to make it speak not just *to* but *about* the *West*. This requires an inversion of the epistemic horizon so that the actual *South* is opened up in order to provide, as, again, the Comaroffs have aptly put it, a 'privileged insight into the workings of the world at large [. . . so] that it is from here that our empirical grasp of its lineaments, and our theory-work in accounting for them, ought to be coming . . .'[98] It is an agenda articulated in various strands of '*South*ern theory' as developed, for instance, by Raewyn Connel (*South*ern Theory), Boaventura de Sousa Santos (Epistemologies of the *South*), Juan Obriarrio (Theory from the *South*), Gurminder K Bhambra (Connected Sociologies), Sanjay Subrahmanyam (Connected Histories), and, indeed, William Twining (*South*ern Voices).[99] All

[96] This engages, of course, one of the central issues of modern (Western) philosophy, and, thus, by far transcends the bounds of this reflection; see here tentatively Hall *Cultures of Inquiry* (n 25); and Bernhard Gill, 'Über Whitehead und Mead zur Aktor-Netzwerk-Theorie: die Überwindung des Dualismus von Geist und Materie - und der Preis, de dafür zu zahlen ist' in Georg Kneer, Markus Schör, and Erhard Schüttpelz, *Latours Kollektive* (Suhrkamp 2008) 47.

[97] See eg Immanuel Wallerstein, 'Eurocentrism and its Avatars: the Dilemmas of Social Science' (1997) Sociological Bulletin 21; Nick Hostettler, *Eurocentrism: A Marxian Critical Realist Critique* (Routledge 2012); but also Ramon Grosfoguel, 'The Epistemic Decolonial Turn' (2007) 21 Cultural Studies.

[98] Comaroff and Comaroff, *Theory of the South* (n 15) 1; see also and recently Anna Leander and Ole Waever (eds), *Assembling Exclusive Expertise: Knowledge, Ignorance and Conflict Resolution in the Global South* (Routledge 2019).

[99] See Raewyn Connell, *Southern Theory: The Global Dynamics of Knowledge in Social Science* (Polity Press 2007); Nour Dados and Raewyn Connell, 'The Global South' (2012) 11 Contexts 12; Boaventura de Sousa Santos, *Epistemologies of the South: Justice against Epistemicide* (Paradigm 2014);

have in common that they see the concrete *South* as much more than merely a theatre in which the effects of colonial and postcolonial violence can be observed (by and from the *West*). In fact, the contention of this inverted epistemology is that (legal) *modernity* only plays out in its fullest sense in the *South*, for it is here that *West* and *South* are conjoined in the hybrid, complex, and contingent *mesclage* that *modernity* always was—but that has been sanitized out of *Western* consciousness. This concrete *South* is, thus, a treasure trove of (comparative legal) knowledge for it reveals the (legal) world behind the *Weberian* façade, the real live of the law, of the state, and of the constitution.

However, such an agenda of epistemic *meridianization* implies a number of methodological moves. In the first place, it requires a *de-Weberization* of the fundamental terms and normative ideals of (comparative) law, for it is the stylized ideal types of the *Weberian* world—from instrumental rationality to the (bureaucratic) rule of law—that frames—and, therefore, blurs—the cognitive horizon of the legal comparativist. They produce a (Eurocentric) model that, much like Ptolemaic cosmology in Thomas Kuhn's well-known example of paradigm shift, seeks to squeeze an actually much more complex and fuzzy 'reality'—of *West* and *South* alike—into a preordained and cognitively closed framework and thereby engenders an often under-complex or contradictory account of how (constitutional) law works 'on the ground'.[100] Hence, ironically, *de-Weberization* means, in the first place, to take the actual Weber seriously and to disassociate the ideal types originally postulated as mere waymarkers in a complex empirical field from the deep structure of the reality behind it.[101] To incrementally—and always only partially—grasp the latter, ideal types can only ever function as heuristic devices against which real phenomena are measured and which must be continuously modified in accordance with these phenomena. Indeed, understanding the life of (constitutional) law on the ground is like piecing together a jigsaw puzzle in which ideas about elements of the final picture orient the assembling of the pieces but must continuously be adapted in accordance with the actual picture that emerges. If, however,

Juan Obarrio 'Theory from the South: Theorizing the Contemporary' *Fieldsights* <https://culanth.org/fieldsights/series/theory-from-the-south> accessed 18 December 2019; Gurminder Bhambra, *Connected Sociologies* (Bloomsbury 2014); Sanjay Subrahmanyam, *Connected Histories: Notes towards a Reconfiguration of Early Modern Eurasia* (CUP 1997); William Twining, *Human Rights, Southern Voices* (CUP 2009).

[100] For the analogy, see Thomas Kuhn, *The Structure of Scientific Revolutions* (University of Chicago Press 1996); as well as Winch (n 61); but also, critically, Paul Feyerabend, *Against Method* (4th edn, Verso 2010); see also Christoph Schönberger, 'Verfassungsvergleichung heute: Der schwierige Abschied vom ptolemäischen Weltbild' (2010) 43 VRÜ/WCL 6.

[101] Berman (n 9).

these ideas are misunderstood as a priori representations of reality, the jigsaw's pieces will be assembled forcefully in their likeness and the result will be a distorted picture in the likeness of the *Weberian* world.

In this vein, a second move in the *de-Weberization* agenda consists of a turn to what Sundya Pahuja and Luis Eslava have termed an 'ethos of ethnography' which calls not only for a focus on the concrete causes, practices, and effects of law 'on the ground' but also for an active deconstruction of the stratification of that ground into an epistemically privileged and normalized 'us' and an observed 'exotic other'.[102] Instead, comparative research has to start from the assumption of an exotic 'us' and open itself to the concrete historical contingencies that have constituted the *West* as much as the *South*. Indeed, it is this ethnographic gaze that connects the 'real' *West* to the 'real' *South*, as it seeks to discern and decipher the myriad ways in which the law operates in the everyday life of states, societies, and people across the globe.[103]

The epistemically privileged place from where to do this discerning and deciphering is the 'real' *South*, as it is here that (legal) *modernity* can be observed in full play, including the complex interactions by which the *Weberian* categories of liberal constitutionalism are manipulated, subverted, sidelined, or re-signified.[104] For only in this 'real' *South* have the *Weberian* categories never been fully naturalized and remain observable before a social and political background that far transcends them in complexity. From a *Southern* optic, comparison, thus, no longer serves to reproduce and reinforce the *Weberian* self-consciousness of the *West* by highlighting the deviance of the *South*, but it becomes a way of making visible the functional logics and deep structures hidden behind the *Weberian* imagery of modernity. What comes into view is, thus, not just a complementary version of legal modernity but a different one altogether, notably one in which the *Weberian* categories are but one of several layers of (self-)reflexivity.[105] For the point is not to artificially take out

[102] Luis Eslava and Sundya Pahuja, 'Beyond the (Post) Colonial: TWAIL and the Everyday Life of International Law' (2012) 45 VRÜ/WCL 195; Nathanael Berman, 'Aftershocks: Exoticization, Normalization and the Hermeneutic Compulsion' (1997) 2 Utah Law Review 281.

[103] There is a growing literature coming from different theoretical premises yet converging on a renewed interest in the 'empirical' in law; see eg Dennis J Galligan and Mila Vertseeg, *Social and Political Foundations of Constitutions* (CUP 2013); Andrew Lang, 'New Legal Realism, Empiricism, and Scientism: The Relative Objectivity of Law and Social Science' (2015) 28 Leiden Journal of International Law 231; or, in the related field of international law, Roberts (n 91).

[104] See Eslava (n 63); Johns (n 63); Jean Comaroff and John L Comaroff, *Law and Disorder in the Potcolony* (University of Chicago Press 2006).

[105] Sujata Patel, 'Beyond Binaries: A Case for Self-Reflexive Sociologies' (2006) 54 (3) Current Sociology 381; Christiane Kraft Alsop, 'Home and Away: Self-reflexive Auto-/ethnography' (2002) Forum Qualitative Sozialforschung/Forum: Qualitative Social Research 3 (3); Ilan Kapoor, 'Hyper-self-reflexive Development? Spivak on Representing the Third World "Other"' (2004) 25 (4) Third World Quarterly 627.

the *Weberian* categories and replace them with equally artificial new (or 'native') ones but to chart their complex and recursive interaction with Southern realities of which they are an irreducible element yet which resist being determined by or reduced to them. Such *Southern* comparativism would, hence, skirt the dual pitfall of constitutional comparativism as outlined by Zoran Oklopcic in this volume, notably of falling either to 'naïve botanism' or to hermetic incommensurability.[106]

The precise contours of this *Southern* modernity are yet to be sketched in terms of a richer, more complex, and mutable set of categories. It will certainly imply a reworking of such key concepts as the rule of law, constitutional government, or democracy, with a view to render a more accurate account of their workings and not-workings.[107] And with this new comparative optic, the history and present of the *West* will also gradually have to be rewritten in the likeness of the *South*.[108] To be sure, this optic must itself resist essentialization, not least by refraining from simply inverting the progress narrative that has informed 'mainstream' comparativism. If, as Amy Allen has argued, 'forward-looking progress with respect to the decolonization of the normative foundations of critical theory [and comparativism] can take place only if we abandon the backward-looking story that positions European modernity as the outcome of a historical learning process',[109] then, likewise, the assimilation of non-*Weberian* forms into a post-Eurocentric Eurocentrism cannot be the way ahead either. Instead a fundamental openness to alterity, hybridity, and contingency as the structural determinants of 'law in practice' is what is at the basis of the *South* and what enables, in a literal sense, the *re-cognition* of the *modern* world in its likeness.

[106] Oklopcic, 'Comparing as (Re-)imagining' (n 3).

[107] A key concept to be addressed in this context is, for example, 'corruption', which tends to hang over the *South* like a (*Western*) 'sword of Damokles' yet in its simplifying use and connotation embodies the Weberian distortion of highly complex realities; see for a recent prominent example Fabia Fernandes Carvalho Veçoso, 'Anti-Corruption Legalism and Moralizing Authoritarianism in Brazil' (2019) Third World Approaches to International Law Review <https://twailr.com/anti-corruption-legalism-and-moralizing-authoritarianism-in-brazil/> (last accessed 27 December 2019) as well as, in the Weberian context, again Thomas 'Re-Reading Weber' (n 26); another is democracy: see eg Andrea Ribeiro Hoffmann, 'Negotiating Normative Premises in Democracy Promotion: Venezuela and the Inter-American Democratic Charter' (2019) 26 Democratization 815.

[108] See eg James G Carrier (ed), *Occidentalism: Images of the West* (OUP 2003); Hassan Hanafi, 'From Orientalism to Occidentalism' (2010) Building Peace by Intercultural Dialogue 257.

[109] Allen (n 58) 148.

3

(Global) Constitutionalism and the Geopolitics of Knowledge

Christine Schwöbel-Patel

A. Introduction

A comparative constitutional analysis that directs a view to the Global South must confront the question of coloniality. Coloniality is mostly concerned with epistemic violence: a violence of omission, exclusion, distortion, and erasure of knowledge that has shaped the relationship between the Global North and the Global South.[1] As knowledge, from the beginning of the colonial era in the sixteenth century, was exported, violently, Western knowledge became dominant, erasing, marginalizing, and invalidating knowledges from the Global South. The approach that considers knowledge and its reproduction as geopolitical emphasizes its material consequences. It not only considers the distributive faculties of knowledge reproduction; it also in particular focuses on the prevention of redistribution of wealth. Given the material (as well as social and cultural) inequalities that continue to prevail across a Global North–Global South divide, an analysis of legal and political constructs which *stabilize* and *reproduce* this divide is critical. Constitutionalism, whether domestic, regional, transnational, or global, is analysed as a legal and political construct that has tended to seek the stabilization of a particular (mostly capitalist) order. In this chapter, the question of coloniality is raised in regard to the origins of a specific way of understanding constitutionalism in the global sphere, namely, the emergent global constitutionalism of the 1990s. I revisit the origins—and the originators—of this project of global ordering in an effort to understand

[1] The Global North and Global South are not exclusively references to geographical terrains, but ones divided along material inequalities. This can mean that there are 'Global Souths' in the Global North and vice versa, as Luis Eslava noted in Luis Eslava, TWAIL Coordinates, *Critical Legal Thinking* (2 April 2019) <http://criticallegalthinking.com/2019/04/02/twail-coordinates/#fn-27281-2> accessed 16 December 2019. Indigenous populations are perhaps the foremost group of Global Souths in the Global North.

Christine Schwöbel-Patel, *(Global) Constitutionalism and the Geopolitics of Knowledge* In: *The Global South and Comparative Constitutional Law*. Edited by: Philipp Dann, Michael Riegner, and Maxim Bönnemann, Oxford University Press (2020). © Oxford University Press. DOI: 10.1093/oso/9780198850403.003.0003

the geopolitics of global constitutional knowledge. Argentinian semiotician Walter Mignolo, who coined the phrase the 'geopolitics of knowledge', emphasizes the necessity to question epistemology as a colonial tool in order to understand and implement *de*colonization strategies.[2] The follow-up question to the coloniality of constitutionalism is then whether it is possible to decolonize global constitutionalism?

If Mignolo provides the methodology and framing of the question for this chapter, then Quinn Slobodian's research provides the relevant intellectual history. Slobodian's book *Globalists: The End of Empire and the Birth of Neoliberalism* draws out critical linkages between neoliberals and early global constitutionalists.[3] Highlighting the intellectual, professional, and personal relationships between neoliberals such as Friedrich von Hayek and early global constitutional scholars such as Ernst-Ulrich Petersmann opens up a view to the institutional (and therefore also material) consequences of global ordering projects. So while intellectual histories are illuminating for the geopolitics of knowledge, they must also be understood within the material conditions in which ideas were allowed to gain currency. A geopolitics of knowledge takes account of the conditions under which knowledge is considered valid and can be reproduced.[4] Interestingly, while the 'ideal' project of global constitutionalism today remains less than a sum of its parts (being mostly a type of Eurocentric thought experiment with global ambitions), the 'material' project of global constitutionalism has had a deep impact on the neoliberal order. The latest generation of advocates of global constitutionalism on the one hand embody the divisions between 'ideal' and 'material' global constitutionalism: They have inherited a project which has mostly dispensed with any questions of redistribution (as material concerns), instead focusing on its ideal qualities only. But, on the other hand, this generation also embodies the unity between the 'ideal' and 'material' global constitutionalism in that some of the ideas of the early global constitutionalists constituted and entrenched the contemporary neoliberal order—just not in the way the original neoliberals had intended. In ignoring the distributive functions of constitutionalism, the contemporary generation of advocates of global constitutionalism is (at times inadvertently) reproducing the status quo, sustaining the division between ideal and material

[2] Walter Mignolo, 'The Geopolitics of Knowledge and the Colonial Difference' South Atlantic Quarterly 10 (2002) 57.

[3] Quinn Slobodian, *Globalists: The End of Empire and the Birth of Neoliberalism* (Harvard University Press 2018).

[4] Daniel Bonilla Moldonado, 'The Political Economy of Legal Knowledge' in Colin Crawford and Daniel Bonilla Moldonado (eds), *Constitutionalism in the Americas* (Edward Elgar 2018) 29–78.

constitutionalism. This division itself deepens the grip of the material *already existing* constitutionalized mechanisms of the global economy. When it comes to the question of decolonizing, it is therefore crucial to appreciate the divide between ideal constitutionalism, which largely ignores material conditions but receives much scholarly attention, and material constitutionalism which has shaped the existing global neoliberal order but is open to far less scrutiny. De facto constitutionalism was built largely through the geopolitics of knowledge of those thinkers and implementers who first conceived of the World Trade Organization (WTO). I hasten to add that global neoliberal constitutionalism is no longer exclusively dependent on the WTO as an institution—and the twin facts of the WTO (appeals system) being disabled through power struggles between competing hegemonic states and there being a growing prevalence of bilateral trade treaties are of little consequence to it. Instead, its logic has become normalized in the financialized and commercialized global structures and the multilateral and bilateral trade and investment agreements that modelled themselves on the key legal-institutional tenets of the WTO. Struggles that aim to both expose and destabilize structures and institutions of inequality and coloniality should therefore be directed less against 'ideal' global constitutionalism and more against 'material' global constitutionalism.

B. The Geopolitics of Knowledge and Constitutionalism

Mignolo posits that colonial epistemology and the idea of 'modernity' are inextricably linked.[5] Modernity is understood as a European narrative about human endeavour and progress. In the Western imaginary, modernity is the more or less linear development of Western civilization from ancient Greece to eighteenth-century Europe, 'where the bases of modernity were laid out'.[6] In Western epistemology, the 'second phase' of modernity ensued with the industrial revolution and the Enlightenment. Knowledge is, according to Mignolo and other decolonial thinkers, therefore limited by epistemic ethnocentricism. With an ethnocentric universalization of modernity, Western thinking has the privilege of being able to speak for the universal while non-Western knowledge is considered 'local' or attributed to 'culture'. Grasping colonial*ity* requires the spatial understanding of knowledge moving and legitimating colonial*ism*.

[5] Walter Mignolo, 'Modernity and Decoloniality' (*Oxford Bibliographies*, 5 May 2017) <https://www.oxfordbibliographies.com/view/document/obo-9780199766581/obo-9780199766581-0017.xml> accessed 16 December 2019.

[6] Mignolo, 'Geopolitics of Knowledge' (n 2) 60.

Spatiality, captured from a material perspective as (primitive) accumulation, links the movement of knowledge to the movement of capital, situating it in the emergence of the Atlantic commercial circuit in the sixteenth century.[7] Key to understanding the geopolitics of knowledge is that coloniality endures today and was not ended or completed with the period of decolonization in the twentieth century.[8] Boaventura de Sousa Santos, another influential decolonial thinker, explains coloniality and its dependency on conceptualizing difference through the idea of the 'abyssal line'—characterized by the line drawn between the Global North and the Global South in which the former is associated with order and the latter with chaos.[9] The Global South in this account is a 'metaphor for human suffering under global capitalism'.[10]

Constitutionalism as a defining political moment is, in Western thought, upheld as the pinnacle of a society's order, sophistication and civilization. The great constitutional moments are generally Western moments of democratic contestation, whether in the French or US constitutions, or the post-war German or Japanese constitutions. In the case of the French and US constitutions, they both stabilized the power of an emergent merchant class, or the bourgeoisie, which had become rich due to colonial enterprises. In the case of Germany and Japan, the constitutions were intended—and still function—as a means of upholding the rule of law, or in the German terminology a *Rechtsstaat*. These constitutions also played a role in stabilization for the purpose of incorporation in a global trading system. The defining constitutional moments in Western consciousness can generally be understood as moments of the entrenching of liberal-democratic power that fixed property rights as central rights and simultaneously excluded redistributional ambitions as extra-constitutional.

Many former colonial states notably experienced constitutionalism for the first time as a means of consolidating the power of their colonial masters. As Upenda Baxi memorably stated, 'modern' constitutionalism was transacted during the early period of colonialism and imperialism. 'That historical timespace', he observed, 'marks a combined and uneven development of the world in the processes of early modernity'.[11] Baxi warns that such 'epistemic

[7] ibid.

[8] 'Decolonization is not completed' is the defining phrase from the 2019 Chagos advisory opinion of the International Court of Justice; Legal Consequences of the Separation of the Chagos Archipelago from Mauritius in 1965, Advisory Opinion [2019] ICJ GL No 169, 25 February 2019.

[9] Boaventura de Sousa Santos, 'Beyond Abyssal Thinking: From Global Lines to Ecologies of Knowledges' (2007) 30 Review 45.

[10] Boaventrua de Sousa Santos, *Toward a New Common Sense: Law, Science, and Politics in the Paradigmatic Transition* (Routledge 1995) 506.

[11] *Upendra Baxi*, 'Constitutionalism as a Site of State Formative Practices' (2000) 21 Cardozo Law Review 1184.

legal racism' must be exposed as the foundational violence of law. Comparative constitutionalism, according to Baxi, risks irrelevance (certainly from the Global South), if it ignores the 'inherent, and at times genocidal violence that accompanies the grand narratives concerning the founding notions of modern constitutionalism: the rule of law, separation of powers, autonomous constitutional review, and guarantees of basic human rights'.[12] He explains that 'these notions still appear tainted to the peoples of the First Nations, or to postcolonial peoples in many parts of the world today; this is because they experience in and through constitutional development the replication of the foundational violence'.[13] Have all moments of constitutionalism in the Global South been moments of epistemic legal racism?

A pivotal constitutional moment in the Global South, perceived to emanate from the *end* of violence of the oppressor, was undoubtedly the South African post-apartheid constitution. The South African Constitution, promulgated in 1996 by anti-apartheid revolutionary and former dissident Nelson Mandela, was particularly celebrated for its incorporation of social and economic rights. Despite its undoubtedly strong symbolic commitment to transitional justice, the South African constitution too has been criticized for its eurocentrism and its coloniality. The absence of redistributive and reparative measures is highlighted by critics, as is the continued social and economic repression of the indigenous black population.[14] Rather than marking the violent imposition of a constitution, as described by Baxi about Indian constitutionalism, this constitution marked the elevated role of the market, and therefore the continuation of economic, social, and cultural inequality.

If one is searching for radical constitutionalism in the Global South, intended to end epistemic legal racism, one is likely to encounter discussions on constitutions which pre-date the South African constitution by almost two hundred years. The 1801 Constitution of Saint-Domingue (later Haiti), and the ones which followed, were promulgated after the Haitian revolution against the brutal and exploitative French colonizers.[15] The 1801 Constitution was promulgated by the former slave Toussaint Lourverture, commonly referred to as the political architect of the revolution. Saint-Domingue was at the time the most prosperous of the French colonies, with profitable sugar and coffee plantations.

[12] ibid 1185.

[13] ibid.

[14] Joel Modiri, 'Law's Poverty' (2015) 18 Potchefstroom Electronic Law Journal 224; DM Davis, 'Is the South African Constitution an Obstacle to a Democratic Post-colonial State?' (2018) 34 South African Journal on Human Rights 359.

[15] Constitution of 1801, art 3: 'There can be no slaves on this territory; servitude has been forever abolished' <https://www.marxists.org/history/haiti/1801/constitution.htm> accessed 16 December 2019.

The 1801 Constitution is mostly remembered for its commitment to abolish slavery. With its emphasis on freedom, the colonized employed the colonizer's tools against them—this was after all a mere twelve years after the storming of the Bastille in the French capital. Apart from the immediate counter-revolutionary measures by Napoleon at the time, the constitutions were interestingly not introduced to Western consciousness until the 1938 publication of CLR James's book *The Black Jacobins*. Even then, it took 'a full generation of [Western] historians to come to terms with the argument'; meaning, even after the historical account had entered Western knowledge, the narrative of slaves as agents in their own story remained uncomfortable.[16] More recently, the constitutions of Haiti have attracted a fair amount of scholarly attention.[17]

In an unhappy reformist twist, and against the background of what we have learned about Western epistemology above, the Haitian constitutions may have eventually attracted the attention of a Western-dominated academy precisely because of the familiarity of the Western form of constitutionalism for making political and legal demands. For although the political drive to transform protests into a revolution were truly radical, the constitutions themselves were also fairly conservative. The 1801 Constitution protected the status quo of Saint-Domingue's status as a colony and dubbed property rights as 'sacred and inviolable'.[18] Although the constitution abolished slavery (in fact a further confirmation of the status quo, as France had abolished it seven years earlier), it did not abolish the plantation system. Furthermore, it established Catholicism as the official religion rather than the indigenous Voudou. Divorce was banned whilst marriage was described as tending 'to the purity of morals'. Much in the image of Napoleon in France, Lourverture gave himself almost absolute power over the island. Later constitutions arguably went further than the first 1801 version, particularly in light of Napoleon reinstating slavery. But, ultimately the promulgation of a constitution can be described as the reformist moment of a revolution. Constitutionalism was invoked *within* not against its liberal tradition—as a liberal tool, applied in order to legitimize the success of previous political, military, and economic battles. The liberal form of the constitution arguably packs the urgent demands of the exploited into a Western format, which can be owned by the Western mind.

[16] James Walvin, 'Introduction' in CLR James (ed), *The Black Jacobins* (Penguin 2001) ch 9.

[17] See eg Philip Kaisary, 'Hercules, the Hydra, and the 1801 Constitution of Toussaint Louverture' (2015) 12 Atlantic Studies 393; Robert Shilliam, 'What the Haitian Revolution Might Tell Us about Development, Security, and the Politics of Race' (2008) 50 Comparative Studies in Society and History 778; Alex Dupuy, *Haiti in the World Economy: Class, Race, and Underdevelopment since 1700* (Westview Press 1989).

[18] Constitution of 1801, arts 9, 10, and 13.

Global constitutionalism shares the Western liberal intellectual and material tradition of domestic, regional, and transnational constitutionalism. But, global constitutionalism also has a distinct history situated in the twentieth century, and more specifically in the 1990s. Indeed, if we look to when and by whom the idea of 'global constitutionalism' was first floated, we find a group of thinkers and policymakers closely associated with key international institutions of the neoliberal order.

C. Global Constitutionalism and Neoliberalism: A Brief Genealogy

At first blush, global constitutionalism and neoliberalism may appear unrelated. Global constitutionalism remains overwhelmingly a statist idea, where the state is the primary, if not sole, actor.[19] A common assumption—and as it turns out misconception—is that neoliberalism is preoccupied with markets and not with states. Generally, this is attributed to the intellectual origins of the so-called Chicago School, associated in particular with US economist Milton Friedman. According to this narrative, neoliberalism means the disappearance of the nation state in favour of laissez faire of the market. In this version of neoliberalism there would be only few touching points between a free market and constitutionalism. However, as many scholars have insisted, the role of the state (and therefore also the role of law) has been critical in the development of a legal-institutional order that protects the market.[20] In particular, Slobodian has uncovered the intellectual history of a strand of neoliberalism which directly links to the emergence of the global constitutionalism debate. In what Slobodian terms the 'Geneva School', a group of economists and lawyers came together who viewed the state as a key component to ensuring a stable global economic order. He suggests calling this group 'ordoglobalists': ordo-liberals who took the idea of an economic constitution to the global level.[21] Building on Slobodian's categorization of the work and influence of two generations of ordoglobalists, I set out two generations of global constitutionalists: the protagonist of the first is the well-known figure of Friedrich von Hayek, and the

[19] A notable exception are the conceptions of societal constitutions, proposed prominently by Gunther Teubner: see Gunther Teubner, *Constitutional Fragments: Societal Constitutionalism and Globalization* (OUP 2012).

[20] Including Sundhya Pahuja, *Decolonising International Law: Development, Economic Growth and the Politics of Universality* (CUP 2011) and Claire Cutler, *Private Power and Global Authority: Transnational Merchant Law in the Global Political Economy* (CUP 2003).

[21] Slobodian (n 3) 12.

protagonist of the second generation is Ernst-Ulrich Petersmann. The third generation in my brief account is the generation that emerged in the late 1990s (after Slobodian's account in *Globalists* ends), who had already normalized the externality of the economy in their visions of global constitutionalism. But let us first turn to the first generation.

1. The first generation of global constitutionalists

The main protagonist in this version of events is the Austrian Ludwig von Mises, who worked at the International Chamber of Commerce in Vienna in the early 1920s and later at the Geneva-based Graduate Institute of International Studies. According to Slobodian, von Mises's preoccupation with economic freedom and market access was motivated by concerns about the fate of the Austrian state after the demise of the Habsburg empire. Von Mises was deeply concerned about the role that Austria would play in a global order that allowed for capital to move across borders—market access had become crucial to this diminished former empire.[22] Von Mises, unsurprisingly, particularly opposed tariff walls. The idea was born of the protection of the market through national and international structures.[23] This view of the legal ordering of the economy came from a deeply rooted idea of economic freedom as tied to rights protection. Rights protection, in other words, could only emerge as a function of capitalism.[24] The idea was later developed by von Mises's famous mentee: Friedrich von Hayek. The Geneva School neoliberals, as Slobodian points out, shared certain affinities with the ordoliberals associated with the Freiburg School. Both schools of thought believed in the separation of the economy from democratic decision-making. In ordoliberalism this was encapsulated in the idea of the 'economic constitution'. The Geneva School took the idea of the separation of the economy to the global scale.[25]

Wilham Röpke, who taught at the Graduate Institute in Geneva for most of his career, similarly placed his hopes in a legal order that protects individuals' market interests. After all, as Jessica Whyte observes, Röpke's view was that 'allowing individuals to pursue their interests through the market leads to social coordination'. Social coordination, according to Röpke, could and

[22] ibid 9.
[23] ibid 6.
[24] Ludwig von Mises, *Human Action: A Treatise on Economics* (1996) 287. As discussed in Jessica Whyte, *The Morals of the Market* (2019) 20.
[25] Slobodian (n 3) 8.

should not be achieved through a political process as it brings 'millions of conflicting interests' into play.[26] Röpke consequently advocated for a minimum of constitutional order on a global scale with a separation of the public sphere from the private domain.[27] Von Hayek similarly envisaged a 'framework for the economy'.[28] The legal-institutional protections of the market—what Slobodian terms 'encasement'—also crucially meant the insulation from democratic processes. Increasingly, and also against the background of the rise of fascism in the 1930s, the Geneva School neoliberals believed that democracy could be problematic for the free flow of capital. All efforts were made to conceptualise norms and institutions that prevented the politicization of the economy, following in particular the liberal model of a strict separation between the public and the private sphere. This was not only an *intellectual* tradition produced and reproduced in academic circles of Geneva; these individuals had substantial influence on the emerging institutions set up to protect the market—of this first generation, most notably the International Chamber of Commerce. Neoliberalism, in short, was from its Austrian branch always an institution-building project in which law had a critical role to play.

2. The second generation of global constitutionalists

Among the next generation of Geneva School scholars, and a student of Hayek's, was Ernst-Ulrich Petersmann. This generation made it their project to develop the constitutional and institutional aspects of ordoglobalism from an international law perspective. Petersmann features most prominently, but he was by no means the only international (economic) lawyer to advocate for a global economic constitution.[29] Petersmann had a keen interest in responding to solidarity of or with the Global South in legalistic and universalizing terms. Already in his doctoral thesis in Heidelberg, published in 1974, Petersmann argued for economic integration of Third World countries, responding directly to the proclaimed New International Economic Order (NIEO) of the 1970s—an alliance of mostly formerly colonized states that wished to revise the international economic order to favour sovereignty over resources and therefore

[26] Whilhelm Röpke, *The Moral Foundations of Civil Society* (Transaction Publishers 2002) 21, quoted in Whyte (n 24) 16.

[27] Wilhelm Röpke, Wirtschaftssystem und international Ordnung: Prolegomena (1951) 4 Ordo 277.

[28] Friedrich August Hayek, 'The Economy, Science and Politics' [1962] in FA Hayek (ed), *New Studies in Philosophy, Politics, Economics and the History of Ideas* (University of Chicago Press 1978) 263.

[29] See also eg John H Jackson, *The World Trade Organization: Constitution and Jurisprudence* (Royal Institute of International Affairs 1998).

address growing inequality between the Global North and the Global South. Throughout the 1970s, global economic integration (and thereby breaking through South–South solidarity agreements) would remain Petersmann's preoccupation. During and after the period of 'decolonization', important South–South solidarity networks were formed, including the Bandung conference of 1955 and the Tricontinental Conference of 1966.[30] A new and strong voice in the UN, seventy-seven developing states established the G-77.[31] They institutionalized this alliance in the first session of the United Nations Conference on Trade and Development (UNCTAD). This collective mobilization prompted important exceptions to the agreement on trade known as the General Agreement on Tariffs and Trade (GATT). Petersmann, and many other international law commentators of the time, attributed great importance to these developments. He worried about the nationalization of resources, and other trade barriers that could work against the globalism he envisaged.[32] It is notable that Petersmann's thesis was completed at the time of the Arab oil embargos of 1973–1974. What became known as the 1973 oil crisis was the price inflation caused by oil-exporting Arabic states refusing to supply certain Western states with oil. The leverage of some resource-rich states was palpable. Petersmann therefore praised efforts of regional integration (envisioning no doubt regional economic constitutions for the Global South similar to the growing European Communities at the time). He also expressed concerns about measures he deemed to be akin to trade unionism. In his view, economic stabilization takes on the role of *politische Schrittmacherrolle*—political pacemaker.[33] Petersmann, crucially, perceives the need to stabilize economic ambitions through legal structures. He viewed trade liberalization as concerning long-term sovereignty concessions which, he felt, the short-term focused Global South countries were unlikely to agree to. In his work, Petersmann laments the inadequate economic infrastructure in the Global South, insufficient competitiveness (due to an insistence on high commodity prices), lack of stability (due to a lack of currency conversions), and protectionism.[34] He finally suggests complementing trade liberalization with legal-institutional structures of harmonization. This should follow, according to Petersmann,

[30] This solidarity is often invoked as the 'spirit of Bandung': see eg Balakrishnan Rajagopal, *International Law from Below: Development, Social Movements and the Third World Resistance* (CUP 2003) 74.

[31] The number rose, but the name stuck. Petersmann eagerly kept tabs on the precise number.

[32] Ernst U Petersmann, *Wirtschaftsintegrationsrecht und Investitionsgesetzgebung der Entwicklungsländer: Grundprobleme, rechtsvergleichende und multidisziplinäre Aspekte* (Nomos-Verlagsgesellschaft 1974).

[33] ibid 33.

[34] ibid 36, 37.

a general international law integration theory.[35] An economic constitution would organize this economic integration.[36] In the conclusion of this thesis, he goes further than the political pacemaker theory, ending euphorically with the description of the law of economic integration as a *Friedensstabilisator*, a peace stabilizer.[37] It is noteworthy that his proposed constitutionalism was effectively a tool to circumvent decision-making in the more democratic institution of the UN General Assembly that provides for the one-state-one-vote model. Neoliberal constitutionalism has tended to work in anti-democratic ways, keeping contestation against the opening of national markets and attendant privatization projects at bay.

From the early 1980s, Petersmann worked on the transition from the GATT to the WTO as part of what Slobodian calls a 'neoliberal legal counterrevolution'.[38] Moving away from the idea of separate economic constitutionalism for the Global South, the new proposal was for global unification and integration of a global market-place through law. The designated legal tool was to reform the GATT. Petersmann was one of the first members of the GATT's Office of Legal Affairs.[39] This scaling up from regional to global integration was intended to create a system where exceptions negotiated in the context of the GATT were no longer possible. It is a vision of uncontested geopolitics of constitutional knowledge. Soon, 'undermining' of the GATT was described as an undermining of the rule of law,[40] utilizing the concept specifically for the purposes of disciplining the Global South states. In the 1980s—a time in which domestic neoliberal policies were to become influential politically through President Ronald Raegan and Prime Minister Margaret Thatcher—Petersmann explained his thinking about the role of law and the market in the following way: 'The common starting point of the neoliberal economic theory is the insight that in any well-functioning market economy the "invisible hand" of market competition must by necessity be complemented by the "visible hand" of the law.'[41] The GATT reformers had in mind the template of the European model of governance. In drafting the reforms (which would eventually lead to the WTO), the European model was to be scaled up to the global,

[35] ibid 46–52.
[36] ibid 50.
[37] ibid 244.
[38] Slobodian (n 3) 242.
[39] Created in 1983: ibid 244.
[40] Slobodian (n 3) 242.
[41] Ernst U Petersmann, 'International Economic Theory and International Economic Law: On the Tasks of a Legal Theory of International Economic Order' in R St J Macdonald and Dougals M Johston, *The Structure and Process of International Law: Essays in Legal Philosophy Doctrine and Theory* (Ronald St J Macdonald 1983) 237 (also cited in Slobodian [n 3]).

all under the auspices of a proclaimed 'international rule of law'.[42] Indeed, once the WTO was in place, with some parts reflecting the ordoglobalist dream (ie the Appellate system), Petersmann praised the WTO system for its constitutional functions in protecting private property. In the first issue of the first volume of the *Journal of International Economic Law*, Petersmann elevates the political-economic project to a project of freedom (echoing and developing his earlier work on economic integration and peace):

> The worldwide guarantees of freedom, non-discrimination, intellectual property rights, and quasi-judicial dispute settlement procedures in WTO law illustrate that liberal international trade organizations can serve 'constitutional functions' for the protection of freedom, non-discrimination, private property rights and access to courts across frontiers.[43]

But the dream of an integrated global economic order, kept in place through a corresponding constitution, was in danger of being the metaphorical baby thrown out with the bathwater. Anti-globalization protesters mobilized against globalization around the 1999 Seattle WTO Ministerial Conference, culminating in the so-called 'Battle of Seattle'. Responding to the Seattle anti-globalization protests, as well as the WTO director-general's call to 'rebrand!',[44] Petersmann adapted the narrative from international rule of law to human rights law. He could not have been more explicit than the opening line of an article from 2000, which begins 'Human rights and liberal trade rules (including WTO rules) are based on the same values'.[45] A version of human rights was put forward which aligned closely with property rights.

In order to defend his vision of social justice emanating from the multilevel constitutional global order, Petersmann recently quoted Thomas Cottier's 'five storey house' of governance.[46] In the typical style of extrapolating from the national to the international, this allegory of constitutionalism draws from the

[42] Ernst-Ulrich Petersmann (ed), *International Trade Law and GATT/WTO Dispute Settlement System* (Kluwer Law International 1997) 18.

[43] Ernst-Ulrich Petersmann, 'How to Promote the International Rule of Law? Contributions by the World Trade Organization Appellate Review System' Journal of International Economic Law 1 (1998) 31.

[44] Quoted in Kirsten Hopewell, *Breaking the WTO: How Emerging Powers Disrupted the Neoliberal Project* (Stanford University Press 2016).

[45] Ernst-Ulrich Petersmann, 'The WTO Constitution and Human Rights' (2000) 3 Journal of International Economic Law 19.

[46] EU Petersmann, Globalists: The End of Empire and the Birth of Neoliberalism. By Quinn Slobodian [Book Review] (2018) 21 Journal of International Economic Law 915, 921.

Swiss model.[47] The five-storey governance house is made up of communes, cantons, the federal structure, the regional (European) integration, and the global trade system.[48] Petersmann defends his social justice and democratic constitutionalism credentials notably through reference to the 'billions of "cosmopolitan market actors"' who benefit from multilevel economic governance.[49] What he fails to see is that the democratic (or the public) has with this vision been collapsed into the private. The scope of the public sphere is defined by the possibilities of the private sphere. Although he resists the charge of his vision 'undoing the demos' (a phrase coined by Wendy Brown), the reimagining of political actors as market actors is precisely what Brown was concerned about.[50]

Indeed, it is this aspect of reimaging social justice as market justice that has constituted the de facto global neoliberal constitution. The geopolitics of knowledge is doing its material work. Trade and investment rules have required the guarantee of open market access in the form of access rights in domestic jurisdictions, leaving the role of the state (in the neoliberal sense proposed here) to defend capital. In *Private Power and Global Authority*, Claire Cutler described this influence of private power in the global political economy as 'transnational merchant law'.[51] International law has created structures to enable and protect commercial law while simultaneously rendering the activities of private actors and institutions politically 'invisible'.[52] Meanwhile, public concerns (around redistribution, for example) are recast as private concerns, and thus are not open to democratic contestation. Such a depoliticizing function of international legal structures for trade and investment is particularly palpable in (albeit contentious) arbitration arrangements skewed in favour of capital and lacking in transparency.[53] Despite repeated statements about the unknowability or 'mystery' of global governance, in fact trade and investment agreements (here is another form of their constitutionalization), introduce

[47] Thomas Cottier, 'Reforming the Swiss Federal Constitution: An International Lawyer's Perspective' in Michael Butler and others (eds), The Making of Modern Switzerland, 1948–1998 (Palgrave 2000) 75.

[48] Thomas Cottier and Maya Hertig, 'Towards a Five Storey House: The Prospects of 21st Century Constitutionalism' in Armin von Bogdandy and Rüdiger Wolfrum (eds), *Max Planck Yearbook of United Nations Law*, vol 7 (Nijhoff 2003) 299, 300.

[49] Petersmann, 'Review' (n 46).

[50] Wendy Brown, *Undoing the Demos: Neoliberalism's Stealth Revolution* (Zone Books 2015). See also David Schneiderman, *Constitutionalizing Economic Globalisation: Investment Rules and Democracy's Promise* (CUP 2008) 191.

[51] Cutler (n 20).

[52] ibid.

[53] One of the main contentious issues with the Transatlantic Trade and Investment Partnership (TTIP) agreement was the proposed 'secret courts': see eg Ferdi De Ville and Gabriel Siles-Brügge, *TTIP: The Truth about the Transatlantic Trade Investment Partnership* (Wiley 2015).

a great deal of constancy. Namely in the 'freezing of existing distributions of wealth, and security certainty for already affluent economic interests'.[54] What has emerged as the de facto global neoliberal constitution cannot of course be solely attributed to Petersmann; but, his work on international economic law and constitutionalism was at the very heartbeat of projects to create neoliberal global constitutionalism. It can also be described as an expansionist project of the geopolitics of constitutional knowledge.

3. The third generation of global constitutionalists

The establishment of the WTO remained, in a sense, the pinnacle of success for global constitutionalists. Since then, the WTO has been subject to deep contestation by its members, particularly the 'constitutionalized' elements of governance and Appellate Body jurisprudence. Despite the contentious institutional form, 'de facto constitutionalism' embraced WTO ideas and arguably raced ahead while the institution limps behind. Indeed, a growth in bilateral arrangements, the failure of agreement regarding WTO reform, and a backlash against multilateralism more generally, seem to indicate that the *formal* institutional global economic order that ordoglobalists envisioned is less likely now than ever. But, overall, the ordoglobalists of the second generation would not be dissatisfied with the de facto global economic order, which continues to protect the movement of capital across borders and continues to prevent democratic contestation of the market. Its model regional counterpart, if also marred by political struggles, is no doubt the European Union.

When tracing genealogies of the global constitutionalist family for the purposes of gleaning the geopolitics of global constitutionalist knowledge, it is interesting to note that the next generation of normative global constitutionalists, the third generation, distanced themselves almost entirely from the economy. This is the 'ideal' project of global constitutionalism seemingly distanced from the 'material'. Also notable is that those who preferred to approach global constitutionalism from the perspective of description and functionalism (although often also normative projects), were more open to discussions regarding the economy.[55] However, even this more economically minded group of observers of global constitutionalism tended to find globalization as

[54] Schneiderman (n 50) 205.

[55] eg Jeffrey L Dunoff and Joel P Trachtman, 'A Functional Approach to International Constitutionalization' in Jeffrey L Dunoff and Joel P Trachtman (eds), *Ruling the World: Constitutionalism, International Law and Global Governance* (CUP 2009) 3–36.

simply *there* and global constitutionalism as *responding* to it, rather than international economic law as creating and legitimizing globalization. This is a clear break with the first and second generation. Among the tentatively yet also resolutely normative generation is, for example, Anne Peters, who studied at the ordoliberal intellectual home of the University of Freiburg in the late 1980s and early 1990s. Andreas Paulus studied law inter alia in the ordoglobalist home of Geneva.[56] This generation also includes Mattias Kumm and Bardo Fassbender. They have all focused on human rights and the rule of law as concepts largely distinct from the market. The scaling up of constitutionalism to the global was to be the ultimate triumph of liberal democracy, not explicitly of the free market.[57] Perhaps not conscious of the intellectual and ideological trajectories they were operating in, these scholars mostly believed that the economy was outside of the remit of their work.[58] In the notable body of work produced by this generation, there is an emphasis on universal human rights, international institutions, harmonization of principles, and the promise of constitutionalism for peace and prosperity. If they did direct attention to redistribution, these scholars found that the discussion had been significantly narrowed.[59] The third generation is grappling with the encasement of the market without realizing that their project had led them to strengthen this very encasement.

So far unmentioned, the proverbial elephant in the room, in the geopolitics of global constitutional knowledge is the prominence of German-speaking thinkers and policymakers. This dominance, I suggest, can be explained through Germanic epistemologies of ordoliberalism on the one hand, as well as an extension of the story of lost empires compensated through legal structures on the other hand. In his account of the Geneva School, Slobodian demonstrates how the ordo*globalist* project arose in the early twentieth century from the 'ashes of the Habsburg empire'.[60] After having had substantial geopolitical influence throughout Europe for several generations, after the defeat of the First World War, Austrians were faced with the status of being a small, and relatively insignificant, state. Small states depend greatly on trade relations with their neighbours. At the same time, small states are usually more exposed

[56] Andreas L Paulus, 'The International Legal System as a Constitution' in Dunoff and Trachtmann, *Ruling the World* (n 55) 69–109.

[57] I critique the scaling up of liberal-democratic constitutionalism to the global in Christine Schwöbel, *Global Constitutionalism in International Legal Perspective* (Brill2011).

[58] I explore this in greater length in Christine Schwöbel-Patel, 'The Political Economy of Global Constitutionalism' in Antje Wiener and Tony Lang (eds), *Handbook of Global Constitutionalism* (Martinus Nijhoff/Brill 2016).

[59] See Mattias Kumm, 'Global Constitutionalism and the rule of law' in Antje Wiener and Tony Lang (eds), *Handbook of Global Constitutionalism* (Edward Elgar 2016) 197–210.

[60] Slobodian (n 3).

to external shocks. The first generation of Austrian global constitutionalists, who insisted on open trade and currency stabilization, arguably continued Empire by other means.

The later generation of German-speaking scholars and practitioners working on the WTO were naturally greatly influenced by the events and tragedies of the Second World War and the rehabilitation of Germany through trade (the *Wirtschaftswunder* no less) and the stabilizing factor of the post-War constitution. The loss of formal Empire, moral confrontation with (legalized) atrocities of the Third Reich, and the move to internationalism following the fall of the Berlin Wall provided fertile ground for an attraction to universalizing legal and political epistemologies. To be sure, there are notable non-German contributors to normative global constitutionalism,[61] whose intellectual projects are motivated by other interests, but the appeal of a constitution, the universalization of legalist-moral principles, and the narrative of the tempering of politics through law have held a pivotal position in the German post-World War II imaginary.[62] Here it is also worth mentioning the work of another important German international lawyer, namely Christian Tomuschat, who has written extensively on the international community as a legal space that limits political power.[63] Stabilizing legal global norms are, in his view, crucial for keeping politics at bay. Peace through law and international institutions is of course not only a German narrative. Whilst German scholars and policy-makers have worked tirelessly at their universalization, learning from the twentieth century has been an enduring narrative of the Western imagination of modernity. This has hardened into a moralist-legal view that the experiences of the World Wars are the prime events from which to learn lessons for the future. Arguably, the focus on learning for the World Wars has displaced—certainly in the German historical narrative, but also beyond—colonialism in the Global South as a period from which lessons must be drawn. Colonial repression, exploitation, and atrocity have been relegated to a more distant past, deemphasizing the need for restitution and reparations. The ideal project of global constitutionalism has therefore narrowed the scope of what must be protected in a universalizing project. Meanwhile, this has opened up the possibilities of a de facto material constitutionalism of inequality in the form of global neoliberal

[61] Dunoff and Trachtman, 'A Functional Approach' (n 55) have already been mentioned.

[62] See in regard to the role of Nuremberg and anti-impunity Christine Schwöbel-Patel, 'The Core Crimes of International Criminal Law' in Kevin Heller and others (eds), *Oxford Handbook of International Criminal Law* (OUP2020).

[63] Christian Tomuschat, 'International Law: Ensuring the Survival of Mankind on the Eve of a New Century, General Course on Public International Law' (1999) 281 Recueil des Cours de l'Académie de Droit International 95.

constitutionalism. The coloniality of (global) constitutionalism is a project of universalizing Western liberalism and creating a moral legitimation of racial capitalism.

D. Decolonizing Global Constitutionalism?

The coloniality of the global constitutionalist project, in both its 'ideal' and 'material' manifestations, is illustrated in its suppression of contestation. Constitutionalism appears as a mechanism for stabilizing the inequalities of the status quo. Both neoliberalism and constitutionalism depend on the separation of the economy from the political.[64] In the neoliberal order, the sphere of the political is shaped by the possibilities of the private sphere. Constitutionalism has been utilized as a means of primitive accumulation in the Global South, expanding the possibilities for capital to flow. The state takes up the role of protecting capital in a prioritization of market values over social values. Historically, this form of protecting capital on a global scale has gone hand in hand with imperialism and the exploitation of the Global South. It is precisely the concept of 'coloniality' that captures continued exploitation.

Decolonial thinking and doing, according to Mignolo, are 'responses to the oppressive imperial bent of modern European ideals projected to, and enacted in, the non-European world'.[65] Given the growing debates about decolonizing the curriculum that are moving from the fringes to the mainstream, and all the co-optations which may come with that, the debate on global constitutionalism is surprisingly archaic. To be sure, in its host disciplines, international law, international relations, and political theory, the calls to decolonize are becoming louder. This is alongside debates on gender, race, class, their intersectionality, and other forms of structural inequality. Global constitutionalism, however, with some notable exceptions,[66] continues to be dominated by a Eurocentric liberal legal rights debate.

If adopting a decolonial project of global constitutionalism, what would this look like? The decolonial project is a 'posture of struggle that takes form and is grounded in modernity's outside, fissures, and borders'.[67] One part of this

[64] See Christine Schwöbel-Patel, 'The Political Economy of Global Constitutionalism' in Antje Wiener and Anthony F Lang (eds), *Handbook on Global Constitutionalism* (Elgar2017).

[65] Walter Mignolo, *The Darker Side of Western Modernity: Global Futures, Decolonial Options* (Duke University Press 2011) 39.

[66] See eg Marco Goldoni, 'Introduction to the Material Study of Global Constitutional Law' (2019) 8 Global Constitutionalism 71, and contributors to this collection.

[67] Walter D Mignolo and Catherine E Walsh, *On Decoloniality: Concepts, Analytics, Praxis* (Duke University Press 2018) 74.

project will be to think outside of given structures and one part will be to think *against* given structures. As to thinking *within* the structures, the question emerges as to a global constitutionalism for the Global South—or in the words of Vidya Kumar, who borrows from Franz Fanon, a 'Constitutionalism for the Wretched'. As already mentioned, Haiti is often invoked as an example of radical constitutionalism. But if one looks a little closer at the constitution(s), events ran up against the *constraints* of constitutionalism, rather than the radical being *enabled* by constitutionalism. Part of the limitation is its liberal form, part of it is also the lack of appeal in the wider population, ie its inherently undemocratic form. This is even more of an issue when constitutionalism is scaled up to the global. So, while constitutionalism may be interesting to radical framers, it is generally not to those ultimately affected. This is not to be misunderstood as a reflection on a lack of political education of the people—given that self-determination, sovereignty, and non-intervention have all served as mobilizers for collective action in the past. Rather, this has to do with constitutionalism often ignoring the material circumstances in its preference for the 'ideal'. A constitutionalism from below may stretch the term so far that it becomes unrecognizable.

Any form of constitutionalism from the Global South is then trapped between two irreconcilable positions described so aptly by Bernasconi:

> Western philosophy traps African philosophy in a double bind. Either African philosophy is so similar to Western philosophy that it makes no distinctive contribution and effectively disappears: or it is so different that its credentials to be genuine philosophy will always be in doubt.[68]

This double-bind is of course no accident, but exists precisely because of the geopolitics of knowledge. Perhaps a radical global constitutionalism can come from the Global South—one emancipated from neoliberalism and its depoliticizations, that is emancipated from the double bind, and can be a true redistributive tool. But, to adapt Balakrishnan Rajapol's conclusions on international law, the prospects of global constitutionalism becoming a purely counter-hegemonic tool are 'bleak'.[69] That is not intended as a reflection of defeatism to the neoliberal order or resistance. Rather, it is an invitation to

[68] Robert Bernasconi, 'African Philosophy's Challenge to Continental Philosophy' in Emmanuel Chukwudi Eze (ed), *Postcolonial African Philosophy: A Critical Reader* (Wiley1997) 188.

[69] Balakrishnan Rajagopal, 'Counter-Hegemonic International Law; Rethinking Human Rights and Development as Third World Strategy' (2006) 27 Third World Quarterly 780.

challenge the global neoliberal order through means which re-politicize and destabilize the given structures rather than to recuperate its core concepts.

E. Conclusion

In considering global constitutionalism as a debate that is both reflective and productive of a particular knowledge about the world as it is and how it should be, we can learn much from Walter Mignolo's suggestion to understand the geopolitical distribution of knowledge. The geopolitics of global constitutional knowledge is situated within the legacies of a group of policymakers and international lawyers who sought order on a global scale for the purposes of separating the economy from the contestations of the political. (Global) constitutionalism is an idea emanating from the West, but not simply geographically, also geopolitically as a form of modernity. Knowledge in this tradition of thinking about colonialism has overwhelmingly worked together with capital's accumulation to disenfranchise the Global South. What has emerged is a de facto global neoliberal constitutionalism.

Given the geopolitics of global constitutional knowledge, one might then think about a radical break with this knowledge—a decolonized global constitutionalism. However, as I have indicated, constitutionalism has tended to be the reformist moment of a radical political movement. Do I think that global constitutionalism can address some of the most egregious problems of our time including inequality, climate change, and the marketization of social and global justice? No. But, a discussion on global constitutionalism, which takes the geopolitics of knowledge seriously, is a productive entry into considering the ways in which international law has contributed to coloniality through constitutionalism and to a de facto global neoliberal constitution.

4

Comparing as (Re-)Imagining

Southern Perspective and the World of Constitutions

Zoran Oklopcic

> Since we assume that words do not speak about nothing, we are compelled to link them to something, to find non-verbal equivalents for them. Just as most rumours are believed by virtue of the saying: 'There is no smoke without fire,' the collection of images is created by virtue of the saying: 'Nobody speaks about nothing' . . . . To compare is already to picture, to fill what is naturally empty with substance.[1]

A. Introduction

Our world is the world of constitutions. Those who compare them often do so from a specific, openly inhabited scholarly 'perspective'. Some of those perspectives are disciplinary. Those who assume them approach the world of constitutions as lawyers, political scientists, or cultural anthropologists. Other perspectives are geographical. Those who inhabit them look at our diversely constituted world from the Asian, African, Latin American, or some other continental, regional, national, or local perspective. Whichever perspective they embrace, some constitutional comparativists will vehemently insist on the exclusively scholarly character and the ideological neutrality of their inquiry. Others, in contrast, will be less preoccupied with those matters, or even more pointedly committed to a particular ideological perspective. A global south perspective—the one that offers the view on the world of constitutions from the 'Southern standpoint'—is the topic of this essay, and the springboard for the meditation on its main theme. That theme is abstract and broad: it concerns the relationship between our understandings of the concepts that we take

[1] Serge Moscovici, *Social Representations: Explorations in Social Psychology* (NYU Press 2001).

Zoran Oklopcic, *Comparing as (Re-)Imagining* In: *The Global South and Comparative Constitutional Law*. Edited by: Philipp Dann, Michael Riegner, and Maxim Bönnemann, Oxford University Press (2020). © Oxford University Press.
DOI: 10.1093/oso/9780198850403.003.0004

for granted as we speak of the world of *constitutions*, their comparison, and the nature of that activity from a particular scholarly perspective.

Before we begin, a note on terminology. In choosing to refer to comparative constitutional *inquiry* I have chosen a term which is both less disciplinarily dogmatic as well as more intellectually ecumenical than those that currently dominate in the debates about scholarly comparisons in the world of constitutions.[2] Unlike the 'law', or the 'studies', comparative constitutional inquiry also evokes the work of an undisciplined mind's eye: roaming around, approaching the familiar, as well as the strange looking objects, turning them mentally upside down, comparing and contrasting them—all in hope of finding the ways in which they resemble, or differ from each other. Thus imagined, 'inquiry' is deceiving—not because of the scenes of snooping around that it conjures, but because of the failure of these scenes to remind us of all that went into their stage-setting. Put differently: irrespective of their outcome, all acts of 'comparative constitutional inquiry' will only ever make sense in virtue of our imaginings of three other seemingly unproblematic acts—of constituting, of comparing, and of perceiving (from a particular perspective). There is more to each of them:

(1) beneath the *constitution* of a polity, the original moment of *foundation*;
(2) before the *comparison* of constitution, a prior act of their *identification*;
(3) within the *perception* of them both, manifold acts of constituent *imagination*.

I will soon begin elaborating on each of the three formulas. Right now, however, it is worth drawing attention to how they relate to the one of the two main points of this article. Even in isolation from its supporting argument, that point is simple and intuitive. Impossible to 'prove' empirically, it comes in the form of a hypothesis—a hopefully intellectually productive theoretical speculation. Formulaically, it reads:

> A scholarly argument that neither refers nor alludes to the hidden 'truths' of comparative constitutional inquiry mentioned above, will most likely be either naively *botanical*, or polemically *quietist*, or rhetorically *timid*—or some combination thereof.

[2] Michel Rosenfeld, 'The Politics of Comparative Constitutional Inquiry: At the Crossroads of Law, Political Science, and Ideology' (2016) 66 (2) University of Toronto Law Journal 273.

This article's second main point emerges from the confrontation of the Southern perspective with the precepts of this formula. That perspective, as we will also soon see, is neither naively botanical, nor polemically quietist, nor rhetorically timid. To the contrary. At the same time, however, those who gazed at the world of constitutions from a Southern standpoint never really confronted three things: (1) the polemical character of the names used to describe its location, (2) the complex work of imagination that ends up being lumped under the rubric of 'perspective', and (3) their endemically Eurocentric imaginary of constitutions and constitutionalism. On our way towards the second, and final point of this paper, let us begin by confronting them in reverse order, beginning with our unexamined imaginations of *the scenes of constituting*—the visuals that inform our contemporary understandings of mostly popular and democratic, if not liberal, constitutionalism.

1. *Constituting*: in contemporary constitutional thought (and beyond)

This section offers a vision of the act of constitution. That vision, as we will see in a moment, remains inaccessible to most of those who engage in comparative constitutional inquiry. We do not get to that vision because we assume (not incorrectly) that living in the world of constitutions confronts us with the inevitable difficulties of comparison. Put differently: rather than to ask, 'How do we imagine the activity of constituting?' we rush to ask, 'Which constitutions are to be compared with which ones—where, when, how, and why?' Today, the answers to these questions—be they explicit or implicit—cluster around three, often intersecting, scholarly projects. Rather than mutually exclusive, these projects are better seen as three faces of contemporary constitutional inquiry. In the literature, the first often goes by the name of comparative constitutional *law*, and is associated with the focus on the exchange of constitutional 'ideas' among presumably unimpeachably legitimate constitutional democracies in North America and Western Europe—an exclusive club which habitually extends its membership to Israel and South Africa as well. Increasingly prominent since the late 2000s, the second project—comparative constitutional *studies*—emerged as a reaction to the empirical obliviousness, methodological deficiencies, disciplinary insularity, and Eurocentric bias of the first. Often blending into 'comparative constitutional studies', *adjectival constitutionalism* is the third face of contemporary constitutional comparativism. In contrast to the former two, the main object of its interest is neither decisions nor provisions, but experiences: not the quiet dialogue among select number of liberal democratic constitutional courts, and not the invisible correlations discernible on the basis of large-N data sets of constitutional provisions from around the world, but the constitutional phenomena of 'Arab', 'Asian', 'African', 'authoritarian', 'Bolivarian', 'European', 'Islamic', 'theocratic', and other constitutionalisms in relation to their presumed comparator: a Western nation-state organized around the template of liberal-democratic constitutionalism.

The imagination that allows comparative constitutionalists to take constitutions, their comparisons, and their perspectival perceptions of both for granted is not simply unreflective. It is also chastened. First, in relying on the historically prevailing normative or ontological understandings of what it means to constitute, contemporary comparative constitutionalists failed to follow the conceptual implications of the most elementary, but thus far under-explored common wisdoms that render the acts of constituting not only intelligible, but also sensible and desirable: that worthy pursuits often take time, that good intentions deserve benevolent patience; that there is something sublime in looking back and concluding: 'I made my modest contribution in helping a worthy project endure.'

Such constitutions may or may not be written, liberal, or democratic. More importantly, nor do they necessarily need to be envisioned as 'founded', 'entrenched', or 'co-instituted' by a popular constituent power. In fact, their very etymology is a testament to a different *vision* of the *scene* of constituting—broader than the images of digging a hole and pouring into it the foundations for a metaphorical constitutional 'building'. Rather than an act that builds a home or a temple—or, more broadly, any kind of a dwelling capable of functioning, at the same time, as the shelter of familial intimacy on the inside, and as the bulwark against existential dangers on the outside—what is evoked by 'con-' and '-statuere' is the scene of *making with-stand*: ensuring that something remains standing, together. Founding and entrenching are only one way of attempting to do the same. If so, we not only still live in the world constituted by constitutions and organized in accordance with the precepts of our constitutional imagination. If so, the world of constitutions will remain our world well into the future—as long as, that is, we remain convinced that giving worthy projects a chance deserves symbolical, institutional, and rhetorical assistance that help them withstand.

Before we move on, consider the following objection, to be expected—in particular—from those who engage in comparative constitutional inquiry as proudly disciplined hermeneuticists, members of their respective disciplines, not as disciplinarily undisciplined imaginers. 'I don't imagine anything, or nothing in particular, in any event'—we might hear them complain—'when I verbalize the texts that refer to the acts of constitution-making'. In many cases, this is patently not true. Very often, the images of a constitution will rely on a familiar metaphor, the choice of which is never innocent. Consider the following, which considers

> [c]onstitutions . . . much like houses . . . bought, inherited, or built according to one's needs, but also rent as a permanent or temporary solution [and often] turned into homes through sentiment [so that they] respond to the basic needs of the inhabitants, [and] provide shelter and protection, while . . . also satisfy[ing] more complicated requirements . . . . The creation of a bond between a home and its inhabitants is a complex process . . . . Functionality of the home is equally important, inhabitants may easily love a home that responds to their needs, while they may feel discomfort when it fails to do so, or it creates problems. A sense of permanence is important with regard to homes. Moving home is always a traumatic experience. Still, every house is a work in process.[3]

This description has implications not only for the way in which we visualize the products of constitution-making, but also for the way in which we quietly imagine more abstract theoretical concepts, such as *constituent power*, that refer to the nature of the agency of constitution-makers. What does the exercise of that power *look* like? Now, our interlocutor may continue to insist that even in this case—when a constitution is explicitly visualized as a 'house'—the nature of the abstract concept of constituent power remains essentially 'aniconic'; impossible to visualize.

That, however, is not exactly true. While it may be difficult to imagine a positive image of constituent power in this case, it is very easy to imagine the picture of its negative space—the picture of possible scenes, phenomena, or objects which definitely make no sense as its representation. Put more concretely, even if one finds it hard to imagine the power needed to build a (constitutional) house, one immediately recognizes that the character of that power becomes unintelligible if we metaphorically represent it as a *wave*. Were that the case, our interlocutor would end up no better than Mr Palomar '[who] sees a wave rise in the distance, grow, approach, change form and color, fold over itself,

[3] Xenophon Contiades and Alkmene Fotiadou, 'The Emergence of Comparative Constitutional Amendment as a New Discipline: Towards a Paradigm Shift' in Richard Albert, Xenophon Contiades, and Alkmene Fotiadou (eds), *The Foundations and Traditions of Constitutional Amendment* (Hart Publishing 2017) 370.

break, vanish, and flow again', as he attempts to detect regularities in the ebb and flow of the waves. His travails—at least among the lovers of Italo Calvino's fiction—are notorious, as Mr Palomar soon realizes that

> isolating one wave is not easy, separating it from the wave immediately following, which seems to push it and at times overtakes it and sweeps it away; and it is no easier to separate that one wave from the preceding wave, which seems to drag it toward the shore, unless it turns against the following wave, as if to arrest it. Then, if you consider the breadth of the wave, parallel to the shore, it is hard to decide where the advancing front extends regularly and where it is separated and segmented into independent waves, distinguished by their speed, shape, force, direction. In other words, you cannot observe a wave without bearing in mind the complex features that concur in shaping it and the other, equally complex ones that the wave itself originates. These aspects vary constantly, so each wave is different from another wave, even if not immediately adjacent or successive; in other words, there are some forms and sequences that are repeated, though irregularly distributed in space and time.[4]

This is a good occasion to draw attention to a particular quality of constituent imagination. That quality is its *stickiness*, which refers not to the inevitability and ubiquity (of always imagining something), but rather to the inevitability of the immediate understanding of that inevitability—once, that is, one manages to draw attention to it. Put differently: even if our anxious hermeneuticist thought that he was never really picturing anything to do with the moment of constitution-making, he will nonetheless be very quick to realize that this moment, together with its outcome, must be imagined somehow.

2. *Comparing*: in contemporary constitutional studies

A constitution is more than just a text. This proposition is non-contentious, even among those who compare constitutions by focusing on what is said in their entrenched provisions, or on what is meant by the decisions which authoritatively interpret them. Though a constitution is more than just a text, those who engage in constitutional inquiry treat it as a Janus-faced artefact: both formal and material. Over the last decade, the latter, material side,

[4] Italo Calvino, *Mr Palomar* (Harcourt Brace 1985) 94.

has increasingly become the focus of those who approach constitutions comparatively. Consider, for example, Ran Hirschl's influential call to abandon the project of comparative constitutional law in favour of more empirically oriented and methodologically rigorous comparative constitutional studies.[5] What animates it—as Vicky Jackson observed—is the ethos of scrupulous scholarship, committed to the production of knowledge that contributes to a particular discipline.[6] What sustains this ethos, however, is not only the picture of scholarly universe consisting of demarcated disciplinary fields, populated by scholars who (whether or not they transgress their boundaries) remain committed to cultivating them, but also the kind of imagination which the proponents of this critique share with the objects of their criticism.

While Hirschl probably wouldn't disagree that '[p]osing a question, defining entities or units, choosing measurements, noticing phenomena, and evaluating models are five distinct junctures at which an observer's decisions structure a scientific investigation', he still maintains that offering a 'detailed taxonomy' remains 'fundamental to any academic endeavor . . . including the study of the yet under-charted terrain of comparative constitutional law'.[7] By unreflectively embracing 'detailed taxonomy' as the standard on which comparative constitutional studies build—one from which they then deviate—Hirschl neglects that the definitions of taxonomized entities remain 'embedded in internal cognitive models', subject only to pragmatic evaluation. More importantly, 'treating definitional entities as empirical entities, or empirical entities as definitional entities, suppresses the fact that experience is always mediated by concepts and measurement scale'.[8]

That imagination is not simply unreflective. It is also—potentially—for lack of a better word, *naively botanical* in its vision of the standard of scholarship from which it consciously seeks to deviate. While contemporary constitutional comparativists uphold detailed taxonomies of presupposed entities, it is contemporary botanists—an irony that should probably not go unnoticed—who treat them as 'multiscaled', so that 'at that scale of perception, the entity appears cohesive, explicable, and predictable relative to some question the scientist asks'. Importantly, as TFH Allen and Thomas Hoekstra argued, 'scaling is done

5 Ran Hirschl, *Comparative Matters: The Renaissance of Comparative Constitutional Law* (OUP 2014).

6 Vicky Jackson, 'Comparative Constitutional Law, Legal Realism, and Empirical Legal Science' (2016) 96 Boston University Law Review 1359.

7 Hirschl (n 5) 280. See also Catarine Walcke, 'Reflections On Comparative Law Methodology: Getting Inside Contract Law' in Maurice Adams and Jacco Bomhoff (eds), *Practice and Theory in Comparative Law* (CUP 2012).

8 Valerie Ahl and TFH Allen, *Hierarchy Theory: A Vision, Vocabulary, and Epistemology* (Columbia UP 1996) 73.

by the observer; it is not a matter of nature independent of observation'.[9] Put differently: 'comparison becomes a problem', as William JT Mitchell argued,

> when it sets itself up as theory, as a foundation for knowledge, or as a methodological guarantee of cognitive discovery. [Such comparison] has had a baneful effect on interdisciplinary work . . . provid[ing] a kind of intellectual house-keeping, rearranging the deck chairs on a sinking institutional structure . . . not mak[ing] any waves, but fill[ing] in the already-existing picture and bureaucratic structure of academic knowledge . . . its family trees of genres and media, with ever more nuanced detail . . . . [T]he real question . . . is not what the difference is between [X and Y] but what difference the difference makes.[10]

That question—'what difference the difference makes?'—is hardly new. More recently, those who have critiqued the project of comparative constitutional studies from the perspective of (a more traditional) comparative constitutional legal inquiry have insisted on the necessity to continue confronting not only the recently fashionable questions of 'explanation and causation', but also the enduring 'category', 'normative', and 'the interpretive questions'. Others, more sympathetic to the CCS project invited its proponents to embrace the spirit 'constructive skepticism', an attitude which, though suspicious of constitutional 'design', would nonetheless embrace 'tentative', 'experimental approaches' the aim of which is distinctly *meliorist*—the improvement of the 'functioning of law in society'. Likewise, the worries about the cognitive and logistical demands which the breadth and depth of CCL imposes on its practitioners may be alleviated by a more collaborative, ' "concentric" approach', with 'different scholars working on the same question from different angles'—and who together, over time, may be expected to generate 'reliable conclusions about cause and effect'.[11] Though sensitive to the question about the point of seeking (and taxonomizing) comparative constitutional (similarities and) differences, it is interesting to note that most contemporary critics of CCS ignore the 'constituent power' of their own contingent imaginings—of constitutions, of comparisons, or of the very field of comparative constitutionalism.[12] What

[9] Timothy FH Allen and Thomas W Hoekstra, *Toward a Unified Ecology* (Columbia UP 2015) 21.
[10] William JT Mitchell, 'Why Comparisons are Odious' (1996) 70 (2) World Literature Today 321.
[11] Rosalind Dixon, 'Toward a Realistic Comparative Constitutional Studies' (2016) 64 American Journal of Comparative Law 193,
[12] See eg Mark Tushnet, 'Saying and Doing in Comparative Constitutional Studies' (2016) 13 (1) American Journal of Comparative Law 13.

they ignore more specifically, as Günter Frankenberg famously argued, are the 'problems of perspective'.

3. *Comparing*: in critical legal studies

Rather than peripheral to the project of legal comparison, Frankenberg argued, they are to be seen as 'central and determinative' for the success of 'critical comparisons'—a more self-aware, and overall intellectually superior scholarly alternative to the traditional way of doing comparative law. First articulated in his eponymous 1985 article—and then over the course of next couple decades, progressively refined and extended to the field of comparative constitutional law—Frankenberg's project may now be understood not only as the most influential critique of the work of juridical comparison from the perspective of critical legal studies, but also as the first attempt to challenge its affective basis: the 'Cinderella complex' of comparative lawyers. Or—as Frankenberg also put it—a compulsion that drives them to privilege 'cognitive control' over the production of 'good', 'non-ethnocentric' abstractions. What's necessary to move beyond the mode of cognitive control is not only a mindset free from the complex of Cinderella, but also a different scopic regime—a way of seeing that hinges on 'distancing' and 'differencing': where the former stimulates 'dialectical learning experience' by decentring us from our pre-existing worldviews, and where the latter contributes to a greater attunement towards 'socio-cultural contexts' that define the perspective of others. In the context of comparative constitutional law—as Frankenberg wrote twenty years later—such comparatist will

> look at (constitutional) law not just as a body of norms but [also] as imaginations of reality . . . an ensemble of 'practical attitudes toward the management of controversy', [that will impel her to] cope with translations of law and constitutions between a language of imagination and one of decision. Guided by such a constitutive theory of law, she will soon discard the fact/law and law-in-the-books/law-in-action distinctions and deal, instead, with how she will represent in her scholarly work the legal representations of local conflicts, contexts, and visions.[13]

[13] Günter Frankenberg, 'Critical Comparisons: Re-thinking Comparative Law' (1985) 26 Harvard International Law Journal 411.

Or—as Frankenberg put it in his famous article on the nature of the migration of constitutional ideas—constitutions are not 'largely invented' by societies . . . but are 'constructed by constitutional elites and experts on the basis of transnational transfers'. For Frankenberg, this ought to result in the reorientation of comparative constitutional inquiry:

> So, the interesting question is not really whether legal transplants are possible (they are not), but how legal transfer happens. Or rather: What happens when it does happen? Which sort of semiotic relationship is established, how are constitutional items de- and re-contextualized, and, most importantly, which elements are excluded for what reasons from a transfer.[14]

But what is it in such 'in-depth comparative studies on constitutional transfers and odd details' that would make them 'interesting'? While Frankenberg claims that 'for comparative constitutional studies to generate more interest they have to deal with both—constitutions as law and order as well as constitutions as culture and as the imaginations of community', why should comparative constitutional scholars *care* to generate more 'interest' for their discipline? How is attracting that interest—attracting, that is, *away* from some other field of inquiry—important beyond the plane of scholarly inquiry? Put differently: what is the purpose of a 'dialectical learning experience': arriving at new 'non-ethnocentric' abstractions for the sake of non-ethnocentric abstractions? Why should comparativists 'cross the boundaries of a legocentrism so prevalent in comparative law', and abandon 'its pathetically narrow focus on legal norms and cases, legal processes and institutions'? Because, unlike an aspiration to produce 'good' abstractions, such crossing would not be predicated on a desire for 'cognitive control'? If so, can there ever be a 'learning experience' ('dialectical' or not) without some kind of cognitive control? If not, what is the specific purpose then of engaging in the work of 'comparative comparison'?

Unlike much of contemporary constitutional comparativism, Frankenberg is much more comfortable to leave that question open. It is to be answered by the one who has to '*cope* with translations of . . . constitutions between a language of imagination and one of decision'; the one who has to '*deal . . . with how she* will represent in *her* scholarly work the legal representations of local conflicts, contexts, and visions'.[15] What will affect her 'coping' and 'dealing',

[14] Günter Frankenberg; 'Comparing Constitutions: Ideas, Ideals, and Ideology—Toward a Layered Narrative (2006) 4 (3) ICON 439.

[15] Mark Tushnet 'The Boundaries of Comparative Law' (2017) 13 (1) European Constitutional Law Review 13.

however, remains occluded from Frankenberg's oblique call for a more purposeful exercise of juridical imagination. As an illustration of what remains in the shadow of Frankenberg's call to overcome one's 'Cinderella complex' and instead of pursuing cognitive 'control' confront 'interesting' questions with an aim of reaching 'good' abstractions by engaging in the work of distancing and differencing, consider William Twining's self-reflective account of the trajectory of his imagination:

> As I pondered the point of the enterprise in various places—including Oxford, Nairobi, Hong Kong, Kampala, Wasenaar (near Leiden), Bangalore, Miami, and Boston—three points became crystallised. First, my primary concern was with the health of my discipline at a particular time—that is the institutionalized study of law—from the point of view of a scholar, educator, occasional activist, and mild agent provocateur. Secondly, although I jet-setted and networked in a number of countries, my home and my main professional base are in England, my working language—even in Kampala, Beijing, Miami, and the Netherlands—is English, and my expertise is largely Anglo-American. Thirdly, words like 'global', 'globalisation', and 'globalism' were a growing part of the barrage of messages from the media and they had begun to become part of the daily vocabulary of neighbouring disciplines.[16]

Twining's diagnostics is important for two reasons. First, it offers a rare example of a theorist willing to put the trajectory of his imagination 'on the record'. Second, it vividly demonstrates that perspectives—whether from Kampala, Boston, or Leiden—are just one among a number of factors that shape the way in which legal scholars exercise their imaginative powers. What shaped his vision of 'globalization' was not only a particular, or a multiplicity of particular perspectives, but also the fact that in shifting between them Twining took care to commit them all to memory, as someone determined to be a good 'citizen' of his discipline (someone who contributes to their 'health'), and as someone willingness to humorously embrace his own personal idiosyncrasies ('mild agent provocateur'). Ignored, for the most part, in serious constitutional scholarship, these professional self-images and temperamental predilections are nonetheless highly consequential. In fact, we might say that they are constitutive—together with other factors that influence the ways in which we practise our theoretical imaginations—if not of the choice of a particular perspective, then at least of what vista is being *reported* from it. In sum: *comparing* the structures,

[16] William Twining, *Globalization and Legal Theory* (Butterworths 2000) 247.

mechanisms, agents, and trends that contribute to withstanding is never just a matter of identification, selection, and detection of the entities, attributes, and the criteria that deserve the label 'constitutional'. More than that, it is always a matter of the observer's purposeful (if not necessarily deliberately and in-advance constructed) *scopic regime*—a matter of the specific protocols of observation and measurement on which he chooses to rely on as she gazes on the world of constitutions.

4. On comparing (from a perspective)

A perspective from which a comparative constitutional scholar allegedly 'approaches' the work of comparison is an analytically imprecise way of referring to a combination of at least five elements that comprise its background scopic regime—*location*, *situation*, *orientation*, *affirmation*, *aspiration*, and *anticipation*—and which can themselves be more precisely defined. The first refers to the geographical position; the second to the circumstances experienced (imaginatively or otherwise) in that position, the third to a specific environment in relation to which those experiences obtain a special meaning that deserves to be recorded and communicated; the fourth to the commitment that introduces side-constraints on how this is done; the fourth, to a broader aspiration that makes that work not simply interesting, or engrossing but also a contribution to a vision of something *better*—and finally, the fifth, to the underlying diagnoses and prognoses of obstacles and opportunities that lead one to contribute to that 'better' by pursuing one 'approach' instead of another.

Instead, the imagination behind constitutional comparativism is *unreflective*; averse to turning its gaze on to itself; disinclined to meditate on a variety of possible ways in which one might imagine the act of constitution, the work of comparison, and the assumption of a particular perspective. When it comes to the debates among the proponents of comparative constitutional 'law' on the one hand, and the proponents of comparative constitutional studies on the other, that imagination is also quietist—as its practitioners metabolize that aversion by the embracing the ideals that keep the disciplinarily disciplined character of their comparativist ideals intact: from methodological rigour to interdisciplinary ecumenism and critical self-awareness.

What is behind this quietism? There are at least two reasons. The first the most general. We do not speak of perspectives in this way not only because we fear that doing so would devalue our scholarship for being 'partisan' but also because we remain 'highly ambivalent' towards broadcasting the imaginative character of its artefacts. Put differently:

> we want to show or tell because we have discovered something important, yet we don't want to show or tell because we 'know' that other people will or may fail to appreciate what we have seen . . . or even criticize us as 'just imagining,' having 'let our imagination run away with us.'[17]

This may also explain the remarkable reception of Twining's own work: though widely admired, discussed, and recommended, it nonetheless did not prove inspirational in the way in which its author had intended.

The second reason behind this pervasive imaginative quietism is more specific and has to do with the 'downcast eyes' of legal scholars, who exercise their imaginative powers anxiously, and, as a result, timidly, privately, and mostly unreflectively. Rather than open to the world of struggle, their imaginations remain (to excuse the pun) *hermeneutically sealed*: their visions of the world must follow from their interpretations of the texts—that is the only way in which they can ever hope to achieve scholarly legitimacy. Today—as in previous historical eras—their embrace of hermeneutics is best seen as a symptom of an underlying anxiety about 'the temptations of baroque vision' and its 'disorienting illusions'. To resist them—on this account—the gaze of legal scholars must remain fixated on the text. When it comes to the eyes of constitutional scholars, their eyes have not only been 'downcast', but also, until relatively recently, parochial—fixated, for the most part, on the texts of national constitutions.

Needless to say, the imaginative circumference of those who work in the field of comparative constitutional law is much broader. It encompasses not only a particular locality, but also—at least potentially—the entire world. At this point, it is important to notice a sharp differentiation between comparative constitutional *law* and comparative constitutional *studies* on the one hand, and a 'Southern' approach to the world of constitutions, on the other. What the former share is the *nature* of the viewpoint from which they observe the developments on the ground. For both, that viewpoint is elevated enough to capture the world of constitutional law. In both cases, that viewpoint *unspecified*. Even though we know where they are—in New York, Toronto, Berlin, London—both

[17] Paul B Lieberman, 'Imagination: Looking in the Right Place and (in the Right Way)' in James Phillips and James Morley (eds), *Imagination and Its Pathologies* (MIT 2003) 27–28.

approaches presume that the global circumference renders the exact location, *from where* scholars observe the world of constitutional law, irrelevant.

While these two 'approaches' are situated *nowhere in particular* (you can crunch your data from Chicago or Hong Kong alike), CGS claims to look at the world of constitutional law *as it is*. In other words, to approach comparative constitutional law from the perspective of the Global South would commit one to inhabit a location somewhere in the Global South; experience a situation typical of the Global South; re-envision the world of constitutional law in light of that experience; broadcast the world picture that appears from there as a *worthy re-description* of the world of constitutional law; promote this picture as the scholarly contribution to the field of constitutional comparativism, (and) as the best way to contribute to the success of concrete political aspirations in the struggles of those on the ground. While these two 'approaches' are situated *nowhere in particular* (you can equally crunch your data from Chicago or Hong Kong) those who embrace the Southern perspective claim to look at the world of constitutional law *as it is*, but *from a particular perspective*. In prefacing their interventions by a pre-emptive disclosure of their partiality, the adherents of the Southern perspective on the world of constitutions give a free pass to those whom they seek to confront polemically. All they need to respond to the Southern perspective is: 'We are simply interested in different things! Our perspective is scholarly and value-neutral, and yours is geographical, and politically committed. Goodbye now, it was nice meeting you!' At the moment, there is no way to respond to this polite dismissal effectively—that is to say, nothing that would impel those who engage in the dominant forms of comparative constitutional inquiry to take the provocations of those who don't seriously. The problem, however, is not only with a specific, Southern perspective. It has to do with the marginal rhetorical utility of the trope 'perspective', as such.

B. Beyond Standpoints: Perception, Location, and Polemical Imagination

Perspective is a name for a defensive rhetorical stratagem. Those who announce it, do so to hide behind it. As they seemingly encourage others, 'Look at it this way!', what they actually say is: 'Please, don't shoot, this is *just* how things appear from my point of view.' This problem will not be remedied by insisting that such standpoint must be understood relationally, as

> a social position of knowing . . . rooted . . . in geopolitics and global social hierarchy [that] captures the position, and hence the activities, experiences, concerns and perspectives, of globally peripheral populations . . . . would thus overcome metrocentrism [and which] does not refer to any singular identity [but rather to] a place in hierarchy. The places can be multiple, because the hierarchies can be multiple too. But because the category 'subaltern' does not refer to an essence, it can accommodate this multiplicity.[18]

Rather than finally providing the Southern perspective with the intellectual respectability it craves, this only gives rise to further questions. What are the polemical advantages of using 'Southern' to refer to the ineluctably multiple and relationally defined peripheral 'positions of knowing'? If 'hierarchy', 'metrocentrism', 'periphery', and subaltern 'multiplicity' always hinge on a way of seeing—why does this way of seeing deserve to be called 'Southern'? To answer this question, consider the terms that historically preceded, and which may be seen as giving rise to this adjective as a shorthand: the Third World and the Global South—both of which may be approached in two ways.

On the one hand, the Third World and the Global South exist as pictures, the rarely reflected-upon *visualizations* of our common world. What do they evoke, more specifically? In the first case, the picture seems to evoke a self-encompassing whole which nonetheless exists as a third member in a set, alongside the first two. In the second case, the image depicts one *specific* side of the world gone global—which, however, continues to be detectable *everywhere* because of our memories of it as it once existed, *somewhere*. Both pictures are strange, but it is not immediately obvious how exactly are they 'problematic'. Though they may be, neither of them is inevitably unclear of fuzzy. Though they seem 'illogical', they only appear as such because we have not grasped their character as 'metapictures'—the pictures which serve as the 'instrument of understanding' not only of the reality which they represent (Third World, Global South) but also of the pictures and seeing in general, and which, in so doing, also 'call into question the self-understanding of [their] observer'. Rubin's vase is one such picture. Wittgenstein's rabbit-duck is another. Irrespective of the way in which they achieve it, '[p]ictorial self-reference' of metapictures is 'a matter of use and context'—their 'pragmatic' and 'functional', not their 'formal' feature.[19] The mark of their (rhetorical) functionality is the

[18] Julian Go, 'Globalizing Sociology, Turning South. Perspectival Realism and the Southern Standpoint' (2016) 10 (2) Sociologica 1, 14.

[19] WJT Mitchell, *Picture Theory* (University of Chicago Press 1994) 57.

multi-stability of the Gestalts that they evoke: a feature that allows a viewer to oscillate between individual pictures: be those the images of the silhouettes and the vase, the duck and the rabbit, or the South in the Globe and the Globe which is the South.

On the other hand, the Third World and the Global South are the concepts which exist politically, and which—as 'all political concepts, images, and terms'—always carry a 'polemical meaning'.[20] What Carl Schmitt didn't state is that not all polemical concepts exist in the same polemical way. Many, if not most of them, belong to the class of 'asymmetric counter-concepts'. To invoke one, as Reinhart Koselleck explained, is to do more than just assert the dignity of the entity in whose name one makes a specific political demand. It is also to allude to—or even to explicitly postulate—the character of that entity (be that the People, the Proletariat, the Christians, or the Hellenes) as the incarnation of the 'universality' that justifies those who invoke its name to 'discriminate against those who have been defined as the "other"' (the tyrants, the bourgeoisie, the heathens, or the barbarians).[21] Likewise, while all asymmetric counter-concepts aim to undermine the legitimacy of those defined as the 'other', not all do so with the same intensity—some do so explicitly and uncompromisingly, others—such as the Third World, or, more recently, the Global South, do so much more allusively and hesitatingly. On the one hand, invoking them sympathetically is a way of affirming the value of cultural diversity, the importance of international solidarity, and the urgency of global redistributive justice. On the other, to refer to them with sympathy is to also uphold the dignity of non-Western visions of political community, as well as a way to denounce the toxic effects of the Eurocentric ideals of sovereignty, legality, and constitutional democracy.[22] What follows from this is an obvious, but by no means trivial and unproblematic conclusion: increasingly frequent calls to approach constitutionalism, or comparative constitutional law from the Global South or the Third World 'perspective' are gestures whose polemical character may only be denied—*polemically*.

At this point we must ask: what is the purpose of resorting to *these* polemical concepts? Schmitt presents us with a simple, general answer to this question: to lend dignity to a part of vocabulary used in the struggles on the ground,

[20] Carl Schmitt, *The Concept of the Political* (Georg Schwab tr, first published 1932; University of Chicago Press 1996) 30.

[21] See generally Reinhart Koselleck, *Futures Past: On the Semantics of Historical Time* (first published 1979; Columbia UP 2004).

[22] As expressed by Alfred Sauvy: 'That Third World, ignored, exploited, scorned like the Third Estate, also wants to be something.' See Alfred Sauvy, 'Trois mondes, une planète' *L'Observateur*, No. 118 (Paris, 14 August 1952), 14.

and in that way, improve—if only marginally—the chances of a particular side in a particular existential struggle on the ground. When it comes to the arguments that lend dignity to 'Third World' or 'Global South' *perspectives*—this cannot be our answer. Though the figure of Global South oftentimes acts as a rhetorical shorthand for a number of ills, deficiencies, historical scandals, and crimes committed either by the West itself or in the name of the universalistic concepts which it had successfully propagated, it is far from obvious to which existential struggle (or even the class of existential struggles!) a Global South 'perspective' on comparative constitutional law could offer a meaningful contribution.

One way to respond to this—admittedly defeatist—claim is to follow Rousseau and assume a self-ironic attitude to the taunts of those on the ground: 'O barbarous philosopher! Come read us your book on a battlefield.' Another is to recoil from the 'barbarous' practicalities of political struggle, and retreat to the reassuring safety of scholarly 'conversations'. In that environment, asking questions about the *purposes* of 'perspective' is a serious transgression; a sign that 'barbarism may be observed to have supervened'.[23] A less extremist version of that approach would be to confront existing constitutional scholarship on Global South (or Global South in general) pragmatically—as a configuration of interventions each of which entail utterances intended to convey an additional meaning not expressed literally. Straddling the fine line between symptomatic reading and insinuation, this approach would probably result in a provisional taxonomy of *Global South-gestures* directed not only towards those who are already half-persuaded by them, but also towards those who find themselves in the position of the Eurocentric, or Western 'other'. In that case, we would probably be compelled to revise our initial assumption about the asymmetric character of 'Global South' as a polemical counter-concept. Intermeshed with the *denunciations* of Western conceptions of nationhood, majoritarian democracy, sovereignty, and constitutionalism, we would encounter the *gestures* that would better be described as exhortations, supplications, disorientations, and re-imaginations.

Of course, 'the refusal to formulate an alternative vision' might allow those who organize around the Southern standpoint 'to exist as a "location" for exhilarating encounters'.[24] The appropriateness of this response—offered by Duncan Kennedy as an answer to the critiques of Critical Legal Studies movement—is

[23] Michael Oakeshott, *Rationalism in Politics and Other Essays* (Methuen 1962) 212.

[24] Duncan Kennedy, 'Afterward' in Duncan Kennedy (ed), *Legal Education and the Reproduction of Hierarchy: A Polemic Against the System (Critical Edition)* (NYU Press 2004) 217.

a matter of timing. Standpoint, perspective—these are badges of recognition, rallying cries, orientation directions; something that in the first phase of a movement, a school, they contribute to the integrity of the project; to something that discursively helps that project with-stand. As time goes by, the sensibility of this response becomes increasingly dubious, however. Once we have assembled ourselves, used the token X to successfully broadcast our political commitments Y, or the aesthetic sensibilities Z—once we kept on using it so as to give our initial staking of the ground some consistency, once the location within the broader intellectual terrain is held for some time—the legitimate question becomes: now what?

1. Global South and the (non-)urban way of life

It is not my aim in this paper to offer a detailed description of these polemical gestures. Nor is my aim—even though I think that pursuing it would be useful, even necessary—to speculate on what do those who make those gestures really hope for, or, more precisely, how do they imagine the relationship between their intervention (once publicized) and the marginal increase in the chances of the success of the political vision of the world towards which they aspire. I hasten to add that these questions provoke a debate that needs to be had, but not on the terms of those who have in advance decided that the Global South perspective is unproductive, in comparison with similarly politically oriented, but otherwise scholarly superior approaches. Nor is my aim to further dwell on the location of Southern gaze, whose elusiveness and contradictions have been—both sympathetically and not—exhaustively critiqued in the literature. Finally, though in agreement with much of Alexandra Kemmerer's admirably self-reflective account of the metaphors that shape our visions of international order, this article does not echo her call to 'look closely', to 'sharpen our eye' and engage in 'diligent observation' for two main reasons.[25]

The first reason becomes obvious once we revisit Schmitt's famous claim about the polemical character of all political concepts. Schmitt's claim—as Leo Strauss was quick to observe—'results in the *unpolemical* description of the political'[26] that '*in concreto* violates this principle'.[27] More important for

[25] Alexandra Kemmerer, 'The Normative Knot 2.0: Metaphorological Explorations in the Net of Networks' (2009) 10 German Law Journal 439, 460.

[26] Carl Schmitt, *The Concept of the Political* (Georg Schwab tr, first published 1932, University of Chicago Press 2007) 109.

[27] ibid 122.

our purposes is Strauss's conclusion about what precipitated this incoherence: Schmitt's contempt for 'a world of amusement, a world without seriousness'.[28] Theorists have not taken this seriously. Schmitt is mostly seen as 'nationalist', 'Nazi', 'devout Catholic', or 'opportunist'. Those who did, saw a reaffirmation of a pastoral world where Mother Earth and 'its fields, pastures, and forests' justly reward the efforts of a 'farmer'.[29] It is this 'way of life' which the members of the political 'entity' defend against the enemy—the one which seeks to destroy it. Which brings to mind an interesting, but for the purposes of this essay, still a cursory question: what would the history of late-twentieth-century political theory look like, had its practitioners spent less energy on the exegesis of Schmitt, and more on a more general question of what it means to be serious? Would our understanding of the political be different had our understanding of the seriousness—and its other—been different? Or, put more generally: how do we *imagine the world of seriousness*—a world hospitable to a serious way of life?

In scholarship, a way of life coincides with 'culture'; with 'interconnected traditions of thought and inquiry'; with 'a set of rule-governed practices, which are at least loosely woven together, and which constitute at least some central areas of social political and economic activity'.[30] Thus understood, ways of life may be nested—individuals may participate in several—and its boundaries are 'inherently imprecise'.[31] Rather than defining it, asking a question seems more urgent for the purposes of this essay: can a way of life be imagined other than *concretely*—without any reference to the scenes in which it manifests itself *daily*? With this question in mind, it appears far less relevant whether Go succeeded in offering a coherent rebuttal of the criticisms of the Southern standpoint. What appears far more relevant instead are the concrete imaginings of 'the position, and . . . the activities, experiences, concerns and perspectives, of globally peripheral populations'.[32] How do we imagine them? What do they do exactly? At which level and in what hierarchy do they find themselves? Which metropolises oppress them? To say that Global South captures 'multiplicity' of those perspectives is an elegant, but a misleading, perhaps even self-deceiving way out. We cannot imagine all of them at once. Even if our picture

[28] Srinivas Aravamudan, 'Carl Schmitt's *The Nomos of the Earth*: Four Corollaries' (2005) 104 (2) South Atlantic Quarterly 227, 231.

[29] Carl Schmitt, *Land and Sea* (first published 1954; Plutarch 1997) 28.

[30] Andrew Mason, *Community, Solidarity and Belonging: Levels of Community and their Normative Significance* (CUP 2000) 23.

[31] ibid.

[32] Julian Go, 'Globalizing Sociology, Turning South. Perspectival Realism and the Southern Standpoint' (2016) 10 (2) Sociologica 1, 14.

of that multiplicity is vague, fuzzy, and shape-shifting its contours evoke some familiar shapes, not others: poor peasants in the Andes fighting the attempts of multinational mining corporations to steal their land; disadvantaged youth playing soccer in a favela in Rio; ordinary citizens of Bogota navigating the administrative classification of the city; etc.[33]

At the risk of oversimplification, the problem—which is also one of the reasons why we cannot immediately follow Kemmerer's call to 'sharpen our eye'—lies less in the hard-nosed character of our imaginative binarism, and more in our unawareness of other, potentially highly consequential, orthogonal binaries. To put it as concretely as possible: as the advocates of the Southern perspective continue preoccupying themselves with defending a relativized socio-economic, political, military, and even quasi-civilizational distinction between the East and the West, the North and the South, the core and the periphery, they neglect another, equally simple, but highly uncomfortable one: the binary between the city and the country, between the resilient urban zones of infatuation with the lifestyles of 'Western' metropolises, and the equally resilient zones of struggles for cultural self-preservation. So, it is a fair question: whose voices are the partisans of Southern perspectives amplifying, modulating, and translating—*really*?

If it is true, as Comaroff and Comaroff argued, that we may find the enclaves of the North in the South (and vice versa) why should we keep recalibrating our visions in a way that continues to perpetuate both, increasingly pockmarked, master-regions of our global political imagination? Because, the South is the name for an eccentric way of looking at the world?[34] There are so many ways to achieve that effect. The most honest argument in its favour—and in virtue of that also the most coherent one—would build on a close reading of Go's claim; to specify not only the *nature* of experiences, the *character* of concerns, and the *location* of perspectives' of the mythical 'globally peripheral populations', but also highlight the objective of their struggle: to overcome 'metrocentrism'. From what was said thus far, metrocentrism is not only a particular symptom for the enduring hierarchical structures of domination, humiliation, and exploitation. If I am right, 'metrocentrism' is also the symptom of the imagination

[33] So even if it may be true—as Vidya Kumar has argued—that '[t]he production of global constitutional theory by global constitutionalists involves the active non-production of the Global South—as an object or as a subject—of the global legal order', the question is of course, so what? More specific question: what kind of GS is imagined and what scholarly project would it serve in a way that the one above wouldn't be able to?

[34] I have accepted this view in my preliminary exploration of the potential of the 'constitutionalism of the Global South' in Zoran Oklopcic, 'The South of Western Constitutionalism: A Map Ahead of a Journey' (2016) 37 (11) Third World Quarterly 2080. In the meantime, I have become more suspicious of the productivity of that gesture, as is plainly manifest in this essay.

of a scholar who conjures it as he attempts to execute an organized retreat from the ambitiously set boundaries of a notionally 'Global', but in reality, a far more sentimentally and aesthetically restricted 'South'.

C. Conclusion: The World of Constitutions beyond Juridical Metaphorology

Perhaps my speculations are completely baseless. Perhaps I am completely wrong to put forward what may be nothing but an unsubstantiated intuition. Perhaps those who embrace the perspective of Global South do not exclude the petit bourgeois and lumpen-proletariat masses of Rio de Janeiro, Sao Paolo, Buenos Aires, Mexico City, Lagos, Cape Town, Jakarta, Kuala Lumpur, and other densely populated zones, organized in accordance to their own, often invisible, locally nesting 'metrocentrisms'. If metropolitan governance over these densely populated areas—whose inhabitants continue to aspire (to a non-negligible extent) towards the style of life broadcasted by the ideological apparatuses whose functional autonomy continues to enjoy the pride of place in the imaginary of Western constitutionalism—is to remain in the focus of a distinctly Southern approach to comparative constitutionalism, the trope of South cannot be expected to forever deflect the reckoning with the large-scale and long-term questions of constitutional *design*. When it comes to the problems that appear at those scales, and within those time frames—and given that there is a sufficient number of those who are successful in their wish to perpetuate them—using the gesture of the South polemically, in order to summarily relegate hierarchy (and its cousin 'metrocentrism') to the dustbin of wicked forms of partial political ordering would not only be intellectually lazy (for the reasons I mention in a moment) but would also probably be a luxury that 'the South'—wherever it is, and whoever it includes—could not easily afford—politically.

In this context, Kemmerer's call to 'sharpen our eyes' is much more welcome. Still, her description of the world picture that confronts the imagination of those who gaze at the world of constitutions needs to be qualified in several important respects. Approaching that world from the perspective of 'metaphorology', Kemmerer writes:

> Our world is a world of pyramid and network and will remain so for some time to come. The contradictions between heterarchies and hierarchies are hence to be negotiated and balanced dialectically, in a permanent process

> of changing perspectives and oscillations, continuously seeking a balance between the universality of the horizontal world of the networks and the particular, spatially fixed worlds of the pyramids. A transparent process of rational deliberation could allow for compromises that could successfully de-escalate collision.[35]

Though Kemmerer usefully highlights mutual non-exclusivity of juridical perspectives, those who gaze at the world of constitutions as critically oriented, and imaginatively self-aware comparative lawyers or political scientists have at least two good reasons to refrain from fully embracing her metaphorology. The first has to do with metaphorology itself. Though highly useful in turning those who engage in comparative constitutional inquiry into more self-aware practitioners of scholarly imagination, it distracts us from appreciating the figurative limitations of metaphorical imagination. By way of example, consider *core-and-the-periphery*—the form of partial ordering that many scholars across disciplinary divides see as alternative to that of hierarchy. Now, the attention to metaphor will be highly useful as we compare and contrast those two templates, because our very understanding of the core, and of the periphery will depend on a metaphorical template that prefigures their relationship, and which we have chosen unreflectively. So, as we identify the world's cores and peripheries we also always inadvertently choose among different cores (on the left), and their respective peripheries (on the right).

(1) OBJECT—SHADOW
(2) PLANET—SATELLITES
(3) DOWNTOWN—SUBURBS
(4) NUCLEUS—CYTOPLASM
(5) HEAD—BODY
(6) TRUNK—EXTREMITIES
(7) HEADQUARTERS—DETACHMENTS

The punchline here is rather obvious: the relationship between two forms of partial ordering—hierarchy and core-and-periphery—will depend, not exclusively, but still constitutively, on which among (1) to (7) governs our imagination of the latter. Embrace (1), (2), (3), (4), and (6) and core-and-periphery become irreducible to hierarchy. Embrace (5) and (7) and they become

[35] Kemmerer (n 25) 460.

different ways to visually represent the networks of command and control.[36] Notice however, that our imaginations of hierarchies, core–peripheries, networks, and other abstract schemes of partial ordering also inevitably hinge on our embrace of specific building blocks—surfaces (levels, layers, fields, boundaries, zones, landscapes), points (poles, nodes, knots), and links (pillars, chains, conduits, flows)—without which those schemes would not be possible. We don't think about them, but that makes them no less constitutive. On inspection, it is obvious: there is no hierarchy, without *levels*, no socio-economic stratification without *layers*, no network without *nodes* and *conduits*, no core-and-periphery without *poles* and *fields*, and so on.

This is all very abstract. Why did I venture this far? Because the relationship between metaphor and these elementary building-blocks is not unidirectional: while it will most often be the case that our choice of metaphors prefigures the identity of a concrete building block, that relationship may always—in principle—work the other way around. This, I think is worth keeping in mind, at least in the case of all those who prepare to challenge the dominant style of comparative constitutional inquiry—naively botanical, polemically quietist, and rhetorically timid, and, on occasion, underhanded. Whatever its other advantages, this style sets limits on the ways in which we gaze at the world of constitutions. It does so, as I suggested earlier, by keeping the assumptions that animate much of contemporary constitutional inquiry intact—that constitutions originate from foundations, that comparing them may proceed without asking what allowed us to identify them, and that the diversity of ways in which we perceive the world of constitution boil down to our different 'perspectives'. Not so; it was this essay's argument.

What prefigures the character of our comparative constitutional inquiries are imaginings—of scenes of constitution-making, of one's professional role in a scholarly community within a wider disciplinary archipelago, of global and local problems, of worthy and unworthy struggles, of lost causes and likely outcomes. In addition to these imaginings—which are mostly vague, and often undetected, but always concrete—comparative constitutional inquiry must also avail itself of the help of others, at different levels of abstraction: from more or less figurally specific, and by now well-worn metaphors of 'migration' and

[36] Of course, each of the metaphorical templates may be concretized further. Today, for example, we are more inclined not to imagine a hierarchical relationship between the city (downtown) and its periphery (suburbs). Had we imagined a city from a different historical era, our conclusion would likely be different. See eg Niklas Luhmann, *Law as Social System* (OUP 2002) 292, 302 . For the discussion about three 'ontological basic structures': 'level', 'section', and 'thicket' see William Wimsatt, *Re-engineering Philosophy for Limited Beings: Piecewise Approximations to Reality* (Harvard UP 2007).

'travel' (of constitutional ideas), to the most abstract, invisible ones. For the most part, these imaginings are simply taken for granted: not only rarely mentioned, but also quietly understood to be 'unmentionable'. To speak of them as the artefacts of our imaginations that may be imagined differently is to imperil the sense and insult the sensibility of scholarly inquiry. Elsewhere, I have attempted to argue why that need not be the case. Here, I conclude with three questions which concern the anticipations, aspirations, and ambitions of those who embrace 'South' as the standpoint from which they gaze at the world of constitutions.

The first question is polemical and practical: is there a point of committing to a Southern standpoint except to broadcast affinity with a cluster of vague and variable commitments? Put differently: what is the anticipated productivity of gesturing to(wards) the 'South', beyond its function as a rallying point for lending dignity to a new form of scholarly antagonism? That is a fair question, because many of those who affiliate themselves with this perspective seem to have no ambition to preach beyond the 'choir' of those who are already, in one way or another, 'converted'. This brings us to the second question: if the ambition of those who engage in comparative constitutional inquiry from the Southern standpoint is not merely defensive—to co-exist, as an idiosyncrasy, among already established, and much more influential approaches—what is it, then? To confront them, in hope of converting those who currently subscribe to them? And if yes, how? Which brings us to a less specific, but more profound final question: how often does one encounter scholars willing to abandon their worldviews after being confronted with the fatal flaws in the arguments that justify them?[37] Those happy to hide their political commitments behind their professional personas have the luxury to ignore these background morphologies of desirable forms of everyday life. Those who make the point of not hiding ether their political commitments, or their partial perspectives, alas, don't.

[37] The obvious answer: not many. Immanuel Kant—woken up, as he admitted, from his 'dogmatic slumber' by David Hume—seems to be one of the rare exceptions to the contrary, which perhaps explains the popularity of his remark.

5

Legal Innovation as a Global Public Good

Remaking Comparative Law as Indigenization

Jedidiah J Kroncke

A. Introduction: A New Paradigm for Comparative Law

This chapter advances a specific paradigm for thinking about comparative law, in service of promoting a truly cosmopolitan global dialogue on legal development. It does so by framing national and transnational legal innovations as an empirical pool of knowledge which is a global public good; a good whose utilization by any domestic legal system requires systemic investments in comparative legal empiricism and training. The primary role of comparative lawyers in this paradigm is that of indigenizers who act to critically guide the translation of legal developments in foreign contexts for domestic use.[1]

These interrelated concepts of legal innovation as a global public good and comparative lawyers as indigenizers are framed in terms of national competition in the context of a multipolar legal order. This framing seeks to directly address the counter-intuitive reality that while a global surge in comparative analysis has followed broad recognition of regulatory institutions and practices as key to national success, the recent participation of comparative lawyers in this surge has been limited, especially in Northern countries. At the same time, faith in universal technocratic solutions to numerous policy challenges has recurrently crashed up against the very central questions with which comparative lawyers have long grappled regarding translation and borrowing between

[1] In many ways, this paradigm partakes in very long-standing debates about 'local knowledge' that has been a mainstay in several social sciences, most notably and centrally anthropology. The fall of various certainties about the 'end of history' manifest in the last two decades has given this debate new expression, even in disciplines where universalist paradigms are dominant, such as economics. See, notably, Joseph Stiglitz, 'Scan Globally, Reinvent Locally: Knowledge Infrastructure and the Localization of Knowledge' in Diane Stone (ed), *Banking on Knowledge: The Genesis of the Global Development Network* (Routledge 2000) 24–44, 26. Note that the presumption in the paper that any time the concept of public goods is mentioned, it is implicitly presumed that this is a 'global public good' in terms that economists such as Stiglitz distinguish the term from nation-state specific public goods.

Jedidiah J Kroncke, *Legal Innovation as a Global Public Good* In: *The Global South and Comparative Constitutional Law.* Edited by: Philipp Dann, Michael Riegner, and Maxim Bönnemann, Oxford University Press (2020). © Oxford University Press. DOI: 10.1093/oso/9780198850403.003.0005

legal systems. The competencies developed by comparative legal training also lean into the nexus of the law/politics divide which implicates the local symbolic aspects of law as well as the distributional contexts of individual polities that often complicate effective cross-national legal adaptation. Thus, while debates in comparative law recur over how to conceptualize itself, critical comparative lawyers are best equipped to deal with the process of indigenization required to realize the potential of global legal innovation.

Comparative lawyers have long struggled over the parochial tendencies of any legal system, and historically felt compelled to advance various shades of legal cosmopolitanism.[2] While humanistic variations of comparative law have merit,[3] in the context of a global order increasingly caught between technocratic universalism and xenophobic nationalism, the functionalist tradition within comparative law is necessarily central to a pragmatic cosmopolitanism which is necessary for attracting broader interest in critical legal comparativism.[4] The alternative is to continue to speak from the margins as numerous fields of regulatory analysis engage in explicit and implicit comparative empiricism with the poor/unintended results catalogued by the legal transplants literature.[5]

The primary implications of this paradigm are twofold. The first implication is that it is in their domestic legal cultures where critical comparative lawyers need to focus their efforts, rather than in transnational or foreign spaces. For both high- and low-income countries, there is a causal relationship between the legacy of Northern legal parochialism which has conceptualized a unidirectional outward flow of legal knowledge and innovation to 'developing' countries.[6] Both in the context of colonialism and other export-oriented projects

[2] For a survey of the possibilities of cosmopolitanism and self-government, see Vlad Perju, 'Cosmopolitanism and Constitutional Self-Government' (2010) 8 ICON 326, 330. Perju's view of comparative analysis as an adjunct to 'self-correction' in constitutional self-government has many consonances with the ideal of domestically oriented comparative analysis outlined in this chapter.

[3] A cogent defence of the humanizing force of comparative legal experience is made in Hugh Scogin, 'Civil Law' in Kathryn Bernhardt and Philip Huang (eds), *Traditional China in Civil Law in Qing and Republican China* (Stanford UP 1994) 53.

[4] As noted later in this chapter, methodological debates within comparative law garner almost a plurality of the energy devoted to comparative legal scholarship. The 'functionalism' invoked here aspires not to any larger claims about legal similarities or difference, or larger projects of potential legal harmonization, but instead is aimed solely at the sensibility that legal experience has the potential to inspire legal solutions or improvements through cross-national conceptual and empirical contextualization. For a different view of functionalism in comparative law, and evaluation of its potential therein, see Ralf Michaels, 'The Functional Method of Comparative Law' in Mathias Reimann and Reinhard Zimmermann (eds), *Oxford Handbook of Comparative Law* (OUP 2006) 339.

[5] Defining what should and can constitute a 'transplant' is often as much an issue of the vector of transmission as it is national source. For a critical inquiry, see Daniel Berkowitz and others, 'The Transplant Effect' (2003) 51 American Journal of Comparative Law 164, 190 ('After two hundred years of for the most part unsuccessful legal transplants, more patience with the development of legal institutions seems to be in order').

[6] The claims in this paragraph are more extensively addressed in Jedidiah Kroncke, 'Law and Development as Anti-Comparative Law' (2011) 45 Vanderbilt Journal of Transnational Law 477.

of reform (sometimes called 'law and development'), the historical detritus of evolutionary thinking has helped vitiate the use of comparative legal empiricism in the North while perpetuating the unconstructive discourse on 'development' sustained elsewhere by still extant intellectual and economic asymmetries. Of notes in a volume dedicated to the impact of the *VRÜ/WCL* are the many parallels and continuities between colonial attitudes about legal knowledge and those still dominant today,[7] long acknowledged and yet seemingly forgotten.[8]

While often cast as legal humanitarianism, Northern legal institutions and academies need to abandon these ideas and recognize that there is still much contested and under examination about the causal factors at play in the historical development of their own legal systems—all of which are now under strain from globalization. Again here we can note that over its long history the *VRÜ/WCL* has called for internal self-critique as a necessary response to these legacies, and not simply chastened but still problematic export mentalities.[9] Escaping the parochial deadweight of the past requires a refocused effort on challenging these norms globally, and using the frame of indigenization to revitalize the relevance of comparative lawyering in the North and elsewhere to the myriad of reform discourses inside and outside of law.

The second implication of this paradigm is that there are a set of both pragmatic and ethical duties that critical comparative lawyers must undertake in service of the public goods concept of legal innovation, and its corollary pragmatic cosmopolitanism. Admittedly, the focus of the duties so advanced lies with necessary emphasis on Northern legal academies which still benefit from systemic inequalities in wealth, status, and the placement of graduates in positions of relative influence.[10] This positional superiority masks and sustains presumptions about the unidirectional flow of legal innovation, and allows many future non-comparative lawyers in the North to rely on anecdotal assurance from foreign legal interlocutors dependent on their social capital to sustain their relative cross-cultural blindness. This means that critical comparativists must not only assertively delegitimize export efforts at home, but they must

[7] Stiglitz (n 1) 26 also noted that current mentalities are 'close cousins' to colonialism which have remade themselves with more formally conceptually neutral veneers.

[8] Gordon Woodman, 'British Legislation as a Source of Ghanaian Law: From Colonialism to Technical Aid' (1974) 7 VRÜ/WCL 19; and Bas de Gaay Fortman and Paschal Mihyo, 'A False Start: Law and Development in the Context of a Colonial Legacy' (1993) 26 VRÜ/WCL 136.

[9] Michaela Hailbronner, 'Overcoming Obstacles to North–South Dialogue' (2016) 49 VRÜ/WCL 353.

[10] While the continued empirical reality of these asymmetries should be beyond dispute, their specific reproduction in global higher education is explored in Simon Marginson, 'Dynamics of National and Global Competition in Higher Education' (2006) 52 Higher Education 1.

also actively seek out interlocutors outside of the common elite juriscentrism of legal academies.

Of great import, the indigenization paradigm also implies a renewed focus on our approaches to domestic and international pedagogy. For domestic students, this requires presenting comparative law not as esoterica but as an essential and natural part of legal reform,[11] if not always relevant to the internal legal perspective of adjudication. It also means presenting these ideas in core courses with the balancing caution that not all Northern legal expertise is effectively transnational. For forging genuine relationships with foreign students and scholars, the paradigm means taking a proactive role in recruitment and teaching, as well as institutional programming. Perhaps more significantly, it implies acknowledging the compromised position of many foreign interlocutors during their Northern educational and professional engagements, as well as their subsequent careers when they often become preferentially embedded in global asymmetries once they return home. As many low-income countries have already had to adopt the indigenization paradigm out of necessity,[12] Northern academics have a duty to facilitate these practices free from the distortions of any export mentality or sense of national mission.

Perhaps no field represents the depth of this challenge better than comparative constitutional law. The rapid proliferation of constitutions over the twentieth century, and almost all modelled until recently on a few dominant paradigms from the Northern, was inflected by a presumptively unidirectional flow of expertise that has often led to some of the worst mismatches in intent and outcome exactly because indigenization was neglected by even those who with critical perspective on law from their home countries.[13] While the rise of transformative constitutionalism as an alternative to liberal constitutionalism in the last few decades was seen in part as a Southern response, its own importation of problematic assumptions about rights and their implementation led to a near complete retreat in the previous Brazilian, Indian, and South

[11] The all-to-common view of comparative law as solely an esoteric exercise is part of what motivated famed American comparativist John Merryman to participate in what is commonly mislabelled as the 'first' generation of law development work carried out by American legal academics in Latin America during the 1960s: John Merryman, 'Comparative Law and Social Change' (1977) 25 American Journal of Comparative Law 457. Merryman ultimately rejected the law and development field *in toto*, for many of the still salient reasons explored by contemporary critics of legal parochialism.

[12] Brian Tamanaha, 'A Pragmatic Approach to Legislative Theory for Developing Countries' in Robert Seidman and others (eds), *Making Development Work* (Kluwer 1999) 145, 156.

[13] Tom Ginsburg, 'Constitutional Advice and Transnational Legal Order' (2017) 2 UC Irvine Journal of International, Transnational, and Comparative Law 5. For the latter proposition see Mary Dudziak, *Exporting American Dreams: Thurgood Marshall's African Journey* (Princeton UP 2009) and Makau Mutua, 'Mary L. Dudziak's Exporting American Dreams: Thurgood Marshall's African Journey' (2009) 31 Human Rights Quarterly 1146.

African exemplars.[14] The current durability of authoritarian constitutions, and rise of authoritarian constitutional discourses more broadly, is a more difficult challenge that itself subverts the traditional North/South divide in regard to who learns from who constitutionally and how. Furthermore, while some countries may have become more formally open to the citation of foreign law in constitutional jurisprudence, this borrowing is still highly path- and status-dependent,[15] and belies the fundamental issues of constitutional design influence taken as the more core concern in this chapter.

Promoting pragmatic legal cosmopolitanism thus includes defragmenting and reconstituting many roadblocks. The task may seem daunting given the currently marginal position of comparative law, but, given the sheer volume of comparative legal analysis implicitly begging for the intervention of comparative lawyers as indigenizers, there are many novel and ongoing apertures. While the response argued for here, grounded in a form of competitive national self-interest, may appear unseemly at first to cooperative cosmopolitan sentiments, it is the only way forward that will avert reproducing the damaging parochialism of the past and present opportunities for inviting investment and reinvigoration of comparative legal practice.

B. Comparative Law and National Competition

Imagine the hypothetical where a government seeks to patent a novel regulatory regime. It makes the public claim that it has invested a great deal of time and money sponsoring empirical research to develop the regime, and hopes that the efficiencies it provides will enhance domestic productivity and attract foreign capital. This government further argues that if a nearby country simply copies its regulatory innovation then the return on investment would be lowered to the point that it would make it difficult to pursue developing further such regulatory innovations. The institutional centrepiece of this novel regime is a well-funded national bureau staffed by comparative lawyers evaluating foreign legal developments and selectively adapting them to their own domestic legal system and regulatory ecosystem. The bureau attempts to perform its

[14] Though debates about the future of transformative constitutionalism still has committed adherents, the empirical evidence is sustainable in the negative; David Landau, 'The Reality of Social Rights Enforcement' (2012) 53 Harvard International Law Journal 190.

[15] Erik Voeten, 'Borrowing and Nonborrowing among International Courts' (2010) 39 The Journal of Legal Studies 547.

operations in secret, though its members regularly circulate internationally, and it seeks patent protections only once its recommendations inevitably go public.

From the outset, numerous challenges could be made against recognizing such a patent, and the reasons for the general international reluctance, outside of the United States, to grant business process patents could all be levelled against the claim.[16] But rather than dismissing the claim out of hand, one would at least have to address the claim from the same mix of rationales that are recurrently fought over in promoting patents more generally even for public law innovations. As many now argue, the complexity of modern society makes state regulatory innovation more important to general economic and political performance than at any prior time in history, and here again constitutional frameworks a key aspect of such performance.[17]

At the level of technocratic intuition, the question is certainly plausible. Beyond the usual cost-benefit analysis tied to how patents may or may not promote innovation, this hypothetical also tests rubrics which cast nations as in competition.[18] Certainly a great deal of intranational political discourse currently frames the international arena as a realm of competition, perhaps with greater intensity than has been seen since the Cold War. Are there not then multiple incentives to scour national and subnational regulatory developments for innovations to interrogate? Private corporations are theoretically exposed to greater market discipline, but some often have global economic and social volume equivalent to many nation states—and the persistence of state-owned enterprises blurs this cleavage further. So while it may seem intuitive that businesses deploy resources to evaluate, even illegally appropriate, intra-market innovations by other market actors,[19] certainly there are still many intuitive analogies for why public entities would now similarly operate even when restrained by political processes.

[16] The enabling of business process patents was achieved in *State Street Bank and Trust Co v Signature Financial Group Inc*, 149 F 3d 1368 (Fed Cir 1998), though later limited by *Bilski v Kappos*, 561 US 593 (2010). For a sustained critique of business process patents as one of many failings of US patent law, see James Bessen and Michael Meurer, *Patent Failure* (Princeton UP 2008). For a general defence of US exceptionalism in this arena, see John Duffy, 'Why Business Method Patents?' (2011) 63 Stanford Law Review 1247.

[17] Volkmar Gessner, 'Introduction' in Volkmar Gessner and others (eds), *Rules and Networks* (Hart 2001).

[18] Erik Reinert, 'Emulation Versus Comparative Advantage' in Mario Cimoli and others (eds), *Industrial Policy and Development* (OUP 2009) 79.

[19] The resources devoted to industrial espionage are re-interpreted as a 'learning strategy' tied to corporate organization in Jason Ferdinand and others, 'Re-Theorizing External Learning: Insights from Economic and Industrial Espionage' (2007) 38 Management Learning 297.

The dominant competitive legal discourse of recent decades has primarily prompted calls for deregulation, which, while far more complicated in practice, has presented a sort of vacuum regarding legal institutional design. The idea that innovative public institutions simply do less, or more with less funding and smaller jurisdictional footprints, is a discourse of negation. However, the fall of the Washington Consensus, often tied to this type of regulatory sensibility,[20] was bookended in the 1980s and 2000s by intense debate over the competitive need to understand the success of emergent Japanese or Chinese regulatory patterns, respectively.[21] Indeed, there has been a huge academic surge in comparative regulatory analysis in recent decades, all while fewer clear abstract models of global emulation have endured empirical investigation.[22]

If the competitive frame is at least plausible and the growing ubiquity in legal comparison across the globe undeniable, the question then arises why such national comparative law bureaus are not more common? There are historical examples, for example the projects carried out in Meiji and post-World-War-II Japan that would be difficulty not to characterize as crucial to their national ambitions.[23] There are even contemporary analogues, as many European Union commissions draw on comparative studies in their work,[24] and the Chinese state has directly sponsored comparative legal analysis following its post-1978 reforms.[25] Moreover, the most noted attempts at meta-historical analysis of civilizations invariably advance openness to new ideas as paramount to civilizational rises and xenophobia an invariable signal of civilizational falls. Why are such basic historical truisms recurrently then ignored? Why is there such a stark gap between calls for global knowledge production and limited public investment in the same?[26]

The most telling answer lies at the very heart of the law/politics divide, and reflects the ever-present cultural context of law. Law is never simply about

[20] More accurately, the policies generally associated with the 'Washington Consensus', or 'neo-liberalism' more generally, are described as promoting private regulation rather than 'no' regulation. See John Williamson (ed), *Latin American Adjustment: How Much Has Happened* (Institute for International Economics 1999).

[21] Respectively, Donald Clarke, 'Nothing but Wind? The Past and Future of Comparative Corporate Governance' (2011) 59 American Journal of Comparative Law 75, 83; and Li-Wen Lin and Curtis Milhaupt, 'We are the (National) Champions: Understanding the Mechanisms of State Capitalism in China' (2013) 65 Stanford Law Review 697.

[22] Weitseng Chen (ed), *The Beijing Consensus*? (CUP 2016).

[23] Luke Nottage, 'The Development of Comparative Law in Japan' in Matthias Reimann and Reinhard Zimmerman (eds), *The Oxford Handbook of Comparative Law* (2nd edn, OUP 2019).

[24] For a criticism of comparative formalism in the realization of European harmonization efforts, see Jule Mulder, 'New Challenges for European Comparative Law' (2017) 18 German Law Journal 721.

[25] Zhaoxing Liu and Jinyuan Su, 'Comparative Law in China' (2013) 1 The Chinese Journal of Comparative Law 158.

[26] Mitchell Stevens and others, *Seeing the World* (Princeton UP 2018).

achieving greater efficiencies on agreed upon quantitative scales, though the lasting durability of GDP growth speaks to their persistent attractiveness.[27] Regulation, whether it regards corporate or family law, always implies distributional concerns which implicate entrenched subnational interest groups and potentially gives rise to new ones.[28] Moreover, the symbolic life of the law is intimately tethered to competing moral values that differentially value the terms of any cost-benefit analysis,[29] and is at the heart of public law discourse even when influenced by universalist frames. As a result, attempts to criticize and interrogate reform justifications premised on aggregate growth have devolved into attempts to better articulate shared moral visions for reform movements or mechanisms for managing legal pluralism.[30]

Critical comparative lawyers have long been caught between more cosmopolitan sensibilities and the need to speak out against the type of universalistic formalism that inspires the technocratic utopianism underlying discourses asserting 'best practices' to be transplanted globally.[31] Thus, even as comparative lawyers have consistently lamented the parochialism of their respective national legal cultures, they have been equally apt to point out that bad comparative legal analysis can be worse than none at all.[32] Even some of the more idealistic contemporary acts of constitutional borrowing carried out with reference to legal cosmopolitanism have been subsequently plagued by issues of ineffective indigenization tied to over-idealism and formalism.[33]

This dilemma places the critical comparativist in a bind as to the notion of a regulatory patent, whether constitutional or financial. Journals of comparative law are still suffused with calls for greater academic comparativism, governmental support for comparative law, and the utilitarian advantages that such commitments would provide. Such calls are so prevalent in academic comparative law that one wonders if their retread is as much collective imaginative therapy as scholarly inquiry. At the same time, debates over 'functionalism' in comparative law highlight the many divides over what the applied possibilities

[27] Most alternatives proposed to replace GDP replicate its essentially quantitative cross-national comparability, most classically the Human Development Index inspired by Amartya Sen, *Development as Freedom* (Penguin 1999).

[28] Stephen Golub, 'A House Without a Foundation' in Thomas Carothers (ed), *Promoting the Rule of Law Abroad* (CEIP 2016) 105.

[29] For a critical overview of contemporary writings on the expressive functions of law, see Matthew Adler, 'Expressive Theories of Law' (1999) 148 University of Pennsylvania Law Review 1363. For a recent restatement, see Richard McAdams, *The Expressive Powers of Law* (Harvard UP 2015).

[30] Jedidiah Kroncke, *The Hedonics of Income Security: The Empty Promise of Employment Law Deregulation* (forthcoming 2021).

[31] Günter Frankenberg, 'Constitutional Transfer: The IKEA Theory Revisited' (2010) 8 ICON 563.

[32] Mathias Siems, 'Malicious Legal Transplants' (2018) 38 Legal Studies 103.

[33] Gunther Teubner, 'Legal Irritants' (1998) 61 Modern Law Review 11.

are for comparative legal analysis, if at all. Thus, while many comparativists would dismiss a regulatory patent as either useless, given the limits of regulatory copying, or unnecessary, given its utilitarian failings in genuinely promoting innovation, taking the hypothetical seriously demands a very precise answer as to how comparative law is conceptualized and promoted.

I believe that contemporary critical comparativists cannot avoid promoting comparativism in a competitive framework, even if they are more inclined to cooperative international visions on other arenas. In fact, the framing of national legal debates has already almost universally accepted this frame, and more humanistic rationales for the value of comparative law are unlikely to persuade or engage outside of minor academic audiences. Without public investments in promoting comparative empiricism cited in our earlier patent hypothetical, these debates are in the feckless sense doomed to be solely academic. Framing legal innovation as a global public good, a good that comparative lawyers are best suited to access, evaluate, and adapt for national consumption, is the best way forward to achieve this end. Fortunately, in a world without regulatory patents legal innovation is still a public good in the classic sense, non-excludable, and non-rivalrous. Yet, it is a global public good difficult to access and far from fungible across legal systems and traditions.

For the remainder of this chapter, two aspects of this paradigm will be asserted as crucial for how comparative lawyers promote the public goods frame. The first is that the fundamentally cultural nature of law means that such a promotion project must primarily be one of domestic contention and institutional development. Critical comparativists in Northern countries need to abandon and aggressively critique practices that are premised on the unilateral flow of legal knowledge along traditional asymmetries in national power and academic legal status. More concretely, this necessarily implicates variations on the Northern academic concepts of 'law and development' or 'rule of law promotion' which are premised on such unilateral flow. It is fundamental to recognize that such practices thoroughly vitiate attempts to achieve domestic promotion of the public goods frame in 'developed' legal systems. Simultaneously, the very notion of North/South dichotomy needs to be eventually abandoned to focus on the central issue of power, which is no longer as asymmetric between North/South nations as in early eras and which obscures parallel parochialisms at the regional and intranational levels.

The second crucial aspect of this paradigm is partially a corollary of the first—namely that comparative lawyers have to acknowledge their national groundings, and that their greatest comparative advantage is not in the analysis of law per se, but in how global legal knowledge can be indigenized locally.[34] The overwhelming current dominance of bad comparative legal analysis, often deeply infused with implicit national parochialism masquerading as universalism, requires asserting our place in this intersection—or simply demonstrating in practice that this space necessarily exists. Recognizing these implications also requires recognizing a number of ethical and pragmatic duties for critical comparativists in their institutional and pedagogical roles.

C. Leaving Behind the Parochial Past, Engaging the Global Present

Most every social scientific discipline initially formed in social contexts they sought to explain, but that the later advancement of the discipline would eventually seek to escape. The nineteenth-century intellectual and cultural assumptions in which modern academic disciplines took shape were invariably enmeshed in the powerful draw of global colonialism and the search for explanatory, usually evolutionary, theories of social change.[35] Some disciplines, such as anthropology, still grapple with these legacies very directly, and others, such as economics, have grown assured that their methodological refinements have transcended these earlier ills. Law has always been amidst and between the empirical methodologies of other disciplines as it has sought to assert its internal coherence as an authoritative and legitimate social practice with an often under-theorized relationship to social facts.

Comparative law's historical roots are no exception to other academic disciplines, and in fact comparative legal reasoning was fundamental to the formation of early social theory as well as justifications for colonialism.[36] The cross-cultural context of comparative lawyers has always made their sensitivity to the production of social facts and assumptions unavoidable, and often set them at odds with the demands of self-referential domestic legal practice. One dynamic emergent from this tension is the debate over whether comparative law should be seen as a distinct academic field, or cast as a methodological practice.[37] Tied up in this debate are implicit and explicit assumptions about

[34] For a modern take on social scientific comparison, see Adam Przeworski and Henry Teune, *The Logic of Comparative Social Inquiry* (CUP 1970) and, for an updated review of classic and contemporary debates in comparative law, see Mathias Siems, *Comparative Law* (CUP 2014).

[35] Peter Stein, *Legal Evolution* (CUP 1980).

[36] Robert Launay, 'Montesquieu' in Annelise Riles (ed), *Rethinking the Masters of Comparative Law* (Bloomsbury 2001).

[37] This is not a new debate within comparative law. For defences of comparative law as a discipline, rather than as a method, see Lawrence Baxter, 'Pure Comparative Law and Legal Science in a Mixed Legal System' (1983) 56 Comparative and International Law Journal of Southern Africa 85; and Catherine

who comparative lawyers should be speaking to. And most often comparative lawyers have struggled to find as receptive an audience with their domestic legal peers as they have found in other disciplines whose methodologies they eclectically borrow from.

These issues of audience and self-definition are central to the claim that comparative lawyers need to portray their craft as the indigenization of the global public good that is legal innovation. The desire to define comparative law as a distinct field or discipline is often motivated by establishing its seriousness and coherence in academic terms, with its own resulting internal preoccupations. The history of this debate is intertwined in the discipline's struggle to free itself from the baggage of its historical origins, where it was integral to forming some of the most lasting misrepresentations of non-Western legal practices still in currency among legal and non-legal scholars alike.[38] While a disciplinary conception of comparative law may lend the appearance of scientific coherence, it places comparative lawyers, already relatively marginal in most legal academic cultures, on a defensive retreat to more self-referential conversations.

In parallel fashion, consider academic debate over the adjunct field of 'law and development' which originated as the study of attempts to transplant Western legal institutions to stimulate legal development in lower-income countries. In its Euro-American academic instantiation, law and development has similarly retreated to recurrent debate over whether it is in fact a coherent disciplinary field of inquiry, or more of a methodological sensibility—all in an attempt to distance itself from its ethnocentric origins. In some ways this movement has been positive, as the invocation of 'law and development' in many lower-income countries has had the practical impact of advancing a domestically oriented engagement with global legal innovation stripped of any expectation of export.[39] Yet, it still persists that while law and development as an academic discourse has become more methodologically or cultural respectable,[40] it has done so by becoming highly self-referential in the North and often fully divorced from the many Northern public and private initiatives which

Valcke, 'Comparative Law as Comparative Jurisprudence' (2004) 52 American Journal of Comparative Law 713.

[38] The negative imprint/misuse of Max Weber's early comparative legal sociology is explored in Robert Marsh, 'Weber's Misunderstanding of Traditional Chinese Law' (2000) 106 American Journal of Sociology 281; and Bryan Turner, 'Revisiting Weber and Islam' (2010) 61 The British Journal of Sociology 161.

[39] See eg Diogo Coutinho, 'Linking Promises to Policies' (2010) 3 The Law and Development Review 3.

[40] The best versions of which are explored in Michael Trebilcock and Mariana Prado, *Advanced Introduction to Law and Development* (Edward Elgar 2014).

still purport to export law across presumed asymmetries in legal development.[41] Even comparative constitutional law continues to struggle with what why foreign engagement in domestic reform is ethical in the first instance, even if again non-academic actors seek to influence ongoing reforms.[42]

This turn to academic self-reference is understandable in the North, as the dissonance between attempts to escape the past sins of comparative legal analysis and their deep popular entrenchment in Northern legal cultures is often more attractive than constant critical engagement. Comparativists who proactively engage with the myriad of export projects, some central to national identity as in the United States,[43] risk being dismissed as irrelevant, especially when such practices are still tied to streams of funding far outstripping those dedicated to comparative law as such. Such institutional pressures leave many comparative lawyers wanting to find a coherent place to speak to the vast proliferation of global academic knowledge production while feeling constrained by the very limited spaces in which most lawyers and non-lawyers expect them to operate.

Here then is the counter-intuitive position of the contemporary critical legal comparativist whose skills seem almost universally applicable to a whole host of global debates, but is often almost completely absent from these same debates. We can see this clearly in the emergence of entire disciplinary debates that are concerned with legal innovation but are also devoid of legal analysis and comparative lawyers.

Take, for example, the tellingly named literature on 'public innovation' which has swept over the globe in recent decades. Often academically centred in the field of public management, the early participants in the field followed much the dominant international sensibility of market supremacy, arguing that governments could innovate if they mimicked aspects of the market discipline faced by the private sector—commonly dubbed 'New Public Management'.[44] The field evolved quickly to include the study of public/private partnerships and a new focus on the collaborative production of improved government with civil society constituencies.[45] Institutionally well supported in Nordic countries,[46] this ideal of public innovation has spread worldwide and has inspired

[41] David Trubek, 'Law and Development: 40 Years after Scholars in Self Estrangement' (2016) 66 University of Toronto Law Review 301.

[42] For an interesting pre-modern take, see Andraan Lanni and Adrian Vermeule, 'Constitutional Design in the Ancient World' (2012) 64 Stanford Law Review 907.

[43] Jedidiah Kroncke, *The Futility of Law and Development* (OUP 2016).

[44] Paul Windrum and Per Koch (eds), *Innovation in Public Sector Services* (Edward Elgar 2008).

[45] Christopher Ansell and Jacob Torfing (eds), *Public Innovation Through Collaboration and Design* (Routledge 2014).

[46] Christian Bason, *Leading Public Sector Innovation* (Policy 2010).

sophisticated models for explaining how government practices change and how further innovation can be induced.[47]

The academic and public investments motivated under the rubric of public innovation would make any comparative lawyer envious. The OECD has established an Observatory of Public Sector Innovation; there are think tanks devoted to its study and promotion, notably Denmark's MindLab; an EU Commission on Public Sector Innovation; a Global Public Innovation Network housed at the Ash Center of Harvard's Kennedy School of Government; and now a dedicated Oxford Handbook on Innovation. What is remarkable about the underlying empirical production of the public innovation discourse is that it is engaged in the direct comparative analysis of legal institutions and practices without ever mentioning law, much less comparative law.[48]

Moreover, the critiques outside and within the public innovation discourse lament the very issues at the heart of the politics/law divide at which critical comparativism ideally operates. Many public innovation scholars have noted how hard it is to define 'innovation' in much the same ways as debates over functionalism contend with what is 'better law'.[49] Others note that similar appeals to ideas such as 'evidence-based policymaking' popularized by third-way political administrations have only elided and exacerbated recognizing the contingency of cost-benefit analysis,[50] with some public innovation scholars still looking for technocracy to achieve politics by another name.[51]

A similar example can be made of the debates within political science that directly address how countries adopt or are influenced by policies in other countries, commonly discussed as 'policy diffusion'.[52] There is a whole host of

[47] Mark Considine and others (eds), *Networks, Innovation, and Public Policy* (Palgrave 2009); Eva Sorensen, The Metagovernance of Public Innovation in Governance Networks (2017) 47 The American Review of Public Administration 826.

[48] Note, for example, the near absence of any discussion of law, or politics, in European Commission, *Powering European Public Sector Innovation* (EC 2013) <https://ec.europa.eu/futurium/en/content/powering-european-public-sector-innovation-towards-new-architecture-report-expert-group> accessed 6 July 2020. More sophisticated practitioners within the field address many systemic issues facing implementing public innovation, and they often end up developing phrases like 'organizational location' which often implicate legal institutions and policies without directly naming them as such. Tima Moldogaziev and William Resh, 'A Systems Theory Approach to Innovation Implementation' (2016) 26 Journal of Public and Administrative Research and Theory 677.

[49] Carter Block and Markus Bugge, 'Public Sector Innovation' (2013) 27 Structural Change and Economic Dynamics 133.

[50] Wayne Parsons, 'From Muddling Through to Middling Up' (2002) 17 Public Policy and Administration 43.

[51] For example, it is still common for some public innovation scholars to openly cast innovative government as necessarily less government; Nikhil Sahni and others, 'Unleashing Breakthrough Innovation in Government' (2013) 11 Stanford Social Innovation Review 5.

[52] Lucie Cerna, *The Nature of Policy Change and Implementation* (OECD 2013) <https://www.oecd.org/ education/ceri/The%20Nature%20of%20Policy%20Change%20and%20Implementation.pdf> accessed 15 March 2020.

competing theories and models advanced within these debates, traditionally focused on geographic and ideological proximity, which have expanded to include subnational and transnational units of analysis.[53] Though strains with open normative presumptions exist, especially within strong federal traditions such as that of the United States,[54] the mainstay of this field aspires to be descriptive in orientation.[55]

Here again, if we look to the emergent critiques within the diffusion literature we see parallel concern with the same classic terrains of comparative law. Participants ask if the adoption of a formally similar regulatory regime is really meaningful for consequential change in regulatory practice, and caution how policy implementation is often ignored in the search for universal causal variables.[56] However, even critiques in policy diffusion debates aimed at moving beyond formalism rarely, if ever, mention law, much less comparative law.[57] Notably, one the most widely commented-upon and well-received recent analyses of policy diffusion was by a comparative legal scholar, Katerina Linos, who attempted to bridge this very divide.[58]

It is less necessary here to explore how comparative lawyers could specifically intervene and contribute to such parallel discourses. It is enough to point out that the increasingly refinement of many global reform discourses have moved their participants to face the core issues of formalism and instrumentalism with which comparative lawyers routinely engage. There are a whole host of discrete academic and professional discourses that have emerged in recent decades where there is now a recognized demand for comparative legal analysis.[59] Importantly, what binds these fields together, and is at the heart of the many investments in 'public innovation', is exactly that they have been made with explicit reference to intranational improvement within the frame of international competition.[60]

53 Frederick Boehmke and Paul Skinner, 'State Policy Innovativeness Revisited' (2012) 12 State Politics and Policy Quarterly 1.

54 William Buzbee (ed), *Preemption Choice* (CUP 2009).

55 Fabrizio Gilardo, 'Four Ways We Can Improve Policy Diffusion Research' (2015) 16 State Politics and Policy Quarterly 8.

56 Cerna (n 52).

57 Louisa Parks and Elisa Morgera, 'The Need for An Interdisciplinary Approach to Norm Diffusion' (2015) 24 Review of European Community and International Environmental Law 353.

58 Katerina Linos, *The Democratic Foundations of Policy Diffusion* (OUP 2013). The acclaim and debate over Linos's work is instructive for comparative law given the variety of qualitative and quantitative methods she uses to construct her argument; see 'Book Symposium: "The Democratic Foundations of Policy Diffusion" by Katerina Linos' (*OpinioJuris*, 24 March 2013) <opiniojuris.org/2013/06/24/book-symposium-the-democratic-foundations-of-policy-diffusion-by-katerina-linos/> accessed 15 March 2020.

59 Francesca Bignami and David Zaring (eds), *Comparative Law and Regulation* (Edward Elgar 2016).

60 Charles Shipan and Craig Volden, 'Policy Diffusion' (2012) 20 Public Administration Review 1540.

Herein, comparative lawyers need to make a much stronger claim of specific expertise than is currently common. While declining in recent years, the popularity of the grouping of Brazil, Russia, India, China, and South Africa as emergent 'BRICS' nations sought to question what was presumed as known about the relationship between regulatory structures and national development.[61] This grouping fundamentally challenged corollary presumptions about what global legal expertise was and from where it could be generated.[62] With little surprise, these were all countries where if one were to invoke 'law and development' it would almost always be presumed to mean critical interdisciplinary study of global legal development for domestic consumption.[63]

Whether or not the BRICS framework endures or produces the alternative developmental models which seem ever alluring to some, critiques of international legal knowledge production have noted how greater global legal transparency made the gaps more evident between the legal models that were often sought to be exported and the actual complexities and debates within many Northern countries. This critique is now well worn, but an important implication of the critique is that when pressed, many Northern exporters could rarely make uncontested causal claims about their own legal histories. How did something like 'judicial independence' evolve in England? How important was industrial policy to European economic development? What is the relationship between locally elected sheriffs, prosecutors, and judges in American law and democratic policing? Even so, are not the lessons of Northern legal failures as relevant as legal successes to arguing for law reform more generally?

Thus, while much faith in technocratic views of law spoke to a desire to escape from the overt chauvinism of earlier eras, universalism has been revealed to often recapitulate older evolutionary and colonial sensibilities, especially when wedded with humanitarian intent.[64] Even the most methodologically rigorous comparative scholars have been shown to fail spectacularly when their attempts to advise others have been carried out with little appreciation for local politics.[65] This is the same naïve self-aggrandizement that has left the

61 Gabriel Garcia, 'The Rise of the Global South, the IMF and the Future of Law and Development' (2015) 37 Third World Quarterly 191.

62 Nicole Bodnar, 'What Toronto's Health Experts Can Learn from Brazil' (*UT News*, 5 October 2010) <https://www.utoronto.ca/news/what-torontos-health-experts-can-learn-brazil-howard-hu> accessed 15 March 2020.

63 Mariana Pargendler and Bruno Salama, 'Law and Economics in the Civil Law World: The Case of Brazilian Courts' (2015) 90 Tulane Law Review 439.

64 Guy Sinclair, *To Reform the World* (OUP 2017).

65 Jedidiah Kroncke, 'An Early Tragedy of Comparative Constitutionalism: Frank Goodnow & the Chinese Republic' (2013) 21 Washington Journal of International Law 533.

international human rights discourse beset by growing criticisms, and now facing reinvention or marginalization.[66]

What now strikes even deeper at the heart of a belief in the unidirectional flow of global knowledge, beyond the rise of BRICS or post-colonialism, is the striking rejection of technocracy within many Northern countries themselves—most evident in the most active contemporary global exporter, the United States, and the most active historical exporter, the United Kingdom.[67] The cosmopolitan instincts of many critical comparativists make them rightly cautious about resurgent nativist versions of populism opposed to global technocracy, but such movements do provide an opportunity to take advantage of the renegotiation between the domestic relationship of the global and local in their home countries.

Here we can consider the other thoughtful contributions to this volume that more explicitly engage in deconstructing the North/South concept and its familial cousins like the 'BRICS'. Florian Hoffman in Chapter Two directly confronts the limitations of any oppositional concept such as 'South' that both overgeneralizes the sameness of countries as distinct as China and Belize, while also serving to blunt understanding the vast, and evolving, diversity within the 'North'. Zoran Oklopcic similarly addresses how the 'South' as a counter-concept obscures the fundamental issue of power which acts across any number of dimensions, carrying with it distortion and misrepresentation in its wake. Both Hoffman and Oklopcic speak in different ways about how theoretically useful ideal types become self-reifying as they can help create the empirical impression that they seek to catalogue.

It is important to note that China, and perhaps much of Asia, rarely classifies itself with the term 'South' both in common belonging and in new instantiations of their own influence in other countries—especially if one considers the oppositional Chinese discourse on Indian development. Furthermore, regional dynamics are often just as crucial to presumptions about legal informational flows. Brazil certainty does not see Ecuador as a discursive equal, even as it may borrow regulatory models from Colombia. Trying to place Japan along in this dichotomy is as telling for its consistent absence as it is for its conceptual misfit. And the term North, as the term Western, belies stark differences between and amidst European and Anglo nations that are quite significant. Power operates in gradients, rather than as a binary, so that European courts

66 Ratna Kapur, 'Precarious Desires and Ungrievable Lives' (2015) 3 London Review of International Law 267.

67 Michael Cox, 'The Rise of Populism and the Crisis of Globalisation' (2017) 28 Irish Studies in International Affairs 9.

may appear more cosmopolitan but rarely cite the legal innovations or developments of but a predictable handful of nations, and American legislatures proactively contemplate near nothing at all. Thus, just as the editors of this volume consider comparative constitutional law 'for', 'with', and 'from', we can consider these perspectives regionally and within countries throughout the world.

Perhaps no field of comparative inquiry better addresses the challenge to traditional notions of expertise than that of comparative constitutional law. In many ways, attempts to universalize constitutional law over the past century have been astonishingly successful, where today even formally communist or non-democratic regimes feel compelled to adopt constitutional documents and language.[68] At the same time, the expansion of constitutionalism was in many ways the earliest form of 'law and development', where Northern models, especially that of the United States, were seen as plausibly serving as global templates.[69] There is some intuitive appeal to constitutional borrowing, as constitutional law is taken, especially in democratic regimes, as the apex legal norm-giver which shapes the rest of a country's legal system. If one deems a legal system a 'success' or 'better', then it naturally flows that its constitution would be the best prospect to begin a transplantation analysis.

However, if we fast forward to the turn of the twenty-first century we can see that there is perhaps less settled about what makes a 'good constitution' than when constitution-making became seen as a set demand of being a modern nation-state.[70] The decline in the global reputation of the American constitution in recent decades is dramatic evidence of this shift,[71] even though its abstract example was central to constitutionalism's historical proliferation. Greater knowledge of American constitutional law helps explain part of this decline.[72] In part, there is again no clear, agreed-upon causal story about how the American constitutional model developed, and how it should further evolve. Broad international contempt for historical decisions such as *Dred Scott* or *Korematsu* and contemporary decisions such as *Citizens United* now limit the global influence of American constitutional law and often casts it as outlier rather than exemplar, especially in the realm of constitutional innovation and

[68] Mark Tushnet, 'Authoritarian Constitutionalism' (2015) 100 Cornell Law Review 391.

[69] George Billias, *American Constitutionalism Heard Round the World* (New York UP 2009).

[70] There is still a great deal of fundamental debate about why countries adopt constitutions, and in what form: Tom Ginsburg and Mila Versteeg, 'Why Do Countries Adopt Constitutional Review?' (2014) 30 Journal of Law, Economics, and Organizations 58.

[71] David Law and Mila Versteeg, 'The Declining Influence of the United States Constitution' (2012) 87 New York University Law Review 762.

[72] Heinz Klug, 'Model and Anti-Model' [2000] Wisconsin Law Review 598.

adaptation.[73] In fairness, critiques of the American constitutional tradition have spawned few alternative models, as the unrealized hopes of 'transformative' constitutions suffused with economic and social rights have similarly revealed that constitutions are far more in dialogue with other legal institutions, norms, and social conditions than their formal roles as apex lawgivers would indicate.[74]

Critically, this shift has presented a crisis for comparative constitutionalism as it has questioned the very expertise required to participate in the field. Like other fields of legal export, actual training and status as a comparative lawyer was often seen as unnecessary for the practice of constitutional export, as the unidirectional flow of constitutional knowledge meant that any Northern constitutional scholar (even law students) could participate fully in such debates. It is not unrelated that the precipitous decline of the status of the American constitution had led to a rapid decline in interest in comparative constitutional discourse within the US. If the world is not heading towards a relative end of constitutional history in the liberal American model, then what expertise do American constitutional scholars have to contribute to international constitutional debates? Potentially still a great deal, but not without significant dispositional modification.[75] But in practice there is no contribution without contemplation that foreign constitutional developments are relevant to domestic debates.[76]

It is key to consider that in constitutional law the gaps between the formal and the social life is perhaps the most extreme. Tying formal elements of constitutional to empirical effects in a given society requires mapping a whole host of contested pathways through which constitutional law is interpreted, enforced, and litigated in the first instance. So much of a constitution's impact is the in the now infamous 'shadow' of law and society scholarship, that it demands even greater local knowledge to analyse, much less predict, what any given change might stimulate. Here again the false hope of technocracy has predominated in recent decades. Another contribution of an academic institution like the *VRÜ/WCL* is showing how much greater recognition was given to power and de-idealization in comparative constitutional law that has only

[73] Richard Albert, 'American Exceptionalism in Constitutional Amendment' (2016) 69 Arkansas Law Review 217.

[74] Upendra Baxi and others (eds), *Transformative Constitutionalism* (University of Pretoria Press 2013).

[75] David Law, 'Alternatives to Liberal Constitutional Democracy' (2017) 77 Maryland Law Review 223.

[76] Mattias Kimm and others, 'The End of the "West" and the Future of Global Constitutionalism' (2017) 6 Global Constitutionalism 1.

recently re-emerged in the field.[77] Similarly, the *VRÜ/WCL* has maintained voice for the more humanistic traditions of comparative constitutional law that question whether the social scientific complexity of legal analysis even allows for large-N studies to produce actionable knowledge.[78]

In each of these diverse instances, the relevance and absence of comparative lawyers is directly tied to traps of the past. Traps tied to comparative analysis's tensions with the inherent parochialism of law as a professional discourse, often seen as tangential or hostile to cross-cultural empiricism, as well as to deep unease about the power and pitfalls of an unequal world. For legal humanitarians wedded to the North's parochial past, there is literally nowhere to go except where asymmetries are so great that some are still strategically compelled to accept the presumptions of export. But such space is shrinking, and competitive frames are increasing in popularity as the global order pluralizes. And herein comparative lawyers can find many opportunities.

If we return to the idea of the regulatory patent, we can see that it is less absurd than at first blush once we move away from the assumptions of the twentieth century. Cross-national legal borrowing is complex, contested, and uncertain in outcome. But it is happening, and will continue to happen as long as there is any aspiration for social improvement. Reframing legal innovation as a public good helps to place comparative lawyers in the role of critical indigenizers rather than sideline academic critics, who are, at a minimum, in the least worst position to mediate the challenges of translating global legal innovation into tangible domestic returns on investment.

D. Institutional and Pedagogical Duties of the Critical Comparativist

In the realms of domestic and international legal reform, various critiques of the legacies of ethnocentric parochialism are now well known but often given affirmation that is frustratingly hollow.[79] Yes, everyone knows that politics matter. Yes, everyone knows that power matters. Culture matters. Even those most wedded to technocratic visions of best practices are aware that they

[77] Paul Brietzke, 'Die Schattenseite der Verfassungsvergleichung: Lehren aus der Dritten Welt' (1982) 15 VRÜ/WCL 5.

[78] Armin von Bogdandy, 'Comparative Constitutional Law as a Social Science? A Hegelian Reaction to Ran Hirschl's Comparative Matters' (2016) 49 VRÜ/WCL 278.

[79] Sherally Munshi, 'Comparative Law and Decolonizing Critique' (2017) 65 American Journal of Comparative Law 207.

must make rhetorical gestures to these cautions, even if in practice they return to universalism and presumptions of the unilateral flows of global legal expertise. This is one of the recurrent frustrations of critiques of the implicit comparativism so commonly at work among international institutions, non-governmental organizations, and public or private aid agencies traditionally centred in the North, but now with participants from a wider variety of nations. The critical work of better-known comparativists can be cited but then rendered meaningless in practice by appeal to the practical dictates of necessity or optimism.[80] And as these appeals emerge from those speaking, or attempting to draw resources, from the privileged side of the still very stark inequalities of the global world, the critical comparativist is relegated to an academic curio who should be listened to but not heard too deeply.

It may be that the rise of China and other forerunners of a more multipolar world will increasingly militate against the legacies of the parochial past as international legal discourse moves forward. The competitive frame of the critical comparativist as an indigenizer is already more and more common in the South, buoyed by the fallout of many failed or partial legal imports. But the general fall of the Washington Consensus, coupled with the recent global financial crisis, has led to less introspection than one might have hoped in the North, with the United States still the apex example of this resistance. However large or small the aperture may be in particular countries, framing legal innovation as a public good is just a starting point for the now well-trodden truism about long marches through institutions. As David Kennedy noted twenty years ago, the marginalization of critical comparative perspectives in international governance was a cultural project of institutionalization.[81]

Much of the recent internal dialogue within comparative law has noted all of the ways in which legal comparativism is now globally rife, but undisciplined.[82] There are countries where comparative empiricism has become commonplace in domestic reform discussions,[83] but even here we see that undertheorized borrowing can lead to practical confusion as much as innovation.[84] A key impact of the distortions of past legal parochialism are the underdeveloped mechanisms for critically evaluating Northern legal experiences elsewhere given how commonly these experiences are idealized, and how often the promotion

[80] Kroncke, *Futility* (n 43) 482.
[81] David Kennedy, 'New Approaches to Comparative Law' [1997] Utah Law Review 545.
[82] Maurice Adams and Jacco Bomhoff (eds), *Practice and Theory in Comparative Law* (CUP 2012).
[83] Zhaozing Liu, 'Comparative Law in China' (2013) 1 Chinese Journal of Comparative Law 158.
[84] Wang Jingen and Larry DiMatteo, 'Chinese Reception and Transplantation of Western Contract Law' (2016) 34 Berkeley Journal of International Law 44.

of formal transplants still occurs while actual comparative study of legislative production and implementation remains both understudied and highly underfunded.[85] Moreover, we need to accept that a domestically oriented version of comparative law is one that may always have difficulty speaking to, or often is orthogonal in concern, with courts seeking to adjudicate concrete disputes.[86]

One first step to combat these trends is to aggressively admit that the transplantation discourse is broken. When Alan Watson gave visibility to the concept in his classic work,[87] he was participating in debates about historical influences and changes that were of a qualitatively different sort than, for example, the literal translation and copying of foreign statutes that occurred during some of the post-Soviet transitions. The rise and fall of the 'convergence' debate has undermined conflating transplantation and influence, and provided, for those open to listening, a rich empirical literature for how foreign influences are indigenized in a variety of contexts.[88] This is true in cases where such indigenization first started out as unmediated copying,[89] or in areas where strong convergence claims are still made, such as corporate law,[90] or when such influence represents recent innovations in the most genuine sense, such as legalizing crowdfunding mechanisms.[91]

The very persistence of cruder forms of the transplant discourse are thus rarely the product of comparative lawyers, but stem from the power dynamics and cultural assumptions which impel, but cannot determine, the course of many legal borrowings. Critical comparativists cannot individually transcend power dynamics, so in their roles as scholars and teachers they can only be vigilant about how they relate to adjacent assumptions. Simply producing good and better scholarship itself will never be enough. As such, a first step is not to ignore comparative legal scholarship we do not like,[92] but actively seek out

[85] Nicola Lupo and Lucia Scaffardi, 'Introduction' in Nicola Lupo and Lucia Scaffardi (eds), *The Use of Comparative Law in Legislative Drafting* (Eleven International 2014) 1.

[86] For the ideal that comparative law is often forced out of mainstream legal discourse, as it 'bites the epistemic hand' that feeds it, see Suryapratim Roy, 'Privileging (Some Forms of) Interdisciplinarity and Interpretation' (2014) 12 ICON 786.

[87] Alan Watson, *Legal Transplants* (University of Georgia Press 1993).

[88] Filomena Chirico and Pierre Larouche, 'Convergence and Divergence, in Law and Economics and Comparative Law' in Pierre Larouche and Peter Cserne (eds), *National Legal Systems and Globalization* (Springer 2013) .

[89] Erdem Buyuksagis, 'The Role of Comparative Law' (2017) 42 North Carolina Journal of International Law 626.

[90] David Cabrelli and Mathias Siems, 'Convergence, Legal Origins, and Transplants in Comparative Corporate Law' (2015) 63 American Journal of Comparative Law 109.

[91] Chang-Hsien Tsai, 'Legal Transplantation or Legal Innovation' (2016) 34 Boston University International Law Journal 233.

[92] For a discussion of avoidance of the influential law and finance literature, see Mathias Siems, 'Review of Comparative Law' (2008) 12 Edinburgh Law Review 334.

where it is being used and where comparative legal empiricism can make the greatest impact.[93] We should not be hesitant to engage other interdisciplinary fields,[94] especially given the earlier discussion about fields looking actively at legal innovation but which, in practice, do not take law seriously.[95]

Such a position does make a functionalist approach implicitly necessary. But this does not mean that we have to make wholly deterministic arguments about the relevance of law. If we take the role of indigenizer seriously, there are many domestic contexts in which we do not have to fight as fiercely as when we deal with international legal reform discourse. If we look at the advancements in empirical comparative constitutional law in recent years, we can see that much of the work of de-idealizing constitutional formation in transitional or post-colonial countries has moved the discourse to grapple with the mix of elite interests, popular mobilization, and the limits of rights-litigation that is the norm within domestic debates,[96] especially with populist movements clawing at more cosmopolitan democratic norms.[97] It is not such a change to admit, for example, that courts are highly circumscribed in their ability to build democratic cultures in post-authoritarian contexts given that pro-democratic certainties about constitutional courts in the North have significantly eroded.[98] Similarly, debates over 'rule of law' promotion, while again still sustained by historical parochial inertia, have grown increasingly ambivalent and approximate domestic debates where legalization is not taken as an inherent good.[99]

There are practical limits as to how much of this work any individual scholar can affect, but the one arena in which comparativists can take on a more aggressive cultural role is in their own institutions. Especially for Northern scholars, there is sometimes a noted shyness about how comparative layers interact with their colleagues on issues of international/comparative/transnational law given that our instinct to militate against parochialism means we are hesitant to criticize any investments in these fields, even those that follow old problematic patterns. However, much of the perpetuation of these patterns occurs because Northern academics continue to be naively or wilfully blind to the status and

[93] Mathias Siems, 'Bringing in Foreign Ideas' (2014) 9 The Journal of Comparative Law 119.

[94] Jaakko Husa, 'Interdisciplinary Comparative Law (2014) 9 The Journal of Comparative Law 28.

[95] Ralf Michaels, 'Transnationalizing Comparative Law' (2016) 23 Maastricht Journal of European and Comparative Law 352.

[96] To say this is a recent realization is only to emphasize that mainstream recognition within comparative constitutional law as a discourse centred around Northern law faculties. This muddier reality already had a well-established pedigree. See eg Paul Brietzke, 'The Seamy Underside of Constitutional Law' (1985) 8 Loyola of Los Angeles International and Comparative Law Review 1.

[97] Kim Scheppele, 'Autocratic Legalism' (2018) 85 University of Chicago Law Review 545.

[98] Tom Daly, *The Alchemists* (CUP 2018).

[99] Bryant Garth, 'Issues of Empire, Contestation, and Hierarchy in the Globalization of Law' in Moshe Hirsch and Andrew Lang (eds), *Handbook on the Sociology of International Law* (Edward Elgar 2017).

monetary imbalances between the foreign students and academics with whom they interact. Almost all non-comparative academics who act out old patterns are buoyed by anecdotal validations of their work, asserted to be validated and confirmed by a foreign interlocutor who has strategic self-interests in not overtly challenging their presumptions.[100] Agitating against this implies a duty to critique programming in our institutions that perpetuates export ideals in theory and practice. It is very difficult to engage with programming outside of universities, as it is easy to be ignored by those who answer to funding sources predicated on export ideals. The draw of relevance and funding moves many comparativists to dampen their true thoughts in order to get some measure of engagement with such endeavours, but the last century of export projects has shown that this gives indirect legitimation without any real modification of practices on the ground.

Again, non-participation and critique can only go so far. The real institutional locus of longitudinal import is that of pedagogy and mentoring. There are long-running struggles over pushing legal education to be more catholic in its orientations,[101] and such claims still often break against the shores of professional training or diversion into variations of legal humanitarianism. For domestic students, the best opportunity is to infuse the public goods perspective into the instruction of core classes, and resist compartmentalizing them into discrete elective courses.[102] Humanistic or disciplinary portrayals of comparative law are the least likely to attract students with professional ambitions, but functionalist invocations of the indigenization approach, explicitly or implicitly couched in competitive national terms, are far more likely to draw attention.[103] Here there are many lessons from the critical legal traditions in the South, where solely political critiques of law have failed to penetrate law school curriculums.[104]

At the same time, there is equal worth for making clear to Northern legal students that not all lawyering expertise is expertise. It should be argued aggressively to future lawyers and scholars that if you do not have a critical empirical

[100] Jon Eddy, 'Book Review of "The Export of Legal Education"' (2011) 61 Journal of Legal Education 330.

[101] Catherine Valcke, 'Global Law Teaching' (2004) 54 Journal of Legal Education 160, 169–70.

[102] Jaako Husa, 'Comparative Law in Legal Education' (2018) 52 The Law Teacher 201.

[103] For a partial counterpoint, see Kevin Davis and Xinyi Zhang, 'Who Wants the Global Law School?' (2018) 3 UC Irvine Journal of International, Transnational, and Comparative Law 71 <https://scholarship.law.uci.edu/ucijil/vol3/iss1/4/> accessed 15 March 2020.

[104] There have been individual efforts to introduce more critical perspectives on law into legal teaching in southern legal academies, but this remains the elite exception rather than the systemic rule; Juny Montoya, 'The Current State of Legal Education Reform in Latin America: A Critical Appraisal' (2010) 59 Journal of Legal Education 545.

means for engaging with your own legal system then you cannot move outside of your system in any genuinely productive way. The fact that so many international reform agencies are staffed by former Northern law students who had deep interests in international affairs, but yet felt it unnecessary to engage in comparative or interdisciplinary training, is a failing in development from the beginning of their legal educations rather than simply the product of the perspectives of their ultimate employers. Beyond public or humanitarian efforts, international commercial interests are staffed by Northern lawyers who engage in aggressive lobbying for legal reform along the very same asymmetries of power and wealth.[105]

The most pressing pedagogical duty critical comparativists then have is in disrupting the dominant sociology of international exchanges and teaching. Anthea Roberts's *How Is International Law International Law?* is a properly lauded recent monograph which shows how even in the putatively cosmopolitan realm of public international law there exists a too-often unexamined entrenchment of dominant Northern asymmetries in professional capital.[106] Roberts's work follows other calls for 'comparative international law' which argue that assertions of universalism inherent in international law cloaked very real differences in the domestic life of international law, and reproduced by omission much legal parochialism.[107]

A great deal of this comparative international law scholarship validates many of the long-standing TWAIL (Third World Approaches to International Law) critiques which tried to outline the often compromised position of 'third-world' legal academics and reformers caught between voicing honest critiques of the North and not undermining their own professional capital often predicated on access to elite Northern legal institutions.[108] Too-strident criticisms of Northern parochialism have often led to subtle and not-so-subtle exclusions. Cynthia Farid's exploration of 'legal scholactivists' represents an evolution of such critiques as she notes the tendency of post-colonial critiques to exteriorize blame while obscuring codependency with elite forms of domination

[105] Melissa Durkee, 'International Lobbying Law' (2018) 127 Yale Law Journal 1.

[106] Anthea Roberts, *Is International Law International?* (OUP 2017).

[107] Martti Koskenniemi, 'The Case for Comparative International Law' (2009) 20 Finnish Yearbook of International Law 1; and Boris Mamlyuk and Ugo Mattei, 'Comparative International Law' (2011) 36 Brooklyn Journal of International Law 2.

[108] Antony Anghie and Bhupinder Chimni, 'Third World Approaches to International Law and Individual Responsibility in Internal Conflicts' (2003) 2 Chinese Journal of International Law 77; César Rodríguez-Garavito and Boaventura de Sousa Santos, *Law and Globalization from Below: Towards a Cosmopolitan Legality* (CUP 2005).

in Southern countries where concepts of seniority and self-interest perpetuate patterns of complicity.[109]

This point of elite complexity is critically important because it helps shed light on why countries that have traditionally been moved to act as 'borrowers' do not necessarily always produce better legal outcomes than exporters. The *VRÜ/WCL* is filled with examples of the type of critical learning that occurred across colonial systems, and continues today.[110] But the genre of critique that Farid represents gives personal substance to Oklopcic's concern with how individuals are caught up symbolic systems that they cannot help to replicate once they secure a privileged position within then. William Twining is often cited as a Northern academic who has been willing to be public about the complexities of his own career, expertise, and presumptions in relationship to the thinkers and students from lower-income countries, and how this impacts their lives once their foreign educations are over.[111]

A systemic result of these individual experiences is that even those countries that may be developing more healthy legal cultures in regard to indigenizing legal innovations from abroad still find their process of reception warped by still-extant legacies of educational dominance and mal-distributions of expertise (and who from them speaks with authority about foreign law). For constitutional law, this is often as acute as in the most technocratic regimes of financial regulation, as international career capital is tied too closely to the constitutional courts of specific countries and thus the academic/educational legal complexes they are embedded in. Such dynamics of self-reproduction thus, in turn, affect domestic students in these institutions about the nature of even their own expertise about foreign countries, and this is a key feedback loop in perpetuating anti-learning norms within traditional 'export' countries.

In concrete terms, such extant realities mean it is wholly unacceptable for critical comparativists not to be at the forefront of the administrative and institutional forums of their home institutions relating to foreign engagement. Too many Northern law schools still select their international students and visitors through processes that involve little to no participation, much less leadership, by comparativists. In parallel, too many foreign students and scholars are still presented with forums where they have little support to express themselves free from the need to assuage Northern sensibilities and presumptions. The

[109] Cynthia Farid, 'Legal Scholactivists in the Third World: Between Ambition, Altruism and Access' (2016) 33 Windsor Yearbook of Access to Justice 57.

[110] Heinz Klug, 'Co-operative Government in South Africa's Post-Apartheid Constitution: Embracing the German Model?' (2000) 33 VRÜ/WCL 432.

[111] William Twining, 'Francis Deng on Dinka Culture and Human Rights' (2013) 46 VRÜ/WCL 197.

tyranny of well-intentioned paternalism is the most recurrent private lament of foreign students in Northern legal programs, a lament quietly passed around for fear of losing the very access they will make use of throughout their careers.

Here again the indigenization frame is relevant. A view of legal innovation as a global public good should reflexively push any scholar to ask what they can learn from, even in purely self-interested terms, the legal expertise of their foreign interlocutors. If there is something to be learned from a Northern legal tradition, a Northern scholar is in fact the one least likely to know what exactly this would be for another nation.

We should be equally ready to push hard against a claim that there is nothing to learn, or that past parochialism precludes Northern legal experience from holding only foreign value. Especially as foreign students and scholars grow more aware of the deficiencies of once idealized Northern legal ideas and institutions, we can take a pedagogical position starting from the same presumption that underlies the public good concept of legal innovation—that learning from failure is as relevant as success. It is only from a position as comparativist cum indigenizer that we can expect to have a productive dialogic conversation with interlocutors who are indigenizers by default.

E. Conclusion: Comparative Law as Domestic Reform Stimulus

It is a not uncommon stratagem of comparative lawyers to make reference to the universalist presumptions of empiricism as tactic to, by inference, draw out the applicability of foreign legal experience to domestic issues in the North.[112] At the same time, many comparativists have a deeply ambivalent relationship to large-N quantitative studies that have rapidly overtaken a variety of regulatory discourses. While critical comparativists rightfully chafe at the often incredible coding decisions that reduce global legal diversity to five-point rankings via limited surveys with low response rates,[113] it has to be recognized that the power of such work is grounded in its relative accessibility.[114] If some comparative lawyers are motivated to ignore post-structuralist or purely

[112] For a critical review of the evolution of empiricism and comparative legal analysis, see Volkmar Gessner and Gerd Winter, 'Empiricism and Legal Practice' (2011) 12 German Law Journal 159.

[113] Ralf Michaels, 'Comparative Law by Numbers?' (2009) 57 American Journal of Comparative Law 765.

[114] John Gerring and Craig Thomas, 'A Question of Comparability' in Bertrand Badie and others (eds), *International Encyclopedia of Political Science* (Sage 2011).

culturalist views of the law, they can take full comfort in the fact that few actual legal reformers are otherwise disposed. Yet, while large-N studies can and are improving, their popularity is more forcefully undermined by the fact that they have, with some striking exceptions, regurgitated old presumptions and prescriptions. While much has been made of the rise and fall (and possible re-rise) of the law and finance literature, the lack of real substance to its early forms was that it was simply old arguments retold in different analytic language.[115]

Herein, the concept of critical comparativist as indigenizer will likely always mean that there will be uphill battles being fought. As George Fletcher noted now twenty years ago, if comparative law is not a subversive, radical discipline then it is not functioning properly.[116] Not just in how we may act to impact domestic legal reforms, but in honestly evaluating our own intellectual projects as we examine the volumes of ongoing global legal change whose indigenous relevance requires no trivial amount of effort to truly uncover.

As any honest teacher of comparative law relays to their students, there are difficulties in comparative legal analysis that no amount of time or erudition fully resolve. While the public good conception may not require the depth of analysis required to fully appreciate the internal positions of legal actors in other national systems,[117] it still militates against easy formalism, naïve instrumentalism, and self-aggrandizing idealization. Yes, there will likely be questions of strategy and representation inherent in making any argument for domestic legal reform that flows through political institutions (democratic or otherwise), but this is no different than that of any legal scholar who implicitly acts to better 'develop' their own legal system through their scholarship.

What the public goods frame ultimately achieves then is not just a better position for escaping parochialism, but in constructing a pragmatic cosmopolitanism divorced from the type of universalism that masks more than it informs.[118] It is a type of cosmopolitanism that emerges from pragmatism rather than idealism, but in doing so better blunts the very real inequalities that naïve forms of cosmopolitanism end up reproducing. It achieves this by setting aside the false binary choice of to transplant or not to transplant, and offers up a discourse that acknowledges the reality of the localized values and ecologies

[115] For an early evaluation of the rapid spread of such studies in comparative legal analysis, see 'Evaluating Legal Origins' [2009] BYU Law Review 1413.

[116] George Fletcher, 'Comparative Law as a Subversive Discipline' (1998) 36 American Journal of Comparative Law 683.

[117] Catherine Valcke, 'Convergence and Divergence between English, French and German Conceptions of Contract' (2008) 16 European Review of Private Law 29.

[118] The 'pragmatic cosmopolitanism' cited here is akin to the ideal of 'rooted cosmopolitanism' advanced by Kwame Appiah: Kwame Appiah, *Ethics of Identity* (Princeton UP 2005).

without resort to isolationism or nativism.[119] If there is a historical unfairness it perpetuates, it is that dominant Northern legal forms have been experimented within so many national contexts that there is an unequal opportunity to learn from these experiments for repatriated, self-interested gain.[120]

As alienated as comparative lawyers at times feel from their domestic legal contexts, the struggle to grow a new cosmopolitan discourse is one that first starts at home. In some countries, this may be very difficult given traditional patterns of scholarly progression and recognition within law, but, again, critical comparativists can speak to challenges that are now near-universal in reform debates across disciplines. Moreover, the personal and pedagogical aspects of the indigenizer frame are not solely utilitarian for the Northern academic, they are ethical. We are facing an era where global inequality is self-exacerbating, and the lack of reform, or significant backtracking, in our home nations continues to have an effect abroad. Whatever our competencies, we are still poorly equipped to impact developments abroad except through promoting self-reform and, in turn, emulation. The emergence of the insufficient and distasteful choices of international technocracy or xenophobic nationalism reshaping global politics speaks directly to the nature of opportunities for intervention.[121] We can continue to produce critiques that echo only at the fringes of power, or we can act to reshape a global legal discourse that speaks with our concepts but rarely our sensibilities.

[119] For one recent attempt to argue for a similar version of 'selective exceptionalism', see Mark Rahdert, 'Exceptionalism Unbound: Appraising American Resistance to Foreign Law' (2016) 65 Catholic University Law Review 537.

[120] For a cogent example, see the discussion of US plea bargaining in the context of its introduction into the German criminal law system in Jenia Turner, 'Plea Bargaining and Disclosure in Germany and the United States' (2016) 57 William and Mary Law Review 1.

[121] For a recent take on comparative law and nativism, see Margaret Woo, 'Comparative Law in a Time of Nativism' (2018) 41 Hastings International and Comparative Law Review 1.

PART II

THEMES OF CONSTITUTIONALISM IN THE GLOBAL SOUTH

6

Transformative Constitutionalism as a Model for Africa?

Heinz Klug

A. Introduction

Over the last decade transformative constitutionalism has been embraced as both a normative imperative and description of the relationship between constitutions and society in the global South and with respect to Africa in particular. First coined by American legal academic Karl Klare to explore the relationship between South Africa's new post-apartheid constitutions and the country's conservative legal culture[1] the term has been widely embraced by jurists, academics, and constitutional activists. For some, the concept represents a jurisprudential tool for ensuring that the last wave of postcolonial constitutions fulfil their promise to transform the political and social conditions of inequality and undemocratic governance that have characterized these societies. Others view the concept as simply descriptive of the aspirations and purpose of these constitutions, which should guide the implementation of these new constitutional orders, whether through legislation, executive action, or judicial interpretation. This latter view relies on a broadly descriptive distinction between constitutional orders that are either aspirational or preservative in character. Significantly, all agree that an essential feature of the constitutions, in which the concept of transformative constitutionalism is invoked, is that there is a significant gap between the explicit terms of these constitutions, particularly with respect to the rights they guarantee, and the social, political, and economic realities faced by citizens in these societies.

Within the field of comparative constitutional law, the concept of transformative constitutionalism has as Michaela Hailbronner notes, become a widely used label to describe the activist constitutional jurisprudence of many

[1] Karl E Klare, 'Legal Culture and Transformative Constitutionalism' (1998) 14 South Africa Journal on Human Rights 146.

Heinz Klug, *Transformative Constitutionalism as a Model for Africa?* In: *The Global South and Comparative Constitutional Law.* Edited by: Philipp Dann, Michael Riegner, and Maxim Bönnemann, Oxford University Press (2020). © Oxford University Press. DOI: 10.1093/oso/9780198850403.003.0006

Global South courts.[2] While Hailbronner recognizes that the concept extends beyond the jurisprudence of the courts she also argues that if transformative constitutionalism means anything it cannot simply describe a distinction between the constitutionalisms of the North and South since the German Basic Law among other constitutions outside the Global South was also transformative in its conception and impact.[3] Similarly, when speaking of transformative constitutionalism in Africa it is essential that we understand what the idea of transformative constitutionalism contributes to debates over constitutionalism on the continent. Furthermore, it will be important to understand how the label, *transformative constitutionalism* might shape both local and global understandings of the relationship between constitutional aspirations and the exercise of governance across African jurisdictions. Whether as a model for Africa,[4] or as a conceptual device to understand or criticize the jurisprudence of apex courts,[5] it is important that we understand the use and scope of this concept. We need to understand under what conditions the concept might provide conceptual clarity, offer jurisprudential guidance, or simply serves as a label that gives the impression that a new constitution heralds dramatic social change, regardless of the social reality it constitutes.

Celebration of South Africa's 1996 Constitution as a *transformative constitution* and the obvious gap between the promise of rights and practise of governance in post-apartheid South Africa has produced an increasing wave of criticism.[6] This criticism includes charges that the very idea of *transformative constitutionalism* may be contributing to the increasing disjuncture between the aspirations of the text and the actual experience of the constitutional order.[7] Even as *transformative constitutionalism* is embraced, and used to analyse the role of apex courts across the Global South—including in Brazil, India, and Colombia—these emerging criticisms make it imperative that we understand the different applications of the concept. This is especially true when it applies to a range of vastly different jurisdictions, as is the case when thinking

[2] Michaela Hailbronner, 'Overcoming Obstacles to North–South Dialogue: Transformative Constitutionalism and the Fight Against Poverty and Institutional Failure' (2016) 49 VRÜ/WCL 253.

[3] Michaela Hailbronner, 'Transformative Constitutionalism: Not Only in the Global South' (2017) 65 American Journal of Comparative Law 527.

[4] Eric Kibet and Charles Fombad, 'Transformative Constitutionalism and the Adjudication of Constitutional Rights in Africa' (2017) 17 African Human Rights Law Journal 340.

[5] Oscar Vilhena, Upendra Baxi, and Frans Viljoen (eds), *Transformative Constitutionalism: Comparing the Apex Courts of Brazil, India and South Africa* (Pretoria University Law Press 2013).

[6] Laurie Nathan, 'Mind the Gap! The Constitution as a Blueprint for Security' in Kristina Bentley, Laurie Nathan, and Richard Calland (eds), *Falls the Shadow: Between the Promise and the Reality of the South African Constitution* (UCT Press 2013) 1.

[7] Sanele Sibanda, 'Not Purpose-Made! Transformative Constitutionalism, Post-Independence Constitutionalism and the Struggle to Eradicate Poverty' (2011) 22 Stellenbosch Law Review 482.

of its use in discussing constitutional developments across a continent as expansive and diverse as Africa. This chapter will first outline the various ways in which *transformative constitutionalism* has been invoked, debated, and criticized before turning to consider how it might be useful in the broader context of constitutionalism in Africa. In taking this approach, I want to explicitly distinguish between the discussion of *transformative constitutionalism* as an interpretative method in constitutional jurisprudence or as a means of categorization in comparative constitutional discussions and the embrace of the concept as a model for advancing social change by constitutional means. While Klare seemed to embrace both these meanings—conceptual tool and model for change—in his initial articulation of the concept, it is only through focusing on the broader use of the concept—distinguishing aspirational and preservative constitutions—that I believe the idea will make a useful contribution to the struggle over constitutionalism in Africa.

B. How to Understand Transformative Constitutionalism?

There are today at least four broad approaches to *transformative constitutionalism*. First, as a project of constitutional interpretation. Second, as a comparative lens through which to distinguish constitutions in the Global North and South. Third, as a means of distinguishing between preservative and transformative constitutions.[8] And fourth, as representing a specific constitutional vision in which the constitution serves as both a symbol, means, and commitment to transform a society. In addition to these four approaches, I want to suggest a fifth approach. Here we might also conceive of *transformative constitutionalism* as providing a conceptual arena in which to develop a socio-legal understanding of how a specific constitutional order emerges. This approach would seek to understand how any constitutional order is constituted—by the institutions, practices, and politics the constitution in any specific society enables, frustrates, or stands in contrast to. This I suggest would serve to promote a sociological understanding of the work that constitutions do.

Most discussions of *transformative constitutionalism* focus on the role of apex courts in interpreting constitutional provisions, especially the jurisprudence of socio-economic and other third or fourth generation rights. It was this approach, framed as the task of interpreting a new constitution that aimed

[8] Daniel Bonilla Maldonado (ed), *Constitutionalism of the Global South: The Activist Tribunals of India, South Africa, and Colombia* (CUP 2013).

to induce significant social change, which was the focus of Klare's original article in which the term *transformative constitutionalism* was first coined. Klare recognized the potential for South Africa's new constitutional order to facilitate a process of peaceful social change but raised concerns about how a legal profession, with judges and lawyers steeped in legal positivism, would manage this interpretative task. The debate that followed in South Africa took various directions. First, many commentators agreed with Klare's description of the Constitution as 'post-liberal', especially in its inclusion of justiciable socio-economic and other positive rights, and therefore requires an interpretative approach that seeks to achieve the transformative goals of the Constitution. However, others, most notably Theunis Roux, argued that a Dworkinian approach to rights is an equally valid, if not a superior approach, to interpretation.[9] A second approach, adopted by justices of the Constitutional Court, embraced the idea of transformative constitutionalism as legitimizing their role in ensuring that the Constitution is central to the building of a post-apartheid society.[10] Finally, Sanele Sibanda and others have taken a more critical attitude to the idea of *transformative constitutionalism*. They ask why, instead of judging the progress of constitutionalism in South Africa from the perspective of the interpretation of rights, including 'questions of how access to courts, the right to equality or socio-economic rights impact upon or are impacted upon by poverty', is it not more important to question what exactly 'the relationship of constitutionalism to the eradication of poverty is?'[11]

The second context in which the idea of *transformative constitutionalism* has become a significant marker has been in the assertion of an alternative approach to comparative constitutionalism, one in which the dominant North/South comparison is refocused to consider the distinct contributions of constitutions and apex courts in the Global South—predominantly the courts of Brazil, Colombia, India, and South Africa.[12] This approach is rooted in the notion that transformative constitutionalism is related to the idea of transitional justice in that these constitutions are 'meant not only to redress past wrongs but also as "an enterprise of inducing large-scale social change through

[9] Theunis Roux, 'Transformative Constitutionalism and the Best Interpretation of the South African Constitution: Distinction Without a Difference?' (2009) 20 Stellenbosch Law Review 258.

[10] Pius Langa, 'Transformative Constitutionalism' (2006) 17 Stellenbosch Law Review 351; Dikgang Moseneke, 'Transformative Constitutionalism: Its Implications for the Law of Contract' (2009) 20 Stellenbosch Law Review 3.

[11] Sanele Sibanda, 'Not Purpose-Made! Transformative Constitutionalism, Post-Independence Constitutionalism and the Struggle to Eradicate Poverty' (2011) 22 Stellenbosch Law Review 483.

[12] Vilhena, Baxi, and Viljoen (n 5).

non-violent political processes grounded in law" '.[13] From this perspective constitutions 'may be considered transformative both in process and product'[14] in that they emerge from processes of political change—whether postcolonial, post-authoritarian, or post-apartheid—and often involve increased public participation or democratic processes in their creation and are transformative as opposed to preservationist in their goals. Upenda Baxi, noting that the claims of transformative constitutionalism 'assign a world historic meaning to the making and interpreting of postcolonial constitutions',[15] argues that while transformative constitutionalism is presented as a promise to recognize 'human rights, democracy and peaceful co-existence and development opportunities' it is equally possible 'that post-colonial constitutional elites may also use this rhetoric to mask constitutional *regression*' (emphasis in original).[16] As such Baxi concludes that '[t]ransformative constitutionalism presents a distorted lens . . . asking "what is transformed and what is left intact" by the acts of making constitutions . . .'.[17]

1. Constitutions as bridges or agents of change

Whether understood as a method of interpretation or as the constitutionalization of fundamental principles to build more equal societies, the central assumption of most of the literature on *transformative constitutionalism* is that the constitution provides an imperative for progressive social change. This is a perspective that stands in direct contrast to those who argue that constitutions are pacts established to preserve particular pre-constitutional interests, especially in post-conflict situations.[18] In the South African debates over *transformative constitutionalism* this imperative has centred around two distinct concepts. First, there has been the metaphor of a bridge introduced by legal academic Etienne Mureinik who suggested that the bill of rights adopted in the 1993 'interim' Constitution would serve as a bridge over which the society would pass in the creation of a society based on the justification of all

[13] Juan E Mendez, 'Constitutionalism and Transitional Justice' in Michel Rosenfeld and Andras Sajo (eds), *The Oxford Handbook of Comparative Constitutional Law* (OUP 2012) 1283.
[14] ibid.
[15] Upendra Baxi, 'Preliminary Notes on Transformative Constitutionalism' in Vilhena, Baxi, and Viljoen (n 5) 20.
[16] ibid 23.
[17] ibid.
[18] Ran Hirschl, *Towards Juristocracy: The Origins and Consequences of the New Constitutionalism* (Harvard UP 2004); Rosalind Dixon and Tom Ginsburg, 'The South African Constitutional Court and Socio-Economic Rights as "Insurance Swaps"' (2011) 4 Constitutional Court Review 1.

forms of public power.[19] A second conception of *transformative constitutionalism* is centred around the inclusion of social and economic rights in the final 1996 Constitution. This latter conception is the one that has been globalized through the idea that the inclusion of social and economic rights as justifiable rights—through explicit inclusion in constitution-making or through judicial interpretation—in Constitutions in the global South has produced a new and dynamic form of constitutionalism in which the global South is setting an example of peaceful, progressive social change for the world.

While Klare initially conceived of *transformative constitutionalism* in response to Mureinik's metaphor of the bridge, his focus was on the limits the existing conservative legal culture would pose. Klare was concerned that the assertion of traditional common law conceptions of legal processes, and the distinction between the public and private exercise of power, could frustrate the fulfilment of the promise of constitutional change. Recognizing that the goal of the post-apartheid constitutional order is to achieve peaceful yet meaningful social change, Dennis Davis later joined Klare in raising important concerns about the limits to legal change inherent within the existing legal system.[20] The academic embrace of *transformative constitutionalism* in South Africa has however taken a number of different directions.[21] The dominant discussion has focused on the implications of a transformative conception of the constitution for the implementation of the social and economic rights guaranteed in the 1996 Constitution.[22] Here there has been both critical and celebratory analysis of the socio-economic jurisprudence of the Constitutional Court as well as discussion of the difficulty of interpreting and applying these rights in the context of the country's vast social and economic disparities as well as an imperative to address poverty.[23] Another line of discussion has focused more specifically

[19] Etienne Mureinik, 'A Bridge to Where? Introducing the Interim Bill of Rights' (1994) 10 South African Journal on Human Rights 31, 32.

[20] Dennis M Davis and Karl Klare, 'Transformative Constitutionalism and the Common and Customary Law' (2010) 26 South African Journal on Human Rights 403; Dennis Davis, 'Elegy to Transformative Constitutionalism' in Henk Botha, Andre van der Walt, and Johan van der Walt (eds), *Rights and Democracy in a Transformative Constitution* (Sun Press 2003) 57.

[21] Henk Botha, Andre Van Der Walt, and Johan Van Der Walt (eds), *Rights and Democracy* (Sun Press 2003) and Solanga Rosa, Transformative Constitutionalism in a Democratic Developmental State (2011) 3 Stellenbosch Law Review 542.

[22] Marius Pieterse, 'What Do We Mean When We Talk about Transformative Constitutionalism' (2005) 20 South African Public Law 155; Sandra Liebenberg, 'Needs, Rights and Transformation: Adjudicating Social Rights' (2006) 1 Stellenbosch Law Review 5; Eric C Christiansen, 'Transformative Constitutionalism in South Africa: Creative Uses of Constitutional Court Authority to Advance Substantive Justice' (2010) 13 The Journal of Gender, Race & Justice 575.

[23] Pius N Langa, 'The Role of the Constitution in the Struggle Against Poverty' (2011) 3 Stellenbosch Law Review 446; Karl Klare, 'Concluding Reflections: Legal Activism After Poverty Has Been Declared Unconstitutional' (2011) 3 Stellenbosch Law Review 865; Malcolm Langford and others (eds), *Socio-Economic Rights in South Africa: Symbols or Substance?* (CUP 2014); Kirsty McLean, *Constitutional Deference, Courts, and Socio-Economic Rights in South Africa* (Pretoria University Law Press 2009).

on the tension between prevailing common law understandings of legal rights, particularly property rights, and the statutory and constitutional imperatives to achieve greater equality, whether through limits on the traditional powers of eviction or in the promise of land restitution and redistribution.[24] A third set of arguments have taken the concept of *transformative constitutionalism* as a tool of critique and even suggested that it provides no single goal but rather suggests that there should be a constant striving for social change within the judicially bound interpretation of the constitution.[25]

In contrast to these more prosaic academic discussions over methods of interpretation and comparative constitutionalism, a third approach to *transformative constitutionalism* has been that taken by justices of the Constitutional Court in South Africa as well as some academics and political leaders. This approach focuses on the Constitution itself as providing a mandate for social change and is best viewed through the prism of constitutional implementation rather than simply interpretation. From this perspective *transformative constitutionalism* is not merely about modes of interpretation but rather involves a 'broader idea of the constitutional project in which the Court is a participant'.[26] This approach is reflected in the views of South Africa's Constitutional Court justices, from the first President of the Constitutional Court and later Chief Justice Arthur Chaskalson, who stated that

> in a society in which there are great disparities in wealth . . . . [where millions live in] deplorable living conditions and poverty . . . a commitment to address and to transform our society into one in which there will be human dignity, freedom and equality, lies at the heat of our new constitutional order.[27]

His successor as Chief Justice, Pius Langa, embraced *transformative constitutionalism* as 'a magnificent goal for the Constitution'[28] which he saw as the 'establishment of a truly equal society'[29] but also noted that 'transformation is

[24] Andre van Der Walt, 'Exclusivity of Ownership, Security of Tenure and Eviction Orders: A Critical Evaluation of Recent Case Law' (2002) 18 South African Journal on Human Rights 371; Frank I Michaelman, 'Liberal Constitutionalism, Property Rights, and the Assault on Poverty' (2011) 22 Stellenbosch Law Review 706; Heinz Klug, 'Decolonization, Compensation and Constitutionalism: Land, Wealth and the Sustainability of Constitutionalism in Post-apartheid South Africa' (2018) 34 South African Journal on Human Rights 469.

[25] Karin van Marle, 'Transformative Constitutionalism As/And Critique' (2009) 2 Stellenbosch Law Review 286.

[26] James Fowkes, *Building the Constitution: The Practice of Constitutional Interpretation in Post-Apartheid South Africa* (CUP 2016) 121.

[27] *Soobramoney v Minister of Health*, KwaZulu-Natal [1997] ZACC 17, 1998 (1) SA 765 (CC) [8].

[28] Langa, 'Transformative Constitutionalism' (n 10) 352.

[29] ibid 353.

not the responsibility that must be borne by the courts alone—it is a task for all three arms of Government to perform in partnership'.[30] Speaking on the implications of *transformative constitutionalism* for the common law and the law of contract specifically, Deputy Chief Justice Dikgang Moseneke noted that

> transformative constitutionalism is certainly not an event . . . [it's] a process that all wielders of public and private power are duty-bound to advance . . . [and as such] courts will increasingly give effect to the ideals of our Constitution and hopefully to the benefit of all concerned.[31]

In addition to these four broad approaches to *transformative constitutionalism*—the interpretative, the comparative, and the symbolic or mandatory—I want to suggest that the idea of *transformative constitutionalism*, particularly in its comparison to preservative constitutionalism, may in addition serve as a useful yardstick in exploring and evaluating different constitutional orders and their implementation. While implicit in the four existing approaches, this approach, in the spirit of the New Legal Realism, asks us to consider and evaluate the role a constitution is playing in any specific social context: whether it is being used to support, challenge, or change the status quo; if it is simply floating above the society; or if its deployment in either a transformative or preservative role is likely to support or undermine the sustainability of the constitutional order more broadly. Significantly, while this use of the idea may be rooted in the recent history of postcolonial or Southern constitutional developments, it makes the concept relevant to socio-legal studies of constitutions more globally. From this perspective, constitutions and their interpretation by courts, social movements, and political elites, have always served as points of reference in social, economic, and political struggles, and the usefulness of the concept of *transformative constitutionalism* is in its normative framing of the direction in which constitutional change is flowing. Unlike the call to see *transformative constitutionalism* as a metaphoric bidirectional bridge or even as a permanent ideal, as a space between an unstable past and an uncertain future,[32] this approach holds up *transformative constitutionalism* as a normative yardstick to explore whether the constitutional order is facilitating processes of social change that

[30] ibid.

[31] Moseneke, 'Transformative Constitutionalism' (n 10) 13; Dikgang Moseneke, 'The Fourth Bram Fischer Memorial Lecture: Transformative Adjudication' (2002) 18 South African Journal on Human Rights 309.

[32] Andre van der Walt, 'Dancing with Codes: Protecting, Developing and Deconstructing Property Rights in a Constitutional State' (2001) 118 South African Law Journal 258, 295–97.

are progressing towards, in Justice Langa's terms, 'the establishment of a truly equal society and the provision of basic socio-economic rights to all'.[33]

C. Constitutionalism in Postcolonial Africa

Before considering *transformative constitutionalism* in Africa, beyond the borders of South Africa, it is essential that we first consider the brief history of formal constitutionalism in Africa. While it is generally accepted that the first round of postcolonial constitutions failed to bring constitutionalism to Africa, the last quarter century has seen constitutional change once again sweep across Africa, with all but nine of Africa's fifty-five internationally recognized states adopting completely new constitutions. Despite these changes, Afro-pessimism[34] leads many to question the salience of these constitutional developments in Africa given the sad history of military dictatorships, corruption, and state failure that characterized the immediate postcolonial era. Regardless of this legacy, any analysis of constitutionalism in Africa must begin from the understanding that Africa is a vast and diverse continent and any notion of a singular culture, historical trajectory or constitutional form would be a gross simplification. Even if it is possible to identify broad historical patterns etched into the political landscape of Africa by the colonial experience and nationalist struggles which produced independent African states from 1957 until the formal end of apartheid in South Africa in 1994, these commonalities overlay vast cultural, economic, ethnic, language, and political differences. Furthermore, the emergence of postcolonial independent states spans a period of nearly half a century and while the cold war was a common element through most of this period, it was the end of the cold war in 1989 that both allowed the decolonization of Namibia and the democratic transition from Apartheid. Simultaneously, this global shift fragmented the established postcolonial order throughout Africa, leading to a second, more autochthonous, wave of constitution-making in sub-Saharan Africa.

This turn to constitutionalism, in which single-party and military dominated states held multi-party elections and installed new democratic governments, sought to address what the World Bank had identified in 1989 as Africa's governance problem. It is in this context that the discussion of *transformative*

[33] Langa, 'Transformative Constitutionalism' (n 10) 353.

[34] Mahmood Mamdani, *Citizen and Subject: Contemporary African and the Legacy of Late Colonialism* (Princeton UP 1996).

constitutionalism in Africa is taking place. At the same time, recent history and continuing civil and military conflicts as well as incidents of state failure, genocide and international interventions, makes it clear that the continent's constitutional malaise lies deeper than the simple design of new democratic constitutions. Reviewing the history of constitution-writing in Africa Martin Chanock argued that the practice of constitution-making has remained top-down, resulting in

> the writing of increasingly complex constitutions, with increasingly sophisticated institutions and rights guarantees, which have, as has been shown time and time again, floated meaninglessly above the societies for which they have been designated, until the bubble bursts in outbreaks of violence.[35]

Chanock's critique is of course only the latest in a series of analyses that have questioned the place of constitutions and constitution-making in Africa. While HWO Okoth-Ogendo eloquently critiqued the first wave of postcolonial constitutions as producing 'constitutions without constitutionalism',[36] other participants in a conference on 'State and Constitutionalism in Africa', held in Harare, Zimbabwe in May 1989—on the verge of the second wave of postcolonial constitution-making—heralded the possibility of a new, popular democratic constitutionalism. Describing this opportunity, Issa Shivji spoke of a 'new concept of constitutionalism [that] should rest on [an] accountable/responsive state and collective rights/freedoms'.[37] Other African voices, including Muna Ndulo, who sees constitution-making in Africa as essential to the establishment of good governance necessary for economic development[38] and Yash Ghai, who as both an analyst and practitioner of constitution-making in Africa promoted popular participation in the constitution-making process,[39] view constitution-making as a path to building effective government and a culture of human rights in Africa. In my own work on South Africa I have reflected on the process of constitution-making and how it took place within a

[35] Martin Chanock, 'Constitutionalism, Democracy and Africa: Constitutionalism Upside Down' in Stephen Ellmann, Heinz Klug, and Penelope Andrews (eds), *Law and Context: For Martin Chanock: Essays on Law and Society* (Federation Press 2010) 126.

[36] HWO Okoth-Ogendo, 'Constitutions Without Constitutionalism: Reflections on an African Political Paradox' in Issa Shivji (ed), *State and Constitutionalism* (SARDC 1991) 3.

[37] Issa Shivji, 'State and Constitutionalism: A New Democratic Perspective' in Issa Shivji (ed), *State and Constitutionalism* (SARDC 1991) 39.

[38] Muna Ndulo, 'Constitution-Making in Africa: Assessing Both the Process and the Content' (2001) 21 Public Administration and Development 101.

[39] Yash Ghai and Guido Galli, *Constitution Building Processes and Democratization* (IDEA 2006) <https://www.idea.int/publications/catalogue/constitution-building-processes-and-democratization?lang=en> accessed 9 December 2019.

global context which framed the opportunities for local innovation as well as a national history and culture that shaped alternatives and imposed a certain path dependency on the options that were embraced.[40]

Adopting Montesquieu's idea that constitutions are reflections of the societies they constitute, Ndulo quotes Ismail Mohammed, the late Chief Justice of South Africa, who described a constitution as 'not simply a statute which mechanically defines the structure of government and the relations between the government and the governed . . . [but as a] 'mirror reflecting the soul', the identification of the ideals and aspirations of a nation'.[41] While this popular and symbolic notion of a constitution is central to the legitimating function of constitutionalism and is regularly embraced by constitution-makers, judicial interpreters of constitutional meaning and advocates of constitutional patriotism, a more sociological conception of constitutions understands them to be social phenomena that serve the essential role of organizing, establishing, and conserving public and social power in society. Drawing from Chris Thornhill's recent book, *A Sociology of Constitutions*, in which he concludes 'that constitutions are functional preconditions for the positive abstraction of political power and, as such, they are also, over longer periods of time, highly probable preconditions of institutions using power: that is states',[42] I would argue that any understanding of constitutional orders in Africa today requires a renewed appreciation of the character of the postcolonial state and specifically its genealogy in colonialism and decolonization.

One explanation for the phenomena of thin constitutionalism in Africa, reflected in both the Harare discussions in 1989 and Chanock's characterization of the products of constitution-making 'floating meaninglessly above the societies for which they have been designated',[43] is that there is a fundamental incongruence between the new institutional architecture they offer and the institutional legacies that remain dominant within those societies. If constitution-makers fail to address the specific institutional and historical forms of governance that dominate society, it should not be a surprise when past legacies frustrate the aspirations of new constitutions and nations.[44] In the literature on the state in Africa there are two key perspectives that I believe are of direct significance to the task of identifying and conceptualizing issues

[40] Heinz Klug, *Constituting Democracy: Law, Globalism, and South Africa's Political Reconstruction* (CUP 2000); Heinz Klug, *The Constitution of South Africa: A Contextual Analysis* (Hart 2010).
[41] Ndulo (n 38) 108.
[42] Chris Thornhill, *A Sociology of Constitutions* (CUP 2013) 372.
[43] Chanock (n 35) 127.
[44] Pierre Englebert, *Africa: Unity, Sovereignty & Sorrow* (Lynne Rienner 2009).

important to constitutionalism on the continent. First, there is the view that the colonial state in Africa has a generally common form and that the specific features of this form defines patterns of governance despite the vast diversity of African societies.[45] Second, that the history of constitutionalism in postcolonial Africa reflects the continued influence of both this colonial legacy as well as the common history of decolonization, or what Crawford Young describes as the code of decolonization.[46]

Despite these and many other contributions to our understanding of constitutionalism in Africa, the puzzle is to explain the similarities in Africa's postcolonial constitutional experience—weak administrations, patrimonial forms of leadership and governance, coups and authoritarianism—despite repeated adoptions of formal democratic constitutions. While Chanock's point, that 'working constitutionalist democracies are rare,' and that '[f]ailure to establish democratic constitutionalist states is not a peculiarly African failure'[47] is well taken, any attempt to understand constitutionalism in Africa must begin by seeking to understand both the sources of commonality as well as possible sources of variation that characterize these constitutional orders. While Africans shared a variety of colonial experiences—depending on the identity of the colonial power and the extent of colonial settlement—they also shared a significant feature of the process of decolonization, a process of constitution-making in which the key element was the transfer of power to those struggling to be free from colonization.[48] Thus, the first postcolonial constitutions were largely negotiated instruments in which the nationalist parties were centrally concerned with their ability to exercise power as representatives of a new nation and thus they accepted many specific constitutional formulations largely designed by the retreating colonial authorities. Even if these constitutions sought, in a variety of creative ways to address what their designers thought were the underlying problems facing the newly independent states—such as ethnic diversity and legal pluralism—their foreshortened lives reflect the fact that they were not embraced—neither by those who were to govern through the institutions and structures they created, nor by the governed, who often rejoiced at their demise, rather than defending them as reflecting their own social and political aspirations.

[45] Mamdani, *Citizen and Subject* (n 34).

[46] Crawford Young, *The Postcolonial State in Africa: Fifty Years of Independence, 1960–2010* (University of Wisconsin Press 2012).

[47] Chanock (n 35) 127.

[48] John Hatch, *A History of Postwar Africa* (Praeger 1965) 387–404; Thomas Hodgkin, *Nationalism in Colonial Africa* (New York University Press 1957) 187–90.

It is in this context that the idea of *transformative constitutionalism* seeks to offer a new model for African constitutionalism, if not for the Global South more generally. Under this conception, model constitutions will serve to drive democratic and economic change to ensure that the aspirations of political and economic participation and security are realized in the relevant constitutional orders. In this vision of a model of *transformative constitutionalism*, in which social change is driven by constitutional imperatives, there is a significant reliance on the recognition and upholding of rights. However, this rights-oriented vision does not rely simply on individual rights but rather places the juridification of collective social and economic rights at the centre of the model. While most sophisticated proponents of *transformative constitutionalism* acknowledge that the implementation of social and economic rights is a complex proposition, the basic premise is that the ability of communities and advocates to challenge the failures of government programmes and implementation in the courts has the important effect of empowering marginalized sections of society. From this perspective, *transformative constitutionalism* not only supports a particular interpretation of the constitutional text but also serves as a symbolic guide to democratic politics in which elected officials and parties are to be judged by their promise and ability to fulfil the constitutional mandate for the progressive realization of a more equal society.

While the post-cold-war embrace of constitutionalism across Africa was greeted with great anticipation and hope, in the years since a greater sense of realism and caution has taken hold. At the same time, there has been a shift, unlike the overthrow or abandonment of constitutions that followed the demise of the first generation of postcolonial constitutions, to a new mode of 'regression' in which ruling elites have made repeated attempts to refashion the existing constitutions to serve their own interests. The most explicit example has been the introduction of constitutional amendments to remove presidential term limits that were originally introduced to ensure that incumbent power did not become too entrenched.[49] Political elites have also learned that judicial control is a relatively weak mechanism and that they can achieve some of their goals by simply gaining control over the levers of state power and engaging in forms of *lawfare* in which they rely on the gradual pace of the law or use the appointment process to get friendly judges,[50] weak prosecutors, and paralyzed

[49] Robyn Dixon, 'Rwandian President Becomes Africa's Latest to Seek Extended Time in Power' *Los Angeles Times* (Los Angeles, 2 January 2016); Alfredo Tjiurimo Hengari, 'Presidential Term Limits: A New African Foreign Policy Challenge' South African Institute of International Affairs, Foreign Policy Programme, Policy Briefing 138, June 2015.

[50] See John Hatchard, Muna Ndulo, and Peter Slinn, *Comparative Constitutionalism and Good Governance in the Commonwealth: An Eastern and Southern African Perspective* (CUP 2004) 317–19.

institutions. Increasingly, they have also embraced different means to tilt electoral contests in their favour, whether through the suppression of the political opposition or through the use by incumbents of both legal and illegal means to guarantee their victory at the polls.[51] As a result, there have been repeated challenges to the validity of elections and cases in which there was either a negotiated outcome, in which governments of national unity were established, or where the results of the election were simply ignored, or the polls officially cancelled. Corruption has also continued to be a major concern with direct consequences for the rule of law and constitutionalism more generally. Even as new constitutions have introduced new independent institutions to oversee elections and combat corruption and even an Implementation Commission in the case of Kenya to ensure that the Constitution is effectively implemented, there remain significant challenges to the consolidation of constitutionalism in Africa.

D. Transformative Constitutionalism and Constitutional Models

Before we assume that *transformative constitutionalism* is, as Eric Kibet and Charles Fombad argue, 'an ideal model to anchor constitutionalism and respect for human rights in Africa',[52] we need to recognize that there are contending constitutional models across the continent. If, for example, we compare apex courts addressing constitutional questions we will find significant institutional differences between constitutional and supreme courts in commonwealth countries in Southern and Eastern Africa as compared to the constitutional councils that are typical among the francophone countries of Francophone West Africa. Despite these institutional distinctions there are even more significant distinctions to be drawn between constitutional orders in Africa. On the one hand, there are a range of constitutional orders that we might consider to be within the realm of democratic constitutionalism, whether we look to the explicitly democratic constitutional orders of South Africa and Kenya or to the constitutions of various African countries that are formally democratic, such as Botswana and Nigeria, but which do not overtly embrace judicial supremacy as a central aspect of their constitutional systems. At the other

[51] Lloyd Sachikonye, *When a State Turns on its Citizens: Institutionalized Violence and Political Culture* (Jacana 2011).
[52] Kibet and Fombad (n 4) 340–66.

extreme are countries in which single families or parties continue to rule in the authoritarian mode that was not completely extinguished at the end of the cold war. Significantly, there is also another post-cold-war model of governance, which features regular elections but is combined with an illiberal or semi-authoritarian constitutional order, framed as non-party states or ones in which a dominant party uses different means to sustain themselves in power. These cases, such as Uganda and Rwanda, have been increasingly advanced as an alternative model of governance in Africa.

Astounded by the economic recovery of post-genocide Rwanda, many commentators praise President Paul Kigame and argue that Rwanda is a viable model for democratic development in Africa. These sentiments both fail to closely examine the structure and workings of Rwanda's constitutional order and serve to undermine the rather messy attempts to promote democratic constitutionalism in Africa by asserting that the semi-authoritarianism of the Kigali government is a productive alternative under the existing conditions of social and economic conflict in Africa. Whether premised on economic envy, guilt for failing to intervene in the genocide against the Tutsi inhabitants of Rwanda in 1994, or because of a concern that violence may overwhelm societies where a strong man is presently seen to be a source of political and economic stability, the outcome is the same—an acceptance of different forms of authoritarianism in Africa today. While the African Union, with its peer review mechanism and commitment to democratic governance among the member states of Africa, was thought to serve as a bulwark for democratic developments across the continent in the last decade of the twentieth century, its inability to challenge this rise of semi-authoritarian regimes and failures of democratic governance across the continent raises serious doubts about the existence of any particular democratic model for Africa let alone the idea of a *transformative constitutionalism* taking root across the continent.

In South Africa, the idea of *transformative constitutionalism* as a model has come under increasing challenge from those calling for the decolonization of the society. These criticisms of the postcolonial legal order have taken two forms. On the one hand there is anxiety over what are perceived to be increasing threats to a 'liberal' legal order that was the celebrated outcome of the 1994 'miracle' credited with saving the country from what many political analysts predicted would be a 'blood bath' or as Mahmood Mamdani noted, if 'Rwanda was the genocide that happened, then South Africa was the genocide that didn't'.[53] On the other hand there is increasing criticism of what is

[53] Mahmood Mamdani, *When Victims Become Killers: Colonialism, Nativism, and the Genocide in Rwanda* (Princeton UP 2001) 185.

perceived to be the 'liberal' legal order created by the historic transition from apartheid and now blamed for its failure to address the legacies of racism and economic inequality that survived the democratic transition.[54] These latter concerns were reflected both in discussions within the ruling ANC about the need for a 'second transition' and in the patterns of increasing political protest and conflict, that erupt across the South African landscape—from Parliament and social media to the streets of towns and cities across the land.

Central to these divergent views of South Africa's postcolonial legal order is a questioning of the 'negotiated revolution' that enabled the democratic transition in South Africa. Speaking to the Oxford Union in late November 2015 Julius Malema, former President of the ANC Youth League and now leader of the opposition EFF in South Africa's Parliament, criticized the legacy of Nelson Mandela stating that: 'the Nelson we celebrate now is a stage-managed Mandela who compromised the principles of the revolution, which are captured in the Freedom Charter.' Explaining this characterization of Mandela and his assertion that '[t]he deviation from the freedom charter was the beginning of selling out of the revolution', Malema argued that while 'perhaps it was necessary to have a cooling off period . . . we cooled off for too long—21 years' and the EFF is 'not going to compromise like Madiba did'.[55] Less rhetorical but perhaps more threatening, given that the ANC remained the dominant political party in South Africa, was the increasing dysfunction within the party. This included a rise in attacks on the judiciary from within the ruling party as well as tensions—over failures to follow the laws governing state procurement; to respond to court orders meant to remedy government failures; or simple intransigence in the face of challenges to government malfeasance—such as the refusal over some time to properly address the findings of the Public Protector in the cases of Nkandla (in which President Jacob Zuma was found to have personally benefitted from security upgrades to his private residence). It is in this context that concerns over the 'rule of law' extend beyond individual legal challenges and begin to raise questions about constitutionalism and democracy in post-apartheid South Africa.

[54] Joel M Modiri, 'Conquest and Constitutionalism: First Thoughts on an Alternative Jurisprudence' (2018) 34 South African Journal on Human Rights 300; Mogobe Bernard Ramose, 'Towards a Post-conquest South Africa: Beyond the Constitution of 1996' (2018) 34 South African Journal on Human Rights 326.

[55] Marvin Meintjies, 'EFF's Malema Takes Aim At "Sellout Black Billionaires" in Oxford Address' *Business Day* (Johannesburg, 26 November 2015).

1. 'Lawfare' and transformative constitutionalism

While understandable as a means of advocacy for progressive interpretation[56] or as a basis for justifying judicial authority and thus as a defence against attacks on the judiciary,[57] *transformative constitutionalism* can serve neither as an autonomous imperative of social and economic change nor to foreclose on democratic decision-making that does not necessarily advance the transformative goals of the constitution-making generation. Once these maximalist claims for *transformative constitutionalism* are set aside it is possible to understand how the concept may be useful as a means of legitimating constitutional review within a constitutional democracy. Within this more chastened conception it is possible to outline at least three useful applications of the concept. First, it might serve as a reminder of the potential threats to legal change from within the legal system, as it was first deployed by Klare. Second, it is a source of justification for progressive constitutional interpretation, including the juridification of social and economic rights as well as the structural elements of the constitution that protect and even advance democratic participation. Finally, it might serve as a bulwark against attacks on judicial authority and provide the legitimacy for a claim that the constitution and the process of constitutional review are essential elements within a democratic order in that they provide opportunities for continued contestation in the face of political malfeasance. It is this last element that allows us to understand the relationship between *transformative constitutionalism* as a claim to a new form of constitutional implementation and application, and the direct role of courts in political conflicts—or what has been termed '*lawfare*'.[58]

We might explore this last approach through the example of South Africa where as conflict grew over the role of Zuma in various scandals—from his home at Nkandla to his relations with the Gupta family—different political parties, non-government organizations, and the then President himself increasingly turned to the courts. After Zuma resisted the Public Protector's decision in her Nkandla report that he 'pay back the money' and Parliament decided that he owed nothing, the question of the Public Protector's constitutionally defined powers was brought to the Constitutional Court. In its dramatic decision—read out on national television by Chief Justice Mogoeng

[56] Glenn Goosen, 'Rights Activism as a Key to a Transformative Jurisprudence' in Jean Meiring (ed), *South Africa's Constitution at Twenty-One* (Penguin Books 2017) 49.

[57] Lwandile Sisilana, 'Constitutionalism: For and Against' in Jean Meiring (ed), *South Africa's Constitution at Twenty-One* (Penguin Books 2017) 83.

[58] Michelle le Roux and Dennis Davis, *Lawfare: Judging Politics in South Africa* (Jonathan Ball 2019).

Mogoeng—the Constitutional Court linked the response to the Public Protector's report on the expenditure of public funds on the President's home at Nkandla to the Constitution's foundational commitment to the rule of law, arguing that

> [o]ne of the crucial elements of our constitutional vision is to make a decisive break from the unchecked abuse of State power and resources that was virtually institutionalised during the apartheid era. To achieve this goal, we adopted accountability, the rule of law and the supremacy of the Constitution as values of our constitutional democracy. For this reason, public office-bearers ignore their constitutional obligations at their peril. This is so because constitutionalism, accountability and the rule of law constitute the sharp and mighty sword that stands ready to chop the ugly head of impunity off its stiffened neck.[59]

Discussing the institution of the Public Protector the Court noted that to achieve its objectives, 'it is required to be independent and subject only to the Constitution and the law'. This requirement the Court notes

> would not ordinarily be required of an institution whose powers or decisions are by constitutional design always supposed to be ineffectual. Whether it is impartial or not would be irrelevant if the implementation of the decisions it takes is at the mercy of those against whom they are made,[60]

and concluded that the 'constitutional safeguards in section 181 would also be meaningless if institutions purportedly established to strengthen our constitutional democracy lacked even the remotest possibility to do so'.[61]

Detailing the constitutional place of the Public Protector the Court argued that '[i]n the execution of her investigative, reporting or remedial powers, she is not to be inhibited, undermined or sabotaged'[62] and '[w]hen all other essential requirements for the proper exercise of her power are met, she is to take appropriate remedial action'.[63] Justifying their conclusions in the name of strengthening constitutional democracy and 'breathing life into the remedial powers

[59] *Economic Freedom Fighters v Speaker of the National Assembly and Others; Democratic Alliance v Speaker of the National Assembly and Others* [2016] ZACC 11, 2016 (3) SA 580 (CC), [1].

[60] ibid [49].

[61] ibid.

[62] ibid [54].

[63] ibid.

of the Public Protector' the court held that 'she must have the resources and capacities necessary to effectively execute her mandate'.[64] Rooting her powers within the Constitution the Court made it clear that legislation is not able to 'eviscerate' the powers provided by the Constitution as the

> power to take remedial action is primarily sourced from the supreme law itself. And the powers and functions conferred on the Public Protector by the Act owe their very existence or significance to the Constitution.[65]

At the same time, the Constitutional Court recognized that the 'Public Protector's power to take appropriate remedial action is wide but certainly not unfettered' and that the 'remedial action is always open to judicial scrutiny'.[66] Furthermore,

> [w]hen remedial action is binding, compliance is not optional, whatever reservations the affected party might have about its fairness, appropriateness or lawfulness. For this reason, the remedial action taken against those under investigation cannot be ignored without any legal consequences.[67]

The reason for this conclusion the Court argued is because 'our constitutional order hinges also on the rule of law. No decision grounded on the Constitution or law may be disregarded without recourse to a court of law. To do otherwise would "amount to a licence to self-help"'.[68] In conclusion, the Court held that due to his manifest failure in disregarding the 'remedial action taken against him by the Public Protector in terms of her constitutional powers' as well as his failure to 'assist and protect the Public Protector so as to ensure her independence, impartiality, dignity and effectiveness by complying with her remedial action' the President has 'failed to uphold, defend and respect the Constitution as the supreme law of the land'.[69]

President Zuma's resignation in 2018 ended the immediate political crisis but highlighted the fact that within the first twenty-one years of South Africa's constitutional democracy two Presidents—Mbeki and Zuma—had been forced from office without use of the formal constitutional mechanisms for removal of

64 ibid.
65 ibid [64].
66 ibid [71].
67 ibid.
68 ibid [74].
69 ibid [83].

the executive. These internal party conflicts reflect the unipolar structure of South African politics, where so long as the ANC remains a dominant party at the national level there exists a form of dual state in which the party and state are deeply entwined. Under Zuma this relationship led to the emergence of a form of 'shadow state' in which corrupt private interests, by attaching themselves to a network of regional and national government leaders within the party, seemed to gain ascendency over even formal party structures. However, the demise of this 'shadow state' under pressure from opposing political factions, with the significant involvement of the courts and the Constitutional Court in particular, highlights the significant role of constitutional review in ensuring the continued functioning of democracy within the South African constitutional order. This I would argue is as significant a dimension of *transformative constitutionalism* as the enforcement of rights or its assertion as a model of constitutionalism and has played an important role in sustaining institutional resilience in the face of such direct attacks on constitutionalism such as the project of 'state capture' in South Africa.[70]

2. The resurgence of African constitutionalism

Beyond the paradigmatic case of South Africa and in addition to the suggestion that *transformative constitutionalism* should serve as a model, it is important to recognize that constitutionalism has become a significant locus of political struggle and debate across the African continent. In addition to repeated processes of constitution-making, public debates over presidential term limits, judicial authority, control over elections, and human rights controversies—from gender to xenophobia—the last three decades have seen constitutions become central to the political life of nations across the continent. Academic production has reflected this resurgence from general discussions of constitutionalism[71] and society[72] to more regionally focused analyses of judicial politics.[73] Amongst the constitutional issues that have been under discussion are many that fall within a broad definition of *transformative constitutionalism* including socio-economic rights,[74] affirmative

[70] Heinz Klug, 'State Capture or Institutional Resilience' in Mark Graber, Mark Tushnet, and Sandy Levinson (eds), *Constitutional Democracy in Crisis?* (OUP 2018) 295.

[71] Hatchard, Ndulo, and Slinn (n 50).

[72] Okon Akiba (ed), *Constitutionalism and Society in Africa* (Ashgate 2004).

[73] Peter VonDoepp, *Judicial Politics in New Democracies: Cases from Southern Africa* (Lynne Rienner 2009).

[74] Mirja Trilsch, 'What's the Use of Socio-economic Rights in a Constitution? Taking a Look at the South African Experience' (2006) 39 VRÜ/WCL 552.

action,[75] environmental justice,[76] and human rights.[77] While much of this literature still focuses on South Africa, there has been some discussion of *transformative constitutionalism* in other African jurisdictions.[78] However, many of the constitutional issues that are under debate across Africa and reflected in academic discussion do not fall within the standard understandings of *transformative constitutionalism*.[79] Whether it is pre-commitment,[80] constitution-making,[81] presidential term limits,[82] or the fate of the political question doctrine in Nigeria,[83] these are all issues of constitutionalism that are not particular to Africa or the Global South.

E. Conclusion

How then does the deployment of the concept and even the imperative of *transformative constitutionalism* as a model for Africa contribute to the idea of a constitutionalism of the Global South? In his contribution to this volume Sujit Choudhry links the concept of a transformative constitution to constitutional transitions, contexts in which there is 'a change in character of the constitutional regime' where the constitution is viewed 'as marking a fundamental break with the previous constitutional order'. While decolonization and the

[75] Ockert Dupper, 'Affirmative Action in South Africa: (M)Any Lessons for Europe?' (2006) 39 VRÜ/WCL 138.

[76] Emmanuel Opuku Awuku, 'The Right to Clean Environment: Lessons from India and Tanzania' (1994) 27 VRÜ/WCL 516; Carola Glinski, 'Environmental Justice in South African Law and Policy' (2003) 36 VRÜ/WCL 49.

[77] Sufian Hemed Bukurura, 'Human Rights in Sub-Saharan Africa: Towards Complementary Enforcement of Social Justice' (1997) 30 VRÜ/WCL 217; M Adekunle Owoade, 'Human Rights as a Resource: The Nigerian Experience' (1990) 23 VRÜ/WCL 152.

[78] Cornelia Glinz, 'Kenya's New Constitution: A Transforming Document or Less than Meets the Eye?' (2011) 44 VRÜ/WCL 60.

[79] See for example the Oxford University Press series *Stellenbosch Handbooks in African Constitutional Law* edited by Charles Fombad: *Separation of Powers in African Constitutionalism* (2016); *Constitutional Adjudication in Africa* (2017); and with Nico Steytler, *Decentralization and Constitutionalism in Africa* (2019).

[80] Dan Jama, 'Pre-Commitment in Contemporary Constitution Making? African and Kenyan Experiences Reviewed' (2011) 44 VRÜ/WCL 482.

[81] Melvin LM Mbao, 'The Politics of Constitution-making in Zambia: Where Does the Constituent Power Lie?' in Charles Fombad and Christina Murray (eds), *Fostering Constitutionalism in Africa* (Pretoria University Law Press 2010) 87; Djedjro Francisco Meledje, 'The Making, Unmaking and Remaking of the Constitution of Cote d'Ivoire: An Example of Chronic Instability' in Fombad and Murray, *Fostering Constitutionalism*, 119; Gregoire Bakandeja wa Mpungu, 'The New Constitution of the Democratic Republic of Congo: Sources and Innovations' in Fombad and Murray, *Fostering Constitutionalism*, 149.

[82] Charles Fombad and Nat Inegbedion, 'Presidential Term Limits and Their Impact On Constitutionalism in Africa' in Fombad and Murray (n 81) 1.

[83] Enyinna Nwauche, 'Is the End Near for the Political Question Doctrine in Nigeria?' in Fombad and Murray (n 81) 31.

demise of authoritarian regimes in both the post-World War II and Cold War eras did indeed produce major constitutional transitions, which were clearly transformative in the reconstruction of the relevant polities, the idea of *transformative constitutionalism* has, in the constitutional imaginations of legal theorists, jurists, and civil society activists, come to mean more than dramatic constitutional change. As Diego Werneck Arguelhes argues in his contribution to this volume, 'transformative constitutionalism' is a distinctive ambition, challenge or feature of 'global south constitutionalism' not unique to the global south but rather 'a combination of a text that contains a blueprint for a better society and the creation of certain institutions to promote it in practice'. Described in more idealistic terms, Marius Pieterse describes *transformative constitutionalism* as 'mandating the achievement of substantive equality and social justice, the infiltration of human rights norms into private relationships and the fostering of a "culture of justification" for every exercise of public power'.[84] Echoing Klare's early concerns, Sam Adelman responds to this vision of *transformative constitutionalism* by noting that it is 'thus a utopian project perpetually in danger of being frustrated by its medium,'[85] liberal legality and constitutional jurisprudence in particular.

To the extent that *transformative constitutionalism* refers, as suggested in the introduction to this volume, to an 'identified . . . range of "transformative" features, such as a constitutional teleology of social change, focus on socio-economic rights/equality, active role for the state, activist judiciaries, innovative legal procedures/remedies, civil society activism, [and the] horizontal effect of rights among private parties' to which I would add the constitutional inclusion of integrity institutions such as independent electoral commissions, auditor generals, and public protectors/ombudspersons as a fourth branch of government, then we might have the basis for claiming a distinct form of Southern constitutionalism. While this is a tempting claim, given the long history of what Boadventura de Souza Santos refers to as the '*epistemicide*' resulting from a Western-centric political discourse,[86] it remains important that we locate any claims to a new conception, such as '*transformative constitutionalism*', within the broader historical development of a contested global political and legal culture that reflects multiple forms of globalization.[87] To this end,

84 Marius Pieterse, 'What Do We Mean When We Talk About Transformative Constitutionalism?' (2005) 20 SA Publiekreg/SA Public Law 155, 156.

85 Sam Adelman, 'Sovereignty, Citizenship and the Universality of socio-Economic Rights' in Vilhena, Baxi, and Viljoen (n 5) 557, 558.

86 Boaventura de Sousa Santos, *Epistemologies of the South: Justice Against Epistemicide* (Paradigm 2014).

87 William Twining, *Globalization & Legal Theory* (CUP 2000); Boaventura de Sousa Santos, *Toward a New Common Sense: Law, Science and Politics in the Paradigmatic Transition* (Routledge 1995).

even as this volume seeks to bring 'Southern' constitutionalism into engagement with the 'Northern' dominated field of comparative constitutional law, it is important as Eve Darian-Smith argues, 'to engage with complex legal processes *beyond nations* and [to problematize] . . . how legal knowledge is constituted *within nations*' but also 'to see these multiple arenas of legal activity as intrinsically related, mutually constituted, and always in dynamic interaction'.[88]

If however we restrict the claims of *transformative constitutionalism* to the jurisprudence of apex courts in Southern jurisdictions, that have broadened our horizons on the justiciability and implementation of social and economic rights, then it may be possible to argue that there truly is a body of law and practical experience in the constitutionalism of the South that forms a unique contribution to global constitutionalism. However, in recognizing this contribution we need to acknowledge that the debate over the role of the judiciary in the implementation of economic, social, and cultural rights is not new or unique to south–south dialogue,[89] although southern voices have long been significant contributors to human rights debates.[90] To this extent, Hailbronner is surely correct when she argues that if *transformative constitutionalism* means anything it cannot simply describe a distinction between constitutionalism in the Global North and South.[91] Similarly, to speak of *transformative constitutionalism* in Africa it is essential that we understand what the idea of *transformative constitutionalism* contributes to debates and struggles over constitutionalism on the continent or how it might shape both local and global understandings of the relationship between constitutional aspirations and the exercise of governance across African jurisdictions.

It is in the light of both these aspirations and concerns, as well as the notion that *transformative constitutionalism* may serve as a model for Africa,[92] that this chapter has suggested an additional approach. Instead of using the concept to describe existing constitutional arrangements or the jurisprudence of apex courts across Africa or the Global South more generally, it may be useful to deploy *transformative constitutionalism* instrumentally as a yardstick to judge and critique the role of constitutions in advancing the cause of social justice, in the form of social and economic rights, equality, and democracy in and across

[88] Eve Darian-Smith, *Laws and Societies in Global Contexts: Contemporary Approaches* (CUP 2013) 10.

[89] Yash Ghai and Jill Cottrell, *Economic, Social, and Cultural Rights in Practice: The Role of Judges in Implementing Economic Social and Cultural Rights* (Interights 2004).

[90] William Twining (ed), *Human Rights, Southern Voices: Francis Deng, Abdullahi An-Na'im, Yash Ghai and Upendra Baxi* (CUP 2009).

[91] Hailbronner, 'Not Only in the Global South' (n 3).

[92] Kibet and Fombad (n 4).

nations. This use of *transformative constitutionalism* would both recognize the aspirational character of constitutions, which is more explicitly acknowledged in the Global South—as compared to the Global North where human rights are assumed to exist—and provide a resource for civil society and political movements as well as critics of existing patterns of exploitation and exclusion, to claim a better future in the name of democratic constitutionalism.

7

Transformative Constitutionalism

A View from Brazil

*Diego Werneck Arguelhes**

A. Introduction

Since it appeared in the 1990s, the multifaceted notion of 'transformative constitutionalism' (hereafter, 'TC') has attracted attention as a distinctive ambition, challenge, or feature of 'global south' constitutionalism.[1] Recent scholarship has broadened the debate by looking for traces of TC in any legal system or tradition in which the constitutional text both requires social change and creates the legal and institutional tools to do so.[2] If what we mean by 'transformative' is, then, the combination of a text that contains a blueprint for a better society and the creation of certain institutions to promote it in practice, it is hard to find a constitution drafted in the last decades that is *not* transformative to some extent.[3] Even within this expanded view of TC, Latin American legal systems are particularly promising places to observe the challenges of enforcing constitutional promises to foster social change.

These unequal societies experience the problem of inequality in different ways. Some societies are unequal, but not poor in absolute terms, and still possess significant state capacity. Others, in contrast, are both poor and unequal.

* This text is based on a presentation in the workshop 'The Global South in Comparative Constitutional Law', 13–15 July 2017, Humboldt University, Berlin (Germany). I am thankful to Phillip Dann, James Fowkes, Ligia Fabris, Jedidiah Kroncke, Roberto Gargarella, and Conrado Mendes for their comments and questions; to Maxim Bönnemann, Natalia Pires de Vasconcelos, and Rafael Lima for comments on a previous version of the paper; and to Renan Oliveira and Gabriela Gattulli for excellent research assistance.

1 See eg Daniel Bonilla Maldonado (ed), *Constitutionalism of the Global South: The Activist Tribunals of India, South Africa, and Colombia* (CUP 2013).

2 Michaela Hailbronner, 'Transformative Constitutionalism: Not Only in the Global South' (2017) 65 (3) American Journal of Comparative Law 527.

3 Hailbronner (n 2). James Fowkes, 'Transformative Constitutionalism and the Global South: A View from South Africa' in Armin von Bogdandy and others (eds), *Transformative Constitutionalism in Latin America: The Emergence of a New Ius Commune* (OUP 2017).

Diego Werneck Arguelhes, *Transformative Constitutionalism* In: *The Global South and Comparative Constitutional Law.* Edited by: Philipp Dann, Michael Riegner, and Maxim Bönnemann, Oxford University Press (2020). © Oxford University Press. DOI: 10.1093/oso/9780198850403.003.0007

Unequal countries with significant state capacities are particularly relevant for comparative conversations on TC. Their domestic laws and constitutions are often full of transformative promises—generous lists of social rights,[4] clauses granting constitutional status to international human rights treaties,[5] and preambles and provisions on national goals pointing to a vision of a more equal society.[6] There are, however, persistent implementation or enforcement gaps regarding these commitments. As the editors of a recent volume on transformative constitutionalism in Latin America have pointed out, in these countries 'admirable legal frameworks are not abided by or they are applied in a selective fashion'.[7] The main challenge these cases pose is not one of building legal or institutional capacity, but rather of changing how existing state capacity is deployed. Institutions *can* be minimally responsive to rights provisions in these countries, while still doing so in a selective way, protecting only a small subset of citizens, thus perpetuating exclusion and inequality rather than fighting it. Constitutional law would have, at least in principle, a better chance of making a difference precisely in such scenarios, as a mechanism to reorient the behaviour of these state institutions.

Against this backdrop, the Colombian Constitutional Court has drawn global attention. It is one of those few global south courts that has achieved widespread visibility as an arguable driver of social change.[8] Although recent studies have provided sobering assessments of what it has actually accomplished, Colombia is still largely seen as case of relative success.[9] In methodological terms, then, Colombia would be considered a 'positive case' for scholars

[4] See, generally, Ángel R Oquendo, 'The Solitude of Latin America: The Struggle for Rights South of the Border' (2013) 43 (2) Texas International Law Journal 185.

[5] See eg Mariela Moraes Antoniazzi and Pablo Saavedra Alessandri, 'Inter-Americanization: Its Legal Bases and Political Impact' in Armin von Bogdandy and others (eds), *Transformative Constitutionalism in Latin America: The Emergence of a New Ius Commune* (OUP 2017) 261–62.

[6] See, generally, Fernando Leal, 'National Objectives' in *Max Planck Encyclopedia of Comparative Constitutional Law* (2017) <http://oxcon.ouplaw.com/view/10.1093/law-mpeccol/law-mpeccol-e391> accessed 21 September 2018.

[7] See Armin von Bogdandy, Eduardo Ferrer-Mac-Gregor, Mariela Moraes Antoniazzi, Flávia Piovesan, and Ximena Soley, '*Ius Constitutionale Commune en América Latina:* A Regional Approach to Transformative Constitutionalism' in *Transformative Constitutionalism in Latin America: The Emergence of a New Ius Commune* (OUP 2017) 10 .

[8] The other two most immediate examples being South Africa and India. See Bonilla Maldonado (n 1).

[9] César Rodríguez Garavito, 'El activismo dialógico y el impacto de los fallos sobre sobre derechos sociales' (2013) 14 (2) Revista Argentina de Teoria Jurídica 489; David Landau, 'The Reality of Social Rights Enforcement' (2012) 53(1) Harvard International Law Journal, 401; Carlos Bernal Pulido, 'The Challenges of Transformative Constitutionalism: A Reply to Jorge González Jácome' (*I-CONnect*, 1 January 2019) <http://www.iconnectblog.com/2019/01/the-challenges-of-transformative-constitutionalism-a-reply-to-jorge-gonzalez-jacome/> accessed 14 March 2019; Carlos Bernal Pulido, 'The Paradox of the Transformative Role of the Colombian Constitutional Court' (*I-CONnect*, 1 November 2018) <http://www.iconnectblog.com/2018/11/introduction-to-i-connect-symposium-contemporary-discussions-in-constitutional-law-part-i-the-paradox-of-the-transformative-role-of-the-colombian-constitutional-court/> accessed 14 March 2019.

looking for manifestations of TC. However, even if we agree that Colombia is, indeed, a success story, there are limits to what one can learn from studying a 'positive' case.[10] In this chapter, I will focus instead of what I consider to be, in several aspects, a 'negative' case: Brazil. Having the second largest population of the Americas, one the region's largest economies, and three decades of democratic elections under a democratically drafted constitution, Brazilian government institutions have long been on the radar of comparative political studies. At the same time, the country still remains somewhat of a blind spot in the specific field of comparative constitutional law.[11]

Brazil has been a 'late bloomer'. In Colombia, the constitutional court immediately positioned itself as a leading force on constitutional transformation in the aftermath of the transition to democracy. The Brazilian Supreme Court (STF), in contrast, initially resisted taking this very role for almost two decades, in spite of having received a broad mandate by the drafters of the 1988 Constitution. Moreover, in recent years, while the STF has increasingly presented itself as a transformative actor, it has yielded much more limited results regarding substantive inequality. The social policies enshrined in the Brazilian constitution have contributed to relevant advances in fighting poverty and securing social rights in many areas. But, overall, judges have at best played a marginal role in driving these changes—and, in the first decade of the transition, the Supreme Court deliberately played no relevant role at all.

In this chapter, I reconstruct Brazil as a 'negative' case along these lines to draw three lessons. The first is related to the interaction between separation of powers arrangements and democratic politics. Courts are part of the broader arrangement of government institutions which are shaped by elections over time, and some of these institutions might (and inevitably will, given enough time) disagree with one another on what the constitution requires, on how to redeem its promises, and on *who* should take the lead in making the necessary changes to the legal status quo. These dynamics may lead to mismatches between blueprints for constitutional transformation, over time and across different actors and institutions.

[10] See, generally, Barbara Geddes, 'How the Cases You Choose Affect the Answers You Get: Selection Bias in Comparative Politics' (1990) 2 Political Analysis 131.

[11] Social scientists have done several 'small-n' comparative studies on legal or judicial institutions using Brazil as one of their cases. See eg Diana Kapiszewski, *High Courts and Economic Governance in Argentina and Brazil* (CUP 2012); Matthew C Ingram, *Crafting Courts in New Democracies: The Politics of Subnational Judicial Reform in Brazil and Mexico* (CUP 2015); Anthony W Pereira, *Political (In) Justice: Authoritarianism and the Rule of Law in Brazil, Chile, and Argentina* (University of Pittsburgh Press 2005); Daniel M Brinks, *The Judicial Response to Police Killings in Latin America: Inequality and the Rule of Law* (CUP 2007).

The second set of lessons is related to how scholars perceive and measure the development of transformative constitutionalism over time. Bold judicial statements attract scholarly attention, nationally and internationally. It is tempting to read these decisions as evidence that something transformative has taken place, especially when a court deliberately adopts the vocabulary and tools of TC in its decisions, presenting itself as fully aware of its transformative task. Treating changes in judicial language as actual change in the judicial role results in what we can call the 'mission accomplished syndrome': because we are satisfied that judges have changed the way they *talk* about a given issue in their decisions, we move to the next item on our list of transformative promises to be redeemed.

The third lesson lies in the intersection between the first two. Following up on their own bold judicial statements would lead courts to the problem of actually enforcing them, but monitoring compliance with ambitious, transformative decisions might lead to actual conflicts between political actors and judges, who would thus attract increased attention, scrutiny, and perhaps retaliation. Even if government officials do not retaliate, just by ignoring the transformative decision they can harm the court's standing before the public. These risks, however, do not mean that courts will be prudent when adopting strong *language* in their decisions. Just by itself and regardless of compliance, a bold decision with a transformative vocabulary gives judges the opportunity to present themselves as fulfilling a transformative role—and, as long the public is not asking whether these decisions have meant anything in practice, the costs of taking these unenforced strong stances are negligible.

Transformative judicial decisions, by themselves, might not be enough to transform existing patterns of inequality, but they can still positively change the court's standing before the public, in general, and scholars in particular. In this scenario, courts might end up fashioning an optical illusion: judges might choose cases with transformative potential and issue rulings requiring major, structural changes in the way the government deals with certain issues—while, at the same time, they refrain from following up on what happens after these decisions are taken. They reap the benefits of being associated with TC discourse and move on to the next issue, leaving the status quo largely undisturbed.

B. Locating Transformative Constitutionalism

Transformative constitutional texts reflect a project to change society into something it currently is not, beyond simply preserving past achievements, or rejecting and breaking with some features of the recent national past. In Latin America, transformative constitutions in this sense are widespread and typically share a common vision. At least on a textual level, these constitutions place emphasis on substantive equality, which, at least in the second half of the twentieth century, established itself in Latin American constitutionalism as a key goal—and as a persistent challenge. Social rights were a very early inclusion in the region's constitutional agenda, and the boundaries of constitutional ambitions had been broadened long before a similar expansion took place in the realm of constitutional adjudication.[12] Current constitutional texts in the region can be read as expressing a common commitment to fighting *exclusion*.[13]

However, while these constitutions promise equality of living conditions, the law and legal institutions have been unequally and selectively applied, leaving large parts of these societies unprotected.[14] This feature has fuelled criticism of these constitutions, as generous provisions of social rights and material well-being coexist with the same poverty, exclusion, and inequality as ever.[15] The generosity of the textual provisions becomes problematic depending on they are perceived and dealt with, over time, by (1) constitution-makers and (2) political and social actors deciding how to redeem these constitutional promises. The novelty and the promise of TC, then, must lie beyond the mere existence of a text that promises health, social justice, education, and the protection of human dignity. They must be connected to legal professionals and political authorities taking these promises seriously, developing policies and arguments around the goals they articulate. Only then we see the markings of transformative *constitutionalism*, beyond simply having a transformative *constitution*. A certain attitude on the part of constitutional interpreters and enforcers is therefore a necessary condition for TC.[16]

[12] Daniel Brinks and Abby Blass, *The DNA of Constitutional Justice in Latin America* (CUP 2018).

[13] von Bogdandy and others, '*Ius Constitutionale Commune en América Latina:* A Regional Approach to Transformative Constitutionalism' (n 7).

[14] ibid 5.

[15] Miguel Schor, 'Constitutionalism through the Looking Glass of Latin America' (2006) 41 Texas International Law Journal 1. In exemplifying his famous 'ontological' classification of constitutions, Karl Loewenstein claimed that 'Latin America is the most favourable environment' for nominal constitutions, which he defines as texts that lack 'existential reality either as whole . . . or at least as to some individual provisions which, though formally valid, have not, or not yet, been activated in actual practice': (Karl Loewenstein, 'Constitutions and Constitutional Law in the West and the East' (1969) 30 (3) The Indian Journal of Political Science 203, 213). In such scenarios, writes Lowenstein, 'the factual situation does not, or does not yet, permit the transformation of constitutional norms into the political reality'. It should be noted, however, that Lowenstein is focusing here more on the structural provisions of the constitutions, which should be expected to constrain the way political power is exercised.

[16] As the recurring debates on constitutional interpretation show, however, the fact that constitution-drafters publicly declared their transformative ambitions might eventually shape how future generations deal with the constitution. See eg James Fowkes, *Building the Constitution: The Practice of Constitutional Interpretation in Post-Apartheid South Africa* (CUP 2016).

The preceding remarks do not add anything substantive to existing definitions of TC. Their purpose is to make explicit three different levels in which the '*transformative*' feature can be located. First, we can look, in a given constitution, for the existence of vision or a blueprint for transforming society, regardless of whether it is explicitly established by the constitutional text or at read into it by interpreters. Second, we can point to a commitment between relevant actors to promote this transformation according to the constitutional document. In this sense, professional legal cultures and political actors in different countries can display different levels of commitments to the constitutional blueprint, making it possible to speak, within certain groups, of transformative constitutional cultures, professional communities, or attitudes.

The third level involves the set of institutional mechanisms or strategies created to transform existing institutions, practices, and realities according to the blueprint. Transformative texts and transformative communities can bet on different institutional mechanisms strategies to redeem constitutional promises. Constitutional review and constitutional courts, for example, can be a mechanism for transformation—perhaps deliberately included in the constitutional text by drafters who expected judicial review to play a key role in favour of their transformative ambitions. But other strategies are also available. Constitutional texts and/or their future interpreters might place their transformative bets on non-judicial institutions and mechanisms, in addition to enlisting courts for this same task. In some designs, courts themselves might be expected to take a secondary or even passive role, at least regarding some of the constitution's promises, as other institutions take the lead.[17]

In this framework, the best opportunity for a transformative text to make a difference in reality would be provided by full convergence on all three dimensions: (1) a transformative constitution is taken seriously by political and legal actors who (2) are committed to transformative constitutionalism and (3) agree on the same set of institutional mechanisms or strategies to promote this transformation. Latin American countries display limited degrees of variation on the first two dimensions. As we saw, most Latin American constitutional texts deserve the 'transformative' epithet. Moreover, if we agree with the standard narratives, in many (if not in most) of these countries, legal professionals—scholars, activists, judges—have adopted an increasingly

[17] See eg Brinks and Blass (n 12).

transformative stance,[18] although at varying speeds, while politicians would seem to be lagging behind.[19]

Variation is much more noticeable in the last dimension. For the purposes of this paper, we can simplify it as a one-dimensional spectrum: some constitutional systems are more *court-centric*, while others are more *government-centric*.[20] Constitution-makers in some countries deliberately empowered courts—and often specifically the constitutional or supreme court—as promoters of change.[21] In other countries, the latest wave of constitution-making placed their bets on political institutions, and especially the Executive branch, as the main agents of constitutional transformation. The most notable examples of this second group are Venezuela, Ecuador, and Bolívia.[22] These constitutional texts and cultures might still speak in a language of rights and social transformation, but they do not emphasize the judicial arena as the main space for making transformative claims or redeeming constitutional promises.[23]

[18] See eg Couso's discussion of the spread of 'neo-constitutionalism' ideas and ideology in Latin American countries: Javier A Couse, 'The Transformation of Constitutional Discourse and the Judicialization of Politics in Latin America' in Javier A Couso, Alexandra Huneeus, and Rachel Sieder (eds), *Cultures of Legality: Judicialization and Political Activism in Latin America* (CUP 2010) 141 .

[19] Von Bogdandy and others, '*Ius Constitutionale Commune en América Latina:* A Regional Approach to Transformative Constitutionalism' (n 7).

[20] For fully developed typologies of constitutional ambitions in the region, see eg Roberto Gargarella, *Latin American Constitutionalism 1810–2010: The Engine Room of the Constitution* (OUP 2013); César Rodríguez-Garavito, 'Beyond the Courtroom: The Impact of Judicial Activism on Socioeconomic Rights in Latin America' (2010) 89 Texas Law Review 1669; Rodrigo Uprimny, 'Las transformaciones constitucionales recientes en América Latina: tendencias y desafíos' in Cézar Rodríguez Garavito (ed) *El derecho en América Latina* (Siglo Veintiuno Editores 2011) 109; see also Brinks and Blass (n 12).

[21] 'Court-centric' means something different in each country, in terms of institutional design. Some countries have a single apex court that combines a host of functions, some of them have more specialized constitutional courts co-existing with a supreme court (and sometimes several apex courts). See Patricio Navia, and Julio Ríos-Figueroa, 'The Constitutional Adjudication Mosaic of Latin America' (2005) 38 (2) Comparative Political Studies 189. Regarding 'government-centrism', with the exception of French-speaking countries, all Latin America countries adopt some variation of presidentialism. Moreover, the region is characterized by particularly strong presidential offices, with many key legislative and other powers at their disposal. See José Antonio Cheibub, Zachary Elkins, and Tom Ginsburg, 'Latin American Presidentialism in Comparative and Historical Perspective' (2010) 89 Texas Law Review 1707; for a more critical appraisal of this trend, see Roberto Gargarella, *Latin American Constitutionalism* (n 20).

[22] For an overview, see Uprimny (n 20). For a sceptical view of these 'executive-centric' constitutions as promoters of social change, see Roberto Gargarella, 'The "New" Latin America Constitutionalism: Old Wine in New Skins' in Armin von Bogdandy and others, *Transformative Constitutionalism in Latin America* (n 13).

[23] In his contribution to this volume, Roberto Gargarella remarks that the 'new constitutional consensus' in Latin America has neglected the lesson that, in dealing with social conflicts generated by inequality, one needs to consider and change the organization of powers in the constitutions (the 'engine room'), and not just to 'fill the Constitutions with more and more of your preferred rights'. Gargarella's criticism of constitutional reforms in the region in the last decades has been twofold: (1) reformers have focused on rights, instead of the organization of powers; and (2) in doing so they left untouched institutional designs that strongly favour the executive, undermining democratic governance and, ultimately, the promotion of equality. My reference to 'government-centric' and 'court-centric' constitutions is independent from (and compatible with) these points, as it centres on the more specific question of whether judicial or political actors are more empowered to redeem constitutional promises within the 'engine room' of the constitution.

Moreover, even within the same country, such institutional strategies for transformation are not necessarily answered in a single voice, once and for all, at a single point in time, by constitution-makers, judges, politicians, and scholars. We find instead potentially different transformative mandates, in the same legal system, depending on whether we focus our attention on (1) the original constitutional blueprints (the drafters' views and ambitions regarding TC); (2) the court's view, which can in itself be disaggregated between different judicial institutions, depending on the country; (3) the political branches' view; (4) the dominant view in the legal community.

This simplified framework highlights the possibility of mismatches on how to promote TC, even when there is convergence between a transformative constitutional text and some of its relevant interpreters. In the next section, I will use the case of Brazil to explore two possible variations on this theme. First, these different actors might not be on the same page, at the same time, regarding the question of the role each institution should play in leading TC. These different dimensions might not necessarily converge towards the same side of the spectrum. Legal scholarship and activists might be court-centric, for example, while courts themselves prefer self-restraint, perhaps even against the constitution makers' expectations for the judicial role.

Second, these actors' views can change over time. The mechanisms by which change takes place are varied—generational changes, external political pressures, and successful media campaigns by activists, for example. But, in some instances, changes in these institutional stances happen (sometimes in a matter of a few years) because of their interactions with each other within the separation of powers framework. A single election can change the point of view of politicians, electing legislators and a president with drastically different views. Even the courts themselves are susceptible to electoral changes, due to the connection between electoral outcomes and the appointments politicians make to high courts. 'Court-centrism' might be the dominant view among judges today, but things might look very different after a few elections.

C. Divergent Paths to Transformative Constitutionalism: The Case of Brazil

The main success story coming out of South America so far is court-centric: the rise of the Colombian Constitutional Court (CC). The story goes as follows: in a country plagued by high levels of political violence, failing state capacity with regard to securing its own territory, a weak political party system, and low levels of political mobilization, the 1991 Constitution-makers deliberately put their promises into the hands of a new, powerful, and independent Constitutional Court.[24] Soon, in its first year of existence, the CC issues decisions making it clear that it has embraced this mandate, announcing new methods of interpretation and subordinating separation of powers to the promotion of substantive constitutional goals. This announcement was consequential, and the Court soon began to redeem these promises in dealing with structural violations of rights.[25]

Politicians resisted the court's new role, and tensions also appeared between the new constitutional court and the old Supreme Court.[26] Over time, however, the CC and the scholarly community—all committed to a court-centric approach—developed tools to overcome this resistance by means of dialogic approaches that give public administrators the chance to make their own choices, to some extent, and open up the constitutional review process to civil society actors.[27] The initial transformative bet of the 1991 constitution was contagious, and successfully so: constitution-makers empowered the court, with the support of scholars; the court accepted this role, and joined efforts with scholars to develop new tools to work its way around the other resisting branches (including the judiciary itself). A wide convergence on court-centrism: constitution-makers, scholars, and the new constitutional judges were on the same page.

The Court played its part. Procedurally, it reinterpreted its own powers to broaden access to its jurisdiction, even to the point of allowing every citizen to trigger its constitutional review mechanisms. Substantively, it has accepted and ruled on cases involving topics that directly deal with social exclusion beyond traditional civil rights cases, like internally displaced persons, sexual workers, and prison reform.[28] Politically, it brought to national policy debates the language of constitutional principles and fundamental rights.[29] Although the court's activism was more successful in some areas than others, and its effect

[24] Rodrigo M Nunes, 'Ideational Origins of Progressive Judicial Activism: The Colombian Constitutional Court and the Right to Health' (2010) 52 Latin American Politics and Society 67.

[25] Manuel José Cepeda-Espinosa, 'Judicial Activism in a Violent Context: The Origin and Impact of the Colombian Constitutional Court' (2004) 3 (Special Issue) Washington University Global Studies Law Review 529.

[26] For a discussion of the tensions between the two courts, see Everaldo Lamprea, 'When Accountability Meets Judicial Independence: A Case Study of the Colombian Constitutional Court's Nominations' (2010) 10 (1) Global Jurist 16 . See also Roberto Gargarella, 'Grafting Social Rights onto Hostile Constitutions' (2011) 89 Texas Law Review 1537.

[27] Rodríguez-Garavito, 'Beyond the Courtroom' (n 20).

[28] Constitutional Court of Colombia Sentencia T-025/2004; Sentencia T-629/2010; Sentencia T-153/1998.

[29] Rodríguez-Garavito, 'Beyond the Courtroom' (n 20).

has shown to be contingent on a series of political and institutional factors, Colombia is overall perceived as a success narrative.[30]

This national experience with TC has drawn more attention of the English-speaking world than its regional counterparts. Consider, for example, that a Colombian Constitutional law casebook has recently been published in English by Oxford University Press.[31] In their preface to the volume, Manuel Cepeda Espinosa and David Landau remark that '[t]he Court's case law is a prime example of transformative constitutionalism aiming to overcome entrenched economic and social inequalities', adding that comparative constitutional scholars might be interested in the CC's '*doctrinal innovations*' on issues such as '*structural remedies for socioeconomic rights*'.[32] Until this release, to the best of my knowledge, there were 'Latin American Law' casebooks in English, but no other 'casebook' on the decisions of a specific court in the region.

Consider now the case of Brazil.[33] Brazil's transition to democracy is, in many ways, a typical case of a 'constitutional new beginning'.[34] Politically, the transition was negotiated with outgoing authoritarian elites. Legally, though, the National Constituent Assembly (NCA) of 1987/88 adopted a new constitution that marked a clear break with the authoritarian legal order on many levels. The 1988 text contained generous commitments to social justice, both in broad principles and in specific rules, as well as new and fundamental checks on executive power. Congressional powers of oversight were expanded, and the *Supremo Tribunal Federal*'s (STF) powers of judicial review over both government action and inaction were greatly augmented.

Just as in the case of the Colombian Constitutional Court, the STF was empowered both by the new constitutional text and by its connection to the 'new constitutional beginning'. In recent years, the Court has indeed played an expansive and growing role in Brazilian politics. It has decided many issues that would most certainly have been considered exclusively political a little more than a generation ago.[35] But things were very different in the 1990s. Beyond merely adopting a posture of self-restraint, the 1990s STF judges interpreted

[30] See eg Landau (n 9); Rodríguez-Garavito, 'El activismo dialógico' (n 9).

[31] Manuel José Cepeda Espinosa and David E Landau, *Colombian Constitutional Law: Leading Cases* (OUP 2017).

[32] ibid x.

[33] This section draws from my JSD thesis: (Diego Werneck Arguelhes, 'Old Courts, New Beginnings: Judicial Continuity and Constitutional Transformation in Argentina and in Brazil' (JSD thesis, Yale Law School 2014) and from Diego Werneck Arguelhes and Mariana Mota Prado, 'Resistance by Interpretation: Supreme Court Justices as Counter-reformers to Constitutional Changes in Brazil in the 90s' in Richard Albert, Carlos Bernal Pulido, and Juliano Zaiden Benvindo (eds), *Constitutional Change in Latin America* (Hart Publishing 2019).

[34] Bruce Ackerman, 'The Rise of World Constitutionalism' (1997) 83 (4) Virginia Law Review 771.

[35] Oscar Vilhena, 'Supremocracia' (2008) 4 Direito GV 441.

the new constitution so as to set aside several procedural and institutional design innovations that would have given the court expanded opportunities to act as an effective check on political power.[36]

Soon after the 1988 constitution was enacted, a host of social actors—social and political entities who had just been endowed with the means to trigger the Court's jurisdiction—eagerly asked the court to deploy those constitutional innovations. The results were frustrating. In some cases, the Court would simply not decide—not by denying it had jurisdiction, but by using its discretionary agenda-setting powers to never assign a given case for plenary deliberation.[37] In other cases, when the Court did issue a decision, the outcome pointed in the exact opposite direction of what the constitution-makers had decided and promised, as the STF judges read the new constitution so as to water down its court-centrism.

One telling example is the STF's interpretation of the president's power to enact *medidas provisórias* ('provisional measures')—executive decrees that become immediately binding like a regular statute, and only then are subjected to congressional approval. In its original wording, article 62 of the 1988 Constitution states that 'in important and urgent cases, the President of the Republic may adopt provisional measures with the force of law and shall submit them to the National Congress immediately'. Because *medidas provisórias* were a kind of statute, they could trigger immediate and abstract review (brought by any party with a seat in Congress) before the STF. In an early case interpreting Article 62, however, the Court frustrated expectations by declaring that it would not second-guess the president's decision of what counted as 'important' and 'urgent', except in the most extreme cases.

Consider another example. In the Brazilian authoritarian constitution of 1967, and in previous constitutions, there were many generous provisions for fundamental rights, including ambitious social rights. Such provisions were not enforced by means of judicial review. Judges considered that they were not self-applicable and required additional legislation by Congress and the President, but Congress and the President would not legislate. These provisions, then, almost never made any practical difference.[38] To deal with this problem of legislative omissions, the 1988 constitution created the *Mandado*

[36] For extended discussion, see Arguelhes and Prado (n 33).

[37] For a discussion of agenda-setting mechanisms in the Brazilian Supreme Court, see Diego Werneck Arguelhes and Ivar A Hartmann, 'Timing Control Without Docket Control: How Individual Justices Shape the Brazilian Supreme Court's Agenda?' (2017) 5 (1) Journal of Law and Courts 105.

[38] Luis Roberto Barroso, *O Direito Constitucional e a Efetividade de Suas Normas* (5th edn, Renovar 2001).

de Injunção.[39] Article 5, LXXI of the Brazilian Constitution states that such an injunction 'shall be granted whenever the absence of a regulatory provision impairs the exercise of constitutional rights and liberties, as well as the prerogatives inherent to nationality, sovereignty, and citizenship'.

Scholars celebrated this procedural innovation as a revolutionary mechanism to promote faster implementation of the constitutional vision.[40] In the leading *Mandado de Injunção* ruling (MI 107) in 1990, however, the STF interpreted this mechanism so as to render it almost useless in practice. The court adopted two assumptions that were worlds apart from the self-understanding of the Colombian Constitutional Court in the 1990s: the plaintiffs were asking for the STF to create legal rules, but (1) only the elected branches could legislate, and (2) the Court could not force the political branches to legislate. On this understanding, the STF could only state that Congress or the President had breached, indeed, a duty to legislate—but there was no concrete remedy associated with the finding of such a constitutional violation. That is, a key constitutional innovation for redeeming constitutional promises became simply a mechanism to certify that a legislative omission was violating a citizen's fundamental rights.

The decision was heavily criticized in the legal community, and it has come to stand as a symbol of the post-transitional court's timidity.[41] The restrictive interpretation of the MI prevailed untouched until end of the 1990s, when the Court started to haltingly tweak it; it was only finally abandoned in 2007.[42] More or less around the same time, the Court would start to become more active in reviewing presidential legislation, until it finally voided a *medida provisória* for lacking 'importance' and 'urgency'.[43]

Many factors have probably contributed to this judicial change of heart, from the restraint of the 1990s to the struggle for expanding powers in the last decade. The generational change in the Court's composition from the late 1990s to the early 2000s is one such factor: it was only in 2003 that the last three military-appointed Justices retired from the STF.[44] The pre-transitional

[39] Usually translated to English as 'Writ of Injunction'.

[40] Henrique Augusto, Figueiredo Fulgêncio, and Alexandre Araújo Costa, 'O mandado de injunção na Assembleia Nacional Constituinte de 1987–1988' (2016) 2 (2) Revista Estudos Institucionais 818; Diego Werneck Arguelhes and Leandro Molhano Ribeiro, 'Nem evolução, nem renascimento?: contingência e captura corporativa em três décadas de mandado de injunção' (2018) 55 (219) Revista de Informação Legislativa 103.

[41] See eg Barroso, *O Direito Constitucional* (n 38).

[42] Alice Bernardo Voronoff de Medeiros, 'Ativismo judicial e democracia: reflexões em torno do mandado de injunção' (2011) 66 Revista de Direito da Procuradoria Geral do Rio de Janeiro 29.

[43] STF ADI 4029 Reporter Judge Luiz Fux 2012.

[44] See Arguelhes, 'Old Courts' (n 33).

generation of Justices shared a somewhat restrictive vision of the role of the Supreme Court in a democratic regime. Indeed, during the constitutional convention, the Supreme Court judges expressed their restrictive ideas on the role of their Court in a democratic system in explicit, public manifestations. After these ideas were mostly defeated in the drafting of the new constitution, they resurfaced in the Justices' efforts to promote—by means of judicial interpretation—the very institutional arrangement of relative judicial restraint that had been rejected by the constitutional assembly, who had opted unambiguously for judicial empowerment.[45]

These restrictive conceptions of the Court's role shaped how that generation of Justices read the new constitutional provisions expanding constitutional review mechanisms. In a series of rulings in the early 1990s, they restricted their own, newly expanded powers of abstract review, both in terms of their scope (the Justices refused to accept abstract review challenges against pre-constitutional laws, therefore insulating, for the time being, statutes enacted by the outgoing dictatorship) and their access (by inventing restrictions on standing rules on abstract review challenges, making it harder for social organizations and social movements to use these mechanisms).[46] The constitution-makers decided to give the STF a central role in the new constitutional order; the post-transitional STF disagreed and deployed constitutional interpretation to resist this change. This was a mismatch on several levels: the constitution-makers' views and the text they enacted had transformative ambitions and were 'court-centric'; the legal community eagerly celebrated the 'court-centric' bet; but the post-transitional judges rejected the transformative mandate.

Note that, in that era, the STF judges did accept wielding power in many high-profile cases. For example, they intervened in the impeachment proceedings of President Fernando Collor de Mello.[47] The problem seemed to be with cases that required judges to assume ambitious, innovative roles in redeeming constitutional promises. Moreover, their decisions restricting the original constitutional blueprint could not, in themselves, be justified as strictly legal interpretations of the constitutional text. They were rather loose judicial constructions of the relevant provisions, much closer to what we could describe as 'activism' than 'self-restraint'. Those judges, therefore, were not simply 'timid', nor 'formalists'—they wanted to play an important role, but in their own terms

[45] Arguelhes and Prado (n 33).

[46] For extended discussion and additional examples, see Diego Werneck Arguelhes, 'Poder não é querer: preferências restritivas e redesenho institucional no Supremo Tribunal Federal pós-democratização' (2014) 25 (1) Universitas Jus 25; Arguelhes, 'Old Courts' (n 33).

[47] STF MS 21.564 (1992); STF MS 21.623 (1992); STF MS 21.689 (1993).

(as a court of cassation and as an occasional reviewer of public policies in concrete cases), and they departed from the constitutional text to achieve this outcome.

D. Separation of Powers, Political Dynamics, and Optical Illusions

Since the 1990s, the STF has abandoned its self-imposed restrictive stance on many different areas. It overruled its case law on (the lack of) judicial remedies for legislative omissions;[48] it has declared that the dire human rights violations in the Brazilian prison system amount to an 'unconstitutional state of affairs';[49] it imposed restrictions on nepotism in political appointments in the three branches of government;[50] it read into the constitution a near-absolute ban on electoral campaign financing by private companies;[51] it interpreted the constitutional clauses of equality and liberty as forbidding the law from treating same sex couples differently from other couples, including when it comes to the right to marry;[52] it has decided that trans people have the right to officially change their names as they wish, without having to undergo any medical procedures before doing so.[53]

In a recent piece, an STF judge, Luis Roberto Barroso, remarked that there are 'several decisions from the Brazilian Federal Supreme Court that contribute to social progress in Brazil', and the court has actually played the role of an 'enlightened vanguard', in the sense that it was 'pushing History forward when it stalls' in some of those cases.[54] While these bold statements are controversial, the current Court is quite far from its 1990s counterpart—more aggressive

[48] Medeiros (n 42).

[49] Vanice Regina Lirio do Valle, 'An Unconstitutional State of Affairs in the Brazilian Prison System' (*I-CONnect*, 25 September 2015) <http://www.iconnectblog.com/2015/09/an-unconstitutional-state-of-affairs-in-the-brazilian-prison-system/> accessed 27 September 2018.

[50] STF RE 579.951 (2008) and *Sumula Vinculante* [Binding Restatement of Case Law] n 8 (2008).

[51] Juliano Zaiden Benvindo, 'Corporate Campaign Contributions in Brazil: Of Courts, Congresses, and the Agendas of Individual Justices' (*I-CONnect*, 3 July 2015) <http://www.iconnectblog.com/2015/07/corporate-campaign-contributions-in-brazil-of-courts-congresses-and-the-agendas-of-individual-justices/> accessed 15 March 2019.

[52] Diego Werneck Arguelhes and Leandro Molhano Ribeiro, 'Courts as the First and Only Legislative Chambers? The Brazilian Supreme Court and the Legalization of Same-sex Marriage' (2017) 50 VRÜ/WCL 260.

[53] Ligia Fabris Campos e Juliana Cesario Alvim Gomes, 'Pessoas trans: o mundo mudou e o Supremo também' (*JOTA*, 1 March 2018) <www.jota.info/stf/supra/pessoas-trans-o-mundo-mudou-e-o-supremo-tambem-01032018> accessed 15 March 2019.

[54] Luis Roberto Barroso, 'Reason Without Vote: The Representative and Majoritarian Function of Constitutional Courts' in Thomas Bustamante and Bernardo Gonçalves Fernandes (eds), *Democratizing Constitutional Law: Perspectives on Legal Theory and Legitimacy of Constitutionalism* (Springer 2016).

vis-à-vis the political branches, and much more engaged with fundamental rights cases. Still, even in this new scenario of judicial assertiveness and creativity, we should be careful before finding evidence of TC being successful in Brazil. First, we must keep in mind how the judicial change took place—the mechanisms by which the Court end up taking the mantle of transformation for itself; second, we must ask ourselves what has actually changed as a result of these decisions.

1. Democratic politics and judicial change

The court's change of heart did not happen at once. Political and electoral changes were decisive. As the last judges appointed by the military regime retired in 2003, Brazil had for the first time a Court fully appointed by democratic governments. The ebb and flow of electoral politics, and regular political conflicts and compromises, lead to the renewal of these judicial offices, and new ideas and commitments—distinctively more 'court-centric' and overall more favourable to expansive uses of judicial power—made their way into the Court. In the 1990s, no judicial decision was made that could be considered truly transformative, even if the constitution itself and the surrounding legal community had transformative ambitions. But even after the full renewal of the Court's composition an actual change in judicial behaviour was slow in coming.

Before the landmark same-sex marriage decision of 2011, it is hard to think of an STF decision that can be considered fundamental in fighting structural inequality in the country.[55] In the meantime, while change was coming to the STF through the mechanism of political appointments, the electoral system also made successive presidents commit to social programmes that did have effects on poverty and inequality.[56] While the Court disagreed with the constitutional blueprint and did not engage with the transformation task for more than two decades, politicians stepped into the gap. Politicians and the STF judges would seem to be in agreement that redeeming transformative constitutional promises was not an issue judges should be too involved with.

[55] On the same sex marriage decision, see Adilson José Moreira, '*We are Family!* Legal Recognition of Same-Sex Unions in Brazil' (2012) 60 (4) The American Journal of Comparative Law 1003; Arguelhes and Ribeiro, 'Courts as the First' (n 52).

[56] See Fábio Veras Soares and others, 'Evaluating the Impact of Brazil's Bolsa Família: Cash Transfer Programs in Comparative Perspective' (2010) 45 (2) Latin American Research Review 173.

If politics and electoral dynamics brought us to the current state of judicial affairs, then, one implication is that the same separation of powers mechanisms can work against 'court-centrism' over time. Judges and politicians diverge, both with each other and among themselves, not only on how to interpret and redeem constitutional promises, but also on who should do so—that is, they can disagree on the 'blueprint' for transformative constitutionalism. It is possible, then, that politicians use their power to appoint judges to change the Court's composition so as to make it less aggressive—to increase the adherence, within the Court, of a more restrained conception of the judicial role. Indeed, such a countermovement seems to have already happened in Colombia, where debates on judicial activism led to a change in appointments to the constitutional court and, consequently, in a relative reorientation of its jurisprudence.[57]

Even if the relevant actors are in agreement, today, on how to promote a certain blueprint for transformation, democratic politics—the contingent environment in which all these institutions, including courts, must operate—presents a challenge for sustaining transformative convergence over time. Respect for rights and constitutional norms insulate some issues from the contingencies of politics in the short run. But, in the long run, there can be no endpoint for disputes on constitutional meaning in general, and on how to approach transformative constitutionalism in particular, because institutions are not themselves insulated from political change. Electoral results and changes in public opinion, which can be affected by contingent factors like economic crises or corruption scandals, can mitigate and perhaps even reverse the direction of processes of legal change. In this scenario, perhaps there is even a hidden trade-off, for actors engaged in promoting TC, between focusing on courts and focusing on political institutions. Focusing too much on the former can divert resources that could be used in engaging with the latter to sustain change over time.[58]

[57] See Landau (n 9) 221–23.

[58] Carlos Bernal Pulido, 'Introduction to I-CONnect Symposium–Contemporary Discussions in Constitutional Law–Part II: The Paradox of the Transformative Role of the Colombian Constitutional Court' (*International Journal of Constitutional Law Blog*, 31 October 2018) <http://www.iconnectblog.com/2018/11/introduction-to-i-connect-symposium-contemporary-discussions-in-constitutional-law-part-i-the-paradox-of-the-transformative-role-of-the-colombian-constitutional-court> accessed 15 March 2019.

2. The 'mission accomplished syndrome'

Sustained interference in the affairs of the political branches can lead to retaliation and, in the long run, reorientation of the Court's jurisprudence through separation of powers mechanisms. But has the Court really been an aggressive promoter of transformative constitutionalism in Brazil? In answering this question, we can be fooled by the court's words. In the 1990s, for example, the Justices would sometimes make strong assertions that a new constitutional era had come, but the change at stake was largely cosmetic. Scholars thought they were seeing change because they focused on the Court's vocabulary. In section C, above, I mentioned the problem of judicial deference to *medidas provisórias* issued by the President. In that long line of cases in which the 1990s Court would inevitably accept presidential judgments of what counted as 'urgent' and 'important', we can still find many strong statements that seemed to express judicial assertiveness over the political branches. For example, the Court asserted that every act by a public official can in principle be reviewed according to the new constitutional values, and in contrast to the authoritarian legal order. These bold statements may sound like the Colombian Court in the early 1990s. But the resemblance begins and ends with the choice of words. In practice, that first generation of Justices announced a distinction without a difference: it would not be until the late 2000s that the court would begin to actually attack *medidas provisorias* that were patently not urgent or necessary.[59]

The risk is that scholars will evaluate the court's stance not by what the judges are doing, but by the ideas they are claiming to be adopting. Here, judges and scholars may converge in praising the court for taking a step in the direction of TC, although no actual step has been taken—only judicial language has changed. We can call this the 'mission accomplished syndrome': because scholars see constitutional judges adopting, in their opinions, the same vocabulary, ideas, and scholarship associated with TC, or the same arguments adopted by other courts that are seen as exemplars of TC, they might experience a feeling of achievement. They may assume that something changed in the world, just because the court changed how it describes its role regarding the constitution. Courts' capacity to bring about social change has been a longstanding topic of debate for decades.[60] The problem I am referring to here is different. Instead of asking what are the potential practical effects of changes in

[59] I discuss these cases in Arguelhes, 'Old Courts' (n 33).

[60] See eg Hailbronner (n 2); Gerald Rosenberg, *The Hollow Hope: Can Courts Bring about Social Change?* (2nd edn, University of Chicago Press 2008); Ran Hirschl, *Towards Juristocracy: The Origins and Consequences of the New Constitutionalism* (Harvard UP 2009).

the law (or in judicial interpretation), the question here is: what does a judicial ruling mean *for the application of the law itself*? Beyond bold words, what kind of stance is the court actually adopting before the other branches? Even when courts change the way they talk, they might still not even change how they actually decide cases involving omissions and violations by the other branches.

Celebrating the adoption of a certain idea, conception, or vocabulary in a judicial ruling is an extremely low bar if we are looking for instances of transformative constitutionalism. Consider a series of decisions made by the Brazilian Supreme Court on prison conditions and prison reform. In Colombia, prison reform was one of the issues that the Constitutional Court framed under used the idea of an 'unconstitutional state of affairs'—a framework to deal with social problems that, involving mutually reinforcing rights violations with multiple causes, requires the judiciary to find ways of spurring public authorities into cooperative action.[61] In 2015, the STF began to decide its own prison reform cases. In August 2015, it decided that, separation of powers notwithstanding, the judiciary could order government authorities to make emergency repairs in prisons so as to prevent violations of the inmates' physical integrity.[62]

A few months later, on an abstract review lawsuit (ADPF 347), the STF asserted that Brazil had a situation of daily violation of the constitution in prisons. Just as the Colombian Court did before, the judges acknowledged that the problem here was not of changing the laws on the books; the laws in place were fine and constitutional, but they were systematically unenforced. The structural nature of the problem meant that changing this situation of daily violations and routine lack of enforcement required large-scale cooperation between government branches. Separation of powers should not be—the Justices made a point of emphasizing in both cases—a protective barrier against long-standing, grave violations of rights.

The STF decision employed strong language, and some of the opinions explicitly adopted the Colombian Court's idea of an 'unconstitutional state of affairs'. However, as noted by both critics and enthusiasts of the decision, the Brazilian Court did not adopt the kind of monitoring mechanisms that had been part of the Colombian Constitutional Court's experiment with the 'unconstitutional state of affairs'.[63] Monitoring mechanisms are acutely needed in

[61] See Rodríguez-Garavito, 'Beyond the Courtroom' (n 20).

[62] STF RE 592.581 (2015).

[63] Valle (n 49); Thiago Luís Santos Sombra, 'The "Unconstitutional State of Affairs" in Brazil's Prison System: The Enchantment of Legal Transplantation' (*International Journal of Constitutional Law Blog*, 30 September 2015) <http://www.iconnectblog.com/2015/09/the-unconstitutional-state-of-affairs-in-brazils-prison-system-the-enchantment-of-legal-transplantation/> accessed 15 March 2019 (stating that the STF adopted the Colombian idea 'The evidence suggests instead that the Brazilian

this kind of ruling because they require the Court to position itself as a coordinator of the other branches, actively seeking to engage a host of stakeholders. The ADPF 347 decision contained no such mechanisms.

The Court described the problem in strong, sweeping language, only to adopt very limited mechanisms to deal with it. In particular, it is remarkable that it only established one requirement for the Executive branch: it forbade the Executive from using the 'National Fund for the Reform of the Prison System' (FUNPEN) for anything other than reforming the prison system. This seemed a very straightforward change, and seemingly easy to monitor. However, in January 2018, the then minister of Justice, Alexandre de Moraes, sponsored a decree-law signed by President Michel Temer that allowed funds from the 'FUNPEN' to be used in public security policies more broadly, and not just in the reform and maintenance of prisons. This was clearly in tension with the court's specific determination. The petitioner, a left-leaning political party, has been trying (still unsuccessfully, at the time of writing) to make the Court revisit the issue and acknowledge a violation of its 2015 decision.[64]

By now, this 'unconstitutional state of affairs' decision has already made its way into the law books and constitutional law classes across the country. A recent review in English of the Court's case law on fundamental rights by one of its judges emphasizes the adoption of the Colombian doctrine as evidence of the transformative role the STF has played.[65] But there is no reason to consider that decision as a fundamental change in how the court faces, in practice, the problem of prison reform. Even the only aspect of the ruling that was directly addressed to the Executive branch—a purely 'negative' obligation not to use public resources for ends other than prison reform—has not been enforced yet, and the court has not revisited the case or addressed the problem of compliance so far.

Court adopted the mechanism as a rhetorical device, without carrying out the necessary monitoring'. For a discussion of the Colombian experience, including the question of monitoring, see Rodríguez-Garavito, 'Beyond the Courtroom' (n 20)).

[64] Breno Pires, 'PSOL pede ao STF que trechos de MP para presídios sejam considerados inconstitucionais' *O Estado de S Paulo* (São Paulo, 9 January 2017). For a comprehensive, critical review of how each branch of government reacted to the ADPF 347 decision, see Breno Baía, 'O Estado de Coisas Inconstitucional na ADPF 347 e a sedução do direito: o impacto da cautelar e a resposta dos Poderes Políticos' (2019) 15 (2) Direito GV 1 .

[65] Luis Roberto Barroso and Aline Osório, 'Democracy, Political Crisis, and Constitutional Jurisdiction' in Christine Landfried (ed), *Judicial Power: How Constitutional Courts Affect Political Transformations* (CUP 2019).

3. Not all judicial wins are victories for transformative constitutionalism

The question of how to measure the actual *transformation* in transformative constitutionalism has become increasingly important with the rise of the activist of 'Global South' courts in countries like Brazil, Colombia, South Africa, and India.[66] Assuming that existing legal rules and principles will be immediately translated into actual social change is a problem for both activists and legal scholars engaged with TC. Recent contributions in the field have tried to engage with the question of impact without falling into this trap—for example, by focusing on the impact of judicial decisions on certain political or institutional *processes* instead of specific cases or outcomes.[67] Perhaps the impact of transformative courts can be found on how they empower national actors to pursue rights agendas and fight social exclusion.[68] And, beyond what is actively done with the output of these courts' engagement with constitutional rights and principles, perhaps just the fact that they decide certain issues is enough to help placing them, with much greater visibility, urgency, and perhaps even legitimacy, in local and national political agendas.[69]

My remarks in the previous section are not meant to be an answer to the broader question of how to ascertain whether legal change has been translated into actual social change. What I call the 'mission accomplished syndrome' refers to a prior challenge: we need, first and foremost, to be sure of what the court is *doing* in its decisions—and this is not the same thing as what the court *says it is doing*. One further complication is that judges might be actively interested in promoting the 'mission accomplished syndrome'. We tend to assume that the court would be interested in making the relevant public authorities comply with its bold rulings. But this assumption only holds if we abstract from the actual costs and risks, for judges, of developing mechanisms to monitor

[66] See Bonilla Maldonado (n 1).

[67] See eg Ximena Soley, 'The Transformative Dimension of Inter-American Jurisprudence' in Armin von Bogdandy and others, *Transformative Constitutionalism in Latin America* (n 13); Oscar Parra Vera, 'The Impact of Inter-American Judgments by Institutional Empowerment' in Armin von Bogdandy and others, *Transformative Constitutionalism in Latin America* (n 13).

[68] The Inter-American Court of Human Rights' impact on amnesty laws in national legal system is one arguable example. On the one hand, the Court's specific decisions on amnesty laws, for example, have been met with resistance and lack of compliance in many countries. On the other hand, national activists, judges, and prosecutors have actively employed decisions such as *Barrios Altos* and *Gomes Lund* to strengthen their legal arguments before national lower and high courts: see Vera (n 67). See also Diego Werneck Arguelhes, 'Transformative Constitutionalism in Latin America' [Book Review] (2019) 17 (1) International Journal of Constitutional Law 464.

[69] Rodríguez-Garavito, 'Beyond the Courtroom' (n 20). Mariana Mota Prado, 'Provision of Health Care Services and the Right to Health in Brazil' in Colleen M Flood and Aeyal Gross (eds), *The Right to Health at the Public/Private Divide* (CUP 2014).

compliance and enforce their decisions. Judicial attempts to force compliance with decisions requiring the government to actively adopt certain measures might give public officials extra incentives to retaliate against the court, or to bypass or ignore the inconvenient decisions.[70] Most importantly, judges can still benefit from unenforced decisions, as long as the lack of compliance does not harm their standing before public opinion and the legal community. Judges might thus have an interest in promoting the 'mission accomplished syndrome' in scenarios where their reputations benefit from the mere adoption of a certain language in their decisions.

If scholars are only paying attention to what judges *say* they are deciding, there is less of a risk that they will investigate what judges are *actually deciding*—not to mention investigate the actual, real-world impact of these decisions on inequality. While scholars and activists can be reasonably assumed to be interested in developing innovative and effective remedies and mechanisms to monitor and enforce transformative judicial decisions, the incentives for specific, individual judges to engage with the same challenge are mixed at best. In the prison reform cases in Brazil, as we saw, the heated scholarly arguments both in favour of and against the STF's self-proclaimed policy intervention were based on an optical illusion. While the court had used strong words in proclaiming an 'unconstitutional state of affairs', it has taken only very mild measures against the Executive, and even these mild measures have yet not been enforced. But, so far, this outcome has not reflected badly at the Justices at all. Quite the opposite: the STF seems to be reaping the benefits of a ruling that was overwhelmingly celebrated by the press and academia, leaving us tempted to move to another issue.

Furthermore, individual members of the court can get positive appraisal—from their peers, from international judicial audiences, from national and international scholars, from public opinion—by saying the right things and by using the words that scholars want to hear, regardless of the effect they have on the world. Regardless of what happens in the few years after a decision, individual judges can obtain these benefits from the ruling, with none of the burdens of non-compliance. By speaking in the language of the 'unconstitutional state of affairs', individual judges can be hailed as a progressive force within the court, while blaming short-sighted or self-interested politicians for not complying with their majestic, well-meaning rulings.

[70] See, generally, Tom Ginsburg, *Judicial Review in New Democracies: Constitutional Courts in Asian Cases* (CUP 2003) ch 3.

The Brazilian Supreme Court gives its individual judges powerful institutional tools to thread this path over time. More than a decade ago, it had been noted that the Brazilian Supreme Court tended to combine strong statements presenting itself as the ultimate guardian of the Constitution with a near total absence of actual engagement with many difficult topics involving fundamental rights.[71] This is possible because the STF has informal and extremely flexible docket control and case selection mechanisms, which have been used to guarantee that the judges do not need to decide cases they do not want to.[72] In the first two decades after the constitution was enacted, the Court used such powers to simply avoid deciding many cases that would put it in collision course with the political branches, and the Executive in particular.[73] Moreover, recent studies have shed light on how judges can deploy these agenda-setting mechanisms for their individual strategies, regardless of whether they have the support of a majority of their colleagues.[74]

The prison reform case point to a new twist in the STF's use of agenda-setting mechanisms to avoid confrontation with the Executive branch. Judges can include high profile, politically sensitive cases on the agenda and decide them in a seemingly aggressive way, while still avoiding confrontation with government actors. This requires excluding from the court's agenda cases that would force the judges to deal with the (lack of) enforcement and implementation of their decisions. In this perspective, the prison reform case appears not as a bold display of judicial power, but as an episode in which the court improves its reputation without actually imposing any costs on the Executive. Judges win praise if they adopt the right doctrinal arguments and ideas, while political actors are not really forced to change their current behaviour. In spite of requests by different plaintiffs involved in the original cases, the STF has, unsurprisingly, not revisited the issue. Doing so would mean actually facing trade-offs and making tragic choices, and perhaps even creating a dent in the

[71] Conrado Hübner Mendes, *Direito Fundamentais, Separação de Poderes e Deliberação* (Saraiva 2011).

[72] Arguelhes and Hartmann (n 37).

[73] For a case study of the privatization cases in the 1990s, see Vanessa Elias de Oliveira, 'Judiciário e privatizações no Brasil: existe uma judicialização da política?' (2005) 48 (3) Dados 559. Many of the recent cases in which the STF won the headlines involved laws from the dictatorship—such as an article from the military penal code criminalizing 'sodomy', or a law regulating the free exercise of the press—or by creating rules to protect rights that Congress was not willing to engage with—like legalizing same-sex marriage. Examples of direct engagement with policies adopted by current governments, in contrast, have historically been much harder to find.

[74] Arguelhes and Hartmann (n 37); Diego Werneck Arguelhes and Leandro Molhano Ribeiro, '"The Court, It Is I?" Individual Judicial Powers in the Brazilian Supreme Court and Their Implications for Constitutional Theory' (2018) 7 (2) Global Constitutionalism 236.

public narrative of the bold court moving beyond separation of powers to fight structural violations of rights.

E. Concluding Remarks: Back to Politics?

While Brazilian courts and the Supreme Court in particular have made advances in some areas, mostly involving civil rights, Brazil provides a cautionary tale against excessive 'court-centric' expectations that are sometimes associated with TC. However, Brazil is not a 'negative case' for the more general idea that constitutions can have a transformative impact. The relationship between the STF and the transformative blueprint set out in the constitutional text since 1988, as discussed in this chapter, has been full of false starts and misleading twists. But there is much more in the Brazilian democratic experiment with transformative constitutionalism than judicial empowerment and a generous list of social rights. The constitution contains a very large number of clauses detailing policies and institutional arrangements for their implementation—regarding health, education, work, and social security, for example—that are not part of the basic structures of government, federalism, or the political system.[75]

Recent empirical studies suggest that, in some areas, public policies contained by the constitution may have made a difference. The comprehensive public health system, for example, has successfully increased and equalized access to health services, contributing to an increase in national life expectancy and decreasing child mortality rates.[76] However, the basic contours of the system and some of its key policies began to be built in the 1980s, before the new constitution. Constitution-makers protected these arrangements in the new constitution, but, so far, it is still unclear to which extent the positive effects are due to their decision to constitutionalize the policy arrangements, or to the substance of the policy arrangements themselves.

A similar question could be posed regarding the impact of the educational system, which allocates responsibilities and positive state obligations across all levels of the Brazilian federation and has contributed to bringing children

[75] See Rogério Bastos Arantes and Claudio Gonçalves Couto, 'Constitutionalizing Policy: The Brazilian Constitution of 1988 and Its Impact on Governance' in Detlef Nolte and Almut Schilling-Vacaflor (eds), *New Constitutionalism in Latin America: Promises and Practices* (Ashgate 2012).

[76] See Rudi Rocha, 'A saúde na Constituição de 1988: Trinta anos de SUS e os desafios pela frente' in Naércio Menezes Filho and André Portela Souza (eds), *A Carta: Para entender a Constituição Brasileira* (Todavia 2019).

to schools and decreasing dropout rates.[77] Moreover, some accomplishments in poverty alleviation have been achieved by means of social policies that, although perhaps inspired by constitutional commitments and specific arrangements, were not necessarily required by the constitution. They are more the expression of well-designed policy choices made by elected officials and perfected over time, in different governments.[78] It is still unclear, then, how exactly the constitution could have shaped these outcomes—by setting in motion political and institutional dynamics, by strengthening policy arrangements that predated it, or by protecting certain policy structures from short-term legislative changes.[79] But, in any event, and although the Brazilian Constitution does assign judicial institutions a prominent role in redeeming these promises, it seems that courts had a limited (and sometimes negative) role in promoting equality across many areas of social policy.[80]

Successful government policies, then, whether due to their presence in the constitutional text or not, have contributed at least partially to redeeming constitutional promises of equality. But politics looms on the horizon of TC in other ways. Institutional bets on transformative constitutionalism reflect political views and ideologies, and are not constructs of universal reason.[81] Contingent electoral results shape even constitutional interpretation, if given enough time. It is crucial, then, that our expectations for transformation take into account the ebb and flow of these processes. These challenges are not linked to dysfunctions of (or threats to) the democratic regime. They are part of democratic politics. The case of Brazil shows that transformative constitutional ambitions are played out within institutional and political arenas whose moving parts, in interacting with one another, will not always move toward greater convergence, within and across institutions, around a specific blueprint for social change. Whatever success TC had in Brazil has been deeply contingent on politics, and this contingency is expressed through the typical mechanisms by which politics influences constitutional law in many other democracies, such as separation of powers, political appointments, and elections.

[77] Naércio Menezes Filho and Reynaldo Fernandes, 'Educação: Avanços recentes e propostas para o futuro' in Menezes Filho and Portela Souza (eds), *A Carta: Para entender a Constituição Brasileira* (Todavia 2019).

[78] See eg Diogo R Coutinho, 'Targeting Within Universalism? The Bolsa Família Program and the Social Assistance Field in Brazil' (2014) 47 VRÜ/WCL 43.

[79] I am indebted to Natalia Pires for making this point to me.

[80] See Rafael Bellem de Lima and Natalia Pires de Vasconcelos, 'O sistema de justiça brasileiro: atores, atuação e consequência do arranjo institucional' in Menezes Filho and Portela Souza (eds), *A Carta: Para entender a Constituição Brasileira* (Todavia 2019).

[81] For an analysis of on how ideology has shaped the scope of constitutional justice and constitutional politics in Latin America, see Brinks and Blass (n 12).

Beyond outright attacks on the court or against its decisions, there are other, subtler ways for politicians to resist court-centrism. Politicians have the means to 're-tune' the vision presented by the court itself over time, by means of political appointments to judicial offices. Consider, for example, that Alexandre de Moraes, the minister of Justice who signed the FUNPEN provisional measure discussed above, was appointed to the Brazilian Supreme Court one month after the enactment of that measure, which arguably eroded an ambitious judicial decision requiring reforms in the prison system. These are real challenges for TC, but they lie in the spectrum of ordinary democratic politics. TC can never be purely 'court-centric', and must be reconciled with separation of powers. A couple of generations of judges and a handful of high-profile landmark cases will not be enough to lock TC in place over time.

A Colombian scholar has rightly warned us against thinking of the 'effects' of transformative constitutional decisions in excessively narrow terms. They can have important 'symbolic' effects. For example, they can draw attention to a given issue, making it relevant in terms of a rights debate and providing a focal point for mobilization.[82] These are important points. But we should not overstretch the idea of an 'effect' so as to be impressed just by victories in the domain of doctrine and judicial language. We need to sceptically monitor the court, just as it should monitor the other branches, to see what (if anything) it is actually doing with these new ideas. Otherwise, we will help fuel a pattern into which Brazil might have fallen: court uses the right keywords; court receives praise by legal scholars and the legal community; court never revisits the issue to face trade-offs or failures associated with its decisions; court moves on to the next set of keywords, and we follow it. In such a scenario, we might consider the possibility of TC leading to symbolic risks: people might stop believing that the constitution, and what the court says about it, will make a difference in their lives. This would be a step towards legitimizing unjust social realities—now with the court's complicity.

[82] Rodríguez-Garavito, 'Beyond the Courtroom' (n 20).

8

Postcolonial Proportionality

Johar, Transformative Constitutionalism, and Same-Sex Rights in India

*Sujit Choudhry**

A. Introduction: Two Conceptions of Transformative Constitutionalism—Anti-Colonial and Cosmopolitan

At its inception, the Indian Constitution was envisioned as a transformative document, in two senses: *anti-colonial* and *cosmopolitan*. The Constitution marked the culmination of one of the great national independence movements of the twentieth century. It gave birth to a radically new constitutional order, which conferred citizenship and political power on the previously disenfranchised living under the yoke of British imperial rule, created democratically elected legislatures and accountable executives, and conferred fundamental rights on citizens that reconfigured their relationship with public power, under which they had been hitherto treated as colonial subjects. Citizens were constitutionally empowered to enforce their fundamental and democratic rights through the twin mechanisms of judicial review by independent courts and regular, periodic elections.

But as Madhav Khosla, Pratap Mehta, and I have argued, the Indian Constitution was also 'a cosmopolitan constitution in its fidelity to the universal principles of liberty, equality and fraternity'.[1] These universal values mandated and framed a vast project of social, economic, and political transformation. Ambedkar argued in the Constituent Assembly debates that the Constitution was transformative because it conferred on the state an express mandate to attack social hierarchies, and to redistribute economic and political power away from elites defined by class and caste towards the hitherto politically powerless

* I thank Gautam Bhatia, Philipp Dann, Menaka Guruswamy, Madhav Khosla, and Tarun Khaitan.

[1] Sujit Choudhry, Madhav Khosla, and Pratap Bhanu Mehta, 'Locating Indian Constitutionalism' in Sujit Choudhry, Madhav Khosla, and Pratap Bhanu Mehta (eds), *The Oxford Handbook of the Indian Constitution* (OUP 2016) 1–14.

Sujit Choudhry, *Postcolonial Proportionality* In: *The Global South and Comparative Constitutional Law*. Edited by: Philipp Dann, Michael Riegner, and Maxim Bönnemann, Oxford University Press (2020). © Oxford University Press.
DOI: 10.1093/oso/9780198850403.003.0008

and economically deprived majority, by legislating across the whole range of political, economic, and social life. This mission flowed from 'constitutional morality'—a term that Ambedkar introduced into the Indian constitutional lexicon to describe and defend the Constitution.

The idea of transformative constitutionalism is part of the grammar of Indian constitutional politics. Arguably, it is also at play in Indian constitutional doctrine. The architecture of rights-based adjudication in India has converged on an emerging global template consisting of elements such as jurisdiction, standing, application, rights-infringement, justification, and remedy. Indian constitutional jurisprudence has developed this template in a distinctive way. The Supreme Court of India (SCI) has construed the writ jurisdiction of the High Court under Article 226 broadly, as well as the direct access jurisdiction of the SCI itself under Article 32. The rules of *locus standi* have been relaxed beyond the person aggrieved to representative standing, citizen standing, and litigation competence. Article 21's right to life has been interpreted broadly to encompass many of the expressly non-justiciable Directive Principles of State Policy under Part IV, giving rise to a rich jurisprudence of economic and social rights that have constitutionalized much of administrative law. Constitutional remedies are aggressive and far-reaching, extending well into the traditional legislative and executive domains of policy design and implementation. Indeed, such remedies are frequently issued on a preliminary basis, and set up a process of judicial oversight of public administration—in theory pending a decision on the merits that in reality may never be taken. Taken together, these elements have vastly enhanced the power of courts to hear, and litigants to bring, challenges to the constitutionality of vast swathes of government action or inaction, and for courts to fashion highly ambitious structural remedies.

The SCI has yet to articulate an overarching theory that unites this collection of particulars under the rubric of transformative constitutionalism, in either its anti-colonial or cosmopolitan senses. In this chapter, I take up this task, by wrestling with the SCI's landmark decision in *Johar*, where it unanimously struck down Section 377 of the Indian Penal Code (IPC).[2] The idea of transformative constitutionalism figured centrally in the various opinions, and the closely related concept of constitutional morality, given real legal teeth for the first time by the Supreme Court. So did another piece of the global template of

[2] *Navtej Singh Johar v Union of India*, Writ Petition (Criminal) No 76 of 2016 (6 September 2018). There were separate reasons provided by Chief Justice Misra (hereafter Misra Reasons), and Justice Fali Nariman (hereafter Nariman Reasons), Justice Chandrachud (hereafter Chandrachud Reasons), and Justice Malhotra.

rights-protection—proportionality, which is relatively new to Indian constitutional jurisprudence.

The unifying thread between transformative constitutionalism and proportionality in *Johar* is that the purposes underlying Section 377 were constitutionally impermissible. The dual mission of the transformative constitutional project defined the scope of admissible reasons for proportionality analysis. Section 377 was unconstitutional on the cosmopolitan ground that mere social morality was an insufficient reason to limit the right to engage in harmless, constitutionally protected activity, the basis on which courts around the world have struck down parallel provisions. On its own, this reason should have been sufficient basis to hold the provision unconstitutional. But the colonial-era origins of Section 377 figured prominently in the submissions and various opinions, as an additional reason why it was unconstitutional. *Johar* does not offer a fully worked-out argument for why the legal origins of the provision should matter at all. I shall argue that Section 377 was also unconstitutional for the anti-colonial reason that it was an element of the Imperial constitutional order in British India in the period after the Indian Mutiny in 1857 of indirect colonial rule.

B. Proportionality, Transformative Constitutionalism, and Constitutional Transitions

Proportionality is a constitutional framework for assessing whether infringements of rights can be justifiable and is a core component of the global template for rights-based constitutional adjudication. The legal test for proportionality consists of a number of components: has the decision been taken for a proper purpose, do the means chosen further that purpose (suitability or rational connection), do the means chosen infringe the right as little as possible (necessity or minimal impairment), and do the salutary effects of the means outweigh its deleterious effect on the rights-claimant (balancing per se). As with any global language, proportionality has its national dialects that reflect different approaches to the interpretation and interrelationship of these components, which in turn have generated and track intramural scholarly debates. For example, as Richard Stacey has explained, courts are divided over whether infringements of the core of constitutional rights can ever be proportional, whether governments must always use the least intrusive means or whether they are owed some deference, and how to structure the final stage of the proportionality test so that it differs from ad hoc balancing.[3]

The Indian jurisprudence on proportionality is in its earliest stages. The idea that fundamental rights are not absolute is expressly contemplated by the text of some of the Fundamental Rights in Part III. Moreover, proportionality has precursors in Indian law, especially the manifest arbitrariness test for Article 14 set out in *Maneka Gandhi*.[4] But it is only recently that proportionality has been expressly adopted by the SCI, in *Anuj Garg*[5] and *Puttaswamy*.[6] It was central to several of the opinions in *Johar*, where the Court held that Article 377 violated several rights (expression, equality, privacy) and failed to meet the test of proportionality.

A foundational question for SCI will be the role of proportionality in the broader Indian constitutional scheme, in particular its transformative character. A similar question confronted the Constitutional Court of South Africa under its post-apartheid constitutional order. An answer was provided was by Etienne Mureinik, in a highly influential article published in 1994.[7] Mureinik took as his starting point the post-amble to South Africa's 1993 Interim Constitution, which described that document as a:

> historic bridge between a past of a deeply divided society characterized by strife, conflict, untold suffering and injustice, and a future founded on the recognition of human rights, democracy and peaceful co-existence and development opportunities for all South Africans, irrespective of colour, race, class, belief or sex.

Mureinik posed the question of 'what [the constitution] is a bridge from, and what a bridge to'.[8] He answered that it was a bridge from 'a culture of authority' to 'a culture of justification'.[9] Under a culture of authority, 'what Parliament says is law' and 'the leadership given by government rests . . . on the fear inspired by the force at its command'.[10] By contrast, under a culture of justification, 'every exercise of power is expected to be justified' and the 'leadership

[3] Richard Stacey, 'The Magnetism of Moral Reasoning and the Principle of Proportionality in Comparative Constitutional Adjudication' (2019) 67 American Journal of Comparative Law 435.

[4] *Maneka Gandhi v Union of India* (1978) AIR 597; 1978 SCR (2) 621.

[5] *Anuj Garg v Hotel Association of India* (2008) 3 SCC 1.

[6] *KS Puttaswamy v Union of India*, Writ Petition (Civil) No 494 of 2012 (SupCt India 24 August 2017).

[7] Etienne Mureinik, 'A Bridge to Where? Introducing the Interim Bill of Rights' (1994) 10 South African Journal of Human Rights 31.

[8] ibid 31.

[9] ibid 32.

[10] ibid.

given by government rests on the cogency of the case offered in defence of its decisions'.[11] In summary, '[t]he new order must be a community built on persuasion, not coercion'.[12]

Mureinik clearly saw the culture of justification as a core commitment of *any* constitutional order. It yields a theory of judicial review, whereby courts require that governments in *any* constitutional democracy explain and justify their decisions. Proportionality is central to such a theory of judicial review. Indeed, Mureinik himself focused on section 33 of the Interim Constitution, the limitations clause, which he argued had the effect of making the rights in the Bill of Rights 'standards of justification'.[13] Moshe Cohen-Eliya and Iddo Porat draw on Mureinik to build a general constitutional theory, whereby the culture of justification requires that governments should provide substantive justification for all their actions, by which they mean justification in terms of the rationality and reasonableness of every action and the trade-offs that every action necessarily involves.[14]

But I want to take Mureinik's argument one step further, as setting out a theory of judicial review for a transformative constitution like South Africa or India's, which describes itself as a radical break from a constitutionally illegitimate past. To do so, I link the concept of a transformative constitution to a democratic transition. By a democratic transition, I refer not merely to the formal replacement of one constitution by another. Rather, I refer to a change in the character of the constitutional regime into a democracy—for example, from an autocracy (South Africa) or colony (India). Moreover, for an initial period, such a democracy is a transitional democracy, as opposed to a consolidated democracy. During this initial period, one question is how the new constitutional regime of a transitional democracy sees itself in relation to the one it has replaced. A transitional democracy views itself as marking a fundamental break with the previous constitutional order, in the manner of a rupture or revolution, even if there has been legal continuity. A transitional democracy is therefore necessarily committed to some kind of version of transformative constitutionalism.

The question of how to interpret a transformative constitution is, in part, shaped by the kinds of cases that arise in transitional democracies. Constitutional courts would undoubtedly hear rights-based challenges to decisions of newly elected democratic governments, acting pursuant to their

[11] ibid.
[12] ibid.
[13] ibid.
[14] Moshe Cohen-Eliya and Iddo Porat, *Proportionality and Constitutional Culture* (CUP 2013).

powers under the new constitutional order. The laws at issue would in many cases be the same as those in any constitutional democracy, concerning the broad array of functions of a contemporary government. In one respect, the constitutional court would be discharging a normal function; a general theory of judicial review, such as one based on the culture of justification, would be a plausible candidate for how it should conceive of its role. Nevertheless, conferring on the courts this role is surely one dimension of what a transformative constitution is; what makes the constitution transformative is precisely the normality of the judicial role, in juxtaposition to the immediate past.

However, in a transitional democracy, constitutional courts are likely to hear challenges to two additional kinds of laws, which are quite different from the legislation that are standard fare in consolidated democracies. Apartheid was an integrated regime of political and economic control that concentrated public and private power in the hands of the white minority. That system was underpinned not just by the Apartheid constitution, but also by the entire legal system, including a vast array of legislation. The adoption of a new constitution could not at a stroke repeal those laws in their entirety, because this would leave a legal vacuum. However, those laws are anathema to the transformative constitution and would almost certainly never be enacted today. So it was envisioned that the National Assembly and provincial legislatures would engage in a systematic overhaul of an authoritarian and racist legal system, to upend it root and branch, as part of a transformative constitutional order. The constitution continued in force this entire corpus of legislation, with no timeline set for its expiry, in order to ensure an orderly transition. Moreover, until repealed, apartheid-era laws continued to be enforced and govern legal relations. This dynamic—of a new constitution, and old-regime legislation that remains in force until repealed—sets up inevitable constitutional challenges.

There is another element of South Africa's transition. South Africa had a 'pacted transition' between the National Party and the African National Congress, like other post-authoritarian transitions that are negotiated by old regime elites and democratic challengers, as occurred in Spain, Chile, and in many of the former Communist republics of Eastern and Central Europe. South Africa also bore similarities to post-civil-war transitions that were concluded by peace agreements—for example, most recently in Colombia. Such pacts often contain measures designed to promote peace that come at the expense of justice. For example, South Africa's pact included reciprocal commitments on transitional justice, specifically language in the post-amble of the Interim Constitution that 'amnesty shall be granted in respect of acts, omissions and offences associated with political objectives and committed in the course of the conflicts of the past'. Although they may be constitutionally mandated, amnesties and other transitional justice measures may require compromises with constitutional principle. For example, an amnesty may violate the rights of victims, for example, the right of access to court—as has been raised extensively under the Inter-American human rights system. Yet amnesties may be necessary to allow transformative constitutionalism to get off the ground at all.

What this means is that a constitutional court in a transitional democracy, interpreting a transformative constitution, performs three distinct roles. Like courts in other democracies, it must adjudicate upon standard legislation that is the bread and butter of normal politics. But it is also a court of the transition, in two ways. It must reckon with evil laws of the prior regime, against which the transformative constitution defines itself, but which nonetheless continue in force. And it must hear challenges to transitional justice laws which may conflict with victims' rights, but which are critical elements of the political bargain that makes the transformative constitution possible.

If we maintain with Mureinik that the culture of justification remains central to transformative constitutionalism and places proportionality at the heart of a theory of judicial review, then the multiple tasks of a constitutional court in a transitional democracy have a radical implication—that proportionality analysis under a transformative constitution is not generic, but heterogeneous. The reason is that proportionality, on his account, is an institutionalized practice whereby the 'leadership given by government rests on the cogency of the case offered in defence of its decisions'.[15] It follows that proportionality analysis requires a governmental interlocutor for the process of justification, which orients the task of the reviewing court. One dimension of that conversation consists of the reasons and evidence for the decision under challenge. But another dimension is the institutional identity of the interlocutor, since an element of proportionality analysis are questions of institutional mission, capacity, and legitimacy, which all go to deference and the standard of review.

Within a constitutional democracy, the institutional interlocutor might vary—the legislature, an expert agency or tribunal, the political executive—but those institutions are all constituent elements of a constitutional democracy. By contrast, under a transformative constitution, the identity of that interlocutor differs fundamentally across categories of cases. In the first kind of case, it is a constitutional democracy that is a creature of, and is presumed to act in compliance with, the transformative constitution. In the second, it is an old guard who governed under a system that the transformative constitution

[15] Mureinik (n 7) 32.

regards as illegitimate. In the third, it is a coalition of old guard and democratizing elites who agreed to a grand bargain that makes transformative constitutionalism possible. The question is how proportionality analysis operates in each different context.

C. *Johar*: Cosmopolitanism and Anti-Colonialism

The issues arising from the interpretation of a transformative constitution within a transitional democracy have implications for the development of Indian constitutional doctrine. The reason is that the SCI—perhaps counterintuitively—is a constitutional court of a transitional democracy. To be sure, India became independent in 1947, and the Indian Constitution came into force seven decades ago, in 1950. The legal dimensions of British imperial rule are now, for the most part, a part of India's distant past. The SCI's docket almost entirely has focused on post-Independence legislation. Thus, the idea that India is a transitional democracy may seem to be no longer relevant. Nevertheless, the SCI remains a constitutional court of a transitional democracy, because of the way the Constitution treats colonial-era law. Under Article 372, all colonial-era laws remain in force indefinitely, until amended or repealed. Indeed, it is pursuant to Article 372 that Section 377, first enacted in 1860 as part of the Indian Penal Code, remained in effect until it was struck down by the SCI in 2018.

The question this raises is how the heterogeneous character of proportionality doctrine should be operationalized in this transitional context, which depends on who the SCI's institutional interlocutors are. The SCI has three institutional interlocutors, in principle, analogous to those of the Constitutional Court of South Africa, for the purposes of its proportionality analysis: pre-Independence British imperial authorities; post-Independence governments; and, arguably, Indian politicians exercising limited powers under the Government of India Act 1935, which de facto amounted to a minimal form of power-sharing.[16] In *Johar*, the first and second interlocutors seemed to be at play. Section 377 was clearly adopted by British imperial authorities, and that provenance provided a reason to condemn it on constitutional grounds. Justice Chandrachud, for example, argued that LGBT persons did not enjoy the full benefits of Independence, because 'Section 377 has managed to survive for

[16] Arudra Barra, 'What is "Colonial" about Colonial Laws?' (2016) 31 American University International Law Review 137.

over 158 years, impervious to both the anticolonial struggle as well as the formation of a democratic India'.[17] He continued:

> Indian citizens belonging to sexual minorities have waited. They have waited and watched as their fellow citizens were freed from the British yoke while their fundamental freedoms remained restrained under an antiquated and anachronistic colonial-era law—forcing them to live in hiding, in fear, and as second-class citizens.[18]

But the SCI's concerns regarding the effects of Section 377 were also very contemporary. For example, Justice Chandrachud placed weight on a report of the International Commission of Jurists, which reproduced government statistics that 1,279 and 1,491 persons were arrested under Section 377, in 2014 and 2015, respectively. These figures considerably diminished the force of the argument that Section 377 had fallen into disuse because there had been very few prosecutions under it, apparently fewer than 200 persons in the 150 years that the provision was in force. By broadening the lens from prosecutions to arrests, and highlighting the gross disparity between the two, Justice Chandrachud buttressed the claim that the harms of Section 377 really arise from harassment at the hands of law enforcement, and impliedly from the threat of selective prosecution. These are abuses of public power. Juxtaposed against *Johar*'s frequent references to social morality (discussed further below), we can take this argument one step further. Although the SCI only discusses social morality to distinguish it analytically from constitutional morality, it likely does so because it considers there to be considerable public support for Section 377, even in the face of the refusal of the Union government to appeal the decision in *Koushal* and defend the provision in *Johar*.[19] It is against this backdrop of public support that law enforcement continues to use Section 377. So another interlocutor is a potential parliamentary majority that could be mustered in support of enacting such a provision today—for example, as part of an electoral coalition with a religiously conservative element.

Proportionality analysis at the first stage was central to *Johar*—ie the requirement that the government has acted for a proper purpose. In most cases, this threshold question is almost always answered in the affirmative, because governments now rarely offer express justifications for decisions that are

[17] *Johar v Union of India* (n 2) Chandrachud Reasons [14].
[18] ibid [24].
[19] *Koushal v Naz Foundation* (2014) 1 SCC 1 (India).

facially illegitimate. In *Johar*, however, the Court reached the conclusion that the Section 377 was 'without any legitimate state rationale'.[20] It did so on two grounds. Section 377 was unconstitutional on the cosmopolitan ground that mere social morality was an insufficient reason to limit the right to engage in harmless, constitutionally protected activity, the basis on which courts around the world have struck down parallel provisions. In addition, Section 377 was also unconstitutional for the anti-colonial reason that it was an element of the Imperial constitutional order in British India in the period of indirect colonial rule after the Indian Mutiny of 1857.

1. Cosmopolitanism

A central distinction that runs throughout *Johar* is that between constitutional morality and social morality. Chief Justice Misra's opinion provides the most fully worked account of this distinction, and an argument for it. He begins with a theory of the Indian Constitution, which he defines as a 'transformative constitutionalism'.[21] The 'revolutionary' mission of the Indian Constitution is 'transforming a medieval, hierarchical society into a modern, egalitarian democracy'.[22] On his account, the principal target of constitutional transformation is not the state itself, but rather, the vast edifice of private social and economic relations—which can be loosely termed social morality. That mission, it stands to reason, authorizes and empowers the state to engage a project of transforming social morality, and presumptively requires courts to defer when constitutional challenges to such measures are raised. Conversely, it would also appear to require that government decisions to entrench, reify, and enforce social morality should be subject to probing constitutional scrutiny.

If social morality is the value system antithetical to transformative constitutionalism, it is to be supplanted with a new value system integral to the constitutional project itself—constitutional morality. The raises the questions of (1) the content of constitutional morality, and (2) the translation of that concept into constitutional doctrine.

Let us first consider constitutional morality's content. At its core, for Chief Justice Misra, is the claim that '[t]he society as a whole or even a minuscule part . . . may aspire and prefer different things for themselves'.[23] The outer

[20] *Johar v Union of India* (n 2) Nariman Reasons [95].
[21] *Johar v Union of India* (n 2) Misra Reasons [95].
[22] ibid.
[23] *Johar v Union of India* (n 2) Misra Reasons [115].

boundary of 'such a freedom to be different' is that it not violate the 'fundamental rights of any other citizen'.[24] Constitutional morality 'urges the organs of the State to maintain such a heterogeneous fibre in the society', and 'to curb any propensity or proclivity of popular sentiment or majoritarianism'.[25] Constitutional morality can 'not be equated with the popular sentiment prevalent at a particular point in time'.[26]

This is a thoroughly modern and cosmopolitan approach to the basis of legitimate public authority. But what does this mean in concrete legal terms? Consider this passage from Chief Justice Misra's reasons:

> While testing the constitutional validity of impugned provision of law, if a constitutional court is of the view that the impugned provision falls foul to the precept of constitutional morality, then the said provision has to be declared as unconstitutional for the pure and simple reason that the constitutional courts exist to uphold the Constitution.[27]

Chief Justice Misra could be read as suggesting that constitutional morality is a free-standing ground of constitutional review, rooted in the idea that that the role of the courts is to ensure that 'constitutional morality prevails over social morality'.[28] However, there is nothing in the text or practice of the Indian Constitution that supports this view. Indeed, even the basic structure doctrine is textually anchored in Article 368. A more plausible reading views constitutional morality—in particular, the imperative that 'the organs of the State . . . preserve the heterogeneous nature of the society and to curb any attempt by the majority to usurp the rights and freedoms of a smaller or miniscule section of the populace'[29]—as a principle of constitutional interpretation underlying *both* the delineation of the scope of Part III's Fundamental Rights and the application of proportionality. *Johar* posits that constitutional morality supplies *both* the justification for the entrenchment of constitutional rights *and* restricts the permissible purposes for proportionality limiting such rights. Governments cannot restrict rights for the very reasons that the Constitution guarantees these rights to individuals.

24 ibid.
25 *Johar v Union of India* (n 2) Misra Reasons [116].
26 ibid.
27 *Johar v Union of India* (n 2) Misra Reasons [124].
28 ibid [121].
29 ibid [253v].

Ronald Dworkin offered a famous account of such a theory of constitutional rights.[30] Indeed, since he did so in the context of Lord Devlin's criticism of the Wolfenden Report, which had recommended the decriminalization of anal intercourse in the United Kingdom, his views merit careful attention in coming to grips with *Johar*. Dworkin begins with the problem of moral disagreement among individuals about what rights people have. His core claim is that some reasons that may be offered for a position 'will be excluded by general criteria stipulating sorts of reasons which do not count'—ie they are inadmissible, and as a threshold matter have no weight at all. One such reason is prejudice against homosexuals, which is inadmissible for the following reason:

> If I tell you that homosexuals are morally inferior because they do not have heterosexual desires . . . you would reject that reason as showing one type of prejudice. Prejudices, in general, are postures of judgment that take into account considerations our conventions exclude . . . . Our conventions stipulate some ground rules of moral judgment which obtain even part from such special contexts, the most important of which is that a man must not be held morally inferior on the basis of some physical, racial or other characteristic he cannot help having. Thus, a man whose moral judgments . . . are based on his belief that any member of these classes automatically deserves less respect, without regard to anything be himself has done, is said to be prejudiced against that group.[31]

Dworkin then applies this framework for moral disagreement to the legitimate basis for the assertion of the *state*'s coercive power, to reason that 'prejudices . . . do not justify restricting another's freedom'.[32] This position holds '[e]ven if it is true that most men think homosexuality an abominable vice and cannot tolerate its presence'.[33] The reason is the distinction between conventional morality in the 'anthropological' or descriptive sense, and in the 'discriminatory' or normative sense, with only the latter admissible as a justification by the state. These two conceptions of a moral position correspond exactly to social and constitutional morality, as Chief Justice Misra uses those terms.

[30] Ronald M Dworkin, 'Lord Devlin and the Enforcement of Morals' (1965–66) 75 Yale Law Journal 986.
[31] ibid 996.
[32] ibid 1001.
[33] ibid 1000.

In his critique of Devlin, Dworkin did not spell out the argument for why individuals should have any rights at all. But elsewhere, he rooted the specific rights that individuals have in an underlying right to equal respect and concern.[34] This has a crucial doctrinal implication—that the same reasons that justify the entrenchment of constitutional rights also operate to circumscribe the kinds of considerations that can legitimately count to limit such rights. This is the most plausible reading of *Johar*. It follows that if constitutional morality requires that we guarantee to everyone 'a freedom to be different', the state cannot justify the limitation of that freedom simply for the purpose of eradicating or diminishing difference—what Chief Justice Misra refers to as 'majority perception or view'.[35] Since that was the only possible purpose for Section 377, he concluded it 'does not meet the criteria of proportionality'.[36]

This is a cosmopolitan argument, because it gives no weight to India's cultural, historical, or political context, either with respect to the rights that individuals have under Part III, or the justifiable reasons for limiting them. In addition to providing a coherent account of Chief Justice Misra's reasons, it also explains and justifies *Johar*'s comparativism. *Johar* cited comparative jurisprudence extensively, from Belize, Ecuador, Fiji, Hong Kong, Kenya, Nepal, South Africa, Trinidad and Tobago, the United States, and the European Court of Human Rights and the United Nations Human Rights Committee. This growing body of case law—to which we must now add *Johar* itself—has found criminal prohibitions on sodomy to be inconsistent with various rights-protecting instruments. But convergence on a common legal position is not necessarily proof of that position's rightness or truth. What matters much more are the substantive reasons offered by courts to reach their decisions—in particular, whether those reasons are cosmopolitan too. Most of these laws were defended on the basis of social morality. And it is of considerable relevance that the authorities discussed in the most depth reached the conclusion that the laws failed the test of proportionality, because of the lack of a proper purpose (eg *Lawrence v Texas*).[37]

[34] Ronald Dworkin, *A Matter of Principle* (HUP 1986) ch 8, 'Liberalism'.
[35] *Johar v Union of India* (n 2) Misra Reasons [34].
[36] ibid [247].
[37] *Lawrence v Texas* (2003) 539 US 558.

2. Anti-colonialism

This cosmopolitan argument would have been sufficient to resolve the case. Moreover, on in its terms, the historical origins of Section 377 in British imperial rule are irrelevant. Whether enacted in the nineteenth or twenty-first century, the provision would have been unconstitutional for the same reason: it breached one or more Fundamental Rights under Part III, and it could not be justified on the basis of a proper purpose. However, history mattered to the submissions of the parties. For example, Menaka Guruswamy, appearing on behalf of the petitioners in the companion case of *Pokkuluri*, submitted that '[i]n a constitutional democracy, a statute that protects and furthers the morality of colonial monarchs is per se arbitrary'.[38] Arvind Datar, on behalf of one of the petitioners in *Johar*, argued that since Section 377 'is a colonial law', and that it was 'wrongfully referred to as representing the will of the people in *Koushal*'.[39] What work did history do here? One answer would appear to be straightforward: to pre-empt any reliance, contra *Koushal*, on majoritarian preferences as a proper purpose for proportionality analysis. Irrespective of whether such an argument is acceptable in *principle*, it could also be rejected *empirically*, on the basis that Section 377 could not represent the will of the majority.

Arudra Barra provides another answer regarding the possible work that history does. He recently observed that in contemporary Indian politics the colonial origins of laws and policies are a sufficient reason to abolish or amend them. He counters that the legacy of colonial-era legislation is complex. On the one hand, there is Section 377. But on the other hand, Provincial Ministries led by the Congress Party under the Government of India Act exercised their executive powers to release political prisoners. The Provincial Legislatures whose confidence they enjoyed repealed public safety and emergency legislation used by Imperial authorities to repress political dissent, and enacted new laws promoting an agenda of agrarian and social reform which continued in force after Independence. He asks:

> Were the executive acts of these Ministries and the legislation passed by the Provincial Assemblies 'colonial'? They were certainly colonial-*era* acts .... If the term 'colonial' is used not just to designate a historical period, but also to designate some particular aspect of that period (defined, for instance, by an opposition to the anti-colonial movement), then it is not easy to describe

[38] Written Submissions on behalf of the petitioners Ankesh Pokkuluri et al, para 1.4.
[39] Written Submissions on behalf of petitioner Keshav Suri, para 6.1.

> the working of the Act [ie the Government of India Act] as either colonial or anti-colonial. And if the identification of these Acts as colonial is problematic then their identification post-Independence as colonial *continuities*, is surely problematic as well.[40]

Instead of condemning laws in terms of their *formal* constitutional origin—ie their enactment pursuant to the colonial legal order—he asks:

> . . . surely it is enough to cite the substantive reasons which make them [colonial-era laws] unacceptable in the present? . . . Calling them 'colonial' may provide an additional rhetorical heft to this attack, but adds little that is substantive, for the colonial origins of a law are by themselves analytically neutral . . . . analytical clarity will be served best if questions and arguments pose in terms of colonial continuities are re-framed so as to remove the reference to the colonial, and focus our attention on more substantive issues.[41]

Barra does expressly address the relevance of the colonial-era status of legislation to those laws' potential unconstitutionality. But the logical implication of Barra's argument is that he would rely solely on cosmopolitan grounds to impugn the constitutionality of Section 377—ie anti-moralism. He would dismiss reliance on the colonial origins of Section 377 as a purely formal argument.

Barra is correct that that the institutional fact that Section 377 was enacted by British imperial authorities is an insufficient reason to constitutionally condemn it. However, there is another set of arguments regarding the colonial-era origins of Section 77 that are distinct from the cosmopolitan objections to that provision, and which go to the anti-colonial dimension of transformative constitutionalism. In his reasons, Justice Nariman provided a standard historical overview of the origins of Section 377. This history begins in 1834, with the establishment of the Indian Law Commission, and the appointment as Thomas Macaulay as its first chair. One of Macaulay's first projects was to draft the IPC. He submitted the first draft in 1837. The IPC then went through several further drafts, prepared and reviewed by a series of entities and individuals including the Commission, members of the Legislative Council of India and Justices of the Supreme Court at Calcutta, the Court of Directors of the East India Company in London, a Council or Committee of the Company, and a Select Committee. The IPC was enacted in 1860, a few years after the 1857 Mutiny.

[40] Barra (n 16) 146 (italics in original).
[41] ibid 169.

For Justice Nariman, the purpose of Section 377 was to impose a Victorian conception of sexual morality on India. While Section 377 prohibited 'unnatural offences', which it defined as 'intercourse against the order of nature'—moral in tone—Justice Nariman noted that Macaulay's original draft defined the prohibited conduct as touching 'for the purpose of gratifying unnatural lust', which clearly expressed a moral judgment on the conduct in question 'in this most prudish of all periods of English history'.[42] Justice Chandrachud provided supporting evidence, in the form of an explanatory note from Macaulay to the 1837 draft in which he described the prohibited conduct in the earlier provision as 'revolting', and justified the omission of an explanation for the provision in order to prevent a 'public discussion' which would injure 'the morals of the community'.[43]

However, this is a reductive account of Section 377 that wrenches it from the broader political project of which it was a part. Mahmood Mamdani provides the larger context.[44] The 1857 Mutiny was a watershed between two models of imperial governance in India. Over the century of the East India Company's rule, from 1757 to 1857, the strategy of imperial governance was *direct rule*. This was a universalist, 'civilizing mission spearheaded by liberal Utilitarian and Christian evangelists',[45] whose core elements were 'to abolish the Moghul court and to impose British laws and technology—along with Christianity—on India',[46] along with the promotion of free markets, in the service of liberal modernity. The Mutiny led Imperial authorities to conclude that this strategy had utterly failed. After 1857, Imperial strategy shifted dramatically, to *indirect rule*, rooted in the protection of culture, custom, and tradition. One part of this strategy included 'setting limits on the operation of the market, thereby protecting the village community from moneylenders, agricultural subcastes from trading castes, and the landlord's estate from division and fragmentation'.[47] Another dimension was the creation of the religious personal codes, one for each community, defended 'in the language of cultural difference and cosmopolitan tolerance'.[48] The census was a crucial political device that enabled imperial authorities to categorize and classify colonial subjects, principally on the basis of caste and religion, which served as the basis for the distribution of political and economic power, in the form of separate electoral rolls for Muslims

42 *Johar v Union of India* (n 2) Nariman Reasons [18].
43 *Johar v Union of India* (n 2) Chandrachud Reasons [21].
44 Mahmood Mamdani, *Define and Rule: Native as Political Identity* (Harvard UP 2012).
45 ibid 9.
46 ibid 8.
47 ibid 27.
48 ibid 30.

and Hindus, and reservations. Although rationalized as a form of minority rights protection, categorization and classification became a technology of Imperial control.

Against the backdrop of the profound shift in imperial governance in India in 1857, the IPC presents a historical puzzle, because of the sharp disjunction between its framing and timing. As Karuna Mantena acutely observes, on the one hand:

> The *Indian Penal Code*, unlike later substantive codes, was not a work of consolidation or digest, that is, it did not take current English law and systematize, simplify, and rationalize it. Rather, it was a self-conscious attempt to construct a code de novo, based upon first principles, taking inspiration from other systematic codes, notably the French Code Penal and Livingston's code for Louisiana. In this respect, the *Indian Penal Code* may be the closest to anything like a pure philosophical code to be enacted in the nineteenth century.[49]

The IPC was the quintessential Benthamite instrument of the civilizing mission. But on the other hand, the adoption of the IPC in 1860 'sits uneasily with the post-Mutiny distancing from ambitious projects for the modernization and assimilation of Indian society'. Mantena argues that the proponents of indirect rule—chiefly Henry Maine—justified the IPC on the basis that during the period of direct rule, the common law courts had displaced or rigidified customary law, which rendered it irreparable. The IPC was the only solution.

However, Section 377 stands apart from the rest of the IPC and is on all fours with other group-differentiated laws, because it targets sexual activity engaged in disproportionately by a group, defined by sexual orientation. Moreover, it was eventually deployed as a tool of indirect rule. The critical link was the Criminal Tribes Act, 1871. The Criminal Tribes Act, and its relationship to Section 377, were previously discussed by the SCI in *NALSA*,[50] although only passing reference was made to those passages in *Johar*.[51] The relevant history is set out in the written submissions of Voices Against 377.[52] The Act authorized the colonial authorities to designate as a 'criminal tribe' a tribe or class of persons 'addicted to the systematic commission of non-bailable offences', through the ascription of a caste-like status. Members of criminal tribes were presumed

[49] Karuna Mantena, *Alibis of Empire: Henry Maine and the Ends of Liberal Imperialism* (Princeton UP 2010).
[50] *NALSA v Union of India* (2014) 5 SCC 438.
[51] *Johar v Union of India* (n 2) Nariman Reasons [49], [55].
[52] ibid [42]–[50].

to be born criminal and were subject to the most extensive system of control, including registration, settlement and resettlement, and detention. In 1897, the Act was amended to encompass eunuchs within its ambit. The amendments established a statutory connection between Section 377 and the Act, by requiring local officials to maintain a registry of all eunuchs 'reasonably suspected . . . of committing offences under Section 377 of the *Indian Penal Code*'. The combined effect of these provisions was to create a status offence, making any eunuch an unapprehended felon.

What are the contemporary constitutional implications, if any, of the Criminal Tribes Act? Voices Against 377 argued that Section 377 imposed on LGBT persons the same harm as persons who were subject to the Criminal Tribes Act—that is, they were unapprehended felons under a status offence. Along similar lines, I have argued that at the root the decision of the Delhi High Court in the Section 377 litigation was the analogy between untouchability and sexual orientation, based on the historical experience under the Criminal Tribes Act.[53] My argument on that occasion was that the treatment which LGBT persons in India experience today is similar in kind to that which 'untouchables' experience, and which prompted the adoption of Article 17 (which abolishes untouchability). But *Johar* allows us to take this argument one step further to the origins of Section 377 itself. Section 377 was legally conscripted into service for the imperial strategy of indirect rule, through classification and control, under the Criminal Tribes Act. It therefore came to serve a *constitutional function* under the colonial legal order. It was indelibly and forever tainted by that role.

Independence—culminating in 1950 with the Indian Constitution—marked the end of the colonial constitutional order and its replacement with an entirely new one. This was one dimension of India's transformative constitutionalism. Article 395 repealed the key statutes of the colonial constitutional order, chiefly the Government of India Act, 1935. In addition, I would argue that we can infer from Article 395, and from the constitutional scheme as a whole, that any surviving colonial-era statute with the purpose of the maintenance of the Imperial system of indirect rule was per se unconstitutional. Article 372 does not change this position. It is simply a technical provision to ensure legal continuity; it has no bearing, either way, on the constitutionality of colonial-era laws—a point made by Justice Nariman.[54] On the anti-colonial account, the

[53] Sujit Choudhry, 'How To Do Comparative Constitutional Law in India: *Naz Foundation*, Same Sex Rights, and Dialogical Interpretation' in Sunil Khilnani, Vikram Raghavan, and Arun Thiruvengadam (eds), *Comparative Constitutionalism in South Asia* (OUP 2012) 45–85.

[54] *Johar v Union of India* (n 2) Nariman Reasons [90].

unconstitutionality of Section 377 lies not in its imposition of *morality*—social, Victorian, or otherwise. Rather, its unconstitutionality lies in its use as a tool for the *maintenance of colonial political power and domination.*

This is a functional argument that allows us, for contemporary constitutional purposes, to differentiate among the mass of colonial-era legislation that remains in force pursuant to Article 372, while nonetheless recognizing the special and distinct constitutional wrong of colonialism in a sovereign democratic republic. This ground of unconstitutionality would not impugn reform legislation enacted by the Provincial Assemblies pursuant to the Government of India Act that lay the groundwork for post-Independence economic and social transformation. Those laws were not designed to perpetuate colonial rule—incorporating Rohit De's insight that it is analytically useful to distinguish between the actions of the earlier and late colonial state in India, as opposed to tarring them with the same nationalist brush.[55]

Nor could this argument put into question the constitutionality of the Imperial enactments that codified the Indian private law of contract and property. Now to be sure, as Shyam Balganesh has persuasively demonstrated, the Indian Transfer of Property Act served Imperial interests. It did so by withdrawing power from the Indian courts, whose judicial creativity 'ran the risk of undermining the control that the British administration had by this time very ably established in India, much of it through complex land revenue schemes, tenancy reform initiatives, and governance policies'.[56] But there is a way to distinguish among colonial-era laws that served Imperial interests, through an analogue to the basic structure doctrine. The question to be posed in each case is whether a colonial-era law that served Imperial interests was core or basic to the post-1857 constitutional order of indirect control. If it was, its very purpose is unconstitutional, and is excluded by implication from the Indian constitutional scheme—a fatal flaw at the threshold stage of proportionality analysis. The Indian Transfer of Property Act was not such a law; section 377 was.

D. Conclusion

Here is the broader lesson of *Johar* and the Indian case. The idea of transformative constitutionalism means two things. First, it implies a radical renovation

[55] Rohit De, *A People's Constitution: The Everyday Life of Law in the Indian Republic* (Princeton UP 2018).

[56] Shyamkrishna Balganesh, 'Codifying the Common Law of Property in India: Crystallization and Standardization as Strategies of Constraint' (2015) 63 American Journal of Comparative Law 33, 43.

in the acceptable grounds for the legitimate exercise of public power. These grounds are common to all constitutional democracies, and what is transformative about a transformative constitution is that it categorically rules out much of what had hitherto been acceptable under an authoritarian or colonial regime. If we imagine judicial review in any constitutional democracy as requiring government to provide reasons to justify all exercises of public powers, and for the doctrine of proportionality to provide the framework for courts to assess those reasons, there is now a single standard of justification across jurisdictions, with a single institutional interlocutor for the court. The cosmopolitan anti-moralism of *Johar* is an illustrative example.

But transformative constitutions must also reckon with the messy and ragged legal legacies of the past in the present, that differ sharply from the image of constitutional revolution. In particular, they must reconcile the continuities of the laws of the old regime that prevent a legal vacuum, and the compromises of constitutional principle that make the transformative constitution possible, with the foundational commitment of the new constitutional order to never again repeat the injustices of the past. Any laws which were integral to the maintenance of colonial domination and control are anathema to the new constitutional order. *Johar*'s condemnation of Section 377 as an instrument of indirect rule is a case in point.

9

Socio-Economic Rights and Expanding Access to Justice in South Africa

What Can Be Done?

David Bilchitz

A. Introduction: Access to Justice, Fundamental Rights, and the Global South

Since the end of the Cold War, there has been a significant expansion of Constitutions that include a bill of rights and, also, allow for the judicial review of legislation and executive conduct on the basis of such fundamental rights. Many of these countries, particularly those in the Global South,[1] have included such provisions following histories of colonialism, foreign domination, or internal oppression. Constitutions have thus been charged not simply with outlining the structures of governance: they provide a blueprint for a different future founded on social justice. This approach to constitutions as designed to enable and encourage the achievement of wide-spread social change has been termed 'transformative constitutionalism'.[2]

One of the features of transformative constitutions that have mainly been enacted in the Global South is the inclusion not simply of civil and political rights but also socio-economic entitlements to such goods as housing, food, healthcare, and education. The backdrop to the inclusion of these rights was a history and present characterized by large-scale poverty—usually of a majority of the inhabitants of a country—arising often from their deliberate exclusion from having access to the socio-economic resources of their own country. As a result, the new orders in these Global South countries did not only seek to

[1] See the discussion around this term in the introduction and theoretical essays in this volume.

[2] Karl E Klare 'Legal Culture and Transformative Constitutionalism' (1998) 14 South African Journal on Human Rights 146, 146–56; Michaela Hailbronner, 'Transformative Constitutionalism: Not Only in the Global South' (2017) 65 American Journal of Comparative Law 527, 527–41; see also the articles in this volume on Transformative Constitutionalism by Klug and Arguelhes.

David Bilchitz, *Socio-Economic Rights and Expanding Access to Justice in South Africa* In: *The Global South and Comparative Constitutional Law.* Edited by: Philipp Dann, Michael Riegner, and Maxim Bönnemann, Oxford University Press (2020). © Oxford University Press. DOI: 10.1093/oso/9780198850403.003.0009

address the political injustices of their past but also needed to engage the poor socio-economic conditions of many of their inhabitants. Thus, 'Global South' constitutions have generally included socio-economic guarantees.[3] Yet, the mere inclusion of a provision does not mean that it is translated into reality: to do so, there is a need to attend both to the substantive content of the provision and enforcement mechanisms.

This chapter focuses on the latter question of enforcement:[4] it adopts the view that if rights are entitlements, then it must be possible for individuals to be able to claim such entitlements (or for someone to do so on their behalf if they are unable to do so).[5] As empirical experience shows, it is not sufficient simply to rely on the promises of governments to realize these entitlements: there must be the possibility of challenging the failure to meet their obligations. Putting people in a position to make claims might be understood under the term 'access to justice', a term whose meaning this chapter will seek to parse in the next section. I shall argue that access to justice should be conceived of as a capability: doing so, involves attending to two crucial dimensions. The first is an internal dimension relating to the empowerment of individuals to make such claims; and the second is an external dimension relating to the design and availability of institutional mechanisms that are set up to hear these claims and adjudicate upon them.

Access to justice in the Global South contexts raises particular challenges: these include the lack of education of many inhabitants as well as the need for new institutional mechanisms that render making claims accessible to the poor. A number of these jurisdictions have included particular innovations to enhance access to justice of their inhabitants. To develop the required depth, this chapter will seek to focus on one jurisdiction, namely, South Africa.

The third part of the chapter will outline the main institutional architecture created by the South African democratic constitutional order that began in 1994 relating to access to justice as well as the shortcomings thereof. The fourth part of the chapter will then turn to considering solutions to these problems and provide concrete policy recommendations to enhance access to justice in South Africa. Some of these are drawn from the comparative experience of Colombia and India. The last part of the chapter will close with a consideration

[3] Daniel Bonilla Maldonado, 'Towards a Constitutionalism of the Global South' in Daniel Bonilla Maldonado (ed), *Constitutionalism of the Global South: The Activist Tribunals of India, South Africa, and Colombia* (CUP 2013) 26.

[4] I have defended this conception of fundamental rights in David Bilchitz, *Poverty and Fundamental Rights: The Justification and Enforcement of Socio-economic Rights* (OUP 2007) but most theories of fundamental rights will share a similar idea.

[5] See, for a similar point, Reni D Segui, 'L'accès à la justice et ses obstacles' (1995) 28 VRÜ/WCL 449.

and response to a possible objection to the approach adopted which is particularly acute in the Global South: given the scarcity of resources in the Global South, should funds be spent on enhancing access to justice or the actual providing of goods and services? Ultimately, I aim to provide a theoretical approach to access to justice drawn from the Global South context which can enable us to generate practical recommendations for enhancing such access in the South African context.

B. Access to Justice as a Capability

The notion of access to justice is at the centre of this paper but what does it in fact entail? As I have indicated in the introduction, it concerns the important ability of individuals to make and enforce claims to entitlements that society is supposed to provide them with. What is involved with exercising such an ability?

In engaging with this question, it is useful to draw on the insights of the 'capabilities approach' developed by Amartya Sen and Martha Nussbaum.[6] The capabilities approach assesses value in terms of whether an individual is capable of doing something or not. The notion of being capable, however, is not simple—Martha Nussbaum, in her development of the approach, identifies several aspects to what is involved in having a capability. For our purposes, it is useful to distinguish between two dimensions she identifies. The first lies in what she terms an internal capability: this considers facets of individual persons which are necessary for the exercise of various functions but which require a certain state of maturity to operationalize. She gives the examples of the use of language, freedom of expression, and sexual maturity. The second is what she terms 'combined capabilities': this involves the internal capability *plus* whether there are suitable external conditions available for its exercise. Thus, individuals in North Korea may have an internal capability to exercise free speech but not a combined capability as the external conditions of state repression render it virtually impossible to do so.[7]

Whilst neither Nussbaum nor Sen expressly recognize access to justice as a capability, neither is committed to the notion that there is a list that is fixed for all time.[8] As has persuasively been argued by Chatterjee and Chowdhury

[6] Amartya Sen, *Inequality Re-examined* (OUP 1992) 39–40; Martha C Nussbaum, *Women and Human Development: The Capabilities Approach* (CUP 2000) 84–85.

[7] Nussbaum (n 6) 86.

[8] Sen (n 6) does not provide a list whilst Nussbaum (n 6) 68 does but views her list as open-ended.

in the context of India, access to justice is a strong candidate for being recognized as a capability.[9] In providing a justification for doing so, they connect the capabilities approach with the idea of basic rights promoted by Henry Shue.[10] Shue contends that a basic right is one that is essential to the enjoyment of all other rights.[11] He identifies the right to security and to subsistence as two central rights of this kind. Chatterjee and Chowdhury contend, however, that 'the right to access to justice is perhaps an even stronger guarantee to the enjoyment of other non-basic rights than the right to security and subsistence, since it goes a step further to guarantee the enjoyment of these two basic rights. Further, it provides an assurance of a fair redressal mechanism in case of the non-availability of the other basic right.'[12] They thus, essentially, highlight the point that having an entitlement is both conceptually and practically tied to the capability to enforce that entitlement.

Apart from these instrumental reasons why it is very basic and tied to other capabilities, access to justice can be understood to have two further components which identify it as a central capability. The first lies in a 'dignitarian justification': this involves the idea that enabling people to make claims is part of what is involved in treating them with dignity and respect.[13] The second lies in a 'relational justification': this involves the understanding that ensuring people can make claims is about building the relationships of individuals in ways which are rooted in respect.[14]

These justifications all provide reasons for thinking that the ability to make claims in official institutions for the guarantee of one's rights is a vitally important capability. Analysing access to justice in this way also allows us to consider what 'real access' involves. That involves first considering the individual and internal factors which render it actually possible for persons to make claims. Secondly, it involves considering the external conditions for making claims and, in particular, the availability and accessibility of institutions. The focus is often placed largely on the latter but the capabilities approach helps us see the necessity of considering the full set of vectors necessary for real access to be granted.

[9] Promit Chatterjee and Sreerupa Chowdhury, 'A Capabilities Approach to Access to Justice' (2013) 4 *Journal of Indian Law and Society* 107.

[10] Henry Shue, *Basic Rights* (2nd edn, Princeton UP 1996).

[11] ibid 19.

[12] Chatterjee and Chowdhury (n 9) 119.

[13] Jeremy Waldron, 'The Rule of Law and the Importance of Procedure' in James E Fleming (ed), *Getting to the Rule of Law* (New York UP 2011) 15–16.

[14] Denise Meyerson, 'The Moral Justification for the Right to Make Full Answer and Defence (2015) 35 Oxford Journal of Legal Studies 237, 259.

This analysis also links well with recent work in the access to justice sector that is critical of the previously dominant top-down framework. Golub, for instance, identifies the dominant model of development agencies on access to justice as involving a focus on courts and law reform. He does not discard the importance of these considerations but instead identifies an alternative 'legal empowerment' model: 'the use of legal services and related development activities to increase disadvantaged populations' control over their lives.'[15] This approach involves a departure from the traditional model in several respects: it involves considering individual barriers to access, such as a lack of education, as well as the possibilities of empowering civil society organizations as well as non-judicial institutions. The focus only on judicial institutions may fail to consider many facets of access to justice, particularly in developing societies. The legal empowerment approach thus offers an alternative that is wholly compatible with the capabilities approach I have sought to defend.

C. Barriers to Gaining Access to Remedies in Socio-Economic Rights Cases: The South African Experience

Capabilities and legal empowerment seek to identify the factors necessary to ensure people are able to make claims if they need to. South Africa is a country which moved from an order that did not enshrine fundamental rights in its constitution to one which did. Its past is one which deliberately disempowered its black population, and its transformative approach to constitutionalism, ultimately, sought to undo these historical injustices through a law-based process that included enshrining both justiciable civil and political rights as well as justiciable socio-economic rights in its bill of rights.[16] This shift provides a fruitful opportunity to consider what changes are required when seeking to ensure individuals can make claims relating to their fundamental rights. I turn now to a consideration of the necessary conditions for access to justice in South

[15] Stephen Golub, 'Beyond the Rule of Law Orthodoxy: The Legal Empowerment Alternative' (2003) Carnegie Endowment Working Papers 41/2003, 5 <http://carnegieendowment.org/files/wp41.pdf> accessed 10 November 2019; see also Stephen Golub, 'Legal Empowerment: Impact and Implications for the Development Community and the World Bank'(2006) 2 The World Bank Legal Review: Law, Equity, and Development 167 <https://openknowledge.worldbank.org/bitstream/handle/10986/6899/568260pub0repl1inal0proof0full0text.pdf?sequence=1#page=181> accessed 31 October 2018; Stephen Golub (ed), *Legal Empowerment: Practitioners' Perspective* (International Development Law Organization 2010) <https://www.myjusticemyanmar.org/sites/default/files/IDLO%20Legal%20Empowerment%2C%20Practitioners%E2%80%99%20Perspectives.pdf> accessed 31 October 2019.

[16] Klare (n 2) 146. See also Klug in this volume.

Africa, its institutional mechanisms, and the obstacles experienced in gaining effective access.

1. The individual dimension

In order to be able to make a claim, it is of course, first critical that one knows that one has such a claim. Constitutional education is thus a central component in enabling individuals to gain access to justice. Looked at in this way, there are a number of obstacles which prevent individuals from gaining access to the institutional mechanisms which are available. The government has in fact made some efforts to advance constitutional literacy.[17] Yet, the knowledge and understanding individuals have about their rights and the Constitution is limited. A 2014 study by the Foundation for Human Rights (FHR) on awareness of the Constitution found that only 46 per cent of the sample had heard of the South African Constitution or bill of rights and that fewer than 10 per cent had read the bill of rights (or had it read to them).[18] Only 40 per cent had heard of the South African Human Rights Commission and 28 per cent of the Public Protector.[19] In a more recent survey conducted by the South African Institute for Advanced Constitutional, Public, Human Rights, and International Law (SAIFAC) of the Gauteng adult population, it was found that 57 per cent of people had heard of the South African Human Rights Commission.[20] Fifty-five per cent knew about the Constitutional Court.[21] Those who knew about these institutions had a very limited idea of what these institutions in fact do. Questions were also asked in this survey testing the knowledge individuals have of the Constitution with a number of basic questions: only six of

[17] Deputy Minister of Justice and Constitutional Development, the Hon JH Jeffery, 'Address' (National Colloquium on Constitutional Rights Education, St George Hotel, 30 July 2015) <https://www.gov.za/speeches/address-deputy-minister-justice-and-constitutional-development-hon-jh-jeffery-mp-national> accessed 10 November 2019.

[18] Foundation for Human Rights (FHR), 'Report of the AJPCR Baseline Survey on Awareness of, Attitude and Access to Constitutional Rights' (FHR 2015) <http://fhr.org.za/files/2114/4249/0340/AJPCR_Baseline_Report_Final_1.pdf> accessed 10 November 2019. The Foundation for Human Rights did not report on whether there is a gendered dimension to this but Kivutha Kibwana, 'Women and the Constitution in Kenya' (1992) 25 Law and Politics in Africa, Asia, and Latin America 6, 19 raises the fact that, in Kenya, women lack even greater awareness of the law than men.

[19] FHR (n 18) 13.

[20] Merle Werbeloff, 'Constitutional Legitimacy: A Survey of the Gauteng Adult Population' (2015) in Institute for Democracy and Electoral Assistance, 'Assessing the Performance of the South African Constitution' (International Institute for Democracy and Electoral Assistance 2016) 24 <http://www.constitutionnet.org/vl/item/assessing-performance-south-african-constitution> accessed 10 November 2019.

[21] ibid.

the eighteen questions were answered generally correctly with the rest being mostly wrong.[22] The latter survey results come from a relatively well-off province—Gauteng—and, it is highly likely that the results would be even worse in provinces with a worse education system (as is suggested by the worse results from the FHR study).

A second major component of being able to make a claim is feeling that one is empowered to do so. One of the major effects of apartheid was psychological and the attempt systematically to disempower the poor. In South Africa, individuals of course have fought against an unjust system but also, on a daily basis, disadvantaged people are still subject to treatment which enhances their sense of disempowerment from the public sphere. There is also a component whereby people see state institutions as in some sense 'foreign' and are inclined to approach traditional leaders or tribunals when they have a complaint more readily.[23]

Apart from these real effects relating to the psychological and educational level of individuals, there are also a number of other concrete factors which inhibit individuals from being able to make claims. A number of these relate to financial and other resources. For many people, the institutions created by the Constitution lack offices close to their homes. To reach them is costly and thus beyond the reach of many. The FHR survey found that people usually had a police station or magistrates' court within an hour of their home though this time varied for those in rural areas.[24] The South African Human Rights Commission (SAHRC) only has one office per province which may be difficult for many people to reach as the distances in South Africa are vast. The same is true of the High Court, which only recently has had branches opened in two of the most economically disadvantaged provinces.

If individuals have the finance for transport, they may of course be concerned with the costs of legal representation should this be necessary. The scope of this paper does not allow for a full overview of the legal aid system in South Africa.[25] A few brief points can be made: South Africa has an extensive system of legal aid. The focus is usually on criminal cases with only a limited availability in civil cases.[26] University legal clinics assist with the provision of legal

[22] ibid 10.

[23] Yetunde A Aiyedun, 'Fair Trial and Access to Justice in South Africa: How Traditional Tribunals Cater to the Needs of Rural Female Litigants' (PhD thesis, University of Cape Town 2013) <https://open.uct.ac.za/bitstream/handle/11427/4677/thesis_law_2013_aiyedun_yetunde_adenike.pdf?sequence=1> accessed 12 December 2019. See also, in the Ivory Coast context, Eugene Assepo, 'Les modes extrajudiciares de reglement des litiges en Cote d'Ivoire' (2000) 33 Law and Politics in Africa, Asia, and Latin America 304, 305.

[24] FHR (n 18) 13.

[25] An overview is usefully provided in Aiyedun (n 23).

[26] ibid 95.

aid but are often, again, geographically far removed from people.[27] Legal aid is also available to people who earn below a certain threshold, which is relatively low:[28] whilst those who are most poor can gain access to a lawyer, many people who earn above this threshold—and still remain economically pressed—in the working classes and middle classes are not entitled to such services. There are also a number of civil society organizations which defend fundamental rights in public interest litigation but they tend to be small and only have the capacity to take on a limited number of cases that might have far-reaching public benefits.[29]

Finally, given the high unemployment rate in South Africa, working people are concerned to hold onto their jobs: taking off a significant amount of time to address fundamental rights violations is just not an option for many. The time investment involved in such cases is thus also a hindering factor on an individual level, particularly, where people are sceptical of the benefits of doing so. The FHR study found that when rights violations had taken place only 10 per cent approached state institutions to try and resolve their problem. This can perhaps be explained by a widespread perception from over 60 per cent of people in the SAIFAC survey that state institutions were difficult to access.[30]

2. The institutional dimension

With the inclusion of rights in the South African Constitution, it was of course necessary to set up the institutional architecture to enable people to claim their entitlements. The Constitution did not envisage that only the courts would address and adjudicate complaints relating to fundamental rights. It sets up a number of special institutions which are described as 'state institutions supporting democracy', created in terms of Chapter Nine of the constitution (referred to in short as 'Chapter Nine institutions'). In relation to socio-economic rights, two main bodies have been important: the Public Protector and the South African Human Rights Commission. Each of these institutions and the court structures will be dealt with in turn.

[27] ibid 97.

[28] ibid 92–93. There is a means test and persons earning above R5000/month or R5500/month (for a household) with more than R75,000 in movable property or R300,000 in immovable property do not receive such aid.

[29] See ibid 97–99 for an overview of some of these organizations.

[30] Werbeloff (n 20) 10.

(a) The Public Protector

The Public Protector was not designed to address issues of rights in general, but rather to focus on conduct in state institutions that is 'improper or results in impropriety or prejudice'.[31] It was also required to investigate such conduct and to take appropriate remedial action.[32]

This wide language of its jurisdiction, however, has the potential to cover conduct of state institutions that infringes upon the fundamental rights of individuals. The Public Protector Act 23 of 1994 provides for an individual complaints procedure for such conduct and extends the powers of the institution in relation both to investigations into forms of corrupt activities but also to harms caused to individuals. Whilst nowhere is the vindication and protection of fundamental rights mentioned as a core competence of the Public Protector, its power to investigate complaints where there is prejudice to a person offers it the opportunity to perform this function. It also, unlike the SAHRC, has the power to take appropriate remedial action. In a recent celebrated Constitutional Court case, a unanimous bench found the Public Protector has the power to issue orders with a binding effect which can only be challenged if subject to judicial review through the courts.[33]

In relation to fundamental rights violations, the Public Protector has become an important institution in small-scale individual complaints against state actors.[34] The Public Protector often deals with failures to provide people with benefits they are entitled to or inadequate service delivery by municipalities.[35] In 2008/9, the last year of the first Public Protector, Adv Mushwana, there were 12,435 complaints.[36] In the 2013/14 period, at the height of its work under Adv Madonsela, the number of complaints had grown to 39,817.[37] One of the key explanations for this difference is that the public trust in the institution grew (largely due to the independence of Adv Madonsela) which led to its greater utilization. Given the many failures of judgment of Madonsela's

[31] Constitution of the Republic of South Africa 1996 (hereafter 'Constitution 1996'), s 182(1)(a).

[32] ibid.

[33] *Economic Freedom Fighters v Speaker of the National Assembly* 2016 (3) SA 580 (CC).

[34] Segments of this evaluation are drawn from Andrew Konstant, 'Chapter 6. Chapter 9 Institutions' in Institute for Democracy and Electoral Assistance, 'Assessing the Performance of the South African Constitution' (International Institute for Democracy and Electoral Assistance 2016) <http://www.constitutionnet.org/vl/item/assessing-performance-south-african-constitution> accessed 10 November 2019.

[35] Private correspondence on file with the author.

[36] Office of the Public Protector, *Annual Report 2008/9* (Office of the Public Protector of South Africa 2009) <https://www.gov.za/sites/default/files/gcis_document/201409/public-protannual-rpt0809.pdf> accessed 10 November 2019.

[37] Office of the Public Protector, *Annual Report 2013/14* (Office of the Public Protector of South Africa 2009) <http://pmg-assets.s3-website-eu-west-1.amazonaws.com/141022public_protectorannual_report.pdf> accessed 10 November 2019.

successor, Busisiwe Mkhwebane, it remains to be seen whether the number of complaints will decrease.

The Public Protector's capacity to fulfil this function adequately is hindered by the failure properly to provide resources to the institution. The highly respected previous public protector, Thuli Madonsela, constantly spoke of the need for more resources to be provided for its operations. According to the Annual Report of 2013/14, the Public Protector was effectively insolvent as its current liabilities exceeded its assets by a significant amount.[38] According to the Annual Report, the financial circumstances of the Public Protector severely limit its ability to investigate all complaints in as expeditious and thorough a manner as they would like. The Public Protector concluded that the 'organisational structure is not fully funded', and that such 'constraints result in cases taking too long to complete and has the potential to erode public trust in the institution'.[39] Parliament has also often been partisan in responding to these problems with the ruling party not appreciating the strong criticism made of certain features of state conduct by the previous public protector. The request for additional funding was only partially fulfilled and the institution was forced to make cutbacks.[40]

(b) The South African Human Rights Commission

The main Chapter 9 body tasked with engaging with fundamental rights more generally is the South African Human Rights Commission (the SAHRC). The purpose of the Commission is specified in section 184(1) of the Constitution and includes promoting respect for human rights and the attainment thereof as well as monitoring the observance of fundamental rights in the Republic. The Constitution provides the Commission with powers to investigate rights violations, to take steps to secure redress where rights are violated, to conduct research, and to educate people about these rights. Interestingly, in terms of section 184(3) of the Constitution, the Commission must require departments of state each year to provide it with information on the measures taken to realize specifically the socio-economic rights in the Constitution. The Constitution also allows for the expansion of these powers by the national legislature. These provisions are elaborated upon in the legislation passed to regulate the

[38] The amount was R38,912,530.

[39] Office of the Public Protector, *Annual Report 2013/14* (n 37) 12.

[40] New 24, 'Public Protector gets R60 million lifeline', 26 February 2015 <https://www.news24.com/fin24/budget/budget-and-economy/public-protector-gets-r60m-lifeline-20150226> accessed 13 July 2020. It has been estimated in private correspondence with senior functionaries that the institution needs about three to four times the budget it is provided fully to meet its tasks which include considering corruption, mismanagement, and failures by the state to meet their obligations.

Commission, namely the South African Human Rights Commission Act 40 of 2013 ('the SAHRC Act').

The SAHRC Act adds a number of powers and functions to the arsenal of the Commission. The most important for our purposes involves whether an individual can prosecute a claim before the Commission. Section 13(3)(a) of the Act allows the Commission on its own initiative or upon receiving a complaint to investigate any violation of fundamental rights. If it finds such a violation has taken place, it can help the person secure redress, which could involve assisting them to approach a competent court or other forum or to do so on their behalf. The Commission is also empowered in terms of section 13(3)(b) to bring proceedings before a court in its own name or on behalf of a class or group of persons. The Commission thus must create a procedure whereby it can receive complaints from individuals. The Commission can investigate a violation: yet the question arises as to what happens once it finds a violation? In reality, the Commission is powerful at the investigatory stage but rather weak at the remedial stage. It is not thus far clear whether the finding of the Constitutional Court relating to the powers of the Public Protector to issue binding remedial orders, applies to the SAHRC. Up until now, the practice has been for it to make a finding but, when seeking to address a violation in a binding way, it approaches another tribunal or court.

Compared to the Public Protector, the number of complaints received by the SAHRC is relatively small: in the 2016/17 financial year, it received around 5012, of which only half were accepted by the Commission (as lying within its jurisdiction).[41] The number of complaints that it took to the courts are very small: around twenty to forty complaints were taken to the equality courts (relating specifically to unfair discrimination) whilst in relation to other rights only one or two cases were taken further.[42] The largest numbers of complaints are concentrated in Gauteng and the Western Cape, provinces that have better educated populations and with a higher level of wealth. The SAHRC itself notes: 'the Commission itself must do more to improve visibility and to initiate investigations of its own accord where complaint volumes are not a true reflection of human rights challenges on the ground.'[43]

[41] South African Human Rights Commission, *Fourth Quarter Variance Report 2016/7* (South African Human Rights Commissions 2017) on file with author.

[42] South African Human Rights Commission, *Annual Trends Analysis Report 2015/2016 Financial Year* (South African Human Rights Commission 2016) 13 <https://www.sahrc.org.za/home/21/files/Annual_Trends_Analysis_%20Report_2015_16.pdf> accessed 10 November 2019.

[43] ibid 22.

We can thus conclude that the Commission itself accepts that there are a large number of fundamental rights complaints that do not reach it. Part of its problems, similar to the Public Protector, flow from a lack of adequate funding. The Commission for instance stated in its 2012/13 annual report to parliament that '[t]he Commission continued to face the challenge of delivering on its objectives in the face of ongoing budgetary constraints'.[44] The Commission cites the lack of adequate budget as preventing it from being able thoroughly to investigate matters in rural areas far from provincial centres, to reach a wider audience through outreach programmes, and adequately to meet the needs of those with disabilities.

(c) The courts

Section 34 of the Constitution protects the right to have access to courts or, where appropriate, another impartial tribunal or forum. Section 38 of the Constitution provides that '[a]nyone listed in this section has the right to approach a competent Court, alleging that a right in the Bill of Rights has been infringed or threatened, and the court may grant appropriate relief, including a declaration of rights'. The standing provisions provided in that section are also very expansive. If someone's rights were violated, the Constitution thus envisages that they should be able to approach the courts. However, when we turn to the actual institutional court structure, there are a number of limitations that prevent widespread access.

The Magistrates' courts hear the majority of cases and are the most accessible to people as they exist across the country. They are, however, not entitled to 'enquire into or rule on the constitutionality of any legislation or any conduct of the President'.[45] Such courts have the powers only expressly conferred upon them by statute and their focus is generally on civil and criminal claims. To the extent these issues engage constitutional rights, they do, of course, have some jurisdiction over such matters: criminal matters clearly, for instance, implicate the right to a fair trial. They also have some specialized powers over such matters as evictions which impact upon constitutional rights. In certain cases, where magistrates have been provided with special training, statutory provisions have also conferred on them powers to engage with specific fundamental rights violations such as where they are designated special equality courts.[46] Similarly, certain courts have been designated as sexual offence courts

[44] South African Human Rights Commission, *South African Human Rights Commission Annual Report 2013* (South African Human Rights Commission 2013) 10 <https://www.sahrc.org.za/home/21/files/Annual%20Report%202012-13.pdf%20October.pdf> accessed 10 November 2019.

[45] Constitution 1996 (n 31) s 170.

[46] Promotion of Equality and Prevention of Unfair Discrimination Act 2 2000.

and some magistrates' courts have been allowed to hear administrative law matters. In general, however, the jurisdiction of such courts is limited in relation to rights matters unless there is a civil claim instituted and the claim does not exceed a maximum threshold.[47] Overall, these courts address day-to-day matters but do not appear to be set up with a wider fundamental rights jurisdiction in mind. Magistrates may well also not be suitably qualified to deal adequately with fundamental rights issues with qualifications to be a magistrate much less extensive than those involved in becoming a judge. The extent to which they are friendly to fundamental rights concerns is also hard to ascertain and is likely to vary.

Most fundamental rights matters are brought to the High Court, which court may rule on the constitutionality of legislation or conduct of the President but the order has no force without being confirmed by the Constitutional Court.[48] There usually are only one or two High Courts per province making them more difficult to access geographically. It is also more expensive to institute proceedings therein and matters can take longer to be heard, though the Constitutional Court has developed the principle that costs, in general, should not be awarded against applicants in matters relating to fundamental rights.[49]

The High Courts in South Africa are also not well equipped for a major influx of cases relating to socio-economic rights. There were only 239 judges in the entire country in 2015, which is not a significant increase since the dawn of democracy when the number was 166.[50] There are thus large rolls of cases which means that they take a long time to be set down and to reach resolution. This is particularly problematic for fundamental rights violations: no special procedures exist other than the general urgent application processes. Yet, it is often risky to take cases on urgency as judges require the applicant to bear the burden of justifying such urgency and often dismiss cases on this basis. It can thus confidently be said that the High Courts are not currently equipped for a massive influx of individual complaints relating to fundamental rights violations.

[47] Magistrates' Court Act 32 1944, s 29(1).
[48] Constitution 1996 (n 32) s 172(2)(a).
[49] *Biowatch Trust v Registrar Genetic Resources* 2009 (6) SA 232 (CC).
[50] Linette Du Toit, 'Chapter 5. The Performance of the Judiciary' in Institute for Democracy and Electoral Assistance, *Assessing the Performance of the South African Constitution* (International Institute for Democracy and Electoral Assistance 2016) 13 <http://www.constitutionnet.org/vl/item/assessing-performance-south-african-constitution> accessed 10 November 2019. It is reported that in 2019, there are 246 judges, including Constitutional Court and Supreme Court of Appeal Judges: see The South African Judiciary, *Annual Report 2018/19* (The South African Judiciary 2019) <https://www.judiciary.org.za/images/Annual-Reports/Judiciary_Annual_Report_2018_-_19.pdf> accessed 30 October 2019.

Once a determination is made by the High Court, appeals lie to the Supreme Court of Appeal and the Constitutional Court and such cases often involve multiple stages of litigation. The Supreme Court of Appeal already has a large case load. Moreover, the Constitutional Court has generally not favoured granting direct access to it and places a high burden of justification for doing so.[51] It reasons that it should not be the court of first and last instance.[52] All judges also sit *en banc* for each case. The Constitutional Court has generally decided a relatively small number of cases per year in comparison with similar courts in other Global South countries.[53] Yet, it can be confidently said that it is not set up well at present for a major influx of cases.

These institutional limitations could perhaps also provide some of the background to the approach adopted by the Constitutional Court towards interpreting socio-economic rights claims. The Court was from its early jurisprudence acutely aware of the fact that many people are living in conditions which could be regarded as a violation of these rights.[54] Its approach to socio-economic rights claims requires applicants to challenge the reasonableness of a government programme in relation to these rights. That challenge, however, is relatively difficult to bring: it is not sufficient simply to claim that one's rights are violated in failing to have a resource provided. Instead, one must rather show that the programme is in some sense irrational, treats one unequally, or fails to address urgent needs.[55] Evidence is required to challenge a government programme, which may be complicated to gather, requiring experts in various fields to attest to the reasonableness or otherwise of the government programme. Even with such expertise, a litigant is not entirely clear what will render a programme reasonable or not.[56] It is not, therefore, surprising that

[51] Jackie Dugard, 'Closing the Doors of Justice: Examining the Constitutional Court's Approach to Direct Access 1995–2013' (2013) 13 South African Journal on Human Rights 112.

[52] ibid 118–19.

[53] The Constitutional Court received 134 applications in 2012, a year before the Constitution Seventeenth Amendment Act came into operation (which extended the Court's jurisdiction), and 232 applications in 2014. Even with this extended jurisdiction, it can nevertheless be argued that the Court's case load is very small compared to comparable courts in the Global South: for instance, the Supreme Courts of Argentina and India decide around 15,000 and 30,000 cases a year respectively. See Siri Gloppen, 'Public Interest Litigation, Social Rights and Social Policy' in Anis A Dani and Arjan de Haan (eds), *Inclusive States: Social Policy and Structural Inequalities* (The International Bank for Reconstruction and Development/The World Bank 2008) 353–354. <https://openknowledge.worldbank.org/bitstream/handle/10986/6409/439630PUB0Box310only109780821369999.pdf?sequence=1&isAllowed=y> accessed 10 November 2019.

[54] *Soobramoney v Minister of Health (Kwazulu Natal)* 1998 (1) SA 765 (CC) [8].

[55] I have analysed the components of the reasonableness enquiry in more detail in David Bilchitz, 'Socio-Economic Rights, Economic Crisis, and Legal Doctrine' (2014) 12 International Journal of Constitutional Law 710, 727.

[56] See *Mazibuko v City of Johannesburg* 2010 (4) SA 1 (CC) where a large amount of expertise and resources went into the case only to find the applicants not succeeding in their claim.

there have been relatively few challenges to the reasonableness of government programmes. This is one of the important factors that has had the effect of substantially reducing the number of claims relating to the positive obligations of government in relation to socio-economic rights. The Constitutional Court may well have been concerned that the existing court infrastructure is just not currently set up in an adequate manner to address the thousands of complaints that may emerge if a more expansive approach were to have been adopted.

D. Widening Access to Justice in Fundamental Rights Matters: Exploring the Possibilities

Conceptualizing access to justice as a capability is important for considering the expansiveness of the measures required effectively to ensure it is realized. Having understood some of the barriers to the achievement of this capability in South Africa, the following section considers some of the possibilities for reform.

1. Expanding internal individual capabilities

As has been mentioned, a central dimension of access to justice is enabling individuals to exercise their capability to approach institutions for redress where their rights are not fulfilled. The first step is to know about the options. If access to justice is to be taken seriously, then a nationwide education campaign is necessary which is conducted in a manner which people with different educational levels can understand. Such a campaign would need to involve at least the following dimensions: first, it would need to educate people about their entitlements and what they can claim; second, it would need to educate people about which possible institutions are available if they feel their entitlements are being abrogated; finally, it would need to make people aware of the methods through which to approach those institutions. Such education could be provided in schools for younger people but it would be necessary also to create a programme of public education targeted at adults too.[57]

[57] See 'We the People Campaign' (*Media Monitoring Africa*) <https://mediamonitoringafrica.org/2012/02/10/we-the-people-campaign-for-immediate-release/> accessed 31 October 2019. 'We The People' was an initiative of Media Monitoring Africa that was aimed at educating the South African public on the role and importance of the Constitution in their daily lives in practical ways. See also Foundation for Human Rights and The Department of Justice and Constitutional Development, 'About Us: Keep it Constitutional' (*Keep it Constitutional* 2019) <https://www.keepitconstitutional.

Such an educational campaign could also help try and address the sense of disempowerment that often allows people to accommodate themselves to rights violations. It could encourage active citizenship, and attempt to counteract alienation from state institutions. It is also likely that there would be an increase in the number of people gaining access to these institutions over time: as individuals see members of their communities having cases successfully resolved, they themselves will be encouraged to approach these institutions.

To enable poorer sections of the population to gain access to justice, it would also be necessary to deal with the very real financial and time barriers discussed above.[58] To address the costs of transport, the availability of redress mechanisms would have to be increased around the country: which institution should take responsibility for this will be discussed further below. Procedures need to be simplified, possibly even allowing initial complaints to be made through letters, as has been done in India.[59] Such a letter could then form the basis for triggering an institutional representative to visit the people concerned (if they are unable to go to specific offices) and investigate their complaint. Where there is a complaint relating to a fundamental right, there needs to be institutional assistance provided whether in the form of a lawyer (if going to court is necessary) or in the making of such a complaint. The Public Protector already allows for complaints via email, letter, and social media, and has outreach officers to assist those who cannot come to its offices:[60] these kinds of programmes need to be expanded upon. This approach will also inevitably require the expansion of legal aid in any case where fundamental rights are threatened.

In terms of time, there needs to be an understanding of the limited time individuals in poorer communities will have to devote to such complaints: ensuring offices can work on certain days after hours or on weekends could help prevent individuals from having to take off whole days of work. A legal duty

co.za/about-us/> accessed 31 October 2019. 'Keep it Constitutional' is a campaign primarily aimed at teaching South African high school learners about the Constitution and their rights under it. However, it also aimed at the larger population of people living in South Africa.

[58] Matthias Nyenti, 'Access to justice in the South African Social Security System: Towards a Conceptual Approach' (2013) 46 De Jure 901; see also Jackie Dugard, 'Court of First Instance? Towards a Pro-Poor Jurisdiction for the South African Constitutional Court' (2006) 22 South African Journal of Human Rights 261, 266. Kgomotso Ramotsho, 'High Litigation Costs Deprive the Poor Access to Justice' (*De Rebus*, 1 November 2018) <http://www.derebus.org.za/high-litigation-costs-deprive-the-poor-access-to-justice> accessed 30 October 2019.

[59] Menaka Guruswamy and Bipin Aspatwar, 'Access to Justice in India: the Jurisprudence (and Self-perception) of the Supreme Court' in Bonilla Maldonado, *Constitutionalism of the Global South* (n 3) 329, 348ff.

[60] Correspondence with a senior official in the Office of the Public Protector confirmed this.

could also be created on private sector employers to allow workers time off to address bona fide fundamental rights complaints and to prevent any disciplinary action being taken against them in such circumstances.

One possible model to consider is the tutela action which is contained in article 86 of the 1991 Colombian constitution. In terms of this action, individuals who believe their rights have been violated can approach a Court in an easy procedure for a writ of protection. Once the individual has provided grounds for the claim that their rights have been violated, the government would have the duty to justify the reasons for its actions. Judges are duty-bound then to make decisions on tutelas within ten days of receiving them and have the discretion to fashion the remedies necessary to protect constitutional rights.[61]

The tutela action has been massively successful in enabling individuals to make complaints where their rights have been violated. Between 1993 and 2004, there was a tenfold increase in the number of tutela actions filed, from 20,000 to 198,000.[62] The Constitutional Court itself ruled on an average of 900 tutelas per year between 2000 and 2010.[63] The expansion of tutela actions is both a success and a failure of the Colombian state: the increased number of tutelas suggests many instances where individuals feel their rights are being violated. That, itself, implies a major crisis in the realization of fundamental rights in Colombia. At the same time, the number of tutelas, and their increase over time, suggests that more individuals are feeling empowered to contest rights violations over time. The increase also represents a trust expressed by individuals that judicial institutions will provide them with a fair hearing and help them to vindicate their rights. The same trend is evident in other Latin American states—such as Brazil—which have instituted a similar easy-access procedure known as the amparo.[64]

No such simple procedure exists within South Africa with the legal process being much more complex and beyond the reach of ordinary citizens. Such procedures have, however, caused major institutional problems for the judiciaries in the Latin American countries that have utilized them. This is perhaps one of the serious worries of doing something similar in the South African

[61] David E Landau and Manuel José Cepeda Espinosa, *Colombian Constitutional Law: Leading Cases* (OUP 2017) 11–14.

[62] Manuel Itturalde, 'Access to Constitutional Justice in Colombia: Opportunities and Challenges for Social and Political Change' in Bonilla Maldonado, *Constitutionalism of the Global South* (n 3) 361, 375.

[63] ibid 376.

[64] The National Council of Justice in Brazil, for instance, released a study which showed that, in 2015, there were around 850,000 lawsuits relating to health in Brazil where an easy-access action is often used to claim treatments not provided: see Conselho Nacional De Justiça, *Justiça em números 2015* (Conselho Nacional De Justiça 2016) <https://www.cnj.jus.br/wp-content/uploads/conteudo/arquivo/2016/07/23fa2e5e06f732d0bb353d2747de333e.pdf> accessed 10 November 2019.

environment. Enabling individuals to gain access to justice thus requires an institutional environment that can cope with such easier access: it is to that issue that I now turn.

2. Institutional solutions

Removing individual barriers, as we saw, is intimately tied to developing responsive institutions capable of addressing the complaints emanating from individuals. The current institutions in South Africa are either struggling to deal with their existing loads or just not institutionally set up in a manner that could cope with a vast influx of cases if access to justice is taken seriously. Ensuring institutions can cope with increased access will require a significant additional investment of financial resources and the expansion of the number of staff employed. Apart from such investment, there are two possible routes that could be followed for expanding access: first, enhancing the capacities of Chapter 9 institutions, or second, enabling these cases to come to the courts and so increasing their capacities. I shall suggest that the preferable approach is a mixture between the two with a division of labour being created between Chapter 9 institutions and the courts. Such a model, in turn, could perhaps be instructive for countries in Latin America whose judicial system is struggling under the weight of too many individual complaints. One further possibility that cannot fully be canvassed in this paper is also to expand funding for strategic public interest litigation and class actions: that would allow for an aggregation of individual claims and thus reduce the demands on the courts through bringing one large action that addresses problems facing multiple individuals. The difficulties of ensuring an alignment of interests between multiple individuals and collective action problems render it unlikely such a solution can replace individualized remedies but it has some potential to ease the burdens on courts and other institutions that expanded individualized access would impose.

(a) Expanding the capacities of Chapter Nine institutions

Currently, the public protector appears to be the institution that hears the highest number of the complaints that individuals have relating to state impropriety or incapacity. Yet, as we saw, it lacks the institutional capacity to deal with a major increase in the number of cases, should access to justice in South Africa be enhanced. To become an effective institutional solution, it would need to develop more than its current 20 offices across the country, enhance further awareness of the complaint procedures it utilizes and employ more staff. The power to issue binding orders recognized by the Constitutional Court comes with the need to include procedural safeguards such as internal appeals processes which again require additional resources. Any binding order made by the public protector is also capable of being challenged in court which has the potential to increase the burden on the courts.

The same is true with the South African Human Rights Commission. Enhancing its capacity to receive complaints and make decisions could also increase the availability of mechanisms for individuals to gain access to justice. It would also, in my view, be highly desirable that there be a division of labour between the public protector and the SAHRC so there is no unnecessary duplication of functions. That would require the two institutions to work together to create certain jurisdictional rules around which complaints each focus upon.

In my view, enhancing access for individuals through these institutions could enable institutions outside the courts to address many of the individual complaints that arise. Yet, inevitably, an increase in cases before these institutions will have implications for an increased load on the courts. This would arise for three main reasons.

First, there would always be the potential to have decisions by these Chapter 9 bodies reviewed. With an increase in access, there will be an increase in the number of appeal cases. Indeed, comparative experience from Colombia suggests the possibility of a massive increase in such appeals.

Second, there may be a virtuous effect created by more people gaining access to mechanisms to enhance their rights and this may encourage more people to approach courts to vindicate their rights too. To address this problem, courts may have to create jurisdictional rules to require the lodging of certain individual complaints first with Chapter 9 institutions.

Finally, the Chapter 9 institutions are likely to be able to provide individualized remedies. However, there are problems which are structural and systemic in nature and often cannot be dealt with on an individualized level and require a more general consideration of governmental programmes. That is indeed a function, arguably, that courts should exercise, and the socio-economic rights jurisprudence of the Constitutional Court suggests that it will be prepared to consider doing so (though on the vague grounds of reasonableness). The increase in the number of individualized cases are thus likely also to highlight a number of the systemic gaps in governmental programmes, which will also increase the load on courts. Providing support for strategic public interest litigation that could aggregate the claims of multiple individuals challenging these systemic problems could also have a virtuous effect in reducing the number of individual challenges reaching the courts around specific matters.

(b) Expanding the capacity of courts and developing their structure

Courts in South Africa already struggle under the weight of the civil and criminal cases that are being brought. There is thus a well-grounded concern that the existing system will be unable to cope with a greater influx of cases on fundamental rights. Indeed, it can be argued that the existing court structure has not properly been designed for a wider jurisdiction on fundamental rights. Special equality courts have been set up to deal particularly with issues of unfair discrimination within existing court structures and there are certain other specialist courts which connect with specific rights (such as labour courts). In relation to administrative law and socio-economic rights, however, there are no courts with a special jurisdiction.

Various options, therefore, exist to address the institutional deficits in the current structure which render access to judicial institutions difficult. All would involve a significant increase in the resources allocated to the judiciary and require an expansion of the number of magistrates and judges. Indeed, South Africa has a tiny number of judges compared to countries that have implemented widely accessible judicial remedies.[65] The following are some of the potential institutional design solutions that could be considered for a more accessible court system[66]:

(i) Create specialist courts

One possibility would be to create specialist fundamental rights courts that adjudicate complaints specifically related to violations of fundamental rights. A critically important point here is that any specialist courts must be created from additional resources as well as additional personnel to staff them. To drain existing courts of resources on these matters would only hamper access to justice on other matters.

Many of the individual complaints that arise are also likely to be capable of being addressed through an administrative law framework. A particular division of Administrative Courts (like in many other countries) could be created to address some of the cases that may arise and which go on appeal.

The one conceptual problem with adopting this approach would be that it suggests that fundamental rights are a separate category of litigation apart from

[65] Mia Lendique, 'Mogoeng: Courts Struggling To Deal With Ever-Increasing Caseload' *Eyewitness News* (Johannesburg, 3 October 2019) <https://ewn.co.za/2019/10/03/mogoeng-courts-struggling-to-deal-with-ever-increasing-workload> accessed 30 October 2019.

[66] I do not consider the possibility of traditional courts which are currently under construction through the Traditional Courts Bill (now in its third iteration). The matters on which they are likely to have jurisdiction will not include the ability to hear complaints of human rights violations. Nevertheless, an understanding of human rights should be required for all those adjudicating in these disputes as well.

other categories. Fundamental rights though are often implicated in civil and criminal matters too. It would be necessary to be clear about which kinds of complaints can be addressed through such a specialist court and where matters should be addressed through the ordinary civil and criminal jurisdiction but, nevertheless, engage with fundamental rights questions.

(ii) Grant fundamental rights jurisdiction expressly to lower courts

As we saw, magistrates' courts only have the powers expressly conferred on them by statute. They are the tier of the ordinary court system closest to the people and with the widest geographic reach, rendering them the most accessible. Individual disputes that cannot be adjudicated by the Chapter 9 institutions could well be included within their jurisdiction. Expanding the jurisdiction of the existing magistrates' courts in relation to fundamental rights would provide individuals with a more accessible avenue to vindicate their claims. Once again, the caveat would have to be made that magistrates' courts would have to be provided with additional resources to enable them to fulfil this function as well as additional training in relation to fundamental rights.

(iii) High court and Appellate jurisdiction focused on structural cases

The worry about swamping the High Courts is real and their current capacity very limited, with long periods of waiting for cases to be heard and to reach completion. To address the appeals coming from Chapter 9 institutions and lower courts in relation to individual complaints, it will be necessary to expand the resources available in this regard. It may well be necessary to appoint a wider array of adjunct justices or law clerks to peruse many of the complaints and provide an indication to judges about which merit their attention.

The jurisdiction of the High Court could also be focused more strongly on cases which go beyond a particular individual complaint and are of a more structural nature.[67] Thus, challenges to any programme or policy of the government for failure to conform to fundamental rights concerns could be reserved for the High Court (and Appellate Courts). This would conform well with the current programmatic approach to the realization of socio-economic rights outlined by the Constitutional Court. Procedural innovations though should be utilized to reduce the burden on the poor in such cases: thus, for instance, the applicant should only have the duty to provide evidence of a prima facie

[67] See Jackie Dugard, 'Forging Space for Pro-Poor Change: The Use of Strategic Litigation by the Socio-Economic Rights Institution of South Africa (SERI) to Advance Equality' (2019) 52 VRÜ/WCL 132 for a case study on SERI's use of strategic, structural litigation.

rights violation taking place through a government programme; thereafter, the government should have the duty to justify its actions and thus adduce the more complex evidence required for an assessment of reasonableness (if this approach to determining the content of socio-economic rights is retained).[68]

Exceptional cases could well still require direct access to the Constitutional Court. The suggestion by Jackie Dugard to widen direct access to the Constitutional Court has both strong merits but also raises serious concerns.[69] The worry with the suggestion that most individual cases of fundamental rights violations be dealt with by other courts is problematic in that many judges (and perhaps magistrates even more) display attitudes and views that do not fully reflect a fundamental rights sensibility. The Constitutional Court still frequently overturns decisions in these courts for failing to do so: the recent case of an eviction performed with the supposed consent of the people where they were not fully apprised of what they were doing is a case in point.[70] These factors would pull in the direction of enabling more direct access. On the other hand, the problem is that, if the Constitutional Court hears many of these cases and there is a wide increase in the number of appeals, the worry of swamping becomes a real possibility. The ability of the court to remain a body which is able to engage in deep deliberation on particular issues may be placed in peril. It is true that the Court at present has a relatively low case load compared to other courts in the Global South. It may also be that its procedure of hearing all cases *en banc* should change and allow for smaller panels for most cases except a narrow category of those which require a large court. An expanded vetting procedure would also likely be necessary, with perhaps many more law clerks hired to assist judges in this regard. Ultimately, it seems that in the current institutional reality, the Constitutional Court would need to retain some jurisdiction over individual cases though institute strong gatekeeping procedures to preserve the character of the institution. Once again, this would have important implications for the resources devoted to the courts.

To avoid the duplication of processes and to ensure proper remedies for rights violations, in many socio-economic rights cases with a structural component, it is recommended that courts exercise supervisory jurisdiction. This will also mean that implementation by other branches can be overseen which is likely to enhance the degree to which orders are implemented. Such orders also avoid the difficulty and inefficiency of individuals having to restart litigation

[68] Sandra Liebenberg, *Socio-Economic Rights: Adjudication under a Transformative Constitution* (Juta 2010) 131.

[69] Dugard, 'Closing the Doors of Justice' (n 51).

[70] See *Occupiers of Erven 87 & 88 Berea v De Wet NO* 2017 (5) SA 346 (CC).

afresh to ensure a case that has already been heard and adjudicated upon is given effect to.[71]

3. Scarcity and access to justice

The approach advocated in this paper requires a major rethinking of how to ensure access to justice for those facing violations of their fundamental rights—and particularly, their socio-economic rights—in South Africa. Yet, it could be argued that there is a potential trade-off between an expansion of access to justice and actual concrete expenditure on the realization of rights. This argument would involve the contention that the changes I have argued for all require a large increase in expenditure in budgets. The focus of my approach lies in building the capacity of individuals and institutions to manage circumstances in which individuals feel that their rights are not being realized. Yet, it could be claimed, why not rather utilize these expanded resources to solve the problems that are likely to be the object of the legal complaints? If access to food is a problem, utilize the resources in question to improve the availability of food to people; if there are problems in healthcare, why not directly attempt to address the challenges faced by the system?

Unfortunately, this argument is flawed for a number of reasons. First, it suggests that we can anticipate, in advance, the claims that are likely to arise in any complaints process and address them before they arise. This would of course be a good idea but part of the reason for the creation of adjudicatory processes lies in the fact that often it is not possible to anticipate fully in advance all the possible legal problems that may arise. Indeed, one of the benefits of legal processes is that they enable individuals to challenge general laws for failing to address their particular needs or interests. The very point of those processes lies in the fact that the mechanism of complaint offers a form of feedback to other branches of government where there may have been a blind-spot.[72]

Second, a related point involves the fact that expenditure on the substance of rights realization is not a substitute for the creation of mechanisms to adjudicate on problems that arise in giving effect to them. Adjudicatory mechanisms exist because humanly created programmes and institutions inevitably run into difficulties. These can arise from the unfair exercise of discretion by an

[71] Ken Roach and Geoff Budlender, 'Mandatory Relief and Supervisory Jurisdiction: When is it Appropriate, Just and Equitable?' (2005) 122 South African Law Journal 325.

[72] On the notion of a 'feedback mechanism', see Stu Woolman, *The Selfless Constitution* (Juta 2013) 176–78.

administrative official, doctor, or teacher; inadequate coverage for vulnerable groups; a lack of consideration of a particular problem; differences of opinion on what should be provided; and many other reasons. This is why the right to gain access to a legal process and to a remedy is recognized as a separate right in international law and, in many jurisdictions.[73] No matter how perfect the attempt to realize a programme is, there is likely to be contestation and issues which require adjudication. Procedural rights guarantee the ability to participate in the decision-making about substance.[74] Substantive realization of a programme is quite different to creating a right of access to an adjudicatory process.

Third, this reasoning seems to rest upon the idea that the legal process should remain rather inaccessible provided we spend a significant amount of money on seeking to realize rights. This approach would mean that individuals should never have their internal capabilities developed to go to courts. It further means that institutions will remain ill-equipped to deal with the possibility that empowered individuals may wish to make complaints. The status quo thus enables those who are able to access the institutions to do so and preserves the inequalities evident in the existing system. This outcome seems fundamentally unacceptable in an environment which seeks to respect the equality of all. It also violates the principle that those who have rights should be entitled to enforce them. Before accepting the notion that a trade-off is necessary between access to justice and substantive outcomes, strong evidence should be provided by the government that indeed a wider access to justice programme is impossible within its available resources. Interventions such as those suggested in this paper need to be experimented with, and so it does not seem possible for it at this point to meet this burden of justification.

Finally, a contextual argument is of particular relevance in the jurisdictions of the Global South. In these contexts, there are widespread institutional failings and often a lack of capacity to design adequate social programmes.[75] The problems are often not based upon monetary resources alone and so the increase in expenditure may often not succeed in addressing the root problems. In the health system of South Africa, for instance, problems arise as a result of widespread mismanagement, lack of attention and care, and poor patient

[73] In international law, see eg Universal Declaration of Human Rights (adopted 10 December 1948) UNGA Res 217 A(III), art 5 <http://www.un.org/en/universal-declaration-human-rights/index.html> accessed 10 November 2019.

[74] See eg Carola Glinski, 'Environmental Justice in South African Law and Policy' (2003) 36 VRÜ/WCL 49, 64.

[75] The description of the African context by Segui (n 5) 463, unfortunately, has not changed majorly.

management systems.[76] Allowing complaints and a multi-institutional approach to address these problems can help avoid replicating failures and bring a fresh perspective to provide solutions to systemic blockages. This approach would see the realization of rights as not being rooted in any one particular institution but involve a multiplicity of institutions, each performing roles which include exercising oversight over each other. Enabling individuals to gain access to mechanisms to highlight such institutional failings is essential, particularly in the conditions of the Global South, in order to address these institutional failures.

E. Conclusion

The reality in South Africa today is that most people would struggle to gain access to processes to address violations of their socio-economic rights (and fundamental rights more generally). Enabling them to do so would not only encourage active citizenship but help highlight deficiencies in existing programmes and institutions. This chapter has sought to move from a theoretical conception of access to justice to the practical task of suggesting concrete interventions that can help address the obstacles faced by many in the country to gain access to justice. Both the capabilities approach and these concrete interventions are also relevant to discussions around access to justice in the Global South more widely. Generating the political will for the reforms suggested in this paper may be a difficult task. Yet, it is one that I hope to have shown is required if we are to take seriously the socio-economic rights (and fundamental rights more widely) contained in the South African Constitution.

[76] Winnie T Maphumulo and Busisiwe R Bhengu 'Challenges of Quality Improvement in the Healthcare of South Africa Post-apartheid: A Critical Review' (2019) 42 Curationis <https://doi.org/10.4102/curationis.v42i1.1901> accessed 30 October 2019.

10

Inequality and the Constitution

From Equality to Social Rights

Roberto Gargarella

A. Introduction: Three Different Approaches

Since the independence years, Latin American constitutionalism has offered different responses to the social conflicts generated by situations of profound political and economic inequalities. Herein I shall examine three of those responses, which I find particularly relevant and influential.

(1) The first response to inequality, which belongs to the nineteenth-century *republican approach* to constitutionalism, demanded the implementation of substantive economic reforms, aimed at reducing economic inequalities, and also required the political democratization of society. Republicans thus suggested the adoption of reforms that were not limited to the legal/constitutional sphere.
(2) The second response, which belongs to the *liberal-conservative approach*, was the one that dominated Latin American constitutionalism between the mid-nineteenth century and the end of that century. Proponents of this view urged to concentrate the available political energies on establishing the material conditions of economic growth. In order to achieve this goal, liberal-conservatives demanded the introduction of constitutional changes, which were mainly directed at modifying one section of the Constitution, namely the one dedicated to the *organization of powers*.
(3) The third response, which belongs to the—presently dominant—*social-conservative* approach, became particularly influential since the beginning of the twentieth century. In order to address the problems created by social inequalities, proponents of this view—like liberal-conservatives—also considered it necessary to introduce changes in the Constitution. However, social-conservatives believed that these changes fundamentally required a substantive reshaping of the (other part of the Constitution, this is to

Roberto Gargarella, *Inequality and the Constitution* In: *The Global South and Comparative Constitutional Law.* Edited by: Philipp Dann, Michael Riegner, and Maxim Bönnemann, Oxford University Press (2020). © Oxford University Press.
DOI: 10.1093/oso/9780198850403.003.0010

say the) Constitution's *declaration of rights*. Typically, social-conservatives demanded the introduction of social, economic, and cultural rights into the Constitution, while leaving the organization of powers basically untouched. Let us explore these different views in some detail.

B. The Republican Approach

The first approach that I shall examine is the one related to the republican approach to constitutionalism. This view was particularly influential during the independence years (around 1810). During the 1850s there was an important re-emergence of Latin American republicanism, which followed the so-called *red* or *democratic revolutions* that took place in Europe, at that time. The republican approach was first inspired by the French Revolutionary ideology, which was extremely relevant during Latin America's revolutionary years. Typically, Constitutions such as those adopted in France in 1791, 1793, and 1795 were seriously read by Latin American legal thinkers of the time. For instance, the Chilean Francisco Bilbao—perhaps, one of the most articulate republican doctrinaires in the region—wrote in his famed *El gobierno de la libertad* (1855) that the French Jacobin Constitution of 1793 was the only Constitution that 'deserves to be remembered'.[1]

Even though there were basically no Constitutions in Latin America that closely followed the French republican model, there were numerous authors and texts (such as the same *El gobierno de la libertad*) of a clear republican character, which greatly enriched the constitutional debates of the era.[2]

Republicans' main goal was the achievement of *collective self-government*, which required, among other things, the achievement of both political and economic freedom.[3] In order to obtain those goals, they proposed numerous initiatives, and here I shall explore only three of them. More specifically, I shall examine (1) their proposal for the adoption of radical economic reforms; (2) their suggestion according to which political, legal, and economic reforms had to be pursued simultaneously (in other words, without assuming

[1] Francisco Bilbao, 'El gobierno de la libertad' in José Alberto Bravo (ed), *Francisco Bilbao 1823–1865* (Editorial Cuarto Propio 2007) 321–22.

[2] In any case, one could mention Constitutions such as those of Venezuela 1811, or Apatzingán in México 1814, among others, as Constitutions that were clearly inspired by the French Revolutionary Constitutions.

[3] Michael J Sandel, *Democracy's Discontent: America in Search of a Public Philosophy* (Harvard UP 1996).

the independence or autonomy of the legal, economic, and political spheres); and (3) their defence of a more horizontal or democratic political organization. I have examined these issues in other writings,[4] so in what follows I will only offer a brief explanation and illustration of these initiatives.

1. Egalitarian reforms, rather than social rights

First of all, I should mention that, when republicans addressed the problems generated by social inequality, they did not immediately think about the Constitution and constitutional rights. Rather, they urged for the adoption of profound economic and social changes, directed at eliminating those fundamental inequalities. This approach was common in the early revolutionary times—for instance, in some of the initiatives promoted by the leader of the *Banda Oriental*, José Gervasio Artigas. In fact, in 1815 Artigas enacted an exceptional *Reglamento Provisorio* which not only ordered a vast redistribution of land, but also organized that redistribution in ways that first favoured the underprivileged—the '*negros, zambos, y mulatos*'—which represented the most disadvantaged groups of society at that time.

Another interesting expression of this republican approach appeared in the Mexican 1857 Constitutional Convention, which was one of the few opportunities in the nineteenth century when republicans had the chance to discuss their viewpoints in the context of a Constitutional Assembly. Not surprisingly, republicans used that occasion in order to first demand the adoption of significant reforms in the property of land. For instance, for Ponciano Arriaga, who was then the president of the Convention, the Constitution ought to simply become '*la ley de la tierra*': by this he meant that the Assembly had to dedicate all its energies to the task of promoting a radical agrarian reform. Many of his colleagues, coming from a similar political origin (they were then called liberal-radicals or '*liberales puros*') emphasized similar ideas. In order to ground their view, these liberal-radicals offered a diversity of reasons.[5] Interestingly, in spite

[4] See eg Roberto Gargarella, *The Legal Foundations of Inequality* (CUP 2010); Roberto Gargarella, *Latin American Constitutionalism* (OUP 2013).

[5] Francisco Zarco, *Historia del Congreso Constitucional de 1857* (Instituto Nacional de Estudios Históricos 1957) 55–56. Some of them maintained that in Mexico there existed enough land for all the members of society, and that, for that reason, there was no reason to keep the Constitution committed to those injustices (Castillo Velasco); others criticized the attitudes of the upper classes, which in a context of poverty continued with the accumulation of property (Arriaga); still others resorted to Christian piety, and maintained that nobody could deny the provision of basic goods (such as water or wood) to those who were in need of them (Olvera); some pointed to the persistent presence of situations of exploitation and oppression towards the most disadvantaged (Ponciano Arriaga, Olvera); some others maintained that the unjust organization of property was directly linked to the existing illegal

of being clearly committed to the cause of the underprivileged, Mexican republicans did not use the opportunity they had for advocating for social and economic rights. Rather, they used the chance they had within the Convention in order to promote radical modifications in the distribution of property.

2. Legal, political, and economic changes

Another interesting lesson that one could derive from the work of early Latin American republicans, concerns their peculiar approach to social reforms. Of particular significance was their understanding that the political and legal reforms that they promoted had to come hand in hand with the introduction of economic reforms. This view was already present in the Mexican Constitutional Convention of 1857. On that occasionmany republicans claimed that the constitutional reform had could not be separated from the adoption of a substantive economic reform.

This particular view—one could claim—was shared by most Latin American republicans, during the early nineteenth century. One remarkable example of this approach can be found in the work of Manuel Murillo Toro—a Colombian intellectual who would then become the President of his country. Together with some of his *radical* colleagues, Murillo Toro strongly advocated for the adoption of universal suffrage in Colombia. The radical group succeed in this fight and universal suffrage was finally adopted. However—and not surprisingly—extreme conservative groups won the first elections that were open to the general public. As a consequence, many of the radicals who had been advocating for universal suffrage decided to revise the actual merits of their initiative. Murillo Toro was one of the few of them who resisted that move: in his opinion there was no point in abandoning the fight for universal suffrage. What was required, instead, was to accompany that initiative with a profound agrarian reform. In other words, Murillo Toro claimed that the fundamental legal reform that they had promoted had to come together with additional economic reforms—it was simply unreasonable to think about the former without thinking about the latter. In his words:

occupations (Olvera); there were also references to the level of inhumanity that characterized the prevailing social organization (Olvera); some denounced the situation of slavery that affected large masses of poor workers (Ramírez).

> Every political reform has to have as its object an economic reform. If we did the former without the later, we would not only run the risk of doing an unfertile work, but also to discredit the reform in the eyes of the people . . . political forms are worthless if they do not come together with a radical reconstruction of the social structure, through taxes and (reforms in the system of property). What would universal and direct suffrage mean (even if secret) in a society where the majority had no guaranteed subsistence . . . ?[6]

3. An anti-presidentialist drive

A final and also significant lesson that can be derived from the work of early republicans, relates to their view about the powers of the Executive—more generally, their view regarding how to organize the distribution of powers within the Constitution. Their approach to the topic was interesting because, among other reasons, of the way in which it challenged the then dominant sentiment of 'distrust towards democracy'. In fact, by the mid-1850s, most liberal and conservative political leaders suggested to concentrate powers in the hands of the Executive—this is the way they found more convenient in order to resist growing impulses directed at 'democratizing' society. This is why the vast majority of nineteenth-century Constitutions in the region adopted a rather peculiar form of the liberal system of 'checks and balances', namely one that was finally 'disbalanced' in favour of the Executive. They created what contemporary legal thinker Carlos Nino described as a 'hyper-presidentialist' constitutional system.[7]

Contrary to this view, and from the early revolutionary years, radical republicans developed an anti-authoritarian and anti-presidentialist approach to the organization of powers. Radicals not only fought against any return to Spanish authoritarianism but, more importantly, against the concentration of political power in the hands of a few. Typically, they attacked Simón Bolívar's exceptional powers in Venezuela; they proposed the curtailment of the powers of the Executive in Peru; they fought against the establishment of a theocratic regime in Ecuador, and in favour of a radically decentralized regime, in Colombia; or battled against the perpetuation of an authoritarian government in Chile. A proclamation by the Chilean *Sociedad de la Igualdad* summarized some of these republican goals. It said

[6] Manuel Murillo Toro, *Obras Selectas* (Imprenta Nacional Bogotá 1979) 70.
[7] Carlos Nino, *The Constitution of Deliberative Democracy* (Yale UP 1993).

> [we are fighting against the future government of General Montt because it represents] the state of siege, the deportations, the expatriations, the military tribunals, the corruption of the Judiciary, the massive killing of the people, torture in the criminal procedures, censorship, usury, repression, and especially the impairment of the national interests and the right of association.[8]

In sum, this anti-presidentialist thrust suggests that for republicans, self-government could neither be achieved in the context of profound social and economic inequalities, nor in situations where only a few (or just 'one', say a monarch or a super-powerful Executive), controlled the entire political decision-making process.

C. The Liberal-Conservative Approach

The liberal-conservative approach to the Constitution became prevalent in Latin America from the mid-nineteenth century. This approach was an expression of the main political compact of the time, namely the one that brought together liberals and conservatives. Curiously or not, until those days the two groups had been disputing political power, usually through the use of violent means. For different reasons (which include the growing threat posed to both of them by the republican alternative), by the 1850s, liberals and conservatives began to work together in most Latin American countries, and also in most Constitutional Conventions of the period.

One of the most sophisticated advocates of this liberal-conservative ideology was the Argentinean legal thinker Juan Bautista Alberdi, who was deeply involved in the discussion of constitutional affairs. Like many of his colleagues, Alberdi considered that it was still not time to directly address the social problems derived from situations of profound inequality. The priority was, for him, the achievement of economic growth, in other words the establishment of the material conditions for economic development. Alberdi claimed that Latin American countries required, most of all, skilled workers and economic freedom; rejected State intervention in the economy; and subscribed to an individualist view of society, as well as economic liberalism.[9] Alberdi considered

[8] Diego Barros Arana, *Un decenio de la historia de Chile*, vol 2 (Encuadernación Universitaria 1913) 520.

[9] Taking into account these antecedents, the noted Argentine historian Tulio Halperín Donghi defined Alberdi's programme as one of 'progressive authoritarianism—a mixture of political rigor and economic activism': Tulio Halperín Donghi, *Proyecto y Construcción de una Nación* (Biblioteca Ayacucho 1980) XXXI.

that his generation had to accept the idea of living under a system of what he called *imperfect liberties*, which is to say a system of *limited democracy*.[10]

In another important book, namely *Sistema Económico y Rentístico*, Alberdi clearly stated: 'I do not share . . . [the fanatic and inexperienced position] that it is necessary to freely distribute political freedom.' By contrast, he deemed that 'economic freedoms'—including the freedoms to 'buy, sell, work, navigate, trade, travel and undertake any industry'—had to be distributed unrestrictedly among 'native and foreigners'.[11] Again, the idea was that the time of political freedom had still not come: first it was necessary to create the material conditions for it, through economic growth.

Alberdi's approach to the topic was widely shared among liberal-conservatives of the time, all across the region. For instance, Alberdi's position was substantially similar to the one expressed by the noted Venezuelan jurist Andrés Bello. Working for the Chilean government in the draft of a Civil Code, Bello maintained that the people were 'less jealous in the preservation of their political liberty, than in the preservation of their civil rights'.[12] As a consequence—he believed—governments should not feel in a hurry to distribute new political rights: it was much more reasonable to concentrate the public energies—as he himself was doing—in expanding economic liberties and ensuring firm guarantees to property rights.

Bello's claim about the people's main interests was not merely descriptive. Rather, it had clear normative overtones. In his opinion, it was totally reasonable for individuals to be much more interested in 'securing their persons and properties' than their political rights. This was so—he assumed—because people were naturally more interested in ensuring the destiny of their families, their honour, and their lives, than in ensuring the destiny of strangers or of abstract entities: 'Strange is the case'—he claimed—of someone 'so lacking in egoism, who would prefer the exercise of any of his political rights . . . to the

[10] For Alberdi, theirs was not the time of expansive political liberties or profound social reforms: those changes had to still wait until the introduction of new changes in external conditions. In his words: 'It is a crime to continue delaying the enactment of a Constitution: a betrayal to the Republic. We need to proceed to organize the Republic, no matter the *caudillos*, the *unitarios*, the federalists, and everything that is still included in our disgraceful Republic: they are all part of the same family. Any exclusion would affect us all: it would imply division and anarchy. You think that it is impossible to have a perfect liberty if we also include the bad guys? Well, then you should know that there is no alternative but to have an imperfect liberty. . . . That would be the only way of obtaining *perfect liberty*. If you want to build up this Hispanic-Argentine ex-colony, this is to say this motherland and not another, then you have to begin with *imperfect liberty*, like the people that have to exercise that liberty. You cannot aspire having the liberty of the North American republics, which our peoples could only obtain after they have the same wealth, culture or level of progress than the peoples and men of New York, Boston, Philadelphia, etc': Juan Bautista Alberdi, *Obras Selectas* vol xiv (Librería La Facultad 1920) 16–17.

[11] See his 'Sistema Económico y Rentístico' in Alberdi, *Obras Selecta* (n 10), vol xiv, 64–65.

[12] Cited after Andres Jaksic, *Andrés Bello. La pasión por el orden* (Editorial Universitaria 2001) 212.

preservation of his interests and his existence'. For that reason, he added, individuals would always be more concerned with the loss of their properties than with the loss of their right to suffrage.[13]

We find an almost identical view in the writings of the Colombian liberal intellectual José María Samper, who would then become, together with the conservative intellectual Miguel Antonio Caro, one of the authors of the 1886 Constitution. Samper stated:

> The Colombian people wanted a government and an organization capable of guaranteeing them national unity and peace; a just liberty; dignity; independence for their religion and Church . . . a government that recognized and made effective diverse and necessary public liberties, and limited—but actual and effective—political and civil rights; capable of suppressing anarchy and constant disorder, which characterize all our institutions since 1858 . . . which suppressed the constitutional and irresponsible despotism of our legislative bodies . . . which returned its liberty to the right of suffrage.[14]

In other words, Samper, like Alberdi and Bello, considered that the time required, for his country, order and stability (against disorder and anarchy), rather than ambitious political rights, or drastic social measures, aimed at protecting the most vulnerable. For the three of them, the coming years were going to be necessarily characterized by restricted political rights and ample economic liberties.

Having reached this point, let me make clear why these views are so important for the purposes of this paper. The liberal-conservative approach offers us a second, fundamental view about how to deal with the problems posed by situations of deep inequality. Of course, for ideological reasons, we may resist the *substance* of their approach, which called for *deferral* in everything that concerned the protection of the most vulnerable. However, it is important not to miss the important methodological or more *formal* lesson that can also be inferred from that view. Taking into account the main divide that characterize most Constitutions—this is to say the division between the declarations of rights and the organization of powers—liberal-conservatives claimed something like the following: *if you are really concerned with protecting certain fundamental rights (say, for instance, property and contracts) the first thing you*

[13] Ivan Jaksic, *Andrés Bello. La pasión por el orden* (Editorial Universitaria 2001) 212.

[14] Alejandro Valencia Villa, *El pensamiento constitucional de Miguel Antonio Caro* (Instituto Caro y Cuervo 1992) 154–55.

should do is re-shape the organization of powers (this is to say the 'other side' of the Constitution) accordingly. In other words, they assumed that it was not of much use to fill the Constitution with long lists of rights. Their suggestion was, instead, to change the power structure of the Constitution so as to honour one's commitment to fundamental rights.

In sum, the substance of the liberal-conservative view was hostile to democracy and majoritarian politics, in general—a view that most of us would tend to reject.[15] However, in formal terms, liberal-conservatives had something interesting to tell us, namely that in order to reform the social and economic basis of society we need to introduce changes in the organization of powers, rather than fill the Constitution with more and more of our preferred fundamental rights.

D. The Social-Conservative Approach

The third fundamental approach to the problems posed by profound inequalities, is the one that became prevalent in Latin America since the beginning of the twentieth century. At that time, the old system of 'order and progress' that had prevailed in the region during the 1880s, came to an end. The price that the region had accepted to pay for achieving economic development proved to be too high, both with respect to the social costs that it imposed, and the level of political exclusion that it required. The downfall of the old system was abrupt, and on some occasions, like in Mexico, it acquired the form of a revolution. Remarkably, the Mexican Revolution of 1910 ended with the enactment of the famous 1917 Constitution that, in a way, changed the history of constitutionalism not only in Latin America, but also in the world.

The Mexican 1917 Constitution, which was written in Querétaro, was exceptionally long, robust in its declaration of rights, and strongly committed to social rights, which was at the time a complete novelty. In fact, the

[15] In fact, Alberdi, Bello, and Samper coincided in defending numerous restrictions for political participation as fundamental guarantees for the preservation of the social order. As a consequence of those types of assumptions, most Latin American countries established severe restrictions to political rights, which for instance included restrictions to the political participation of women, the poor, single people, or domestic servants (Marcela Ternavasio, *La revolución del voto. Política y elecciones en Bue.nos Aires, 1810–1852* (Siglo XX1 2002); HildaSábato, *Pueblo y política. La construcción de la Argentina moderna* (Capital Intelectual 2010); Hilda Sábato and Alberto Lettieri (eds), *La vida política en la Argentina del siglo XIX. Armas, votos y voces* (Fondo de Cultura Económica 2003). In addition, the new liberal-conservative Constitutions introduced numerous counter-majoritarian devices, assuming that the main threat to liberal, classic rights, came from 'unchecked majorities' and unbridled political institutions.

Mexican Constitution became pioneer in the entire world in the development of so-called *social constitutionalism.* It accompanied the enactment of the Constitution of the Republic of Weimar, in 1919; the creation of the International Labour Organization (ILO) in 1919; and the development of the Welfare State and the Keynesian economic model.

Since the enactment of the Mexican Constitution, and little by little, most countries in the region began to change their basic constitutional structure. In fact, and following Mexico's early example, most countries began to include long lists of social rights in their Constitutions: Brazil modified its Constitution in 1937; Bolivia in 1938; Cuba in 1940; Uruguay 1942; Ecuador and Guatemala in 1945; Argentina and Costa Rica in 1949. This was the way in which Latin American Constitutions expressed, through the use of the legal language, the main social change that had taken place in the region during the first half of the twentieth century, namely the incorporation of the working class as a decisive political and economic actor.

Now, it is worth pause for a while to examine in some detail the remarkable Mexican example, which offers interesting insights in order to understand this 'new' Latin American approach to the 'social question'. There are at least two things that I would like to highlight from the Mexican case.

First, it is worth mentioning that the Querétaro Convention was the result of a long process of violent political disputes (motivated by a situation of extreme economic inequality), which followed at least two significant but finally unsuccessful attempts to introduce constitutional reforms—one in Ayala, and the other in Aguascalientes. These first two meetings were dominated by radically revolutionary forces—the *Zapatistas* forces (commanded by Emiliano Zapata) that came from the South, and the *Villistas* troops (commanded by Pancho Villa) that came from the North. These forces, which represented the marginalized indigenous groups of the Nation, demanded the nationalization of natural resources and the adoption of a profound agrarian reform. By contrast, the Querétaro Convention, which came after those two radical experiences, was controlled by the military group of the *Constitucionalistas*, which responded to General Venustiano Carranza. Carranza, it must be noted, did not subscribe the previous wave of radicalism. Rather, he was more concerned with the re-establishment of peace and order. In other words, the Querétaro Convention, which he promoted, did not come to provide constitutional status to the radical demands that had prevailed during the initial years of the Revolution, but rather to re-establish political order.

And here comes the second element that I wanted to highlight from this process, and which becomes manifest when we read Carranza's Inaugural Speech before the Querétaro Assembly. Carranza's speech revealed the new constitutional approach that since then has been prevalent in the entire region. In that opportunity, Carranza first returned to the recurrent topics of regional constitutionalism: he criticized the old constitutional model for being too idealized, and based on 'general principles' that had no actual utility;[16] he claimed that previous legal thinkers had been unable to adjust constitutional law to 'the needs of the Mexican people';[17] and he also referred to the uselessness of the old legal order to ensure to the benefits of the division of power, federalism, and republicanism.[18] However, and at the same time, Carranza made clear that the main objective of the Convention was the re-establishment of law and order, through the presence of a strong political authority.

Those are, I believe, crucial elements to be examined in the context of this paper. On the one hand, the so-considered 'revolutionary' Mexican Constitution (which in some respects undoubtedly was), could also (or better) be described as the final and moderate result of a long revolutionary process. On the other hand, and more significantly, the Mexican Constitution deserves widespread attention not only for the *novelties* that it introduced in its text, namely a robust list of social rights, but also for the elements that it *preserved* from the 'old' constitutional order, this is to say a political system that concentrated authority in the hands of the Executive. In this way, the 'new' constitutional model reproduced, at least in part, the liberal-conservative constitutional model that had been dominant in the previous decades.

In sum, this 'new' constitutional project has two faces, like Janus: one face is oriented towards the future and calls for social reform, inclusion, and political participation, while the other is oriented towards the past and calls—like old, nineteenth-century Latin American Constitutions—for the concentration of political authority and the preservation of the old, elitist, unequal order. For this reason, I do not refer to this project as the project of *social constitutionalism*—as most people call it. I rather consider this constitutional project as the project of *social conservatism*.

The social-conservative constitutional model became the standard Latin American model for constitutional design, from the beginning of the

[16] Emilio Rabasa, *El pensamiento político y social del Constituyente de 1916–1917* (IIJ-UNAM 1986) 196.

[17] ibid.

[18] ibid 197–98. Although he was clearly open to the consideration of previously unattended social issues, the legal program defended by Carranza in Congress was still very distant from the one that finally became enacted by the Convention. Carranza's project barely mentioned the agrarian problem; (simply) authorized the Legislature to pass laws related to labour and the progress of the working classes; and favoured the 'frank intervention' of the State in the economy.

twentieth century to the present. Think, for instance, about the case of the so-called *New Latin American constitutionalism*, this is to say the new or reformed Constitutions that were enacted by the end of the twentieth century.[19] Many of these renewed Constitutions have basically reproduced what could be called the *'old' model of Latin American constitutionalism*. For instance, the new Constitutions of Venezuela 1999, Ecuador 2008, and Bolivia 2009, are Constitutions that in their basic structure look very much like the old ones. On the one hand, these new Constitutions include strong, long, even spectacular lists of social-economic-cultural and multicultural rights. On the other hand, these new documents reaffirm the old model of concentration of powers, which characterized Latin American Constitutions in the mid-nineteenth century. In sum, both in what concerns the rights that they included, and the organization of powers that they established, these 'new' Constitutions reproduce what was already common in the 'old' Constitutions (the ones that had been enacted in the region during the first half of the twentieth century).

Worse still, in my view, these 'new' documents—like the 'old' ones—keep the doors of the *engine room of the Constitution* closed; this is to say that they keep the old structure of powers unmodified.[20] The 'new' declarations of rights look thus innovative, modern, advanced; while the organization of powers still reproduce the basic features of the nineteenth-century-style Constitutions—this is to say an institutional schema that was elitist, exclusive, hierarchical, hostile towards democracy.

E. Conclusions: Lessons Learnt (or Not): How (Not) to Defend an Egalitarian Constitutional Approach

In Latin America (as well as in other parts of the world), contemporary, progressive legal scholars seem to be obsessed with social, economic, and cultural rights. Consequently, legal scholars interested in social change tend to devote most of their intellectual energies to imagining new rights to be included in the new Constitutions; to finding new arguments for the judicial enforcement of social rights; and to suggesting new and alternative judicial remedies and responses, directed at implementing those social and human rights, both at the

[19] Detlef Nolte and Almut Schilling-Vacaflor (eds), *New Constitutionalism in Latin America* (Ashgate 2012); Javier Couso, 'Radical Democracy and the New Latin American Constitutionalism', manuscript on file with the author (Yale University, *SELA* 2013).

[20] Gargarella, *The Legal Foundations of Inequality* (n 4); Gargarella, *Latin American Constitutionalism* (n 4).

national and international level. Obsessed with the inclusion of new rights into the Constitution, they forget about the importance of changing the rest of the constitutional document accordingly, so as to facilitate the political enforcement of those new rights. As a result, many of the region's Constitutions began to offer very generous declarations of rights, together with an institutional structure that continued to work in favour of the concentration of powers. In that way, the new declaration of rights ended up being dependent on the criteria of the president in office: if the president had both good will and sufficient economic resources, those rights became viable, but if any of these conditions did not exist, those constitutional rights became pure poetry.[21] Everything, in the end, seemed to become dependent on the discretionary will of the President.[22]

This peculiar approach to rights and the Constitution has been the product of a new (now old) constitutional consensus that gained force in the twentieth century, which seems to have forgotten or neglected some of the important constitutional lessons taught by the 'founding fathers' of Latin American constitutionalism. Surprisingly or not, progressive constitutional scholars in the twentieth century have acritically subscribed to and even promoted this renewed view. Let me make reference to some of those missed lessons of modern Latin American constitutionalism.

In the first place, this new consensus runs against the important lessons offered by *republican* intellectuals, in the early nineteenth century. Contrary to what many of our contemporaries have been doing, republican doctrinaires—at least in principle—tended to think about the 'social question' without resorting immediately to the idea of 'rights'. Republicans were deeply concerned with social and economic inequalities, but this profound social concern that

[21] These claims should not be read as a critique of the inclusion of social, economic, or cultural rights in the Constitution. By contrast, in the context of formalistic legal cultures, like the ones that prevail in the Americas, it seems particularly important to make judges understand that the Constitution cannot be merely interpreted as a 'negative' document. In other words, I am not saying that Latin American Constitutions went too far in terms of the efforts they made for the enforcement of social rights, but rather that they did not go far enough.

[22] If we pay attention to the recent socio-economic history of Latin America, we find cases where the President on duty promoted significant social reforms, for instance in terms of racial and ethnic integration (President Lula in Brazil; President Evo Morales in Bolivia). However, those socially reformist initiatives were usually the result of political decisions, rather than the product of social rights-litigation. In other words, the presence of new social rights in the Constitution did not seem to make much difference, in the context of a system of concentrated authority. Some remarkable illustrations of what I am saying can be found in Ecuador, particularly during the government of Rafael Correa, where almost every civic initiative aimed at implementing some of the participatory rights included in the 2008 Constitution was resisted by the President, through the use of his veto powers: see Julio Echeverría, 'Plenos poderes y democracia en el proceso constituyente ecuatoriano' in Julio Echeverría and Cesar Montúfar (eds), *Plenos poderes y transformación constitucional* (Ediciones Abya-Yala 2008), Ramiro Avila Santamaría, *Desafíos constitucionales* (Tribunal Constitucional del Ecuador 2009); Gargarella, *Latin American Constitutionalism* (n 4).

they had did not necessarily or exclusively move them to think about the inclusion of social rights in the Constitutions. Rather, those worries motivated them to promote radical economic reforms (typically, agrarian reforms) that, in their view, were indispensable for achieving social justice. Also, and very significantly, those old republicans viewed those economic reforms as integral parts of a wider reform, which usually included a broad constitutional reform (in no way be limited to the declaration of rights), but also went beyond the legal/constitutional sphere. This was another important lesson that doctrinaires of our time could have taken from our old predecessors: political, economic, social, and legal (constitutional) reforms need to be promoted together. As Murillo Toro claimed: political independence required economic independence—one thing without the other tended to become meaningless. Does this mean that only comprehensive or super-ambitious reforms are worth pursuing? Not necessarily. The point our predecessors wanted to make was that social reformers should not think about the economy, the law, or politics as if they constituted autonomous realms, independent from each other.

Unfortunately, many among our colleagues have tended to dismiss those lessons. Worse still, they have usually preferred to address the problems generated by social and economic inequalities through the *liberal language or rights*, thus forgetting the republicans' critical and sceptical approach to rights. What is still more surprising, numerous progressive doctrinaires have begun to approach to the organization of powers, adopting—in one or another way—the old *conservative understanding* of the separation of powers. Conservatives—we should remember—had developed this view in order to defend monarchical and authoritarian governments: for them, the only reasonable way to organize powers in divided, unequal, and conflictive societies, was through the concentration of powers in the hands of one or a few (typically the monarch or a hyper-president). In this way, twentieth-century progressives had also forgotten the old republican aversion to monarchy and other varieties of the concentration of powers.

In addition, the new constitutional consensus contradicts other, important lessons that were left to us by our *liberal-conservative* antecessors regarding how to protect constitutional rights. As we have learned, the liberal-conservative view on the subject claimed something like the following: 'if you want to protect fundamental rights, you do not need to fill the Constitutions with more and more of your preferred rights. Rather, you should move to the other side of the Constitution and change the organization of powers accordingly.' Now, the new constitutional consensus seems to have neglected that lesson. At the present time, legal scholars who are concerned with social rights tend to fill the Constitution with more and more social rights, rather than change the organization of powers in agreement with their renewed social commitments.[23] Our contemporaries seem to claim: 'if you care about rights, what you need is more rights.' This is, I believe, a gross mistake, which in part explains the unsuccessful story of social rights in recent Latin American history.[24]

As I said before, present Latin American Constitutions tend to show 'two different souls': one more progressive, social in its spirit, and democratic in its aspiration, which looks like a twenty-first-century Constitution; the other more regressive, reactionary, and elitist, which still resembles the old nineteenth-century model of constitutionalism. In spite of their interesting promises, these new Constitutions are unnecessarily filled with internal tensions and contradictions, which tend to generate wrong expectations and unnecessary inefficiencies. Once and for all, it is time to abandon the mistaken approaches that still inform Latin American constitutionalism.

[23] Imagine, for instance, that you want to favour the inclusion of more participatory rights in the Constitution. Then, it would not be a good idea to leave the organization of powers untouched, thus preserving the hierarchical, vertical, elitist nineteenth-century model of the Constitution. It seems clear that the new participatory rights would thus become—sooner or later—in tension with the old organization of powers, which concentrated power in the hands of the Executive and which—consequently—was not consistent with the idea of having an autonomous and active civil society.

[24] Things have been changing a little in recent years, but nothing denies the decades of pure frustration that followed the adoption of this imperfect strategy: (Víctor Abramovich and Christian Courtis, *Los derechos sociales como derechos exigibles* (Trotta 2002); Martín Abregú and Christian Courtis (eds), *La aplicación de los tratados internacionales sobre derechos humanos por los tribunales locales* (Del Puerto-PNUD 1998); Varun Gauri and Daniel M Brinks, *Courting Social Justice: Judicial Enforcement of Social and Economic Rights in the Developing World* (CUP 2009); Malcolm Langford, *Social Rights Jurisprudence: Emerging Trends in International and Comparative Law* (CUP 2009). In any case, we still need to explain both why social and economic constitutional rights became transformed into 'dormant clauses' during so many decades, and also why and how, in some cases, they became 'enforceable' rights, little by little, and after so long. One possible explanation—among many—that is consistent with my analysis so far, would be the following. The 'globalization' of law, the examples of more active foreign courts, and, most of all, the introduction of some important changes in the 'engine room' of the Constitution (including changes in legal standing and in access to justice; the adoption of new doctrinal criteria; and the emergence of some new legal instruments—such as the *actio popularis* or the right to *amparo* in Colombia or Costa Rica) had a significant impact on the region's legal culture. See eg Mauricio García Villegas and Maria Paula Saffón, 'Is there Hope in Judicial Activism in Social Rights? Assessing the Dimension of Judicial Activism in Social Rights in Colombia' (documento de trabajo, Dejusticia 2005); Manuel José Cepeda-Espinosa, 'Judicial Activism in a Violent Context: The Origin, Role, and Impact of the Colombian Constitutional Court' (2004) 3 Washington University Global Studies Law Review 529; Manuel José Cepeda-Espinosa, 'The Internationalization of Constitutional Law: A Note on the Colombian Case' (2008) 41 (1) VRÜ/WCL 61; Roberto Gargarella, Pilar Domingo, and Theunis Roux (eds), *Courts and Social Transformation in New Democracies* (Ashgate 2006); Camila Gianella and Bruce Wilson, 'LGBTI Rights' in Juan Bertomeu and Roberto Gargarella (eds), *The Latin American Casebook* (Palgrave 2016).

11

Same Bed, Different Dreams

Constitutionalism and Legality in Asian Hybrid Regimes

*Weitseng Chen**

A. Introduction

Authoritarianism in the Global South has been associated with poverty, cronyism, and corruption, *except* for in a cluster of Asian states. The difference in this cluster of Asian states is believed to account for the Asian economic miracle after the Second World War. These states, including Japan and the Asian Tiger countries, with potentially emerging cases such as Vietnam and China, embraced the ideas of legality and constitutionalism in the early stages of their nation-building and economic development. After their GDP per capita had increased by several dozen times, they transited their authoritarian legality/constitutionalism towards a more liberal and/or democratic regime. For the Global South, it is vital to conceptualize such authoritarian legality/constitutionalism and the subsequent transitions, as these countries have proved that constitutionalism is not limited to certain geographic areas and Western liberal democracies. They are arguably the most successful examples of constitutionalism-making in the Global South thus far.

However, existing literature is scant. For example, we know that constitutionalism functions well in these countries, but our knowledge about the process of the evolution and conditions under which it evolved is very limited. Similarly, we know that liberal transitions took place in some of these countries down the road, but we do not know sufficiently the underlying dynamics and mechanisms of such transitions. From a comparative perspective, we do not know either why this model of authoritarian constitutionalism but not others has worked in East Asia. This chapter aims to provide an analytical framework and selects a few crucial topics to elaborate.

* The author gratefully acknowledges the financial assistance of NUS Center for Asian Legal Studies and AcRF Tier 1 research fund (R-241-000-163-115).

Weitseng Chen, *Same Bed, Different Dreams* In: *The Global South and Comparative Constitutional Law.* Edited by: Philipp Dann, Michael Riegner, and Maxim Bönnemann, Oxford University Press (2020). © Oxford University Press.
DOI: 10.1093/oso/9780198850403.003.0011

This chapter seeks to answer the following three questions and is organized accordingly. First, why would authoritarians accept the idea of legality and what exactly do they mean by legality? Second, what makes authoritarian legality functional and stable? Third, what are the factors that provide the conditions for the transition towards a more liberal and democratic system?

B. Constitutionalism and Legality in Asian Authoritarian States

Henry Ford, the American car industry tycoon, once said, 'A customer can have a car painted any color he wants as long as it's black.' This line fits nicely into the discourse of constitutionalism and legality in the authoritarian context. Rhetoric differs from actual acts. On paper, authoritarian constitutions may look very similar to their democratic counterparts.[1] This is not surprising as democratic constitutions serve as a rich source of constitutional borrowing by authoritarians. For example, while Taiwan's constitution was modelled upon Germany's Weimar Constitution, American influence was paramount in the drafting of Japan's 1946 Constitution, South Korea's 1948 Constitution, and the Philippines' 1935 and 1973 Constitutions. Moreover, democrats and authoritarians sometimes share the same constitution after regime changes, and Tom Ginsburg's empirical studies also found no evidence of commonly believed-in Asian constitutional characteristics such as 'Asian values' or relatively unconstrained executives.[2] As such, a more meaningful approach for studying Asian authoritarian constitutions is to figure out what exactly authoritarians mean by legality and constitutionalism, and how constitutional institutions really operate in the authoritarian context. What is needed are functionalist, historical, and empirical approaches to studying what different patterns of behaviour exist and how legal institutions function in non-liberal and authoritarian contexts.[3] In this way, we will achieve a more intimate understanding of both non-liberal constitutions and liberal democracies.

To begin with, constitutionalism and authoritarianism seem to absolutely contradict one another, at least notionally. While the former emphasizes the

[1] Zachary Elkins, Tom Ginsburg, and James Melton, 'The Content of Authoritarian Constitutions' in Tom Ginsburg and Alberto Simpser (eds), *Constitutions in Authoritarian Regimes* (CUP 2013) 141–64.

[2] ibid; Tom Ginsburg, 'East Asian Constitutionalism in Comparative Perspective' in Albert HY Chen (ed), *Constitutionalism in Asia in the Early Twenty-First Century* (CUP 2014).

[3] ibid; Günter Frankenberg, 'Comparing Constitutions: Ideas, Ideals, and Ideology—Toward a Layered Narrative' (2006) 4 International Journal of Constitutional Law 457, 457–59.

importance of the rule of law, accountability, human rights, and checks and balances, the latter embraces rule by law and centralism, and dislikes the idea of human rights and checks and balances. That said, some authoritarians are pragmatists and do not mind accepting legality and constitutionalism for practical reasons, especially for the sake of economic development and better government performance, or simply to give an appearance for the sake of legitimacy. Some may go even further and hold elections if they are confident of winning the elections. By the same token, if they are able to stay in power even in a democratic system, they would be willing to democratize the country. As a result, such pragmatism leads to what political scientists call 'hybrid regimes' in Asia, that is having some form of notional form of democratic institutions in place while the authoritarians continue to wield centralized political control over the country.

Hybrid regimes are commonly seen in Asia. They are either partially democratic without political liberalization (eg regular elections are held but both political and civil society is not fully liberalized), or partially liberal without democratization (eg civil society is liberalized but without democratization in political society).[4] A hybrid regime is a product of global political economy where authoritarians often borrow ideas from their liberal counterparts (and vice versa, sometimes).[5] The majority of East Asian states are, or once were, hybrid regimes, including, for example, Hong Kong, Thailand, Malaysia, Indonesia, Singapore, South Korea, Taiwan, and Japan. Even in China, which remains as a one-party regime, public discourse about law and constitutionalism is common, albeit more restrictions have been imposed by the Xi Jinping administration. When asked to name five vital topics that journalists should report about if there is no pressure, Chinese opinion leaders and journalists selected their top five: unconstitutionality of law and policies, government's infringement of rights, judicial independence, rights of disadvantaged people, and civil society.[6] All of them concern varying dimensions of constitutionalism and legality.

Against this backdrop, the mentality of hybrid regime leaders demonstrates an instrumental commitment to constitutionalism and legality, as opposed to a

[4] Larry Jay Diamond, 'Thinking About Hybrid Regimes' (2006) 13 Journal of Democracy 21; Terry Lynn Karl, 'The Hybrid Regimes of Central America' (1995) 6 Journal of Democracy 72.

[5] Terry Lynn Karl, 'Imposing Consent? Electoralism vs Democratization in El Salvador' in Paul Drake and Eduardo Silva (eds), *Elections and Democratization in Latin America, 1980–1985* (Center for Iberian and Latin American Studies, University of California 1986).

[6] Ya-Wen Lei, *The Contentious Public Sphere in China: Law, Media, and the Dilemma of Authoritarian Rule* (Princeton UP 2017). Nonetheless, it is not uncommon to find some of these opinion leaders and journalists being cooperative with the government and imposing self-censorship to preserve the limited freedom of the public sphere in China.

normative commitment.[7] Modern authoritarians are adaptive, pragmatic, and strategic in developing the means of governance. For them, legality provides the unity and certainty necessary for modernizing their economic and bureaucratic systems. However, legality and legitimacy are separated. Legality and constitutionalism are merely a means of governance, whereas authoritarianism is where legitimacy ultimately lies. This should not be surprising. Historically, democracy is far from the only source of legitimacy, and authoritarianism is also part of Weberian concepts about legitimacy. Similar to being adapted to innovations and technology, borrowing the idea of legality does not disqualify authoritarians as authoritarians.

That said, one underlying question remains: why is the authoritarians' instrumental commitment to legality credible? While some patriotic and nationalistic citizens are inclined to follow whatever the political leaders would say, business people, foreign investors, and legal professionals are not that willing to put their wealth at risk if they consider these commitments merely empty or excessively uncertain. In this regard, Asian authoritarian regimes, many of which are developmental states at the same time, have proved to be able to conduct a 'commitment engineering'. For example, authoritarians would make credible their commitment to contract enforcement, property rights security, and other laws necessary for business in various ways. They may align their interest with investors by creating various forms of public–private alliances (eg joint-invested commercial entities or jointly developed industries), thereby making investors trust that their economic interests are bound and that authoritarians have no incentive to revoke this business-friendly legal environment. As demonstrated in practice, many investors consider such commitments 'good enough' for business purpose and are able to distribute any residual risks of uncertainty through market mechanisms (eg to charge a higher risk premium) or change in business behaviour (eg to shorten the payback period).[8]

Notably, a few Asian hybrid regimes eventually transitioned towards a more liberal and democratic regime, but their experiences suggested that it took decades to transform an instrumental commitment to law into one with a normative nature, commonly seen in genuine democracies. Taiwan accepted the idea of liberal constitutionalism as early as in the 1920s when forming its constitution, yet genuine practices of constitutionalism did not happen until after its democratization in the 1990s.[9] Similarly, Japan during Meiji years (1868–1912)

7 Mark Tushnet, 'Authoritarian Constitutionalism' (2015) 100 Cornell Law Review 391, 425, 445.

8 Weitseng Chen, 'Arbitrage for Property Rights: How Foreign Investors Create Substitutes for Property Institutions in China' (2015) 24 Washington International Law Journal 47.

9 Weitseng Chen, 'Twins of Opposites: Why China Will Not Follow Taiwan's Model of Rule of Law Transition toward Democracy' (2018) 66 American Journal of Comparative Law 481.

adopted an illiberal form of constitutionalism, which helped to stabilize and modernize the country. A normative commitment to constitutionalism that constrains both the rulers and the ruled, however, was not existent until years after World War II when liberal democracy was imposed by the United States on this country.[10] Similarly, under pressure from the US, South Korea created its own constitution right after World War II, but that did not change the regime's authoritarian nature until its democratization in the late 1980s.[11] In Hong Kong, the British introduced a Diceyan idea of the rule of law to their colony, with a focus on social stability and executive branch's power.[12] Ever since, it has possessed a typical form of authoritarian legality and constitutionalism, with occasional turbulence as a result of democratic movements.[13]

These transitions, however, do not imply that a move towards a liberal and democratic regime will always materialize. While it is true that an increasing number of people—especially the middle class, intellectuals, and the less privileged—would require the authoritarians to live up to their commitment to legality and constitutionalism and therefore borrow varying legal concepts to challenge government actions they consider illegal or unconstitutional, this remains a demand-side story. On the supply side, some authoritarians have appeared to be able to defuse such tensions successfully.

A common tactic employed by political elites is to propose alternative concepts to those under liberal constitutionalism. While some of the concepts are part of a necessary process to localize transplanted constitutional norms,[14] they functionally help to defuse the tensions and conceptualize what political elites really mean by legality and constitutionalism. Some of these concepts could also explain certain behaviour patterns of the regimes. For example, political tutelage theory, guided democracy, Economic Hong Kong (as opposed to undesirable Political Hong Kong), paternal democracy, Asian values, and

[10] Tom Ginsburg, 'From Signal to Legality: Meiji Japan and Authoritarian Constitutionalism' in Weitseng Chen and Hualing Fu (eds), *Authoritarian Legality in Asia: Formation, Development, and Transition* (CUP 2020).

[11] Kim Hakjoon 'The Influence of the American Constitution on South Korean Constitutional Development Since 1948' (1992) 16 Asian Perspective 25; Yoon Dae-Kuo, *Law and Political Authority in South Korea* (Westview Press 1990).

[12] Richard Cullen and David Campbell, 'Understanding Authoritarian Legality in Hong Kong: What Can Dicey and Rawls Tell Us?' in Weitseng Chen and Hualing Fu (eds), *Authoritarian Legality in Asia: Formation, Development, and Transition* (CUP 2020).

[13] Michael Davis, 'Constitutionalism in Hong Kong: Politics Versus Economics' (2014) 18 University of Pennsylvania Journal of International Law 157, 167.

[14] Cheryl Saunders, 'The Impact of Internationalization on National Constitutions' in Albert HY Chen (ed), *Constitutionalism in Asia in the Early Twenty-First Century* (CUP 2014); Mark Tushnet, 'The Possibilities of Comparative Constitutional Law' (1999) 108 Yale Law Journal 1225, 1307–08.

democratic centralism.[15] From a scholarly perspective, these concepts might pluralize our understanding of constitutionalism and lead to a more diverse typology of constitutionalism around the world, such as communitarian constitutionalism,[16] and authoritarian constitutionalism.[17]

C. Conditions for Stable and Functional Constitutions and Legality in Hybrid Regimes

Asian authoritarian regimes have proven to be more stable than many liberal democracies. What have been the conditions for such stability and functional institutions? To begin with, there must be formal rules, announced in advance, that genuinely constrain rulers on important issues and correspond to some degree to the exercise of actual power in the political system.[18] Most importantly, these rules have to be self-enforcing among the major political actors, in the sense that no powerful actor wishes to overturn them and most actors feel better off within than without the system.[19] For example, although the election rules in hybrid regimes are likely to be unfair, participants would uphold the rules provided they consider that it is still possible to win the election next round. So long as these conditions are largely met, the rules are likely to be stable. Below are several characteristics that this chapter would like to highlight.

1. Fragmentation

One characteristic of authoritarian legality and constitutionalism is that the legal system is fragmented and non-unitary. It is fragmented in that the markets and society are not only governed by laws but also social norms (or, informal rules). It fails to be unitary because there exist multiple layers of laws,

[15] Sarah Biddulph, 'Democratic Centralism and Administration in China' in Fu Hualing and others (eds), *Socialist Law in Socialist East Asia* (CUP 2018); Thio Li-ann, 'We Are Feeling Our Way Forward, Step by Step' in Albert HY Chen (ed), *Constitutionalism in Asia in the Early Twenty-First Century* (CUP 2014); Ginsburg, 'East Asian Constitutionalism' (n 2).

[16] Thio Li-ann, 'Constitutionalism in Illiberal Polities' in Michel Rosenfeld and András Sajó (eds), *The Oxford Handbook of Comparative Constitutional Law* (OUP 2012).

[17] Tushnet, 'Authoritarian Constitutionalism' (n 7).

[18] Ginsburg, 'From Signal to Legality: Meiji Japan and Authoritarian Constitutionalism' (n 10).

[19] ibid; Barry R Weingast, 'The Economic Role of Political Institutions: Market-Preserving Federalism and Economic Development' (1995) 11 Journal of Law, Economics, & Organization 1.

rules, and norms that co-exist and co-evolve together.[20] Considering their uneven market development and underdeveloped legal system, authoritarians usually prefer such fragmentation and inconsistency as they could maximize the flexibility of law enforcement, which is usually selective. One case in point is China, where dual-track legal arrangements exist across the board, between state-owned enterprises and private firms, domestic and foreign entities, urban and rural jurisdictions, and central and regional governments. Multiple layers of law, which might contradict each other on specific issues, would be created simultaneously. For example, conflicting tax codes or rules about property rights in land widely exist between the central and regional levels.[21] As tax break and precious property resources (eg land) are commonly used as incentive packages by local governments to compete for foreign capital, such multiple layers provide great latitude for political leaders in choosing the 'right' law to apply according to its changing policy preferences.

Similar practices can also be observed during the process of legal transplantation. In Japan, for example, critics argue that the Supreme Court selectively borrowed some American constitutional doctrines to develop their judicial interpretations in order to legitimize government acts.[22] While in Hong Kong, it is interesting to find that the pro-Beijing parliamentary members called for the adoption of the American judicial appointment system because it engages in a political review that scrutinizes the political background of judicial nominees.[23]

As a matter of fact, the regulatory regime fragmented between laws and social norms resonates with an oft-discussed topic among law and economics scholars. That is, shall we invigorate social norms by using law or, conversely, invigorate legal changes by way of social norms?[24] Existing literature focuses on the former perspective, discussing the role of law in changing social norms.[25] In the context of authoritarian legality, however, political elites may opt for the

[20] See eg Tamir Moustafa and Tom Ginsburg, 'Introduction: The Functions of Courts in Authoritarian Politics' in Tom Ginsburg and Tamir Moustafa (eds), *Rule by Law: The Politics of Courts in Authoritarian Regimes* (CUP 2010).

[21] Shitong Qiao, *Chinese Small Property: The Co-Evolution of Law and Social Norms* (CUP 2017) 143–44.

[22] Okudaira, Yasuhiro, Kenpo-sosho no kiseki to riron [The Trajectory of Constitutional Adjudication and Constitutional Adjudication Doctrines], in Kenpo-Sosho [Constitutional Adjudication] (special issue of Hogaku Seminar) (Nihon-hyoron-sha) (1983).

[23] Waikeung Tam, *Legal Mobilization under Authoritarianism: The Case of Post-Colonial Hong Kong* (CUP 2013) 177.

[24] See Qiao (n 21) 182.

[25] See eg Robert Ellickson, *Order without Law: How Neighbors Settle Disputes* (Harvard UP 1991) 284; Richard H Thaler and Cass R Sunstein, *Nudge: Improving Decisions about Health, Wealth, and Happiness* (Yale UP 2008).

latter approach, at least in the early stages. This is in part because authoritarian leaders, unlike their counterparts in democracies, do not have to always satisfy their followers and therefore often succeed in creating norms in line with the goals of the authorities.[26] It is also in part because of the limited capacity of their legal systems and uneven market development, which often render a top-down, unitary legal reform less effective than a bottom-up, pluralist approach for legal experimentation.[27] In fact, in the context of the Global South, unless social order is established through legitimate and capable government, strict enforcement of law will tend to cause conflicts because different actors will resort to competing laws, rules, and social norms to support their positions.[28]

2. Reconfiguration

Unsurprisingly, authoritarians would try to control laws or legal institutions that may have more political impact on their regimes. Such controlling mechanisms could be unveiled by studying how exactly legal institutions operate in the authoritarian context. A functionalist and institutionalist analysis is therefore needed. In doing this we will also be able to pinpoint the ways in which authoritarians manipulate legality and constitutionalism for their political benefit.

It is common for hybrid regimes to reconfigure the functions of various legal institutions. Property law, for example, might not be used to protect the property rights of existing owners but to serve the national agenda of social equality or economic growth, by for instance confiscating and reallocating owners' land to other parties, some of whom might have better capacity in utilizing these limited resources.[29] Company law could also become a vehicle to formalize the government's immense interests in state-owned firms rather than to protect

[26] Eric A Posner, *Law and Social Norms* (Harvard UP 2002) 32.

[27] For a further discussion about non-unitary approach for legal reforms, see eg Mike Dowdle and Mariana Prado, 'Dialogus de Beijing Consensus' in Weitseng Chen (ed), *The Beijing Consensus? How China has Changed the Western Ideas of Law and Economic Development* (CUP 2017) 15; Michael Dowdle, 'China's Present as the World's Future: China and 'Rule of Law' in a Post-Fordist World' in Leigh K Jenco (ed), *Chinese Thought as Global Theory* (SUNY Press 2016).

[28] Daniel Fitzpatrick, 'Evolution and Chaos in Property Rights Systems: The Third World Tragedy of Contested Access' (2006) 115 Yale Law Journal 996.

[29] For a further discussion, see Frank Upham, 'Lessons from Chinese Growth: Rethinking the Role of Property Rights in Development' in Weitseng Chen (ed), *The Beijing Consensus? How China has Changed the Western Ideas of Law and Economic Development* (CUP 2017); David Kennedy, 'Some Caution about Property Rights as A Recipe for Economic Development' (2011) 1 Accounting, Economics and Law 1.

minority shareholders or improve corporate governance.[30] Authoritarian rulers also commonly justify the violation of people's rights by taking a legal positivist approach. The state often converts a political issue into a legal one and asks courts either to adjudicate in its favour or defuse the tension through a lengthy procedure. Ironically, one mechanism is judicial review. For instance, Taiwan's Constitutional Court defended the authoritarian Kuomintang (the Nationalist Party, or KMT) for decades by justifying the KMT's suspension of nationwide legislative elections, thereby freezing the liberal part of Taiwan's Constitution via a constitutional approach.[31] Similar patterns have also been observed in other jurisdictions, such as the Supreme Court in South Korea, and other parts of the Global South.[32]

A related characteristic is the development of functional substitutes for their corresponding institutions in Western liberal democracies. For example, when existing property laws failed to facilitate the transfer of property rights in China, firms and individuals would piggyback the company law so as to transfer land at issue by transferring the shares of the companies that own the land.[33] Also, to curb corruption and political favouritism, instead of the judiciary, various forms of institutions, including taskforces, independent commissions, party organs, and government-affiliated non-profit organizations would step in to serve as effective mechanisms for improving public and private governance as well as law enforcement. These functional substitutes are crucial for capacity-building in authoritarian states, and, in fact, demonstrate the convergent effects even where significant differences between the hybrid regimes and Western democracies remain at the formal level.[34]

Similarly, while the courts serve as a dispute resolution mechanism, their role could be redefined in a way significantly different from that of their counterparts in Western countries.[35] In many Asian hybrid regimes, courts are not expected to check the government but to assist the executive branch in

[30] Donald Clarke, Peter Murrell, and Susan Whiting, 'The Role of Law in China's Economic Development' in Loren Brandt and Thomas G Rawski (eds), *China's Great Economic Transformation* (CUP 2008).

[31] Chang Wen-Chen and Yeh Jiunn-Rong, 'The Emergence of East Asian Constitutionalism' (2011) 59 American Journal of Comparative Law 805.

[32] See eg Yeh and Chang (n 31); Clark B Lombardi, 'The Constitution as Agreement to Agree: The Social and Political Foundations (and Effects) of the 1971 Egyptian Constitution' in Denis J Galligan and Mila. Versteeg (eds), *Social and Political Foundations Effects of Constitutions* (CUP 2013) 398–425; Anil Kalhan, '"Gray Zone" Constitutionalism and the Dilemma of Judicial Independence in Pakistan' (2013) 46 Vanderbilt Journal of Transnational Law 1.

[33] Weitseng Chen, 'Arbitrage for Property Rights: How Foreign Investors Create Substitutes for Property Institutions in China' (2015) 24 Washington International Law Journal 47.

[34] Curtis J Milhaupt, 'Nonprofit Organizations as Investor Protection: Economic Theory and Evidence from East Asia' (2004) 29 Yale Journal of International Law 169, 201.

[35] See also Moustafa and Ginsburg (n 20) 14.

facilitating policy implementation. For example, Japanese judges produced a high quality of judicial decisions but they rarely went out of their way to challenge the Liberal Democratic Party's dominance. In fact, Japanese courts are often cited as the prime example of a timid and passive judiciary in that they are expected to help the government to improve governance and correct social irregularities.[36] In China and during the authoritarian era of Taiwan, courts are not independent as they rely on the support from the governments and supervision from senior officials to improve judicial capacity, which is considered more urgent than judicial independence.[37] As a matter of fact, in China, the nature of courts and judicial adjudications is likely to be redefined entirely by integrating the judiciary into the overall executive branch. By doing so, the courts could report and handle social conflicts early and be in active cooperation with local state entities to obscure and defuse social tensions.[38] In cases relating to prevailing transactions of illegally created land properties (eg private properties illegally built upon state-owned land), courts were instructed not to express clear opinions about illegality or at least avoid deciding the consequences of such illegality until the administration gives a green light.[39] Before then, the courts in fact worked with local governments to work out various practical solutions and legal policies to defuse social tensions and minimize the impacts.[40]

Such practices of reconfiguring the functionality of legal institutions can also be observed at the level of supreme courts and constitutional courts. In South Korea, Taiwan, and Japan, however capable these courts were, they were not *proactive* compared to their US counterparts. However, they were *reactive* to social and political needs and helped to put through reform initiatives that had proved to be feasible.[41] Overall, there might also exist a shift in style of judgments, from terse to expository, forgiving of procedural flaws, and patient with immature constitutional argument.[42]

When the judiciary occasionally crossed the line to check the executive branch, punishment would follow. For example, former South Korean

[36] John Haley, 'Constitutional Adjudication in Japan: History and Social Context, Legislative Structures, and Judicial Values' (2011) 88 Washington University Law Review 1467; J Mark Ramseyer and Eric B Rasmusen, 'Why Are Japanese Judges So Conservative in Politically Charged Cases?' (2001) 95 American Political Science Review 331.

[37] Weitseng Chen, '"Sir, We Suggest You Be Fired!" Lessons for China from Taiwan's Judicial Reforms' (2014) 2 The Chinese Journal of Comparative Law 289.

[38] Frank Upham, 'Reflection on the Rule of Law in China' (2011) 6 National Taiwan University Law Review 251.

[39] Qiao (n 21) 168–80.

[40] ibid.

[41] Yeh and Chang (n 31); Dae-Kuo Yoon, *Law and Political Authority in South Korea* (Westview Press 1990); Haley, 'Constitutional Adjudication in Japan' (n 36).

[42] Thio, 'We are Feeling Our Way Forward' (n 15).

President Park expressed opposition to a court's decision to strike down a controversial provision of an Act; subsequently, when he revised the Constitution to centralize power, he excluded every judge who had voted in favour of that decision.[43] Similarly, after Taiwan's Constitutional Court announced that an ad hoc committee in charge of the investigation of an attempted assassination of the then President Chen Shui-Bian was partially unconstitutional, the opposing legislators retaliated by cutting the budget of the Court and, also, the travel and research funding of the grand justices.[44]

3. Performance accountability

Most importantly, authoritarians are bound to a performance-centric legitimacy, which does not include legality and thus could justify illegality and unconstitutionality in the name of better economic development. It is crucial, therefore, that authoritarian states are able to deliver such expected economic performance, on which their legitimacy ultimately rests. Otherwise, political crisis can happen and the equilibrium of authoritarian legality can be broken.

This is especially clear in Asian developmental states associated with economic success such as Taiwan, South Korea, and China. Particularly in the realm of economic matters, the leaders of these countries during the authoritarian era are indeed sensitive to the voices of people although they are not held accountable to the people. This is similar to what Susan Rose-Ackerman calls 'performance accountability', which requires the state to carry out public programmes competently, using professionals and well-trained civil servants, and assuring a high level of efficiency in public service.[45]

In South Korea, Taiwan, and China, such top-down performance accountability seems to derive from their shared Confucian tradition under which rulers are held accountable not by the people but by 'the mandate of heaven'.[46] According to such a conceptualization of political legitimacy, the consequence of the emperor's failure to deliver public goods would see the onset of natural disasters and revolutions, which signal the loss of political legitimacy

[43] Tom Ginsburg, 'Introduction: The Politics of Legal Reform in Korea' in Tom Ginsburg (ed) *Legal Reform in Korea* (Routledge 2004).

[44] Weitseng Chen and Jimmy Chiashin Hsu, 'Horizontal Accountability in a Polarised New Democracy: The Case of Post-Democratisation Taiwan' (2014) 15 Australian Journal of Asian Law 1, 6.

[45] Susan Rose-Ackerman, 'Regulation and Public Law in Comparative Perspective' (2010) 60 University of Toronto Law Journal 519, 523.

[46] Bui Ngoc Son, *Confucian Constitutionalism in East Asia* (Routledge 2016) 86–87; Francis Fukuyama, *The Origins of Political Order* (Profile Books 2011) 133.

and therefore justify civil rebellion. Until that happens, these authoritarian regimes, which are based on social hierarchy and meritocracy, would be sustained. Outside this circle of Confucian culture area in East Asia, authoritarian hybrid regimes, such as the Philippines, Malaysia, and many others, do not seem to be very successful.

That said, in addition to cultural factors, institutional designs definitely matter too. We have also seen many positive examples in these Asian developmental states that are able to avoid state capture and ensure economic efficiency. Dan Puchniak and Luh Luh Lan suggest that the corporate governance structure of Temasek Holdings, the mighty sovereign wealth fund of Singapore, accommodates the government's role in the organization but also vigorously prevents any cronyism and excessive intervention that would do harm to the profitability of the firm.[47] The interaction between the Singapore government and government-linked companies has also been constitutionalized, as the country's constitution is arguably the only one in the world that provides detailed provisions about the President's supervisory powers over these firms and the auditing procedure required.[48] The outcome of such institutional and constitutional design has been evidenced by the success of a number of Singaporean government-linked companies in competitive markets globally.

However, outside this small circle of East Asian countries, an authoritarian constitutional framework does not necessarily guarantee economic development. To the contrary, it usually leads to predatory states and failing economies as we have witnessed elsewhere in the world.[49] One example is the Philippines between 1965 and 1986 under President Ferdinand Marcos. Like Park Chung Hee in South Korea (1963–1979) and Chiang Kai-Shek in Taiwan (1950–1975), Marcos announced the enactment of Martial Law, concentrated bureaucratic powers, vowed to implement land and property rights reforms, and built up similar public–private alliances in the marketplace. However, unlike his counterparts, Presidents Park and Chiang—who were obsessed with national economic development—Marcos, a charismatic lawyer, did so mainly through his inspiring speeches and remarkable diplomatic skills, and concentrated his attention solely on the interests of his family clans, cronies, and patrons.[50]

[47] Dan W Puchniak and Luh Luh Lan, 'Independent Directors in Singapore: Puzzling Compliance Requiring Explanation' (2017) 65 American Journal of Comparative Law 265.

[48] For example, Constitution of the Republic of Singapore, art 22B.

[49] Daron Acemoglu and James Robinson, *Why Nations Fail: The Origins of Power, Prosperity, and Poverty* (Crown Business 2012).

[50] Paul D Hutchcroft, 'Reflections on a Reverse Image: South Korea Under Park Chung Hee and the Philippines Under Ferdinand Marcos' in Byung-Kook Kim and Ezra F Vogel (eds), *The Park Chung Hee Era: The Transformation of South Korea* (Harvard UP 2011).

Eventually, this authoritarian constitutional regime gave rise to state capture, corruption, poverty, inequality and poor economic growth.

At the end of the day, there remains a long-lasting and inconclusive debate about the relationship between economic development and the political system. In considering the debate between pro-democracy and pro-authoritarianism theories, these Asian experiences seem to suggest a third possibility—that there is no strong causation between the nature of polity and the success of economy. What is more important is pragmatic policies.[51]

4. Discussion

Several assumptions about legal institutions, which we usually take for granted in Western democracies, would change mainly due to the fact that legality in Asia is usually promoted by a strong state and takes root thanks to the government's support (or tolerance). Take the example of the courts. First, unlike in normal democracies, we cannot presume courts would act as an intermediary between the state and society. Dynamics of social changes would not be reflected into state policy through court decisions. In fact, courts are arguably the least important indicator of social changes due to citizen's preference to avoid litigation. As critical issues and social tensions would not be channelled through the courts, social tensions would be guided into other diverse channels, such as executive branches, mediation, police, or security bureaus, or even street protests.

Second, litigation could be limited to certain areas which are usually related to commercial activities, such as company law, intellectual property, and contracts. For other types of issue, many states would actively discourage litigation with procedural barriers, limits on the number of legal professionals, and institutional alternatives such as government-sponsored mediation. The reason for this is that litigation could exacerbate social conflict and engender political opposition. In this way, the states hope to avoid the presumptively divisive role of litigation, which would explicitly articulate contradictory arguments, interests, and principles and then explicitly choose winners and losers.[52]

[51] See eg Michael Trebilcock and Mariana Prado, *Advanced Introduction to Law and Development* (Edward Elgar 2014); David S Law, 'Constitutions' in Peter Cane and Herbert M Kritzer (eds), *The Oxford Handbook of Empirical Legal Research* (OUP 2010); Ran Hirschl, 'The "Design Sciences" and Constitutional "Success"' (2009) 87 Texas Law Review 1339, 1360.

[52] Upham, 'Reflection on the Rule' (n 38).

As courts do not act as a main mechanism to challenge or serve as checks on other political institutions, the performance of the judiciary should be evaluated differently. The former Chief Justice of Singapore Chan Sek Keong suggests that

> [t]he objective of administrative law as not (primarily) to stop bad administrative practices but to encourage good ones. [Such] 'green-light' views of administrative law do not see the courts as the first line of defense against administrative abuses of power; instead, control can and should come internally from Parliament and the Executive itself in upholding high standards of public administrations and policy.[53]

Similarly, the judiciary in Japan is well known for being conservative in checking the executive branch despite the high-quality decisions it often produces.[54] The most extreme, and perhaps controversial, example comes from China. One would be disappointed if evaluating Chinese courts against their ability to check the governments at both central and local levels. However, if focusing on everyday justice, which accounts for the majority of judicial cases, one would find positive and incremental improvement.[55] In forgoing land disputes, Chinese courts generally fail to prevent illegal land-taking by local governmental officials; however, with respect to land disputes between private individuals, they from time to time provide innovative legal opinions to improve the property regime incrementally.[56]

More radically, the premise that law matters could be questionable. In the Global South, law may not matter as much to social and economic development. In terms of economic development, for example, the key drivers of success may lie in neither the nature of polity nor the constitutional framework, but in a number of factors that reflect exogenous advantages and constraints (such as resources, population size, and geographic locations), historical foundation (eg colonial legacies, culture, and races), pragmatic policies (eg investment in science, education, healthcare, and a stable electoral system), and informal rules and social norms.[57] To put this thesis in context, Taiwan's

[53] Chan Sek Keong, 'Judicial Review: From Angst to Empathy' (2010) 22 Singapore Academy of Law Journal 469, 480.

[54] See sources cited in n 36 herein above.

[55] Benjamin Liebman, 'Leniency in Chinese Criminal Law? Everyday Justice in Henan' (2015) 33 Berkeley Journal of International Law 153.

[56] Qiao (n 21) 167–81.

[57] See sources cited in n 48 herein above; see also Kevin E Davis and Michael J Trebilcock, 'The Relationship between Law and Development: Optimists versus Skeptics' (2008) 56 American Journal of Comparative Law 895, 932–38.

and Japan's most impressive economic development took place during a period when the government intentionally limited the role of law by limiting the number of lawyers.[58] More recently, Frank Upham of New York University also argues that China's economic growth would have been impeded if a well-defined property rights regime were in place at the beginning of its economic transition because it would have limited the state's latitude in reallocating its limited resources.[59] At the end of the day, the allocation of property rights is a political process and growth requires constructive destruction of incumbent interests and outdated ownership structure.[60]

D. From Authoritarian Legality towards Liberalism and Democracy

Legality could gradually become part of legitimacy when people begin to expect the judiciary to adjudicate cases impartially and require governmental agencies, including the highest leaders, to be subject to law too. In this regard, there exists a risk that authoritarian rulers may be trapped in their own success in introducing legality. This is related to the last question this chapter would like to address—whether there is an inevitable transition from authoritarian legality towards liberalism and democracy.

1. Linear theory

Many presume that authoritarian legality and non-liberal constitutionalism is merely transitional, in that domino effects take place when further governance and political reforms are necessary to make the initial legal reforms effective. For example, once the idea of property rights protection is adopted by law, effective courts and legal professionals are needed in order to enforce the law. From this, a degree of judicial independence must be accepted to ensure that the courts are trustworthy. Down the line, more rules are incorporated and all stakeholders, including political elites and governmental officials, are

[58] eg Frank Upham, 'Mythmaking in the Rule of Law Orthodoxy' in Thomas Carothers (ed), *Promoting the Rule of Law Abroad: In Search of Knowledge* (Carnegie Endowment for International Peace 2006) 77–79.

[59] Upham, 'Reflection on the Rule' (n 38).

[60] Frank Upham, 'Chinese Property Rights and Property Theory' (2009) 39 (3) Hong Kong Law Review 611, 616; Kennedy (n 29).

inherently expected to comply, thereby restraining the arbitrariness of state power and creating spill-over effects in the political system. One may call it the 'Trojan horse effect' deriving from the inherent tension between constitutionalism and legality, on the one hand, and authoritarianism, on the other.[61]

Interestingly, some reformist elites and governmental officials may welcome certain levels of the Trojan horse effect to the extent that their power base is not undermined. It could serve as an external force to bulldoze their way through obstacles, especially those from the conservative establishment. Nonetheless, similar disruptive effects could also seriously undermine the legitimacy of authoritarian regimes when the state cannot live up to its promises of genuine constitutionalism, rule of law, and even democracy. Indeed, such a Trojan horse effect reflects the inherent defect of authoritarian legality, and, therefore, is inevitable.

In line with this linear theory, a number of transitions from authoritarian legality to genuine rule of law and democratic constitutionalism have indeed taken place. In Taiwan and South Korea, for example, the trajectories of transitions in the 1980s and 1990s largely followed the forgoing pattern of chain reactions. A performance-driven legitimacy, under which illegality could be justified in the name of facilitating economic growth, evolved gradually to incorporate legality. People discovered that they could sue the government and win, and therefore the accountability and supremacy of the judicial system gradually increased. In both countries, legal professionals were the crucial agent of democratic transitions and bar associations served as an important platform for their collective actions.[62] That said, they often sided with the government at earlier stages due to their elite status and thus some critical legal reforms took place only during or after the democratic transition. Furthermore, public interest and non-government organizations, which often resorted to constitutional rhetoric to frame their arguments and mobilize followers, also mushroomed before such transitions. From time to time, international factors, especially the United States, also facilitated this process.[63]

[61] Matthew C Stephenson, 'Trojan Horse Behind Chinese Walls? Problems and Prospects of US-Sponsored "Rule of Law" Reform Projects in the People's Republic of China' (2000) 18 Pacific Basin Law Journal 64; Chen, 'Twins of Opposites' (n 9).

[62] Kim Jae Won, 'Legal Profession and Legal Culture during Korea's Transition to Democracy and a Market Economy' in William P Alford (ed), *Raising the Bar: The Emerging Legal Profession in East Asia* (Harvard UP 2007); Wang Tay-Sheng and Tseng Wen-Liang, *Ershi Shiji Taipei Lushi Gonghui Huishi (廿世紀臺北律師公會會史) [The History of Taipei Bar Association in the 20th Century]* (Yu Shan Publishing 2005).

[63] Jacques deLisle, 'International Pressures and Domestic Pushback' in Bruce Gilley and Larry Diamond (eds), *Political Change in China: Comparisons with Taiwan* (Lynne Rienner Publishers 2008).

2. Pitfalls of the linear theory

This linear theory, however, is theoretically problematic and empirically questionable if we examine it carefully in context. Comparative democracy studies have shown that not only are there diverse factors, endogenous or exogenous, affecting the evolution of authoritarian regimes, but the trajectories of transitions are also diverse in terms of the sequence of various development objectives such as accountability, rule of law, economic development, social mobilization, and nation-building.[64] Hybrid regimes can be enduring or revert to a more authoritarian form, such as one-party authoritarian state or dictatorship.[65] When the language of rights is adopted in framing individual or collective grievances, it may reflect not 'rights consciousness' but 'rules consciousness'—where the latter indicates people's seasoned sensitivity to the signals of change in rhetoric by the powerful state, instead of state vulnerability.[66] Just within the greater China area, we have seen different trajectories. While Taiwan demonstrates that the rule of law is dependent on democratic institutions, Hong Kong does not. China has developed in a resilient way and seems to have been able to cope with inherent tensions of authoritarian legality. As such, any unilinear approach to forecasting the future of such regimes is oversimplified and questionable.[67]

Indeed, Trojan horse effects are inevitable, but a matter of scale. The actual impact depends on how capable the state is of containing such effects. The authoritarian state could paralyze the mechanisms of domino effects by setting up firewalls between areas where legal reform is seen desirable (eg commercial laws or arbitration concerning foreign businesses) and where it is considered suspect (eg administrative litigation or fully independent courts).[68] As said above, alternative constitutional concepts would be proposed to defuse the tension. Certainly, this battle of doctrinal paradigms itself signals a change in the political and legal culture as both the state and reformist community are compelled to frame their respective political claims in legal terms.

[64] Fukuyama (n 46) 474–75.

[65] Andrew J Nathan, 'Authoritarian Impermanence' (2009) 20 Journal of Democracy 37; Larry Diamond, 'The Democratic Rollback' (2008) 87 Foreign Affairs 36; Steven Levitsky and Lucan Way, 'The Myth of Democratic Recession' (2015) 26 Journal of Democracy 45; Minxin Pei, 'The Chinese Political Order: Resilience or Decay?' (2014) 21 Modern China Studies 1.

[66] Elizabeth J Perry, 'Studying Chinese Politics: Farewell to Revolution?' (2007) 57 The China Journal 1.

[67] Andrew J Nathan, 'The Puzzle of the Chinese Middle Class' (2016) 27 Journal of Democracy 5; Chen Jie and Chunlong Lu, 'Democratization and the Middle Class in China: The Middle Class's Attitudes Toward Democracy' (2011) 64 Political Research Quarterly 705.

[68] Upham, 'Reflection on the Rule' (n 38).

However, these changes do not necessarily imply a transition that will materialize. Some competing dynamics have been unveiled by empirical and historical studies. For example, in the context of cause lawyering in Hong Kong, Waikeung Tam argues that economic modernization has hindered the efforts of the middle class to pursue liberal, democratic reforms due to the pressure from a stronger coalition between large corporations and the authoritarian government.[69] It is effective for Beijing to suppress activist lawyers via the well-established legal system it inherited from British colonial rule, and thus politically easier to live with it than to overturn it.[70] Additionally, international contexts also matter. For example, the international factors during the Cold War era, in fact strengthened the authoritarian rule in Taiwan—until after the late 1970s a reverse trend took place when the KMT faced a legitimacy crisis caused by the US–China rapprochement.[71] Also, commonly seen in Asian hybrid regimes with a civil law system, the role of judges is mechanical and limited. This leads to the phenomena in these countries where the more prestigious judges become (eg high court judges), the less power they control (compared to their counterparts in other agencies with the same level of seniority), as they are expected to focus on doctrinal analysis instead of policy review.[72]

Furthermore, the domestic political economy also injects more variables into the arena. For example, as opposed to the 'middle class' thesis that predicts a transition triggered by a rising middle class, empirical studies show that the middle class in China have not and probably will not serve as agents of democratic reforms, largely because Chinese middle-class wealth has depended highly on the state sector, which explains what Andrew Nathan calls 'the puzzle of the Chinese middle class'.[73] Moreover, the size of the country may also affect the efficacy of social control, flow of information, and the cost of collective actions. In a comparative study of lawyer advocacy between Malaysia (a population of 23 million people) and Indonesia (215 million), it has been suggested that the size of countries and its population has largely determined the distinct role of lawyer advocacy in both countries.[74]

[69] Tam (n 23) 150.
[70] ibid 182.
[71] deLisle (n 63) 185.
[72] Yves Dezalay and Bryant G Garth, 'International Strategies and Local Transformations: Preliminary Observations of the Position of Law in the Field of State Power in Asia, South Korea' in William P Alford (ed), *Raising the Bar: The Emerging Legal Profession in East Asia* (Harvard UP 2007) 81–106.
[73] Nathan, 'Authoritarian Impermanence' (n 65).
[74] Daniel S Lev, 'A Tale of Two Legal Professions: Lawyers and State in Malaysia and Indonesia' in William P Alford (ed), *Raising the Bar: The Emerging Legal Profession in East Asia* (Harvard UP 2007).

3. The neutrality of legality

At the end of the day, the maintenance of authoritarian regimes depends on more than just the unrestrained and arbitrary use of power. Authoritarian regimes increasingly adopt institutions that are commonly associated with liberal democracy. In this regard, legalization could serve to organize and thus prolong the authoritarian party's hold on power. Legality can institutionalize the division of powers within the authoritarian state and create de facto checks and balances in various forms, thereby stabilizing the authoritarian rule and enhancing legitimacy. Even if the regime fails to adjust to new demands for larger constitutional space, this failure does not necessarily lead to democratization. Conversely, it could also lead to a military regime or a totalitarian regime depending who wins over during the political turmoil.[75] Empirically, authoritarian regimes also learn from each other's experiences. Knowing that activist lawyers are the drivers of democratization in South Korea, Taiwan, and other East European countries that embraced legality during their authoritarian years, China may well rationally suppress rights-protection movements to limit the Trojan horse effect.

As such, from a functionalist perspective, the neutrality of legality needs to be emphasized. Authoritarian legality should not be presumed to be merely transitional. At most, legality does create a new platform, where actors, including liberals and authoritarians, are to compete with each other with their newly learnt legal concepts and vocabularies. This process could be rocky in the short term or during a certain period of development, until it reaches a new institutional equilibrium. However, the nature of the new equilibrium remains open, on condition of varying determinants in addition to legality.

E. Conclusion

Recent years have seen increasing discussion about concepts relating to authoritarianism, such as state capitalism, developmental state, illiberal democracy, authoritarian legality, authoritarian constitutionalism, and, more recently, democratic recession and authoritarian diffusion. These concepts are developed along similar lines: the relationship between economic development and

[75] For a discussion, see eg Larry Diamond, Francis Fukuyama, Donald L Horowitz, and Marc F Plattner, 'Reconsidering the Transition Paradigm' (2014) 25 (1) Journal of Democracy 86, 96–97.

authoritarianism equipped with legal and institutional innovations (ie legality and constitutionalism), which may outperform liberal democracies.

However, our knowledge about how legality and constitutionalism operate in non-liberal contexts remains limited. As demonstrated in East Asia, authoritarian legality and constitutionalism is not only possible but actually exists in many Asian states associated with reputed prosperity. What we do not know well is how varying institutions operate, how actors behave, and what the mechanisms of its creation, development, and transition are. This essay is not to defend any authoritarian practice normatively, but aims to highlight several characteristics of these legal systems empirically and pinpoint the mechanisms that make authoritarian legality functional. The label 'authoritarian' should not be the end of intellectual exercise, but rather the beginning of further constitutional studies for this peculiar type of hybrid regime, which accounts for the majority of Asian countries. It would be equally problematic to assume these regimes are transitional. This is not only naïve but also a shame in that we would miss the opportunity to understand better the democratic and constitutional values we cherish.

Eventually, it is the beginning of the battle of ideas rather than the end of history. Amartya Sen once pointed out that the constant famines in India under British authoritarian rule disappeared suddenly with the establishment of a multiparty democracy and a free press.[76] Interestingly, famines indeed happened in authoritarian China, causing millions of deaths—but China also lifted 800 million of people out of poverty at unprecedented speed. At the end of the day, it is about state capacity-building, crucial for both democracy and authoritarian countries. Legality and constitutions appear to be a means that neither can claim sole ownership over. This essay earlier cited Henry Ford to describe authoritarian legality: 'A customer can have a car painted any color he wants as long as it's black.' If he knew about this open-ended competition between authoritarians and liberals, he would have revised it to: 'A customer can have a car painted any color he wants, as long as he believes the chosen color is better than black.'

[76] Amartya Sen, 'Democracy as a Universal Value' (1999) 10 (3) Journal of Democracy 3, 8.

12

The Challenge of Transforming Mexican Authoritarian Constitutionalism

Roberto Niembro Ortega[*]

> The conclusion that I am warranted in drawing from these observations is, that a mere demarcation on parchment of the constitutional limits of the several departments, is not a sufficient guard against those encroachments which lead to a tyrannical concentration of all the powers of government in the same hands.[1]

A. Introduction

In recent years, we have read a handful of studies on democratic erosion, democracy's death, democracy's crisis, and so on. The paradox of this democratic erosion is that their leaders use the institutions of democracy to kill it.[2] This democratic decay is present in the US, Europe, and Latin America. For a long time, Mexico has been considered an autocracy or a weak democracy. However, Mexicans reached the year 2018 with the will to change our country's situation, wanting to leave behind the severe and complex humanitarian crisis we live in. In order to achieve that, we have democratically chosen a government that has promised to accomplish this. In this context, we live in a moment of change in which a national transformation is being announced. This change

* I want to thank the participants of the Global South in Comparative Constitutional Law conference for their comments and critics. Moreover, I want to thank Stephen Holmes, Mark Tushnet, Roberto Gargarella, Luis Pomed, Lewis Kornhauser, Micaela Alterio, and my colleagues at the legal theory seminar 2013–14 at NYU School of Law for their comments on and critiques of a prior version of this paper.

[1] James Madison, *The Federalist Papers* (Clinton Rossiter (ed) No 48, Signet Classics 1961) 313.

[2] Steven Levitsky and Daniel Ziblatt, *How Democracies Die* (Penguin Random House 2018) 8; Tom Ginsburg and Aziz Z Huq, *How to Save a Constitutional Democracy* (University of Chicago Press 2018) 26, 43, 75; Mark A Graber, Sanford Levinson, and Mark Tushnet (eds), *Constitutional Democracy in Crisis?* (OUP 2018).

Roberto Niembro Ortega, *The Challenge of Transforming Mexican Authoritarian Constitutionalism* In: *The Global South and Comparative Constitutional Law.* Edited by: Philipp Dann, Michael Riegner, and Maxim Bönnemann, Oxford University Press (2020). © Oxford University Press. DOI: 10.1093/oso/9780198850403.003.0012

has meant an alternation of political elites and a different way of doing politics, at least.

The starting point to outlining a constitutional transformation is not a trivial matter, because the proposed change concerns the existing situation. That way, if our starting point is that the system currently in force is that of a more or less functional democracy, then there is no need for a transformation but for reform instead. However, if the status quo is a sort of authoritarian constitutionalism, there is no other choice but to make a transformation. Even more, understanding authoritarian constitutionalism as a starting point can prevent us from erring upon that path, because it shows that a series of reforms is not enough to carry out this transformation. In fact, in this new phase, it will be crucial not to make the same mistake of the past, which is to consider that some liberal and democratic legal modifications are enough to eradicate our authoritarian culture and practices.[3]

The Mexican Constitution turned 100 years old in 2017. The 1917 Mexican Constitution indicates the end of the Mexican Revolution and the beginning of a new era. In the aftermath of this historical process, a continuous confrontation between revolutionary leaders took place, leading in 1929 to the foundation of the *Partido Nacional Revolucionario*, predecessor of the *Partido Revolucionario Institucional* (PRI). Afterwards came the stabilization of the regime and the predominance of one political party for the next seventy years. Since 1977, electoral competition has slowly opened to the opposition by legal and constitutional amendments to include representatives elected by proportional representation. With this legal change, Mexico moved to a multiparty system. In 1989, the right-wing *Partido Acción Nacional* (PAN) won a first gubernatorial election, and in 1997 the PRI lost control of Congress for the first time. Some years later, in 2000, the PAN won the presidency. After twelve years of PAN's government, the *Partido Revolucionario Institucional* returned to *Los Pinos*. With the return of PRI to the presidency, there was an authoritarian backlash in the country.

In 2006, Zamora and Cossío argued that with the rotation of the presidency in 2000, Mexico turned to a new constitutional order in which separation of powers became an effective mechanism. According to these scholars, the Congress and the Supreme Court began to make binding decisions and were not subordinated by the president. They argued that Mexico was

[3] On the types of law reform and its justifications for Latin America see Keith S Rosenn, 'The Success of Constitutionalism in the United States and Its Failure in Latin America: An Explanation' (1990) 22 University of Miami Inter-American Law Review 1; Jorge L Esquirol, 'The Failed Law of Latin America' (2008) 56 American Journal of Comparative Law 75.

experiencing a new era of constitutionalism in which authoritarian government or 'Presidentialism' was unlikely to reappear any time soon.[4] Moreover, they pointed to two important characteristics of this moment. On the one hand, the PRI's lack of ideological focus produced a flexible authoritarianism that allowed it to respond opportunistically to political forces without undermining the basic power structure. On the other hand, the Mexican president became the supreme coalition-builder.[5] Unfortunately, they did not envisage what would develop from these two characteristics.

In my opinion, these authors' trust in the idea that authoritarian government was unlikely to reappear was misguided. However, they noticed two characteristics of the new kind of authoritarian constitutionalism that followed in 2012 to 2018. First, accordingly with the PRI's flexible authoritarianism that allowed it to respond opportunistically, the party began to use the liberal democratic Constitution as a façade of democracy. It used the Constitution as a written discourse for legitimation and stabilization, but not as a real attempt to limit power. Second, the President, in fact, became the authoritarian coalition-builder. I propose to call this very sophisticated way in which Mexican ruling elites with an authoritarian mentality exercised power as authoritarian constitutionalism. Authoritarian constitutionalism's reliance on the Constitution as a discourse explains why it was so important for Mexican political elites to have a written Constitution and establish almost every public policy in it, while disregarding liberal democratic ideology.[6] Since 1917, it must be noted, there have been more than 600 constitutional amendments, and the Constitution has become extremely large and disorganized.

This chapter goes as follows. First, I identify the features pointed out in the literature that characterize authoritarian constitutionalism. Then I propose my own understanding of authoritarian constitutionalism according to the Mexican reality between 2012 and 2018. My purpose here is to understand the sort of authoritarian constitutionalism that existed in those years in Mexico as a starting point to begin a constitutional transformation. As Omar El Manfalouty says in relation to the Islamic world, we *seek to understand the enemy in order to defeat it*.[7] Third, I will focus on what functions a constitution

[4] Stephen Zamora and Jose Ramón Cossío, 'Mexican Constitutionalism after Presidencialismo' (2016) 2 International Journal of Constitutional Law 411; *contra* this, see Jesus Silva Herzog Márquez, *El antiguo régimen y la transición en México* (Planeta 1999) 150.

[5] Zamora and Cossío (n 4) 415–16.

[6] Octavio Paz, *El laberinto de la soledad, postdata, vuelta al laberinto de la soledad* (Fondo de Cultura Económica 1994) 133–34; José Antonio Aguilar Rivera, *La geometría y el mito. Un ensayo sobre la libertad y el liberalismo en México, 1821–1970* (Fondo de Cultura Económica 2010) 12.

[7] Omar El Manfalouty, 'Authoritarian Constitutionalism in the Islamic World: Theoretical Considerations and Comparative Observations on Syria and Turkey' in Helena Alviar Garcia and

accomplishes, according to authoritarian constitutionalism, and explain how ruling elites use the discourse of constitutionalism for authoritarian purposes. Finally, I present some conclusions.

B. Common Features of Authoritarian Constitutionalism

I want to clarify at the outset that I do not intend to present a conceptualization of authoritarian constitutionalism applicable to all countries.[8] My understanding of authoritarian constitutionalism has been influenced by the Mexican reality between 2012 and 2018, and maybe it will be useful to understand other realities since Mexico shares some common features with other Latin American countries that sustain authoritarian constitutionalism, such as a restrictive view of ideals of autonomy and self-government. As Gargarella points out, Latin American conservatives favour a particular conception of the good and a restrictive and elitist approach of the organization of public affairs, having adopted a system where the Executive branch prevails over the rest.[9] However, we have to keep in mind that authoritarian constitutionalism is a global phenomenon with different manifestations that change over time.[10] Mexico is not the exception. Moreover, it is not just a phenomenon of the Global South, but one present in other countries—such as France and Japan[11]—as well.

In my opinion, authoritarian constitutionalism should not be used in reference to a distinctive regime; rather, it is a concept that refers to a very sophisticated way in which ruling elites with an authoritarian mentality exercise power in not fully democratic states.[12] In this case, the regime's liberal democratic

Günter Frankenberg (eds), *Authoritarian Constitutionalism: Comparative Analysis and Critique* (Edward Elgar 2019) 96.

[8] Günter Frankenberg, 'Authoritarian Constitutionalism: Coming to Terms with Modernity's Nightmares' in Helena Alviar Garcia and Günter Frankenberg (eds), *Authoritarian Constitutionalism Comparative Analysis and Critique* (Edward Elgar 2019) 4.

[9] Roberto Gargarella, 'Authoritarian Constitutionalism in Latin America: From the Past to Present' in Helena Alviar García and Günter Frankenberg (eds), *Authoritarian Constitutionalism Comparative Analysis and Critique* (Edward Elgar 2019) 121–29.

[10] Frankenberg (n 8) 4.

[11] See Eugénie Mérieau, 'French Authoritarian Constitutionalism and Its Legacy' in Helena Alviar Garcia and Günter Frankenberg (eds), *Authoritarian Constitutionalism Comparative Analysis and Critique* (Edward Elgar 2019); Hajime Yamamoto, 'An Authoritarization of Japanese Constitutionalism?' in Helena Alviar García and Günter Frankenberg (eds), *Authoritarian Constitutionalism Comparative Analysis and Critique* (Edward Elgar 2019).

[12] Elkins, Ginsburg, and Melton have used the Unified Democracy Scores to identify authoritarian regimes. Country-years with a Unified Democracy Scores (UDS) score greater than or equal to 0.16 are coded as democratic, and country-years with a UDS score less than 0.16 are coded as authoritarian: Zachary Elkins, Tom Ginsburg, and James Melton, 'The Content of Authoritarian Constitutions'

constitution, instead of limiting the power of the state and empowering those who would otherwise be powerless,[13] is used for practical and authoritarian ideological functions.

For Mark Tushnet, authoritarian constitutionalism is an intermediate normative model between liberal constitutionalism and authoritarianism that has moderately strong normative commitments to constitutionalism.[14] According to the author, this is a conceptual possibility that has some connection to empirical reality, but not a precise claim about any system.[15]

The literature on authoritarian constitutionalism identifies the following common features. We come across conservative values—such as order, community bent, and value consensus rather than contention;[16] however, it is not clear that there is a distinctive authoritarian ideology. We also find that there is an intermediate level of protection of liberal freedoms,[17] which is why I use the term 'not full democracies'. More importantly, we encounter constitutions with an authoritarian content,[18] even though there is no agreement on what that content is.

in Tom Ginsburg and Alberto Simpser (eds), *Constitutions in Authoritarian Regimes* (CUP 2014) 141, 144–45. I want to emphasize that authoritarian constitutionalism takes place in countries that score greater than or equal to 0.16, and in that sense they are democratic according to Elkins et al. However, they are countries with low or intermediate level of democratic development. Maybe there should be a different threshold to distinguish between authoritarian constitutionalism and democracies.

[13] Jeremy Waldron, 'Constitutionalism: A Skeptical View' (2012) NYU School of Law, Public Law Research Paper No 10-87 <http://papers.ssrn.com/sol3/papers.cfm?abstract_id=1722771> accessed 25 September 2019; Keith E Whittington, 'Constitutionalism' in Keith E Whittington, R Daniel Kelemen, and Gregory A Caldeira (eds), *The Oxford Handbook of Law and Politics* (OUP 2008) 281. I recognize that this understanding of constitutionalism could be very limited and there are dramatically different forms of constitutionalism: Cass R Sunstein, 'Constitutions and Democracies: An Epilogue' in Jon Elster and Rune Slagstad (eds), *Constitutionalism and Democracy* (CUP 1988) 327–28.

[14] Mark Tushnet, 'Authoritarian Constitutionalism' (2015) 100 Cornell Law Review 391, 397.

[15] ibid 395. There are very useful studies in the literature on authoritarian constitutionalism, the most helpful for our purposes being studies about constitutions in authoritarian regimes. They show us, for example, that the constitutions of democratic and authoritarian regimes do not differ much. Differences extend to marginally fewer rights, specificity, and the lack of judicial independence in authoritarian regimes: see Elkins, Ginsburg, and Melton (n 12) 141, 143. Very relevant is Loewenstein's distinction among normative, nominal and semantic constitutions, the latter being a formalization of status quo: see Karl Loewenstein, *Teoría de la Constitución* (Alfredo Gallero Anabitarte tr, Ed Ariel 1964).

[16] Li-Ann Thio, 'Constitutionalism in Illiberal Polities' in Michel Rosenfeld and András Sajó (eds), *The Oxford Handbook of Comparative Constitutional Law* (OUP 2012) 144; Turkuler Isiksel, 'Between Text and Context: Turkey's Tradition of Authoritarian Constitutionalism' (2013) 11 International Journal of Constitutional Law 710, 726; Samuel Tschorne V, 'Authoritarian Constitutionalism and Political "Stability" in Chile: The Role of Law and Institutions in the History of Chile 1820–1925' (SELA paper, Yale University 2014) 29.

[17] Tushnet (n 14) 396.

[18] Alexander Somek, 'Authoritarian Constitutionalism: Austrian Constitutional Doctrine 1933 to 1938 and Its Legacy' in Christian Joerges and Navraj Singh Ghaleigh (eds), *Darker Legacies of Law* (OUP 2003) 361–62; Isiksel (n 16) 702, 709.

Authoritarian constitutionalism emphasizes the tension between the exercise of power within ill-defined limits, lack of accountability, the way the ruling elite executes and masks its violence under the forms of the constitution,[19] and the idea of constitutionalism. This tension makes authoritarian constitutionalism a perplexing—but not absurd—category, for it points out certain inconsistencies and helps us both understand and critique. These inconsistencies exist between the functions that some constitutional provisions fulfil in a liberal democracy (limiting the power of the state and empowering those who would otherwise be powerless) and the liberal democratic ideology behind constitutionalism, on the one hand, and the functions that those same provisions and a constitutionalist discourse fulfil in authoritarian constitutionalism, on the other. It is worth noting that I do not hope to hide or justify these authoritarian functions. On the contrary, this concept is a tool that helps us understand, uncover, and critique those functions. In this sense, authoritarian constitutionalism is normatively attractive as a critical tool.[20]

Now, we have to keep in mind that we are talking about authoritarian constitutionalism instead of, for example, electoral authoritarianism[21] or competitive authoritarianism.[22] These categories differ in two main ways. First, electoral authoritarianism and competitive authoritarianism refer to a distinctive regime; authoritarian constitutionalism, as I have said, does not. Authoritarian constitutionalism, as I understand it, emphasizes *a way in which ruling elites with an authoritarian mentality exercise power* in not fully democratic states, where the liberal democratic constitution in place, instead of limiting the power of the state and empowering those who would otherwise be powerless, is used for practical and authoritarian ideological functions. The second difference is the emphasis that authoritarian constitutionalism places on the constitutional facet instead of on multiparty elections or unfair electoral competition. In this sense, my understanding of authoritarian constitutionalism differs from other authors who use this category to describe a distinctive regime.

[19] James Madiso, *The Federalist Papers* (Clinton Rossiter (ed) No 10, Signet Classics1961) 75.

[20] cf Tushnet (n 14) 460: 'Singapore is not a bad place to live .... Yet, of course, it is not a liberal democracy .... From a normative point of view the central question, probable unanswerable now, is whether a Singapore without authoritarian constitutionalism would be a liberal democracy or fully authoritarian state. If the latter, authoritarian constitutionalism may be normatively attractive for Singapore.'

[21] Andreas Schedler, 'The Logic of Electoral Authoritarianism' in Andreas Schedler (ed), *Electoral Authoritarianism: The Dynamic of Unfree Competition* (Lynne Rienner Publishers 2006).

[22] Steven Levitsky and Lucan A Way, *Competitive Authoritarianism: Hybrid Regimes after the Cold War* (CUP 2010).

C. Authoritarian Constitutionalism Reconsidered

1. Constitutions with an authoritarian or a liberal content?

As has been said, one of the features of authoritarian constitutionalism described by the literature is a constitution with authoritarian content. In my opinion, the cases in which this has happened—such as Austria from 1933 to 1938, Turkey from 1982 to the present, Chile from 1830, and maybe Singapore[23]—are examples of *constitutional authoritarianism* rather than *authoritarian constitutionalism*. In the former, the practices follow a constitution with an authoritarian content. There is no constitutional commitment to constitutionalism through which practices can be confronted and criticized. On authoritarian constitutionalism, there has to be a liberal constitution in place, at least, if we want to call it *constitutionalism*.

Maybe this difference seems pedantic and for sure we should keep thinking of *constitutional authoritarianism* and *authoritarian constitutionalism* as categories that pose similar difficulties. In fact, *constitutional authoritarianism* and *authoritarian constitutionalism* are very similar. However, if our purpose is to find analytical clarity, this may be a good place to start. Moreover, the difference between the two—the existence or non-existence of a liberal democratic constitution—is very relevant. Indeed, a liberal democratic constitution is part and basis of a constitutionalist discourse with authoritarian purposes. This discourse makes the exercise of power more sophisticated.

In brief, *authoritarian constitutionalism* refers to the exercise of power within the framework of a liberal democratic constitution. Of course, a constitution that does not fulfil the promises of constitutionalism[24] makes authoritarian constitutionalism a *thin* constitutionalism.

[23] Since we can find provisions like the following: Constitution of the Republic of Singapore Aug 9, 1965 art *5A(1) Subject to Part III, the President may, acting in his discretion, in writing withhold his assent to any Bill seeking to amend this Constitution (other than a Bill referred to in Article 5 (2A)), if the Bill or any provision therein provides, directly or indirectly, for the circumvention or curtailment of the discretionary powers conferred upon the President by this Constitution.

[24] HWO Okoth-Ogendo, 'Constitutions without Constitutionalism: Reflections on an African Political Paradox' in Douglas Greenberg and others (eds), *Constitutionalism and Democracy: Transitions in the Contemporary World* (OUP 1993) 66.

2. Practical and ideological functions of liberal democratic constitutions in authoritarian constitutionalism

In a liberal democracy, where power is widely and evenly distributed, the provisions that theoretically have the purpose of limiting power do have the *effect* of constraining it.[25] Conversely, authoritarian constitutionalism turns liberal democratic constitutions inside out.[26] Elites use constitutions to achieve certain goals, such as control of political opponents or to bolster a regime's claim to legal legitimacy insofar as it serves the regime's interests.[27] Consequently, the application of the constitutional provisions varies according to the interests of the ruling elite. Therefore, to understand the continuity or effectiveness of authoritarian constitutionalism we must look beyond constitutions.

This instrumental use of the constitution may tell us something about the ideologies of the ruling elites. According to Linz, authoritarian ruling elites have no elaborate or guiding ideology and prefer to call it mentalities. Linz, who follows Theodor Geiger, explains:

> [I]deologies are systems of thought more or less intellectually elaborated and organized, often in written form. Mentalities are ways of thinking and feeling, more emotional than rational, that provide noncodified ways of reacting to different situations. Mentality is an intellectual attitude; ideology is intellectual content. Mentality is physic predisposition, ideology is reflection, self-interpretation; mentality is previous, ideology later; mentality is formless, fluctuating—ideology, however, is firmly formed. Ideologies have a strong utopian element, mentalities are closer to the present or past . . . . It is more difficult to conceive of mentalities as binding, requiring a commitment of the rulers and the subjects irrespective of costs and of the need of coercion to implement them.[28]

The distinction between mentalities and ideologies emphasizes the weakness of the commitment to political ideas, the looseness of ideas, and the flexible approach mentalities allow. These pragmatic mentalities of authoritarian elites allow them to adopt and implement constitutional provisions that serve a limiting purpose according to the necessities they have across time and space.

[25] Stephen Holmes, 'Constitutions and Constitutionalism' in Michel Rosenfeld and András Sajó (eds), *The Oxford Handbook of Comparative Constitutional Law* (OUP 2012) 207.
[26] ibid 211; Isiksel (n 16) 714.
[27] Tushnet (n 14) 422.
[28] Juan Linz, *Totalitarian and Authoritarian Regimes* (Lynne Rienner Publishers 2000) 162–63.

Their pragmatic mentalities adapt to the realities and situations in a non-codified way. So, to the extent these constitutional provisions benefit them in some way, they will adopt or implement them. In this sense, there is a more flexible approach to the constitution far away from the strict commitments of ideologies.[29]

Besides this pragmatic approach, what distinguishes authoritarian constitutionalism is that those provisions, which in a liberal democracy usually serve as a limitation to power and empower those who would otherwise be powerless, do not work here. Moreover, these kinds of provisions are used for different practical purposes and to perform authoritarian ideological functions, serving the necessities of the ruling elite in a specific time.[30]

Let us begin by identifying the different kinds of provisions of most liberal democratic constitutions. Using the Mexican Constitution as an example, we find: (1) rights and liberties; (2) rules that attribute and separate power in different branches of government; (3) rules that distribute power among federal and state governments; (4) rules that establish causes of officials' liability, procedures, and sanctions; (5) rules that regulate elections; (6) provisions that grant governmental powers over the economy, regulation of property, public goods, etc; (7) provisions that design representative institutions and procedures, and (8) rules to amend the constitution.

In a liberal democracy, these provisions have several functions. They may empower institutions that allow people to cooperate and coordinate, or they may serve as tools to gather information and expose it to the people, but they also have the purpose and the effect of limiting power by establishing what can and cannot be done, or *how* things can be done.[31] Moreover, some of these provisions empower people that otherwise would be powerless.[32]

Thus, what distinguishes authoritarian constitutionalism is that those limiting and empowering functions disappear. We can guide our inquiry about the purposes that liberal democratic constitutions fulfil according to authoritarian constitutionalism by thinking of the functions that constitutions have in authoritarian regimes. Since the content of constitutions in democratic and authoritarian regimes do not differ too much, what makes the constitutions fulfil different functions is not the content but the context in which they are applied.

According to Ginsburg and Simpser, constitutions in authoritarian regimes have the following functions: coordinate multiple actors, control subordinates,

[29] ibid 162–64.
[30] Frankenberg (n 8) 14.
[31] Waldron (n 13) 20–21.
[32] ibid 24–25.

elicit cooperation from subjects, establish instructions, make advertisements, obfuscate actual practices, provide signals of ideological legitimacy to particular voices, enhance credibility, demoralize would-be opponents, describe things as they might be, structure authoritative discourse, and provide a political idiom.[33]

Now let us imagine how the provisions of a liberal constitution can fulfil the same functions that constitutions in authoritarian regimes do. For example,

- Provisions that regulate elections can help to coordinate political elites by establishing the way of peaceful succession among them.
- Provisions that separate power among different branches, distribute power among the federal and states governments, establish representative procedures, and delineate the process to amend the constitution serve to coordinate elites by assigning different tasks to different groups, without serving as mutual checks and balances or pauses for reflection.
- Rules imposing officials' liabilities help to control subordinates.
- Rights and liberties help to elicit cooperation of the powerless and provide a political idiom.
- Regulation of the economy and public goods, such as oil and energy resources, make advertisements to national and foreign investors.
- Procedural democratic rules can obfuscate actual practices, provide signals of legitimacy, and describe things as they might be in order to generate an illusion.
- Elections are used by the ruling elite to gather information about the preferences of the people and engender the belief of legitimacy without being an effective mechanism of accountability.

We can classify these functions as practical and ideological. Among the practical functions are coordinating actors or controlling subordinates, making advertisements, eliciting cooperation, etc, and among the ideological functions are obfuscating actual practices, providing signals of legitimacy, etc. As I said, in a liberal democracy cooperation and coordination are also fulfilled by the constitution, and the constitution serves to legitimate the regime. The difference is that, under authoritarian constitutionalism, constitutions do not effectively limit power nor empower those who would otherwise be powerless. However, as we will see, that does not impede ruling elites from trying to use

[33] Tom Ginsburg and Alberto Simpser, 'Introduction' in Tom Ginsburg and Alberto Simpser (eds), *Constitutions in Authoritarian Regimes* (CUP 2014) 1, 2–14.

the constitution as a legitimizing force. If that is no longer possible, they use the constitution to stabilize the regime by generating continuous aspirations while making implausible any real change.

Thus, ruling elites are not strongly constrained by the liberal constitution in place. According to their pragmatist mentality, they do with the constitution whatever they need.[34] In that sense, the standard justifications freely invoked by the ruling elites do not do any good. Perhaps they make things even worse, since liberal democratic standards are used to cover authoritarian functions.[35]

3. Constitutionalist discourse in authoritarian constitutionalism

I have pointed out the practical and ideological functions that a constitution fulfils for authoritarian constitutionalism. Now I will focus on the ideological functions of the constitution. To understand these ideological functions, it is helpful to switch our perspective. Instead of considering the constitution as an instrument of government we have to look at it as a discourse.

A constitution is a written ideological discourse upon which the ruling elites adopt a spoken discourse of constitutionalism. Commonly, they appeal to the constitution, the rule of law, and respect for human rights or the life of democracy. In that sense, the text matters insofar as it gives the ruling elite the material basis—making it more credible—to use the spoken discourse of constitutionalism in their benefit.[36] Of course, there is no normative architecture—that is, conventions and practices, principles and understandings[37]—that makes constitutionalism a reality. In the mentality of the ruling elite, there is no commitment to the limitation of power.

This is a superficial constitutionalist discourse because it does not further the liberal democratic ideology that is needed for constitutionalism to work

[34] In Nonet and Selznick's classification, this is a political repressive constitution because it is subordinated to politics: Philippe Nonet and Philip Selznick, *Law and Society in Transition* (Routledge 2001) 16. I do not deny that. What I mean is that constitutions have to be responsive in some degree to social needs *in order* to be repressive.

[35] We may attribute mentalities and not ideologies to the elites in authoritarian constitutionalism because it is compatible with all the observation evidence about their behaviour, and makes the evidence more comprehensible to us: Raymond Geuss, *The Idea of a Critical Theory: Habermas and the Frankfurt School* (CUP 1981) 93.

[36] As Alan Hunt says, law is important in that it exhibits symbolic or ideological dimensions. Law mobilizes important ideological symbols: Alan Hunt, *Explorations in Law and Society: Towards a Constitutive Theory of Law* (Routledge 1993) 4.

[37] Graham Walker, 'The Idea of Nonliberal Constitutionalism' in Ian Shapiro and Will Kymlicka (eds), *Ethnicity and Group Rights* (New York UP 1997) 165.

properly. I mean values such as individualism, plurality, neutrality, participation, and disagreement. As with the cases of authoritarian constitutionalism, its pillars are the conservative cultural values of order, community bent, value consensus rather than contention, etc, and, of course, ruling elites do not make any attempt to undermine them by spreading liberal democratic values.

The ruling elite uses this constitutionalist discourse—written and spoken—for ideological purposes. The goal of this discourse is to stabilize domination or engender the belief of it being legitimate.[38] Stabilizing domination might be easier than engendering the belief of its legitimacy, and it is possible that the younger the regime, the greater possibilities exist for generating this belief. Conversely, as time goes by and people realize that the constitution is not respected and the discourse of constitutionalism is just a sham, its legitimating force would tend to reduce. In the end, to engender the belief of legitimacy and stabilize a regime, ruling elites need to produce continuous aspirations to keep the people in the game of authoritarian constitutionalism, even though at the same time they make implausible any real change, as I will describe next.

(a) Creating constitutional aspirations

To achieve this purpose, ruling elites have to create an illusion of possible change. This can be accomplished, for example, by granting rights that formulate the interests of the powerless without changing the conditions—social, economic, and institutional power relations—to make them effective.

Commonly, this granting of human rights is accompanied by theories advancing the idea that the dogmatic and organic parts of the constitutions are independent or interrelated in a peaceful way.[39] Accordingly, it is possible to make some progress just focusing on human rights. However, as has been argued by Roberto Gargarella based on the Latin American experience, this thesis seems doubtful. Constitutions should be seen as comprising related and interdependent components, recognizing the special influence that the organization of powers has on the functioning of the entire constitution, and, in consequence, the necessary attention that has to be paid to it.[40] The lack of acknowledgement of this difficult relation among the components of the constitution may hide failures of the political branches to comply with the constitution, blind the presidential hindering of social rights implementation, or ignore the inactivity of Congress to implement participatory clauses.[41]

[38] Geuss (n 35) 15. Of course, constitutional discourse is not the only one used for stabilizing and legitimizing a regime: see Hunt (n 36) 117, 134–35.
[39] Roberto Gargarella, *Latin American Constitutionalism 1810–2010* (OUP 2013) 157–58.
[40] ibid 157, 159, 161, 172, 184, 186, 187, 205, 206.
[41] ibid 158.

This logic may explain why, for example, constitutional amendments in Latin America have focused on granting more human rights during the last decades, even though there has not been any substantial change in the vertical organization of power.[42] Moreover, in the cases where the organic part of the constitution has been amended to establish more democratic procedures or vehicles for popular participation, in the statutes or in practice, these have not been respected.[43]

In those cases, rights reflect powerless interests but further elite interests.[44] The logic is that the law has to be responsive to some degree to social needs in order to be repressive, that is, to secure control by ruling elites.[45] In effect, the powerless make some minor gains and the elites maintain control over the state.[46]

In fact, without any respect for or inclusion of the powerless, it would be very difficult for any constitutionalist discourse to be persuasive.[47] Creating constitutional aspirations depends on the identification of real but partial freedoms and equalities.[48] Delusion is plausible and effective because norms selectively articulate real needs, relations, and potentials of the powerless.[49]

This real, but feigned, achievement of constitutionalism creates an illusion of living in a constitutional state.[50] It is an illusion because there is no overwhelming evidence that the belief is false. On the contrary, the inclusion of human rights, separation of powers, and some respectful practices make people believe that it is possible to achieve a constitutional state. The discourse satisfies the wish of the people to live in a place where power is limited. However, under the existing conditions it is implausible that this could happen.[51] In other words, there is no evidence that under the existing conditions the constitution will limit power and would be respected without relying on the varying considerations of the ruling elite.

[42] ibid 148, 172, 185, 186.

[43] According to Roberto Gargarella this has happened in Ecuador and Venezuela: ibid 173–77.

[44] For the distinction see Geuss (n 35) 38.

[45] I use the categories of Nonet and Selznick in a slightly different way. For them, repressive law 'gives short shrift to the interest of the governed, that is, when it is disposed to disregard those interests or deny its legitimacy': Nonet and Selznick (n 34) 29.

[46] Hugh Collins, *Marxism and Law* (Clarendon Press 1982).

[47] Terry Eagleton, *Ideology: An Introduction* (Verso 2007).

[48] Mark Warren, 'Liberal Constitutionalism as Ideology: Marx and Habermas' (1989) 17 Political Theory 511, 525.

[49] ibid 526.

[50] As EP Thompson says, the essential precondition for the effectiveness of law, in its functions as ideology, is that it shall display an independence from gross manipulation and shall seem to be just. On occasion, by actually being just: EP Thompson, *Whigs and Hunters: The Origin of the Black Act* (Phanteon Books 1975) 263.

[51] Geuss (n 35) 42.

(b) Making any real change implausible

For this purpose, ruling elites have to conceal and reproduce reality.[52] This could be attained, for example, by hiding politics behind the scenes using democratic procedures as a façade,[53] presenting group interests as the interests of the whole,[54] hindering or obstructing the creation of opposition powers through manipulated electoral rules, and co-opting them if they come to existence.[55]

Likewise, ruling elites have to dissimulate the conditions under which normative potentials might be realized,[56] masking the conditions of realization of a desirable political situation. They also focus on some kinds of social contingencies or power relations and suppress others.[57] For example, they may highlight the importance of human rights provisions while disregarding the organic provisions of the constitution or the uneven power relations in society. Or they may point to frequent elections without considering any other auxiliary precautions.[58] This way, elites use the constitution to provide symbols and generate appearances in order to mask contrary practices.[59]

Moreover, elites may make sham constitutional attempts to counteract the conditions that allow them to implement the constitution according to their varying wishes. These conditions are wide corruption, weak civil society,[60] rigid verticality in the political system, popular ignorance of the constitution,[61] material inequality,[62] etc. Among these conditions, one of great importance is the creation of an authoritarian coalition.[63] This coalition is made up of the provision of benefits to other officials, the opposition, political parties, and

[52] Schedler (n 21) 1.
[53] ibid 9.
[54] Geuss (n 35) 14.
[55] ibid 13.
[56] Warren (n 48) 512.
[57] ibid 514.
[58] Even though frequent and fix elections were very important for the framers of the American Constitution, they also knew that 'A dependence on the people is, no doubt, the primary control on the government, but experience has taught mankind the necessity of auxiliary precautions. This policy of supplying, by opposite and rival interests, the defect of better motives . . .': James Madison, *The Federalist Papers* (Clinton Rossiter (ed) No 51, Signet Classics 1961) 319.
[59] Malcolm M Feeley, 'Review: Law, Legitimacy, and Symbols: An Expanded view of Law and Society in Transition' (1979) 77 Michigan Law Review 899, 905.
[60] It is worth recalling that according to Madison restraints need constitutional laws and the vigilant spirit of the people: James Madison, *The Federalist Papers* (Clinton Rossiter (ed) No 58, Signet Classics 1961) 350.
[61] Mark Tushnet (n 14) 429 says that 'if the participants in the system cannot unambiguously identify actions as violations [of the constitution], the breaches of the constitution cannot serve as a signal that people should now coordinate cooperative action against the leader'.
[62] Gargarella, *Latin American Constitutionalism* (n 39) 206.
[63] Tushnet (n 14) 431.

social powers such as mass media.[64] Therefore, the lack of virtue among men make it possible to create an authoritarian coalition between several members of government and private fortunes. This authoritarian coalition renders the constitutional means ineffective.[65] To use the words of the Federalist Papers, there are no longer any personal motives to resist encroachments or violations of rights and liberties, there is no ambition to counteract ambition, no opposite or rival interest or mutual checks.[66]

Finally, ruling elites may want to misidentify and justify existing power relations.[67] By falsely identifying the causal origins of social phenomena, they are removed from the realm of possible political action.[68] Examples in this regard include pointing to the constitution as the legal impediment of change, making a subsequent constitutional amendment and subverting the purpose in the laws or in practice. On the other hand, justification of existing power relations makes the prevailing distributions of power something right, proper, and good[69]—by, for example, appealing to the existence of more or less regular elections and formal representative procedures to justify decisions adopted behind the scenes and without public deliberation.

D. Some Examples of Mexican Authoritarian Constitutionalism

I want to exemplify how authoritarian constitutionalism worked in Mexico. The first example is the incorporation in 2012 of the right to public consultation and the right to run as an independent candidate, in the Constitution. In the case of public consultation, the amendment established various restrictions that severely limited the importance of public consultations. In this regard, article 35 of the Constitution requires public consultation to be requested by at least 2 per cent of the citizens, but limits the object of the consultation; this way, public consultation cannot deal with limiting human rights, the principles of article 40, electoral procedures, revenues

[64] For a similar idea about networks see Scott Newton, 'Plus ca change. . . The Riddle of All Central Asian Constitutions' in Helena Alviar García and Günter Frankenberg (eds), *Authoritarian Constitutionalism Comparative Analysis and Critique* (Edward Elgar 2019) 209.

[65] Remember that for republican governments to function properly private fortunes should not be sources of danger. James Madison, *The Federalist Papers* (Clinton Rossiter (ed) No 58, Signet Classics 1961) 345.

[66] ibid 319.

[67] Warren (n 48) 514.

[68] ibid.

[69] ibid 513.

and expenditures, and national security and the armed forces. The Supreme Court is in charge of reviewing the constitutionality of the consultation beforehand. Because these excluded topics are related to almost every public policy, there has not been a single consultation considered constitutional. The most striking consultation denial was the one massively required after the approval of the amendment establishing private investment in oil and hydrocarbons. In the case of the right to run as an independent candidate, article 116 delegates the regulation of independent candidates to state legislatures that have, in practice, narrowly restricted them.

Another, and more recent, example is the creation of a national anticorruption system in 2015. The system was introduced by a constitutional amendment some months after the widely publicized corruption scandal involving former President Enrique Peña Nieto and its very expensive 'white house' built by one of the main construction companies hired by the government, which was reported in detail by a prominent Mexican journalist.[70] Even though civil society pushed for this constitutional amendment, the timing of its approval was no coincidence. The political purpose of the publication was clear in the transitional articles. These articles established that the amendment would be in force 180 days after its publication, once the laws were passed. In other words, the constitutional amendment was an immediate response to the crisis derived from the scandal without any real intention to implement it. The anticorruption public prosecutor has not yet been appointed. Moreover, the journalist who published the report was fired some months after the publication, for no reason.

E. Conclusions

The term constitutionalism can be used to refer to an ideology, a theory, a narrative, or some sorts of institutions. Identifying the different *uses* of the concept helps us to understand that we may be discussing different things when talking about constitutionalism. In the case of authoritarian constitutionalism, we use it to criticize a way in which ruling elites with an authoritarian mentality exercise power in not fully democratic states, where the liberal democratic constitution in place, instead of limiting the power of the state and empowering those

[70] Aristegui Noticias Editorial Staff, 'La casa blanca de Enrique Peña Nieto (investigación especial)' (*Aristegui Noticias*, 9 November 2014) <http://aristeguinoticias.com/0911/mexico/la-casa-blanca-de-enrique-pena-nieto/> accessed 9 November 2014.

who would otherwise be powerless, is used for practical and authoritarian ideological functions.

After reviewing the very few articles written about authoritarian constitutionalism, we find some common features: (1) an intermediate level of authoritarian practices, (2) conservative values, and (3) a constitution with an authoritarian content.

I have argued that if we want to talk about authoritarian *constitutionalism*, there has to be a constitution with a liberal democratic content rather than with an authoritarian content. This distinction allowed me to distinguish between *authoritarian constitutionalism* and *constitutional authoritarianism*.

In both cases, there are constitutional practices and cultural values that, if assessed by a liberal democratic perspective, would fail. The difference is that in an *authoritarian constitutionalism* these practices fail to achieve the potentials expressed by the constitutional provisions, while in *constitutional authoritarianism* it is the constitution, among other variables, that allows and promotes those practices.

Moreover, I argued that ruling elites hold an authoritarian mentality. To demonstrate it, I focused on the functions that liberal democratic constitutions fulfil according to authoritarian constitutionalism as instruments of government, and the ideological functions they serve in written discourse. In my opinion, once we appreciate the whole picture, we are able to support the thesis of a distinctive ruler's authoritarian mentality and understand how authoritarian constitutionalism operates.

As has been said, in authoritarian constitutionalism the provisions that theoretically have the purpose of limiting power or empowering those who would otherwise be powerless are ineffective. Constitutional provisions that theoretically create incentives for powerful actors to control each other and constrain them—separation of powers,[71] checks and balances, federalism, rights, and liberties—do not work to limit power or to empower those who would otherwise be powerless. Instead, in authoritarian constitutionalism the constitution is used for other practical functions, such as coordination, eliciting cooperation of the powerless, and gathering information.

Regarding the ideological functions of constitutions and constitutionalist discourse, I focused on the power-interests they serve and the political effects generated by them.[72] This constitutionalist discourse creates an illusion where,

[71] Holmes (n 25) 210, 211.
[72] Eagleton (n 47) 9.

even though the constitution is not merely an expression of the needs and will of the ruling class,[73] the interests of the powerless become law because they serve the interests of the ruling elite. Moreover, the conditions that could make constitutional aspirations effective remain hidden and are misidentified by the same constitutionalist discourse.

[73] Hunt (n 34) 7.

Index

For the benefit of digital users, indexed terms that span two pages (e.g., 52–53) may, on occasion, appear on only one of those pages.